Paul of Tarsus

Joseph Holzner

Paul
of Tarsus

SCEPTER
London

This edition of *Paul of Tarsus* is published in England by
Scepter (U.K.) Ltd., 21 Hinton Avenue, Hounslow TW4 6AP;
e-mail: scepter@pobox.com

This is a translation of *Paulus, sein Leben und seine Briefe,* published by B.
Herder Book Co, St Louis, 1945 under the title *Paul of Tarsus*. Reprinted
here with revisions to the translation.

ISBN 0906138 61 2

Nihil obstat: Arthur J Scanlan, STD, Censor Librorum
Imprimatur: ✚ Francis J. Spellman, Archbishop, New York
Date: 20 January 1944

Cover: *St Paul preaching at Athens*, Cartoon by Raphael, Victoria and
Albert Musuem Picture Library, London.

Cover design, text revision and typeset by ISV Intermedia, and printed in
Singapore.

CONTENTS

CHAPTER ONE

THE INFLUENCE OF GREECE

"But Paul said to him: I am a Jew of Tarsus in Cilicia,
a citizen of no mean city" (Acts 21:39).
"And the tribune answered: I obtained the being free of this city with
a great sum. And Paul said: But I was born so" (Acts 22:28).

The city of Tarsus lies on a plain upon which the savage peaks of the jagged Taurus mountains cast their sombre, brooding shadows. "I am a Jew of Tarsus in Cilicia." Thus Paul once identified himself before a Roman governor during one of his imprisonments. Tarsus was an important traffic point in the commerce of the ancient world. Here two ancient cultures touched upon each other; the Graeco-Roman culture of the West and the Semitic-Babylonian culture of the East. The city lay in the foothills of the Taurus mountains whose snow-covered peaks encroached on the Cilician plain as did the Libanus range in Galilee. By the northern pass, the Cilician Gate, Taurus was united with the cultures of Asia Minor, by the eastern pass in the Amanus mountains, the Syrian Gate, it drew upon the cultures of the Oriental Semitic world, while through the great harbour on the south Tarsus communicated with all the countries of the Mediterranean Sea. St. Paul's native city lay in the fruitful plain of Cilicia, protected alike from the raw

winds of the north and the pirates of the Levant, and yet it was
a city to lure a boy to colourful adventures in the wide world.
Paul was, indeed, to see much adventure; his whole life was
one great adventure.

Tarsus was a free commercial city, a reloading place for
the commerce of the world. Here the world obtained the wood
needed for its buildings, floated down from the sides of the
Taurus on its swift mountain streams. Through the city flowed
the navigable Cydnus, lined on both shores with loading places
and ramps and vast warehouses. Here Paul played his boyish
games with his schoolmates, crying out to the crews of the
passing ships, climbing atop the crates and bales that came
from all parts of the world, running between the foreign dealers
and merchants as they haggled and gesticulated on the wharves.
Paul knew these strangers from Ephesus, Corinth, Alexandria,
Rome, and Spain in their gaudy costumes and he heard the
strange sounds of their dialects.

The wild melody of the sea that echoes in the psalms and
hymns of Israel, sounded also in Paul's youthful dreams and
accompanied him through his whole life. The sea seemed to be
an essential part of the fulfillment of his great adventure, as
indeed it almost came to be the end of his career. His letters
refer frequently to pictures drawn from the commerce and
traffic of the world. Certainly it was part of God's design that
he who was to be the missioner of the pagan cities of the world
should himself be reared in a pagan metropolis. He was to
know no difference between Jew and Gentile, between Greek
and barbarian, or between free and slave, partly because he was
reared in a prosperous city in which the varied populations of
the Roman Empire mingled, and not on the idyllic hills of
Galilee.

The tourist who visits Tarsus today has the same experience that he would have if he went to Ravenna. What was
formerly a fine inner harbour, uniting the city with the sea, a
placid lagoon filled with a forest of masts and sails, is now a

dismal swamp. Because of the neglect of the Turks the stream and its mouth have been covered with sand. Now the city is some twelve miles from the little harbour of Mersina. But the fertility of the Cilician plain still remains; the fields still produce bumper crops of grain, and the orchards are filled with luscious fruit-bearing trees. Like Damascus, Tarsus has an inexhaustible water supply. Once the ancient river Cydnus rushed through the city; now called the Tarsus Tschai, it meanders dreamily a mile from the city between its shores covered with poplars, plane trees, and weeping willows. About a mile upstream from the town, the Tarsus Tschai forms a magnificent waterfall, tumbling in foaming torrents over mighty granite blocks and sending great clouds of mist into the air.

The atmosphere of this city in which Paul grew up and in which he spent many years after his conversion was unmistakably influenced by Hellenist culture, and not even the little Jewish boy reared in separate schools and an alien home could be kept from that influence of ancient Greece. If we are to understand the person who wrote the Pauline Epistles, their various moods and the similes and references he uses, we must look back briefly on that Hellenistic world. We know today that Greek thought and Greek culture had a considerable influence on St. Paul and that he lived for some time in Tarsus. Greek was his mother tongue; he thought, spoke, and wrote in Greek. He did not suffer St. Peter's handicap, for when Peter went beyond the boundaries of his own land he needed an interpreter, especially when he wrote a letter.

The predominant religious idea in Tarsus at this time was the concept of the divine power which resided in a superior god, distinguished from a lower god who laboured. This sublime god was called Baal Tars, the Lord of Tarsus, and was later identified with Zeus. The difference between the superior god and the working god implied the transfer to the divinities of human relationships. The Oriental always pictured the majesty and dignity of the divinity as something that could not be separated from quiet, repose, inactivity, and inaccessibility. The superior god came into contact with the exterior world only through his ministers and servants. Thus the great Baal of Tarsus was given an assisting, labouring deity, who was highly revered by the people of Tarsus.

This lesser god was the native deity Sandan, who was later merged with the Greek Heracles into one god. Sandan was a bucolic god, represented on coins and reliefs as a farmer, and was probably the old genius of the pioneer farmers of Cilicia. As everywhere in the Orient, Baal Tarsus and Sandan were vegetation gods as is evident by the bundles of wheat, the bunches of grapes and flowers with which they are pictured.

The high point of the year in the worship of Baal and Sandan was reached with the annual funeral-pile observance. The funeral pile represented the idea of the death and resurrection of the god of vegetation, an idea found in all the mystery religions of the Orient. A picture of the deity was placed high on a decorated float and paraded through the streets of the city and then burned on the funeral pile. This ceremony represented the death of vegetation under the scorching rays of the summer sun and the subsequent resurrection in the spring. The funeral observance was followed by the feast of the living, in which the resurrection of the god was acclaimed triumphantly while the devotees of the god gave themselves over to all kinds of excesses. Outside the city of Tarsus we can still see the remains of a forbidding structure said by some to be the monument of Sardanapal, the mythical founder of Tarsus, but which is probably the original site of these pagan rituals.

As a young man, Paul may have stood and watched from a distance how the autumn sky was reddened when the flames rushed upward from these nocturnal orgies. He heard the shrieks of the whirling mob as the image of the god was launched into the fire and the flames reached to greater heights. And the next day his companions told him of their feast, while within his heart he felt sorry for these poor pagans who did not know the great God of Israel. Later when he came to preach the gospel he may have referred to these feasts as an expression of man's natural disposition to believe in the mystery of death and re-surrection. These dark presentiments found in various forms in all pagan religions were portents of the death and resurrection of Christ. Paul passed the grim monument often enough and as he passed he tried to decipher the old Assyrian inscription until someone translated it for him and told him it was taken from Strabo's writings: "Pilgrim, eat, drink, and be merry; nothing else has any value" (Strabo 19, 5). Later when he was writing his first letter to the Corinthians (15:32) he may have recalled that inscription as he was quoting Menander and referring to Isaias (22:13).

In his letters, Paul often gives evidence that he was acquainted with the old pagan mysteries. As a boy in Tarsus, he had opportunity to see how the worshippers of Isis would appear before the people attired in the garb of the god. These mystics wrapped themselves in the peculiar garment of the god; if the god was represented as a fish, his worshippers put on a dress to make them appear as a fish. St. Paul's peculiar expression "to put on Christ" may refer to that custom of the pagan mystics who dressed in the symbol of their god. Paul used such expressions because they were understood by the pagans to whom he was speaking and writing. When he so often compares the redemption by Christ to the freeing of a slave, he is referring to a scene he witnessed often in his childhood in Tarsus. The slave brought into the temple the purchase price which he had saved. The master came with the slave and received this money and thus sold the slave to the god. The god then freed the slave, and the slave became the god's freedman (1 Cor. 7:22).

"I am a Jew of Tarsus, a citizen of no mean city." Paul's answer rings out with all the ancient Greek's pride in his native city. Tarsus was then competing with Alexandria and Athens as the city with the highest culture. Tarsus supplied the tutors for the imperial princes in Rome. Living in a city of such high culture, Paul's personality must have been influenced by it. Here Greek refinement and the Greek language held sway; here ruled the statutes of Roman law and the stringent regulations of the synagogue; here were felt palpably the subtle Greek attitude towards life, its love of sports and physical excellence, all the decadent forms of Oriental magic and mysticism with their obscured notions of a divine redemption.

A few decades before Paul's day, Cicero had been governor of the province of Cilicia. When Paul was still a boy, the bent figure of the aged Athenodoros was a familiar sight in the streets of Tarsus and, as he walked by, people nudged each other and said: "There goes Athenodoros. He's a famous man. He is the old friend and tutor of our Emperor Augustus." Athenodoros had been a simple farm boy from the countryside back of Tarsus, whose teacher had been the great Poseidonius. In Appolonia, in Epirus, the youthful Augustus had sat at the feet of Athenodoros and there he had promised the old man undying loyalty. Athenodoros had often admonished his royal pupil, warned him against intemperance and, so went the rumour, once had saved him from a grievous marital scandal. For the last twenty years Athenodoros lived in Tarsus. He reformed the city government and started a great movement for education. His fellow citizens built a temple in his honour and every year on the anniversary of his death they had a funeral meal at his grave.

His moral principles would have done honour to any Christian moralist. "Know this: you will not have freed yourself of all your passions until you do not ask anything of God that you cannot ask in public." "Every man's conscience is his God." "Live with your fellow men as if God saw you; and speak to God as if men heard you." We know these sayings of Athenodoros only from the writings of Seneca, who was his great admirer. From Athenodoros, Seneca learned the importance of conscience. "There is a holy spirit in us," wrote Seneca, "that observes and records our thoughts, both good and bad. If you do something honourable, everybody may know it; but if you do something shameful, what difference does it make even if no one knows it since you yourself are conscious of it?"

Young Paul did not need to attend the lectures in advanced literature in order to become acquainted with the sayings of Athenodoros. In all the public places and on the street corners, and especially in the shady groves along the banks of the Cydnus, the Stoic and Cynic wandering lecturers discussed and debated all the current questions in philosophy, ethics, and religion. As he walked home from school in the evening, Paul undoubtedly stopped to listen to their harangues. Later, when he returned as a man to Tarsus, he probably entered into discussion with some of these public debaters. And while he listened and argued, he acquired some of the Cynics' ready turns of speech and learned some of their rhetorical strategy. A careful examination of St. Paul's style leads us to believe that he had mastered the language of the man in the street as well as that of the intelligentsia of his time. He had at all times a high regard for the Greek of the Septuagint, but that did not hinder him from appropriating expressions from the current language whenever it suited his purpose.

As a youth, Paul was interested in wrestling and in military drill and parade, as is evident from the similes he uses about the runner in the race, about the prize awarded to the winner, the Roman sentinel, and the triumphant march. And the pictures he derived from legal affairs indicate that he grew up in a large metropolitan city, just as the Gospels reflect the rural village life of Palestine.

In some respects Tarsus was an extremely rigid and conservative city with certain ideas of moral strictness and discipline. In some of the Ionian cities that had no great reputation for morality, the women went about in the streets in scanty attire, but in Tarsus they were always veiled when they appeared in public. The custom of veils for women originated with the Persians, who even at this time exercised great influence in matters of public deportment. The veil was considered a wall of security for a woman in public since it protected her from the public gaze. Moreover, it was a symbol that a woman was under the power and protection of her husband. The veil was also the symbol of a woman's dignity and honour; only when she was veiled could she command the respect of others. St. Paul had known this custom from his youth and therefore he wrote to the unveiled women of Corinth: "Therefore the woman ought to have a power over her head . . . But if any man seem to be contentious, we have no such custom" (1 Cor. 11:10, 16).

The city of Tarsus was not without historic and romantic connections that would intrigue the adventurous spirit of a boy like Paul. Just below the great cataract outside the city was supposed to be the place where Alexander had pitched his camp after crossing the mountains in his pursuit of the Persian King Darius. Heated by his strenuous march through the mountain pass, he plunged into the icy waters of the Cydnus fed by the melting snow of the peaks of the Taurus range, as Barbarossa did later in another mountain stream of these Cilician mountains. Soon the King lay on his camp bed in a violent fever. Except Philip, 'a disciple of the famous Hippocrates, the royal physicians did not know what to prescribe. Philip said he could save the King with his medicine; but Parmenio, one of Alexander's generals, warned the King that Philip would poison him because he was in the pay of Darius. With one movement Alexander grasped the potion prepared by Philip and drank it while he thrust Parmenio's letter of warning into the physician's hand. The life of the King was saved, and here the course of history might have taken another turn. Had Alexander died there by the Cydnus, Hellenism would not have been born, there would have been no Oriental Greek culture to prepare the way for Christianity. All that had happened near Tarsus.

In the same city of Tarsus was born that man who, himself saved by the royal adventure of faith, would travel across the known world and announce that faith was the great way by which a man could be saved.

Often the population of the city rushed out to see the fabulous Cleopatra as she sailed up the Cydnus on her royal barge, clad as Aphrodite, like the ancient Queen of Saba, come to capture the heart of Mark Antony. Filled with his puritanical horror for all this luxury and voluptuousness, Paul's father warned him to hold himself aloof from these pagan festivities.

Paul's boyhood world was therefore the world of Greek culture, of the Greek language, and round about him was the atmosphere of Greek community life as it was lived in the Greek *polis*, that unique instrument of Greek colonization through which Alexander had hoped to conquer and penetrate the entire East. Inspired by his genius, his successors, the Ptolemies and the Seleucides, with their great talents for organization, established flourishing cities of culture and education like Rhodes and Tarsus, Antioch and Alexandria, Ptolemy and Tyre, Ascalon and Gaza, Gadara and Gerasa. All these cities swarmed with peripatetic lecturers and students who travelled from town to town as did the professors and students of Europe during the Middle Ages. It was impossible to escape the artistic, intellectual, and moral preachments of Greek culture; the ordinary citizen came into contact with them at every turn in his life. Paul, no doubt, had already found himself at variance with much that he heard, he who afterward wrote: "But prove all things: hold fast that which is good" (1 Thess 5:21).

Since the days of the Scipios all this wealth of the Greek spirit became allied with the genius of world-conquering Rome, which sought now to Romanize the Hellenized Orient through the Roman franchise and thus create throughout the Empire a superior caste that would be loyal to Rome.

Paul was born a Roman citizen. His family possessed

both the Tarsian and the Roman franchise. In Tarsus the citizenry was divided into clans and guilds which, like those in the Middle Ages, had their own temples and their own peculiar religious observances. The higher-class Jews who were able to pay at least 500 drachmas could purchase citizenship and thus took part in the rule of the city. No strict separation existed between Jew and Gentile. They were bound together by their common interest in the city and the state, and they prayed, although separately and in different ways, for the welfare of the emperor and the city. Paul, therefore, did not come from a ghetto. He looked out upon the world with an unrestricted view; he had none of the repression and narrowness of the ghetto dweller. In Tarsus the Jews were not an underprivileged minority and therefore Paul was entirely loyal to the civil authority and that loyalty prompted him to speak so sympathetically of the state and to urge his followers to pray for those who ruled the state.

A Roman citizen was really a member of the lower nobility. He generally bore the name of that person to whom he was indebted for his citizenship. The fact that St. Luke never uses St. Paul's given name, Saul, points to St. Luke's historical reliability, since in these Greek cities a Roman citizen was never called by his first name. Among the people of his native city Paul was always called Paul, but at home, in the family circle, like every Jew he was called by his religious name, Saul, i.e., the desired one.

The Greek cities differed from the Roman in being allowed greater freedom for the development of an individual's personality and in being more receptive of alien cultural influences. In this free atmosphere the future herald of Christian liberty spent his boyhood. Here as a boy and as a young man, Paul evidently acquired that trait of character which made him the preacher of a religion that surmounts all races and all classes. All this was yet latent in him. Another greater than he would come to call him, another birth would occur to deliver him from the womb of synagogal Jewish narrowness. But even now he was being well prepared for his great task: to tear down the wall that separated Jew and Gentile. "And I became to the Jews, a Jew," and to the Greeks he became a Greek, "I became all things to all men" (1 Cor. 9:20 ff.).

These are some of the more important features of Hellenic culture which influenced Paul during the time he lived in Tarsus. All such natural gifts and advantages which God bestows on a man through his environment can later be used and expanded by grace and inspiration to form the material for a higher supernatural structure of thought and knowledge. We need not conclude that Paul knowingly drew from the Hellenistic world; but a boy of Paul's mental receptivity and alertness would have absorbed many ideas whose origin he would not be able to account for in later life. The man who drew such a detailed and incisive picture of the pagan world in the Epistle to the Romans gave evidence that he possessed sharp powers of observation and that as a boy he did not walk the streets of Tarsus with blinkers on.

The more we study Paul's personality the more we are amazed at how wonderfully grace and nature are intertwined to make him a most unusual instrument of Providence. Paul himself realized with reverence that the whole course of his life was a miracle of divine guidance (Gal 1:15 ff.). In retrospect, we may say that Tarsus seems to have been predestined to produce that man who was to accomplish Alexander the Great's dream of spiritually uniting East and West and of realizing the Lord's vision: "Many shall come from the east and the west, and shall sit down with Abraham and Isaac and Jacob in the kingdom of heaven" (Matt 8:11).

CHAPTER TWO

JEWISH TRAINING IN TARSUS

"Being circumcised the eighth day, of the stock of Israel, of the tribe of Benjamin, an Hebrew of the Hebrews; according to the law, a Pharisee"
(Phil. 3:5).

Much more important than the Hellenic influence in the formation of his character was that other influence of the thousand-year-old Jewish tradition, his Jewish descent and early Jewish training.

The Jewish communities spread over the whole world were much larger and wealthier than the original communities in Palestine. Since the days of that King Antiochus of whom we read in the books of the Machabees, the Jews in Tarsus formed a kind of separate division in the city, a kind of political corporation with rights equal to those of the Greeks. They became a sort of state within a state. In ancient times no one could become a citizen except through membership in some tribe or clan *(phyle* or *thiasos),* and therefore Paul's family like other Jewish families had a certain patrician pride. In the Epistle to the Romans, Paul sends greetings to Andronicus, Junias, and Herodian, his "kinsmen" (Rom. 16:7, 11). These kinsmen are really fellow members of his clan and were probably either distant relatives or schoolmates in Tarsus.

"Of the tribe of Benjamin." St. Augustine has a beautiful passage in his commentaries in which he applies to St. Paul the symbolism of the name of Benjamin as expressed in the prophecy pronounced by the dying patriarch Jacob: "Benjamin a ravenous wolf, in the morning shall eat the prey, and in the evening shall divide the spoil" (Gen. 49:27).

As a Pharisee, Paul's father was a man with the strictest religious and patriotic sentiments. He conscientiously taught his son the ancient sacred language of the Bible about which Paul was learning at school in the Septuagint translation. Otherwise the family spoke Greek at home. The Jews had an excellent domestic system for the education of children. That was the secret of their strength. When a boy was in his fifth year he learned the principal contents of the Law as found in the fifth and sixth chapters of Deuteronomy, the great Hallel (Ps. 113-118) which was chanted on great feasts, and the significance of the important days of the religious year.

When he was six years old, Paul was sent to the "Vineyard," a school like our kindergarten, which was attached to the synagogue school. Every morning a slave (*pedagogue*) went with him, leading him across the busier thoroughfares and carrying his school satchel and writing materials. At the Vineyard, Paul sat on the floor with the other pupils and learned to write with his iron stylus on the wax tablets. For a number of years the boy devoted his time at school to studying the Sacred Scriptures. Now he learned how important his people were among all the nations of the world. His youthful imagination was stirred by the story of his people's triumphs, and he grieved to learn of their sufferings and humiliations. Every day he came home from school with another stirring tale from the history of his people. The canticles of Sion and the lamentations of Israel re-echoed in his ear. His teachers told him, too, of the future of his people. Some day the Messias as a great king would come and conquer the whole world with his miraculous sword, a weapon more radiant and powerful than Apollo's lance which was the most cherished treasure of the city of Tarsus. After that victory the whole world would come to adore in Jerusalem. Even the emperor would leave Rome to kneel in Jerusalem.

Perhaps Paul's Greek school companions looked down on the little Jewish boy, but Paul knew that his people had already had a glorious history behind it when shepherds were still pasturing their flocks on the sites of Rome and Athens. While his companions were playing at the game of "Scipio and Hannibal," while they recalled the glorious campaigns of Alexander and Caesar, Paul was wandering with the patriarchs Abraham and Jacob and their camel herds through the desert, he stood with Joseph looking up at the pyramids on the Nile, or he was alongside David and Samson when they slew the giant and the thousand Philistines. The other boys in school were writing essays about the questionable adventures of Jupiter and trying to write poems lamenting the troubles of Dido, but Paul trembled at the thought of the almighty Jahve of his people whose name was ineffably holy.

When Paul was ten years old he began the second and less happy stage in his education. At that age Hebrew boys were introduced to the so-called "oral law". Every day he was obliged to learn a new list of sins. The rabbis had erected a great wall of oral laws, purification prescriptions, and fine-spun distinctions around the law of God, and these commentaries and corollaries were taught to be equally binding in conscience with the Ten Commandments. The heavy thud of these horrifying laws must have had a most depressing effect on a nature as delicate and sensitive as Paul's. Later Paul expressed himself about these days when he was robbed of the happiest days of childhood (Rom. 7:9-11): "And I lived some time without the law. But when the commandment came, sin revived, and I died. And the commandment that was ordained to life, the same was found to be death to me. For sin, taking occasion by the commandment, seduced me, and by it killed me."

Until that time the boy had looked with reverence and

awe at the mute letters of the law in its richly embroidered cover, but now the law began to call out to him and warn him at every step, "Don't do that! Beware! Don't touch that!" His spirited nature rebelled against the maddening restraint, it seemed that a terrible fraud had been foisted on his conscience, and he thought that he had tasted the foulness of death: "And I died." What terrifying experience did Paul have in his childhood? Knowing more today about the facts, we do not, like the psychologists of an earlier day, immediately jump to the conclusion that Paul had fallen into some great sin or that he had no sunny, joyful childhood. But these revelations help us to understand the older Paul better, the depression of spirit of those "born under the law," and of the great joy at the redemption by Christ, which he describes in the Epistle to the Romans. Because of brutal treatment by his father, Luther developed a diseased complex in his youth and later transferred that attitude to God the Father. He was right when he thought that the solution to his difficulty was contained in the Epistle to the Romans. But because he cast aside all direction, he hit upon the wrong solution, which has had its effects down until our own time: the great deluding power of autosuggestion.

The atmosphere in Paul's childhood home was a thoroughly religious one, although it was somewhat heavy and sombre. In this atmosphere the national pride of the Jewish youth developed and bound him closely to the mother country of the Jew. His father was probably a quiet, serious, righteous man. He was deeply recollected when he put on his broad prayer band and walked solemnly to the synagogue, a man of the cast of the stern Puritan Scot. We may suppose that in the case of his youthful son Paul he did not spare the rod, and it may be that Paul deserved such punishment especially when we remember the wild and reckless man who persecuted Christ before grace had subdued him. Paul may have been a wilful, stubborn boy, hard to manage. Was Paul thinking of his father when he was writing to the Ephesians: "And you, fathers, provoke not your children to anger"? (Eph. 6:4). That problem of tyrannical parents and high-spirited sons, of old-fashioned parents and modern youth, existed even then.

We know nothing of Paul's sisters and brothers, except that he had a sister who later married in Jerusalem (Acts 23:16). Unfortunately we know nothing of Paul's mother. It is always interesting to learn about the mothers of great men and their influence on their famous sons. The Apostle never referred to her. Probably she died early, and Paul grew up without the benefit of a mother's love. Perhaps that circumstance explains the thoughtful gratitude and appreciation he showed for the feminine services he received from the mother of Rufus (Rom. 16:13).

In Pharisee circles men used to quote the saying: "It is a praiseworthy thing to join the study of the Torah with a gainful, secular occupation." Apparently Paul's father was a well-to-do cloth merchant and tentmaker. At that time, as even now, tent making and especially the weaving of tent cloth were an important industry in Tarsus.

The rabbis had indeed declared that weaving and tanning were unbecoming occupations for a Jew, but people paid little attention to that. At Joppe, Peter was the guest of Simon the tanner (Acts 9:43). Thus Paul learned how to weave tent cloth out of the famed Cilician goats' hair; from the craftsmen and the slaves employed in his father's factory, he learned to make tents out of the finished cloth. Even today the Cilician shepherds wear waterproof cloaks made of goats' hair. These cloaks are so stiff that they can be used for tents. In his journeys through Asia Minor in later years, Paul may have used such a goats' hair mantle (cf. 2 Tim. 4:13).

Often the boy came away with bleeding hands from handling this Cilician goats' hair. Why engage in this hard work? Was he not to become a famous rabbi? But Paul did not yet see the day when he would have to depend on the work of his hands and that this very trade would help open the doors of Aquila and Priscilla and permit him to sit at their workbench.

He did not yet know of those wonderful nights in Ephesus when his hands would glide mechanically over the rough cloth on his knee while he talked to Apollo about the weaving of the Holy Spirit in our souls, and how the eternal Logos had become man and pitched His tent among us. In this way nature and grace join hands, man's free choice and God's disposition work together and like the weaver's shuttle speed back and forth to leave the divine woof in the human warp. Many years later when he was able to look back on the course of his own life and that of his people, his fingers trembled as he wrote: "O the depth of the riches of the wisdom and of the knowledge of God! How incomprehensible are His judgments, and how unsearchable His ways!" (Rom. 11:33).

In the evenings Saul sat with his sister on the roof of their house and looked up to the snows on Mt. Taurus. His father used to tell about the Lycaonians and Galatians who lived beyond those mountains and how they were all doomed to destruction because they did not know the God of Israel. Saul's youthful mind had not yet heard of that enrapturing ideal of the kingdom of God's love which was to embrace all men. Sometimes caravans of camels and donkeys came over the Taurus, pounding the ancient mountain trails. Even as today the caravan was led by the surefooted donkey. Some of the merchants found their way into the establishment of Paul's father, where they sold large balls of sheep's wool and goat's hair. The boy listened to their rough dialect with its crude Celtic expressions. Little did he think that some day these coarse Galatians would find a place in his affections.

While Paul was working in his father's factory and while he went home tired after washing his hands and dreamed of these strange peoples, far away in another town another Boy, somewhat older, was also laying aside his tools to go to rest. The boy of Tarsus, of course, knew nothing of that young Man in Nazareth. But while Jesus went to rest on his hard pallet, He may have breathed a prayer for the little boy in Tarsus.

CHAPTER THREE

AT THE FEET OF GAMALIEL

"I am a Jew, born at Tarsus in Cilicia, but brought up in this city,
at the feet of Gamaliel" (Acts 22:3).
"And I made progress in the Jews' religion above many of my equals
in my own nation, being more abundantly zealous
for the traditions of my fathers" (Gal. 1:14).

According to an old rabbinical tradition, every Jew at the age of five was to be introduced to the reading of the Torah (the law), at ten years of age he was to be taught the Mishnah (the oral tradition), at fifteen he was to learn the Talmud, and at eighteen he should be led to the Chuppa (the bridal chamber).

As a strict Pharisee, Paul's father had probably taken him to Jerusalem for the celebration of the Pasch. But about the time that he reached his fifteenth year he began to live in Jerusalem in order to attend the famous Temple high school.

It is not easy for us today to realize what an impression the first sight of Jerusalem made on a young man of Paul's religious background. For every religious Jew, Jerusalem was the cherished goal of his youthful ambitions. As the traveller approached the city from the north, he beheld a breath-taking view. To the right of the Mount of Olives, the massive pile of Herod's temple reared itself from the steep valley of the

Kedron. It was like a mountain of shimmering marble covered over with the blazing glory of its golden roof. In the west appeared the city with its palaces, above which Herod's new palace rose in haughty grandeur.

Just as memorable as the day of his arrival in this holy city was the youth's first day at the Temple college of which Gamaliel, "respected by all the people" (Acts 5:34), was the venerated rector. He was a member of the Sanhedrin, and an intellectual leader of great magnanimity whose influence even permitted him to take the Apostles under his protection. At that time Jerusalem was filled with students, and the rabbinical schools left their imprint on the city in the same way that the Sorbonne gave character to medieval Paris. The rabbis who taught in the school, however, were not paid officials. Besides their teaching in the schools, each rabbi engaged in some trade in order to earn his frugal sustenance. Thus the great Hillel was a day labourer; another teacher, Jehoshua, was a charcoal burner. It was the latter who once said: "You do not know the need of these scholars, how they support themselves and on what they live." Paul, too, may have been forced to lead an austere existence, especially if his father limited his allowance. Later, on his missionary journeys, this training in frugal living stood him in good stead and made it possible for him to live without the alms of his Churches.

The theologians in Jerusalem at that time were divided into two schools: the sympathetic and conciliatory school of Hillel, who was always able to find a way to circumvent the harshness of the law, and the school of Shammai, who fanatically insisted on the letter of the law. Gamaliel was a worthy successor of his uncle Hillel. Paul matriculated as a student in the school of Gamaliel and soon "made progress in the Jews' religion above many of my equals in my own nation" (Gal. 1:14). In this religious atmosphere at Jerusalem, Paul's literary and artistic interests which had engaged his attention in Tarsus gradually receded even though Gamaliel encouraged his pupils to study Greek literature. In the classroom the students sat in a semicircle on the floor or on very low benches surrounding their teacher just as they do today in the Arabian university mosque of El Azhar in Cairo. Thus Paul literally sat at the "feet of Gamaliel." We are fortunate in knowing the details of classroom procedure at that time. A passage was chosen from the Old Testament. It was first read in Hebrew and then in the vernacular Aramaic. Then the teacher reviewed the various explanations which had already been given or which might be given. Finally the teacher invited the students to enter the discussion by questions and answers, in a way resembling the seminars at our universities. Thus the lecture concluded in a spirited discussion during which the argument often became heated and the clamour grew louder and louder.

The subject matter of the theological course comprised two groups of subjects: the Halakah, that great mass of interpretations and explanations of the law, and the Haggada, those religious truths derived from the history of the Old Testament and the many legends that had grown up around it. We might call it a course in canon law and moral theology, and a course in dogmatic theology and Church history. Paul pursued both these courses as is evident from the various examples of symbolic explanations of historical events which he gives us in his Epistles (Phil. 3:6; Gal. 1:14). In ancient times the study of history as we consider it today was unknown. The rabbis were less interested in the history of men than in the history of mankind. They were concerned about man's relationship to God as it was known through certain typical personalities and important events of the past.

An example of the freedom with which historical details were treated is given by St. Stephen, who apparently went to the same school as that attended by Paul and may have been his schoolmate. Stephen's references to the training and miracles of Moses, to the mediation of the angel in his calling near the burning thorn bush and at the promulgation of the Ten

Commandments on Mt. Sinai were all parts of the old Jewish tradition. So too are the references to Jannes and Mambres (in 2 Tim. 3:8), and the legend about the Archangel Michael who fought the devil for the body of Moses (Jude 9). Paul had mastered the art of weaving together a mass of details in order to illustrate an entirely independent matter. He did not base his gospel on the Old Testament, but once he had received it by immediate revelation, he tried to corroborate it through his mystical exegesis of the Old Testament.

We discerned two influences in Paul's education: his religious training and the Hellenic culture of Tarsus. His exegetical training and the mastery of the threefold sense of the Scriptures which he achieved in Gamaliel's school are a third influence of his formative years. Without a knowledge of these typical (symbolical), accommodated, and allegorical senses, we will not be able to understand Paul's letters. Following Father Prat,[1] we may define these senses as follows. The typical sense is a secret, spiritual, and prophetic meaning which is a kind of overlay on the literal meaning. Thus the Scripture is in a special sense a prophetical work of the Holy Spirit. According to this sense, St. Paul speaks of Adam, the first man, as the type of Christ, the last man. These are the two great personalities between which, as between two poles, the history of mankind moves. In the same way, the law of Moses, the paschal lamb, the rock in the desert, the synagogue, and marriage, have a symbolical meaning.

Since the Bible is a book written for all times, its meaning can be accommodated to the needs of any time. This accommodated sense is the particular meaning which any preacher or devout reader may discern according to the light that is given him. St. Paul makes use of this sense when he is recommending the collection for the brethren in Jerusalem; he compares the common need of all the brethren to the common need of all who gathered manna in the Old Testament (2 Cor. 8:15). He

---

[1] *Prat, S.J., La theologie de Saint Paul, Paris, 1929*

applies a scriptural text to an analogous instance of the present.

Besides these senses, a scriptural text may be used in a rhetorical or allegorical manner in order to illustrate a point. The mastery of this sense of the Scriptures by the great preachers of the past, St. Bernard, Bossuet, and Segneri, may have accounted for the peculiar effectiveness of their preaching. St. Paul gives us an example of the use of the allegorical sense in the letter to the Romans (10:6-9). He recalls the words of Moses' farewell sermon which had become a proverb among the people: "This commandment, that I command you this day, is not above you nor far off from you. Nor is it in heaven, that you should say: Which of us can go up to heaven to bring it to us, and we may hear and fulfil it in work? Nor is it beyond the sea: that you may excuse yourself, and say: Which of us can cross the sea, and bring it to us: that we may hear, and do that which is commanded? But the word is very near to you, in your mouth and in your heart, that you may do it" (Deut. 30:11-14).

St. Paul says that the gospel which is the faithful adherence to Christ through justification lies within every man's possibilities. Do not say therefore: "Which of us can go up into heaven to bring Christ down to us?" He is here in our midst, He became man. Do not say: "Who can go down into the earth to bring Christ back from the dead?" Christ rose from the dead and lives again among us. All you need to do is make a sincere effort to live according to your faith and make a sincere confession of Christ, who became man and rose from the dead. This is no proof from the Scriptures; it is merely a rhetorical reference to a parallel instance in the Old Testament. St. Bernard and St. Bonaventure were masters of this allegorical sense, because they were filled with the spirit and imagery of the Bible. For the modern preacher who meditates, this use of Scripture is an inexhaustible fountain into which no vessel descends without being filled with gold.

For a young man engaged in his studies in Jerusalem far from his parental home, the social life of the metropolis was not without its dangers. The more select circles, to which Paul because of his intellectual gifts soon found admittance, united the grossest bigotry with the most refined luxury. The upper classes in Jerusalem spoke an affected form of Aramaic. They were busy about an exaggerated social life in which they displayed their wit and culture while they were always ready to lionize foreign celebrities. In their houses the stranger met the attractive women of the city from whose wrists and ankles gold spangles and bracelets dangled while their softly draped robes wafted vague perfumes about their persons. They modelled themselves after the famous Berenice who had tried to seduce Titus himself, and set the fashions in clothing and jewellery for the visitors from the provinces. But Paul's consuming interest in religion made him blind to everything else. He remained unmarried even though marriage was a special obligation for a Pharisee. It was a singular thing to do, although some precedent existed for it in Elias and Jeremias. A famous rabbi who had not married justified himself by saying: "What shall I do? My soul cleaves to the Torah. Let others, keep the world going." Paul may have reasoned similarly. Later, as a Christian, he based his celibacy on his mystical betrothal to Christ and the Church.

The Bible was his consuming interest. The Bible again and again. He memorized it in two languages. He knew most of the Septuagint version before he left Tarsus. On his journeys on foot later he was certainly not able to carry with him the large and expensive rolls of the Scripture. He would have suffered their irreparable loss in his several shipwrecks. But in spite of all this, his letters are filled with quotations and references to every book of the Old Testament. Scholars have counted about two hundred Scripture references. Can anyone doubt that it was the Bible that formed his mind and made him the great man he was? For him the Bible was the earth's greatest treasure. "What advantage then has the Jew?" he asks; and he answers: "First, indeed, because the words of God were committed to them"

(Rom. 3:1). The Jew's love for the Bible is unexampled in the history of the human race.

Two hundred years before the destruction of Jerusalem a Jewish sage expressed the sentiment of his people, a sentiment that lived in the youthful soul of Paul of Tarsus. "This is the book of the covenant made with the great God. From this book wisdom flowed like the waters of the Pison when it is in flood and like the waters of the Tigris when it goes over its banks. From it has come understanding flowing like the Euphrates when it is swollen large and like the Jordan in the time of the harvest. From it has come discipline like a light and like the water of the Nile in the autumn. No man has lived that has exhausted its learning and no man shall ever search out its depth, for its meaning is as full as the sea and more profound than the deepest abyss." When the Temple was destroyed by Titus, the Jews, who certainly have a keen understanding for values, abandoned the gold and silver vessels for the sacrifice, the candelabra and the lamps, and even the high priest's breastplate with its precious stones, in order to save the Bible. This was indeed the true treasure of the Temple, which they snatched from the flames of destruction.

CHAPTER FOUR

STEPHEN AND SAUL

Ten years have passed since Paul left the college at Jerusalem after his farewell to Gamaliel. As a "young man" (Acts 7:57), about thirty, he now returns to Jerusalem. We have no way of knowing where and how he spent the years after his departure from Gamaliel's school in Jerusalem. He may have returned to the Diaspora to begin his career as a rabbi. Perhaps he even returned to the synagogue of his native Tarsus. Here, at any rate, he would have had an opportunity to study the Hellenic mind from the vantage point of his recent training. Since he appears to be well acquainted with the Sanhedrin in Jerusalem, he may have visited the outposts of the Jewish world at their direction, returning to make his report at intervals. But he never stayed long enough in Jerusalem to meet Jesus. Paul never makes the slightest reference to any personal meeting with our Lord, even when his apostleship was questioned. A man of his impulsive character could not have remained passive or indifferent toward Jesus; he would either have been one of His antagonists or he would have become an enthusiastic disciple. The famous passage in the Second Epistle to the Corinthians (5:16): "And if we have known Christ according to the flesh;

but now we know him so no longer," declares merely that Paul
no longer sees Jesus with his earthly, nationalist prejudices, but
with the eyes of supernatural faith. It is therefore highly
probable that Paul never knew our Lord personally.

During these years the most tremendous event in the
history of the world took place: Christ redeemed the world on
Golgotha. With true Jewish pride and arrogance, Paul had
concerned himself little about the squabbles of Galilee. This
carpenter from Galilee would go the way of all visionaries.
These movements were always put down eventually; only
recently a certain Theodas with four hundred followers was
slain and also a certain Judas of Galilee (Acts 5:36 ff.). But as
time passed, it appeared that this movement was different from
the rest. This time it seemed that the Lord was roaring from
Sion and had "uttered His voice from Jerusalem" (Amos 1:2).

Saul heard the rolling of the thunder from afar. Three
Cilician travellers, Andronicus, Junias, and Herodian, who had
spent Pentecost in Jerusalem, told of the strange occurrences on
a certain Friday; and others came back saying that this affair
with the Nazarene could not be put down. After He was dead
He was more dangerous than alive, and His followers were still
increasing. True, most of His followers were pious Israelites
from the poorer quarters of Ophel who came every morning
and evening to the inner Temple court and to the Hall of
Solomon. Recently, however, some priests of the lower classes
had gone over to them (Acts 6:7). They were not a troublesome
crowd; in fact, most people looked with favour on them. A
certain Levite of some standing in the community, Joseph of
Cyprus, had become a Nazarene and now called himself Barnabas. It was said that he had gone so far as to sell his property
and give the money to the new sect (Acts 4:36 f.). When Paul
heard that his old college friend, Joseph of Cyprus, had
apostatized, he could no longer remain aloof from the affair.
Perhaps, too, he may have been invited by the Sanhedrin to
take a hand in suppressing the new sect.

The Hellenistic Jews from the Diaspora had their own organizations and synagogues in Jerusalem. Even more than today the city was filled with national synagogues; some scholars enumerate about 480 alien synagogues.'[2] These synagogues provided rooms for prayer, instruction, and some offered bathing facilities and an underground prison for the synagogal penalties, particularly scourging. St. Luke speaks of one of the more important synagogues as that of the Libertines who were the descendants of those Jewish prisoners of war that Pompey had deported to Rome and later set free. Besides this great synagogue the Jews of Alexandria, Cyrene, Asia Minor, and Paul's native Cilicia had synagogues in Jerusalem (Acts 6:9). Among all these national groups, especially in the Cilician group, violent arguments arose about Jesus whenever they gathered for services.

If we accept A.D. 30 as the most probable year of our Lord's death and then allow a few years for the new religion to grow until the death of St. Stephen, it was probably about A.D. 33 when Paul returned to Jerusalem. His first visit in the city was to his old teacher Gamaliel, who during these years had turned grey and now lived in the past. Since the day of that execution on Golgotha, the city was no longer the same. A heavy weight seemed to lie on the conscience of the people and the priesthood. The disciples of Him who had been crucified continued to assemble, as it were, about some mysterious thing, some invisible thing which no one could see excepting those who belonged to Him. They grew in numbers, too; many of the more broadminded Greek-speaking Jews, the Hellenists, from the Diaspora flocked to their meetings. Because of this growth the new Church made a progressive step in its organization which was of far-reaching importance. A man called Stephen, renowned for his exceptional knowledge of the Bible, and a certain householder, named Philip, who had four daughters with the gift of prophecy, were elected as members of a new

---

[2] Cf. H. F. B. Mackey, *The Adventures of Paul of Tarsus,* London, 1931

seven-man college, and soon we find them preaching and working miracles (Acts 6:8; 8:6; 21:9).

Contrary to what we might think today, the infant Church was not a complete and independent organization separate from Judaism. In the early years it had merely that loose juridical form possessed by many of the alien synagogues in Jerusalem. Without its own building, but with a new and unheard-of belief in the Messias, great fraternal love, and a mystic, Eucharistic cult of Jesus practised together with a peculiar love banquet (Acts 2:42-46). It was Stephen who first recognized the independent character of the new Church and pointed out that it must develop and grow of itself. In Stephen, Paul found a representative of this new movement and an adversary who was not to be underestimated.

Let us pay a visit to one of the synagogues of Jerusalem. Over the entrance we might find the inscription in Greek and Aramaic: "Synagogue of the Cilicians." Almost every Cilician in Jerusalem seems to be present today; the auditorium is packed because today is the day of the great discussion. The Scripture lesson is read and the sermon follows, and now the debate begins. Peter and John are watching the scene from behind a pillar in the rear of the hall. Stephen can be seen standing on a raised podium near the front, and opposite him is the small, emaciated figure of the man from Tarsus. The two greatest minds of the early Church are about to cross swords.

Stephen had a deep-seated hatred of the subtleties of the law. He handled the matter calmly, referring to the historical background. He recalled what the prophets had said: that the Messias would suffer and die. And he declared that the crucified Jesus was that servant of God pictured by Isaias.

That picture of a suffering man, dying a slave's death on the tree of shame as the promised Messias, was an utterly repulsive thought for Saul. He began now to visualize the horrible scandal of the cross. Today he recalled the scriptural curse, "He is accursed of God that hangs on a tree" but later he was to take this weapon of attack and turn it against the foes of Christ: "Christ has redeemed us from the curse of the law, being made a curse for us" (Deut. 21:23; Gal. 3:13). As spokesmen for such extreme views of the Messias, we can understand with what fury Paul and Stephen rushed in for the attack. Paul was a debater of unusual keenness, but Stephen had the advantage of a calmer poise. "They were not able to resist the wisdom and the spirit that spoke" and they could only retort with one scant argument from the law: "He is accursed of God that hangs on a tree" (Acts 6:10).

Stephen saw that it was necessary for him to proceed to an attack on the whole position of the law. The law and the Temple here in Jerusalem were only a passing stage in the great scheme of redemption which extended farther back into the past and into the future than the law. The monstrous historical error of Judaism consisted in the fact that it tried to barricade the course of human history with the great block of the Temple and the law and thus seal up the course of the dispensation of God's grace. When Stephen flung his words about the passing of the law and the Temple into the ears of his audience, they rose outraged and stood on the benches.

The debate turned into a trial; angry fists threatened above the heads of the crowd. Someone snatched Stephen and whisked him away through the narrow streets past the old-clothes dealers' booths to the council chamber in the Temple where the Sanhedrin, the venerable fathers of Israel, were assembled in their sacred semicircle. His accusers had no trouble in twisting his words. Once more Stephen explained his concept of the Messias and its relationship to the story of the redemption, concluding with the fearful accusation, "Of whom you have been now the betrayers and murderers" (Acts 7:52).

Bestial fury leered out from every face, but Stephen seemed to be in an ecstasy with his eyes on something above him. The high priest, that hard man Caiphas (A.D. 16-32), wanted to proceed immediately to taking a vote. "Guilty or not

guilty?" Paul, who as a member of the Sanhedrin and a scribe
had the right to vote, was about to cast his pebble into the urn,
but he was too late. Jews from all the synagogues in the city
were dragging Stephen through the chamber and out to the
Damascus Gate. The place for stoning was a ramp about twice
a man's height. Paul came storming after the mob and stood to
watch the bloody business as the only scribe witness. The first
witness against Stephen threw him from the ramp in such a
way that he fell on his back. If the victim fell on his face, the
witness turned him over and then the second witness took a
large stone and threw it with all his force on the heart of the
victim. The blow failed to kill. Now, according to the law
(Deut. 17:7), it was the people's turn. The men took off their
white mantles and put them down at Paul's feet, in order not to
be impeded in their bloody work. Stephen raised himself from
the ground and looking heavenward, stretched out his arms and
prayed: "Lord Jesus, receive my spirit." The first stones began
flying through the air; Stephen fell to the ground. His eyes
found Paul, and amid the hail of stones he cried out: "Lord, lay
not this sin to their charge." The deed was done. The young
hero lay motionless in his blood. Paul was content: he had
earned his spurs.

This was the kind of lynch justice that the high priests
themselves feared. The whole Sanhedrin prudently stayed in
the background so that it would not come into conflict with the
governor. Paul, however, never forgot that day. All during his
life that scene haunted his conscience. Again and again the
scene of Stephen's stoning rises in his memory (Acts 22:20;
26:10; Gal. 1:23; 1 Cor. 15:9): "I am not worthy to be called an
apostle, because I persecuted the Church of God." When he
recalled that day in his later years, he may have recognized it as
one of the most decisive days of his life.

When he returned that evening from the stoning and went
to bed, was he able to sleep? Did he perhaps hear the hushed
voices of the men who went out with their torches to bring back

the body of the youth? Did he hear the weeping women who came to comfort Stephen's mother in her sorrow? Or did he put down these pangs of conscience as temptations of the devil? He had not yet learned the discerning of spirits.

St. Stephen's death was the price which the early Church paid that she might break through her national Judaistic shell and go on her way as the universal Church, and in order to win for herself her greatest Apostle who would consummate the separation from Judaism, *"Non sine sanguine"* (Heb. 9:22). No great victory is won without the shedding of blood. That is a principle in the kingdom of God. Stephen made that sacrifice and became the Church's first soldier pioneering the way into a worldwide future. The Church needed such a champion who would "fill up those things that are wanting of the sufferings of Christ" (Col. 1:24). Sometimes God allows his co-workers to fall in battle, but the work goes on. Stephen is dead; he who was the great hope of the Church is gone. But the truth cannot die, for God is ever with the truth.

And within a year of his death, one of his murderers took Stephen's place and fought his fight to victory. St. Augustine once said that Paul stoned Stephen with the hands of all the rest because he watched their clothing. Therefore St. Stephen's prayer was meant especially for him. *Si martyr Stephanus non sic orasset, Ecclesia Paulum non haberet* ("If Stephen had not prayed thus, the Church would not have had Paul") (*Sermo* 382).

CHAPTER FIVE

THE PERSECUTOR

*"But Saul made havoc of the Church, entering in from house to house: and
dragging away men and women, committed them to prison"* (Acts 8:3).
*"Who before was a blasphemer and a persecutor and contumelious:
But I obtained the mercy of God,
because I did it ignorantly in unbelief"* (1 Tim. 1:13).

Truth can be reached by different routes. God gives it to
some men without any fight or crisis; others, like St. Augustine
and Dante, must go through fearful inner distresses. St.
Augustine looked on his own conversion as a symbol of the
road which guilt-laden humanity travels, and in his immortal
Easter chant he praises in bold hyperbole the sin of our first
parents as a blessing, "a happy fault," because it led the way to
the Redeemer. Saul, too, travelled through sin and darkness
before he found Christ. How momentous his early hatred of
Christ and his vision of the Saviour were to him is evident from
the fact that he speaks of them repeatedly in his letters and
sermons. When a man makes a radical break with his past he is
likely to see it afterwards in a very sharp light, and sometimes
he finds it difficult to be fair to himself or others. That was true
of St. Paul, St. Augustine and Luther. St. Augustine manifested
an exaggerated consciousness of guilt, and Luther indulged in

excessive reproaches against the Church, while Paul seemed to reproach and blame himself beyond measure. As an old man, the Apostle was able to judge more mildly when he said that he had acted "ignorantly in unbelief."

The death of Stephen was the upbeat of a new wave of suffering; it was the signal for the bloodiest persecution of the infant Church, but that persecution only accelerated the growth of the Church. We know from experience that an unjust persecution merely awakens sympathy for the cause of the persecuted.

Where was Paul? A seemingly casual remark in the Acts of the Apostles, "and Paul was consenting to his death," arouses our interest; on further thought we are inclined to doubt the accuracy of the translation. Paul was a man of refined feeling and high culture. He saw how Stephen died amid the glory of martyrdom; he saw reflected in his face the light of another world; he saw him die with a prayer for others on his lips. Could Paul have turned away from this sight unmoved? Something stirred in his soul that made him feel uneasy, he was conscious of something that he was afraid to face, and his "consenting" was certainly not an unmixed feeling of approval. Here was the first goad that pressed into his soul. His sensitive soul must have suffered increasingly from self-reproaching, but as he suffered he thought he was suffering, "zealous for the law" (Acts 22:3). When a man feels the burden of guilt on his soul, he tries hard to justify himself before his own conscience and before others by increasing his false zeal, and thus he sinks yet deeper into evil.

But Paul soon pulled himself together. He had a job to do: this cursed heresy must be rooted out and destroyed. He was to play the principal role in this proceeding against the Christians. His method was clever. First the fanaticism of the people was stirred up by circulating accusations, and by throwing fuel on national prejudices and hates. All that was done at the secret behest of the Sanhedrin, which remained behind the scenes; when public opinion was ripe, Paul went into action.

A kind of inquisition was established, and Paul was named the grand inquisitor. He was given spies, Temple soldiers, legal processes, at his disposal. Nocturnal arrests, sudden searches of house and persons, forced confessions and incriminations by means of torture applied in the subterranean rooms of the synagogue, floggings of thirty-nine lashes, as he himself would receive later, were the order of the day (Acts 26:11). The prisons were filled. Those who could do so, fled with their wives and children and a few pitiable household possessions to the country, but even there Paul suddenly appeared with his henchmen.

How was it that the apostles were able to remain un-disturbed in Jerusalem? What of those Christians who escaped persecution and for whom the apostles remained? It seems that the line of separation did not run between Jews and Christians, but between those Jewish Christians who held fast to the Mosaic law and the more liberal, Greek-speaking Hellenist Jewish Christians who came mostly from the Diaspora. The distinction was made between the conservative wing of the original apostles and the more radical wing led by Stephen. This is the beginning of that vexing problem which runs through Paul's whole life: on one side a Jewish Church bound to the law; on the other side, a universal Church emancipated from the law. Those Pharisees who had been converted to Christ without taking off their Pharisaical garments, could remain undisturbed in Jerusalem, and the apostles were under the protection of James, who was universally respected as being faithful to the law.

"Saul made havoc of the Church." A most unusual pro-cedure for a future apostle! How can one reconcile such brutal action with Paul's character? Perhaps it will always remain a psychological riddle, but we must attempt to penetrate the mystery. We have seen what a great change the incidence of the law made in the life of an adolescent Jew. After he came under the law, he was under an uncanny power, he lived continually under "sin," or the fear of sin. This fear of sin was a tyrant that insinuated itself into every department of life, into his material as well as his spiritual being and it produced a depressed, enslaved consciousness. Paul suffered intensely under the weight of this fear. Once he cried out: "Unhappy man that I am, who shall deliver me from the body of this death?" (Rom 7:24.) A great sword of uncertainty was suspended over his head, an uncertainty about the coming day of doom.

Two things dominated the Jewish religion at this time: the law and the coming day of judgment. Life was regulated down to the smallest detail of everyday routine by the law's 248 prescriptions and 346 prohibitions, besides uncounted oral interpretations. Every possible case was provided for; nothing was left to the individual's responsibility. The more hopeless the present seemed, the safer they thought they were behind the palisades of the law. Here, hedged in by the law, the Jew awaited the day of judgment which was pictured for him in lurid colours by many apocalyptical writers. Anyone who dared to shake even one of the posts of this structure of the law was to be destroyed.

Out of the law, Judaism wove for itself a garment like that of Nessus, which ultimately caused its own death. For the Jew every commandment of the law, every cultural and moral prescription, was of the same divine validity. He who violated one rule, violated the whole law. The inviolability and solidarity of the law was in itself a dogma of religion. Paul, no less than Peter, knew that no matter how much he tried, his effort would be far behind what the law required. At the Council of Jerusalem, Peter said: "Now, therefore, why tempt your God to put a yoke upon the necks of the disciples which neither our fathers nor we have been able to bear?" (Acts 15:10) When Paul says that he lived "without blame," he is referring to a blamelessness in observing the outward requirements of the law as compared to his companions (Phil. 3:6). Within his soul he was perpetually tortured by the discrepancy between his willing and doing. How disconsolate was the spirit of every devout Jew may be seen from the moral pessimism of the author of the Fourth Book of Esdras, written sometime after this period.

"Ah, Adam, what have you done?
You have sinned. But the consequences
Of your sin fell not alone on you,
But on your children.
What does it avail us that eternity
Is promised us?
For we do the works of death."

In that analysis of his own soul in the Epistle to the Romans, Paul gives us a detailed description of the soul's helplessness and its consequent misery. That self-analysis has rightly been called one of the most touching confessions in human history. A genuine pearl such as is cast up on the shores of human life only by the severest inner trials and by the storm of violent inner battles.

But no man can live long in a spiritual vacuum, in a negative attitude toward life. Thus, many who lived under the law tried to make a virtue out of necessity with a slavish observance of the letter of the law, an indulgence in pettifogging exegesis of the law, and a pitiful attempt to make themselves believe that their racial connection to the people to whom the promises were made was of some avail. But all this hypocritical subterfuge was intolerable to a man of Paul's character. From his letters we know that his nature was one that had an irrepressible urge for perfection, a desire for complete dedication to a goal and a willingness to seek its own dissolution in the accomplishment of any task assigned by God. Paul was an uncompromising enemy of all mediocrity. Only by such an inner all-consuming fire of restlessness can we explain his headlong leap into the work of persecution. His extraordinary zeal was kept pitched at the highest point in order to make up for the defections in the observance of the law. That is a form of "super-compensation," as it is called by psychologists, arising from a feeling of inferiority and guilt under the oppressive force of the law.

And now as he looks into the eyes of these dying Christians, Paul discerns something he has never seen before. He sees a mildness, an expression of inward blessedness, of a higher life, of a union with the risen Christ which is disturbed by no pain and no horror inflicted by men; they seem to be in communication with Christ who assures them that they are passing over to a new life and not to death. He caught a momentary glimpse of something that surpassed anything he had ever known, of something the law could not give.

The vision of this inner bliss written on the faces of his victims was the second goad that pressed into his soul, and against it he rose in rebellion; but the more he fought it, the more it bored into his being. Only later, as a Christian, was Paul able to realize the terrible craftiness of "sin." An erroneous religious training can be the source of much suffering and result in a fateful distrust in God. In the letter to the Romans, Paul speaks of the cure for such error. An entirely new and positive basis for a relationship with God must be found. The bands that held the soul captive must be released. It must take an aggressive attitude against evil; it must come to know a childlike trust in God in which it will pray with joy and cry out with spontaneity, "Abba, Father."

CHAPTER SIX

THE GREAT REVERSAL

"For God, who commanded the light to shine out of darkness, has shone in
our hearts, to give the light of the knowledge of the glory of God,
in the face of Christ Jesus" (2 Cor. 4:6).
"For neither did I receive it of man: nor did I learn it
but by the revelation of Jesus Christ" (Gal. 1:12).

When he looked back on his life, Paul saw it divided into
two parts: the days without Christ and the days "in Christ." We
are approaching that moment in his life that separates these two
parts. In three momentous occurrences that follow swiftly on
each other's heels, Paul's life storms on. First the murder of
Stephen, then the persecution of the Christians in Judea, and
finally the ride to Damascus. From there he hurries on to the
moment of the great reversal, to that moment when his life will
be turned into another channel; and from then on it will no
longer be a life of destruction but a life pouring out all its
energies to support, to fructify, and to bless all mankind.

How he arrived at this point of reversal and what mental
processes were behind it, will perhaps always be a mystery to
us. He himself always maintained staunchly that his conversion
was a supernatural occurrence, a miraculous event when Christ
strode mightily into his life. To try to convince him that in this

most important moment of his life he had been deluded would have been a foolhardy undertaking. The veil that covers such a supernatural event as Paul's conversion must remain. Yet it must not become a barrier, obstructing our way to a psychological and historical study of what occurred.

Jerusalem had now been purged of Christians. Some had fled to Joppe where Peter taught them; others went to Samaria where Philip took charge; while others had gone as far as Damascus in the heart of eastern Syria; and still others fled to places as distant as Phoenicia, Cyprus, and Antioch. A large number took refuge in Damascus, which was one of the largest Jewish colonies where, since the days of King Achab, the Jews had obtained the right of erecting their bazaars, those long lines of merchants' booths in the streets. By this migration thousands of true Israelites were in danger of contamination by these Christians. That nest of Christians must be destroyed.

At the head of a well-armed troop, Paul rode out one morning through the Damascus Gate, past the fresh mound of Stephen's grave, out to the north. From Jerusalem to Damascus at that time was a journey of about one week. The traveller could choose one of three routes, each being about 150 miles long. Paul chose the shortest route, which led across the barren, stone-strewn Judean plateau, close by Bethel in the country of Benjamin, on through the bleached fields of Samaria. On these fields the Saviour, journeying this way years before, had said: "See the countries. For they are white already to harvest" (John 4:35). Perhaps he, too, like the Saviour, stopped at Jacob's well. Did he notice the unfriendly looks of the Samaritans or the way they breathed more lightly as they saw him gallop off, down past Dschennin to the green plain of Esdrelon across which the cool breeze from the sea was blowing? He rode by the mountains of Gelboe where his royal ancestor had lost his crown and his kingdom. Soon he beheld the drawn-out peaks of Mount Hermon with their coat of snow; here he passed by Scythopolis (the ancient Beth Sean) where the Philistines had hung up the bodies of Saul and Jonathan, and he crossed the Jordan to the wilderness of Gadara. Now his route took him up to the ancient "sea road" the *via maris* on which Abraham, Jacob, and Rachel had once travelled. How delightful this journey would have been under other circumstances! How delightful these cool nights when the travellers gathered about the crackling fires under the stars that shone from the dark velvet skies. But Paul was a city man; he had little taste for the beauties of nature. In all his letters there is nothing of the thrill of natural beauty. Paul was too intent on spiritual things and psychological problems. Man was far more interesting to him than nature, and besides this, God was the axis of all his thinking.

But now he was a hunter driven on by an insatiable thirst for the prey. He was not, however, the only hunter in these days of the ride to Damascus. Another, the Master of these disciples he is hunting, is on his trail. Paul thought he was the hunter while he himself was the quarry. In his *The Hound of Heaven* Francis Thompson speaks of the hunt for souls. Christ is the divine hunter, and here on the road to Damascus he is running down his most precious quarry, and the quarry will not be able to escape. Paul was now outside the whirl of the metropolis, where many hide from God. He was alone without one of his own kind to talk to. He had six days and six long nights for reflection. Whether he willed it or not, he must stand at the bar of his own conscience.

Those who baulk at whatever is supernatural try to explain Paul's conversion and his new concept of Christ as the psychological result of his Hellenistic mysticism and a mythological image of some heavenly person, accentuated by his Stoic spiritualism and the enlightenment he received in Gamaliel's classes and his own prophetic disposition. These ingenious scholars speak of a "pre-Christian Christianity" in Paul's mind. What, we may ask, was the picture of the Messias entertained by the Jews of that time and by Paul? One group of Jews, a small number of sincere, religious Jews without "guile," lived in the true spirit of the prophets and awaited the coming of the Messias as a religious renewal and reconciliation, and through the light of the Holy Spirit these men attained to the faith in Jesus. To this small group belonged such men and women as Mary, Elizabeth, Zachary, and Simeon, and the great canticles of the *Magnificat, Benedictus,* and *Nunc Dimittis* are the expression of this faith.

The popular, rabbinical concept of the Messias was painted over with political ambitions that were derived from certain misunderstood passages of the Bible, especially from the apocryphal writings, such as the Psalms of Solomon, the Book of Enoch, the Fourth Book of Esdras, and the Apocalypse of Baruch. When a nation has been in subjection for centuries, it begins to dream of liberation just as the prisoner who has been long confined in a dungeon. The Jews began to long for a political Messias, and thus the religion of Judaism had a false development which was a repudiation of the religion of the prophets. The injection of political hopes despoiled the Jews of their religion and thus robbed them of their most valuable heritage. This heterodox outgrowth of Judaism had no longer any understanding for the idea of the atonement of the Messias; the Messias was now no longer the suffering "servant of God" spoken of by Isaias, but some ineffably glorious warrior and statesman who was far above human weakness and suffering and death.

This hero and superman could never succumb to his enemies; he could never submit to such a degradation as crucifixion. He was to bring dominion and victory to the Jews; he was to establish world dominion and world peace. "For his enemies his countenance would be more terrifying than any man could imagine... Whatever he looked upon trembled before his gaze and wherever his voice reached, things melted as wax before the sun" (Enoch 46:4; Esdras 13). The idea that the Messias would be capable of suffering was entirely unacceptable to the great mass of the Jews, but especially repugnant to the scribes and Pharisees, the "Chaberim" or official guardians of religion.

The poor and humble, the "Amha'arez," those who "labour and are burdened," were more ready for the idea of suffering. But even among Christ's disciples, some were dreaming of earthly glory (Mark 9:33). Did they not hope for seats to the right and left of the throne of the Messias? (Mark 10:37) Did not Peter reproach our Lord when he foretold his passion? (Matt. 16:22; Mark 8:32) Even after he was risen from the dead, how difficult it was to open the eyes of the disciples on the road to Emmaus: "Ought not Christ to have suffered these things?" (Luke 24:26)

Such was the idea of the Messias that dominated the mind of Paul. Christ's death on the cross proved that he was a false Messias, and it was a certain sign that his disciples were deceivers. And this idea of fraternizing between Jews and peoples of other nations in one kingdom! It was a monstrous thought. We must keep all this in mind if we wish to estimate the magnitude of that event on the road to Damascus when the Christian spirit broke in on a man of Paul's mentality.

He was now eight days on the journey from Jerusalem with the legal papers and warrants in his pocket for the arrest of the Christians in Damascus. Again and again he was thinking of those words the Christians spoke in prayer as they died; those words of the prophet about the Lamb that was led to slaughter; about the Messias who by suffering and dying would save his people in their religious and moral need. This was the third goad. He fought furiously within himself against such an idea of a Messias. Never would he, the scion of ancient Jews, apostatize to such heresy. And yet the thought refused to leave; it became the companion of his ride. It fanned the flame of his hatred against that sect whose victory, he knew, would be the end of the Jewish religion and the Jews' plan for world dominion. He knew that if the Nazarenes were right, his cause was lost. Everything seemed to stand or fall with that. In fact, now it suddenly became a question of his own spiritual position. He did not yet know that already the arrow of the hunter had hit the mark. Already the new life was struggling within him; until now he had not lived at all. Later, when he looked back on those moments as he approached Damascus, he saw that it was then he began his "being in Christ."

Such was Paul's mental state on the ride to Damascus. Of himself he would never have become a Christian; this state of mind does not of itself lead to Christ. He might have fallen from this point into the abyss of despair. But within him there was a mighty ferment; a storm was raging as he rode on to the scene of new violence against the Christians.

Here at last lay before him the green oasis of the plain of Damascus, watered by the crystal-clear Barada and Parphar. The pearl-grey city, surrounded by its necklace of pomegranate, palm and myrtle trees, slumbered beneath the white shimmering rays of the midday sun. Looking out from under his coloured head-dress, his eyes began to pain as he held them fixed on his goal. Was it like this long ago when Moses saw the flames swimming and lambent above the thorn bush in the desert sun? Then suddenly that inexplicable thing happened.

From above came a blinding flame of fire. The horses pawed the air and turned off the road; a crash of metal, and Paul lay prostrate on the ground. The flames closed over him, and in the flames he saw the face of a man from heaven, heavenly (cf. 1 Cor. 15:48). And he looked into eyes that seemed to have the sea of eternity behind them, eyes that were serious and sad, mild, sublime. In the presence of that face, all opposition melted, and a voice spoke to him in the sacred language of his fathers (Acts 26:14), a voice as soft as "a whistling of a gentle air" like that which Elias heard when the Lord commanded him to go "through the desert to Damascus" (3 Kings 19:12, 15). Like the sad lament of Good Friday, he heard his name called twice: "Sha-ul, Sha-ul, why do you persecute Me?" And with lightning speed, the thought burst upon his mind: "My cause is lost. Stephen is right. Jesus lives."

Is it surprising that Paul was stunned by the blow of that thought? How long was it until he was able to overcome his unspeakable amazement and ask: "Who are you, Lord?" Then he heard the words he knew he must hear: "I am Jesus," and in the tone of gentle reproach: "whom you are persecuting." At that moment he beheld the face of Jesus.

Like a stream that gushes forth from hidden springs, a light burst forth within him and flooded his mind, "the light of the knowledge of the glory of God, in the face of Christ Jesus" (2 Cor. 4:6). The light of faith was lit within him. Mysterious powers had stirred themselves. A new life had begun. A higher world had been revealed, and it seemed that the withered fragments of the shell that confined his soul were falling away. His high arrogant spirit had completely capitulated. The battlements of his soul that had tried to withstand the Lord lay in ruins and he became a prisoner in obedience to the Lord. "And every height that exalts itself against the knowledge of God, and brings into captivity every understanding to the obedience of Christ" (2 Cor. 10:5). Never afterwards did he doubt about what had happened in those few short moments; it was his adamant conviction that he had seen the risen Lord and had spoken with Him.

He now took hold of himself. He had never been an idle dreamer; his was not a pale and melancholy Hamlet soul. He was always the man of action. Immediately he asked, "Lord, what will You have me do?" He had defended himself like a hero, but now, when he realized that his valour had served the cause of error, he resolutely joined the army of his victor. He had no time for lament and reproach; he had no thought of falling on the sword of despair. He went on to new action, a new cause, a new banner; he immediately re-formed his line of battle. Another great soldier, Ignatius Loyola, prepares his disciples for thirty days before he ventures to ask them to make the heroic step of self-surrender in the declaration, "Take, O Lord, all my freedom." But Paul made the magnanimous act of surrender after these few minutes. "Lord, take me from myself and give me Yourself. I desire to be Your bondsman, Your slave." Thus he described himself in signing his letters afterwards. The heavenly hunter had caught him and brought him to his knees like the pioneer that snares the wild prairie horse. And from now on he, too, will be obedient to the slightest pressure of the heavenly rider. Rising from the ground by the side of the Damascus road, Paul was the true and faithful bondsman of Jesus forever.

Out of that contact with Christ in this most gracious act of his condescension, he gained an important idea for himself and for the Church, that "it is not of him that wills, nor of him that runs, but of God that shows mercy" (Rom. 9:16). Out of that vision of the risen Saviour came not only the overwhelming knowledge of the Messianic mission of Christ, but an inner conversion from his errors, from his old moral paralysis, from his old religious despair. Out of it came the conviction that Christ is the Saviour of sinners, the Redeemer and reconciler who brings those "who some time were afar off" and makes them "nigh by the blood of Christ" (Eph. 2:13). If he had not had the vision of the risen Saviour, he would never have been able to rise above the "scandal of the Cross," above that ancient Jewish conviction that the cross was the tree of shame. Only the Resurrection could remove that stumbling block for him as it had also removed it for the other disciples. He had seen Christ not as an avenging and punishing God, but as the good and kind Saviour (Tit. 3:4), and because of that gracious vision he was convinced that the anger of God had been transmuted in the Crucifixion into love and that the crucified Jesus was really the Lamb of God spoken of by the prophets.

From this moment on the Damascus road to the ardent acclamation of the Cross in the Epistle to the Galatians, "God forbid that I should glory, save in the cross of our Lord Jesus

Christ," is but one short step. Now the Cross is the sign of salvation, now the scandal has become the power of God; the old
pitiful failure of the Cross is now seen as the heroic act of
obedience out of which came a glorious victory. He saw a new
world; everything had a different value now. He now affirmed
everything that the Jew denied, and all that the Jew valued he
now counted as dung (Phil. 3:8).

Every attempt of psychology to explain Paul's conversion
has failed. No one has been able to illuminate the interior of the
occurrence. It was a mystic death that occurred in a mystic darkness. It was as mysterious as the inception of a new life in the
womb of a mother; it was indeed a rebirth in the truest sense. So
it seemed to Paul himself, "He was seen also by me, as by one
born out of due time" (1 Cor. 15:8). He could say no more about
it, for what can a man say about the moment of his birth?

Hostile critics have made desperate attempts to explain
the occurrence on the Damascus road as the vision of a
hysterical weakling. The whole thing, they say, is questionable
but certainly not miraculous. But against all the critics, Paul
himself said on five occasions that it had all happened by the
power of God, that it was the revelation of the living Christ,
and with an absolute conviction he averred that "He was seen
also by me" (1 Cor. 15:8). Paul's was not a diseased, abnormal
soul. The almost incredible activity of thirty years contradicts
that conclusion. If any man ever had sound sense and judgment
and a knowledge of reality, it was Paul. If any man was ever
certain about his cause and willing to give his life for it, it was
Paul. If we accept the psychological law that new developments in the soul presuppose certain dispositions without which
such developments are devoid of any permanence, the suddenness and permanence of Paul's conversion are proofs of its
supernatural character. After all, such, mysterious occurrences
as Paul's conversion concern only two, God himself and that
individual upon whom God has bestowed his grace.

It would be wrong to try to derive everything in Paul's

life from this miraculous meeting with Christ near Damascus, as if this meeting had set his mental being in motion to form the whole Pauline theology. He had learned much from his disputations with Stephen and the Hellenists, at the hearings held in court about the teachings of the Christians, and later from the disciples in Damascus and Jerusalem. Jesus himself advised him to seek the teaching of tradition from the mouth of Ananias and to wait for "those things wherein I will appear to you" (Acts 26:16). Actually Paul received those visions in which certain truths were revealed, such as the resurrection of the dead at the second coming of Christ (1 Thess. 4:15; 1 Cor. 15:51-52).

From the miraculous meeting near Damascus, however, Paul received four great concepts. The first was the realization that the risen Christ was the Messias in whom the prophecies were fulfilled; the second, that the Jesus who walked on earth is identical with the pre-existing eternal Son of God; the third, that Christ dwells mystically in his followers as in another physical body (Acts 9:5; 1 Cor. 12:13; Eph. 5:30); the fourth, his own calling as the Apostle of the Gentiles. The Damascus vision was the vision that gave him his calling, and it can be compared to the visions in which the prophets were called. Because of that vision he was unable to be silent about Christ, "for a necessity lies upon me. For woe to me if I preach not the gospel" (1 Cor. 9:16).

But above all this was one thought suppressing every other emotion of his being: the penetration of his being by the all-forgiving love of Christ. That the Lord should visit his beloved disciples after his Resurrection was understandable; but that He should appear to him, his ruthless enemy, that God should have "separated me from my mother's womb, and called me by his grace," that Christ should have loved him with such a tender love, this was truly overwhelming and incomprehensible. And from then on, that love of Christ's was the unfailing inspiration of his gospel.

It was a mysterious duel between Creator and creature. God is a mighty hunter who will have only the strongest as his quarry. There is no escape from the chase; the quarry must either surrender or be done to death. The fact that the chase ended in Paul's conversion was not owing to any historical or psychological situation. It was another instance of the impenetrable mystery of grace and freedom. St. Augustine, who had experience with these things, said of Paul's duel with grace: "Grace struck him down and then lifted him up" *(percutiens eum et sanans, occidens et vivificans) (Sermo* 14*),* like that sacred lance of the legend that healed the wounds that it made.

CHAPTER SEVEN

IN DAMASCUS

*"And whereas I did not see for the brightness of that light,
being led by the hand by my companions, I came to Damascus.
And one Ananias, a man according to the law, having testimony of all the
Jews who dwell there, coming to me and standing by me, said to me:
Brother Saul, look up"* (Acts 22:11-13).

Every true conversion has two phases, the conversion of the intellect and the conversion of the heart. Without understanding, the pride of the human heart and its arrogance against God remain unconquerable. But besides this understanding, the heart itself must be seized by grace, it must be shattered and shaken in order that the will may be rectified. These two phases, as in St. Augustine's case, may be separated by a period of time.

When Paul arose at the Lord's command, he opened his eyes which he had pressed shut against the glaring light; but as he raised his lids he saw nothing – he was blind. Now the great terror of the Christians stood helpless by the road, groping about for an arm or a sleeve of one of his companions. They took hold and led a broken, silent man through the myrtle grove up to the gate that ever since has born his name. They went down the street called "Strait," a beautiful avenue with a Corinthian colonnade whose ruins can even now be seen amid

the confusion of modern houses. A small mosque marks the
place where the house of Judas stood.

Still ignorant of what had happened to their leader, Paul's
companions went to the Jewish quarter to announce his arrival
with terrible threats of what was to come. But Paul went to his
room in Judas' inn, refusing all refreshment that was offered by
the solicitous innkeeper. For three days he ate or drank nothing;
he was dead to the world. For three days he fell into a mystic
sleep, a sleep of expectation. For what was he waiting? Christ
had told him that he would learn what he was to do in the city.
In the same way the other apostles had waited before Pentecost.
At any rate, he was waiting, and to think that until this time no
one would have dared to keep him waiting. He was waiting in
God's ante-room; and waiting, too, is often a beautiful virtue
because grace has its own time.

When a human soul is suddenly wrested by the roots from
its old circumstances and environment and a new principle of
life is infused into it, the change never happens without great
sorrow and contrition. No psychology of religion will ever be
able to explain the reconstruction of Paul's religious world.
Now he was in a period of breaking down old things and ideas
– a process in which his human pride was being ground down,
in which the pure metal of his soul was being refined from the
dross in order that he might become a suitable instrument in the
hand of the Lord. Just as in that old legend the pagan idols in
Egypt toppled from their pedestals when the divine Child
arrived, so now Paul's old world was falling in ruins. Round
about him lay everything that he had held dear, the whole
structure of his world had come down, and the foundations of
his being were laid bare. But nothing that was worth while was
lost. God saw to that. The basic fabric of his temperament, the
original solidity of his character, his hair-splitting dialectic, his
cosmopolitan polish: none of this was lost or destroyed by
grace. All of it was salvaged by the delicate fingers of the
divine Physician to be knitted together into a new creature.

In the presence of the flaming countenance of the risen Lord, whatever was hard and rigid was softened and made pliable. Inhibited emotions and dormant powers were set free, fanaticism was transformed into a glowing zeal which later often appeared as a womanly tenderness alongside a granite-like resolution (Gal. 4:19). For three days Paul was clearing away the debris of his old mental world, but he did not leave in its stead a smoking, scorched place of desolation. Something new was breaking forth beneath the ruins; a new life had started, the new life in Christ. When we read his letters, those spiritual documents whose like cannot be found in all the literature of the world, we hear on every page the cry: "But I obtained the mercy of God" (1 Tim. 1:13).

According to a principle of the economy of salvation, man is always led to God through other men. In the kingdom of nature as well as in the kingdom of grace God makes use of secondary causes, except in the instance of the original creation. Perhaps it happened that while Paul sat, blind and broken, in his room in the inn, someone told him about the miraculous power possessed by some of the faithful, and perhaps he asked for one of them to come to him. At the same moment, God was informing a certain good and faithful man, Ananias, about the condition of him whom they feared so much. God chose a quiet retiring man, a man like Moses many years before, who shrank back from his assignment. According to an old Syrian tradition, Ananias was one of the seventy disciples of the Lord who had fled from Jerusalem when Paul's persecution first broke out. Therefore he hesitated about this meeting with Paul.

His anxiety, however, was overcome by the assurance: "For behold he prays" (Acts 9:11). When a man prays, he thought, he cannot be very dangerous. But it required courage nonetheless for the old man to venture into the lion's den. He heard a knock on the door. Someone told him of the summons to Judas' house. He started out immediately and entered the inn

with considerable trepidation. But once he had come into
Paul's presence, he was confident, and his confidence begot
confidence in Paul. The gnarled hands of this simple man of the
people were laid on Paul's head, and thus Paul received the
baptism of humility. He laid on hands and prayed, for so the
Master had taught him. As one of the Lord's disciples he had
the gift of healing, and as he prayed the scales of pride fell
from Paul's eyes. "Brother Saul," said Ananias, "Do you
believe in Jesus, that he is the Messias and the Son of God?"
And when Saul heard the word "Brother," something was
touched in his inner being; now he had been received into the
sacred brotherhood of the Lord's disciples.

There he sat, the terror of the Christians, like a child at
the feet of the simple Ananias whom he had come to arrest.
Perhaps as he sat there he remembered the warrants he carried
in his pouch. Perhaps the scene here in Judas' inn came back to
him in later years when he wrote: "Where is the wise? Where is
the scribe? Where is the disputer of this world? Has not God
made foolish the wisdom of this world?" (1 Cor. 1:20).

"What shall I do, Lord?" he had asked. The Lord would
show him that he was to suffer much. But that was thoroughly
un-Jewish; for the Jew, suffering was a punishment, while the
Christian regarded it as a sublime act, a mystical participation
in the world-redeeming suffering of Jesus, a means to attain
moral perfection.

Saul had already received a spiritual baptism. Now he
was to receive sacramental baptism and be admitted into the
holy brotherhood of the Christians. But to be a Christian means
to be baptized in Christ's death and it implies a complete
surrender of oneself to Christ, even to the baptism of blood in
martyrdom. Quickly his keen intellect saw all the consequences
of this act, and he may have felt some portent that his life
would follow that course from this baptism to the baptism of
blood. So with Ananias and some of the brethren Paul went
down to the Barada which, by means of its hundred canals and

branches, watered the gardens of Damascus and supplied the splashing fountains in a thousand courtyards, bestowing its blessing on the palaces of the rich and the houses of the poor. Thus this lonely man became a member of the communion of saints, for even the greatest man remains useless outside this community. Ananias called the disciples of Jesus "saints," following the prophet Daniel who called the members of the Messianic kingdom "saints of the most high God" (Dan. 7:18).

Paul's immediate admission to baptism was not unusual. All that was required for baptism was a contrite acknowledgment of Jesus; as the Messias, as the Son of God, of the redeeming power of his death on the Cross, of his Resurrection and the sending of the Holy Spirit (Acts 2:41; 8:37; 16:31; 19:5). Instruction about the life' of Jesus and about the sacramental and moral doctrines was added after baptism. Things were happening so quickly about him that Paul was unable to grasp it all. He realized with amazement that strange things were taking place within him as his old methods of thought seemed to fall away like scales. Writing to the Romans in the years to come he described this rebirth as a mystic death and burial and resurrection in Christ (Rom. 6:3-7). We have no reason to conclude that out of this experience on the Damascus road Paul retained a weakness of his sight. Indeed, St. Luke refers on two occasions to Paul's piercing look (Acts 13:9; 14:8).

On the following Sabbath, Paul felt that it was his duty to go to the synagogue and give an account of the change in his loyalties. He felt obliged to announce to the synagogue that Christ was the fulfilment of the hopes of Israel, the reformer of humanity, and the desired of all times and peoples. The newly formed community of Christians in Damascus consisted mostly of refugees and continued its old connections with the synagogue, trying to avoid any open conflict with the other Jews. They were deeply embarrassed when Paul appeared and thrust his dynamic personality into the scene and announced his recent decision with heavy emphasis. Paul was beginning to be

a dangerous companion. Here already was born that bitter
hatred in the souls of his Jewish compatriots, who quickly
sensed that Paul was the future enemy of the national religion
of the law. Here, too, was the beginning of that patient anxiety
in the minds of his fellow disciples, who urged him now to
leave Damascus as quickly as possible. It was his first flight.
From now on his life would be a series of flights and hasty
farewells like that of His divine Master.

CHAPTER EIGHT

UNDER THE CLOUD

"At Damascus, the governor of the nation under Aretas the king, guarded the city of the Damascenes, to apprehend me. And through a window in a basket was I let down by the wall, and so escaped his hands" (2 Cor. 11:32).
"Neither went I to Jerusalem, to the apostles who were before me: but I went into Arabia, and again I returned to Damascus. Then, after three years, I went to Jerusalem to see Peter; and I stayed with him fifteen days" (Gal. 1:1).

For a long time the great personages of Christianity were presented to us in an artificial, transfigured light. The saints were made to walk across the stage of history as if they were impossible wax figures. The modern flair for realism broke violently with the old tradition of the legends of the saints that was willing to sacrifice truth in the cause of piety. According to that old tradition, Paul was a scoundrel one minute and the next he had been transformed into an impeccable saint who grasped the whole Christian teaching in that one moment and went out to preach as an apostle on the very next day. But these instantaneous miracles of grace are always the easy product of the imagination and they present an erroneous picture of how God's grace actually works.

Certain apparent discrepancies exist between the account given by St. Luke and what Paul himself has to say in the Epistle

to the Galatians about the next few years. There seems to be a
gap in the narrative of the Acts. The period of time described as
"for some days" seems not to be sufficient as the preparation
for a large-scale missionary career. It is not likely that Paul
began his missionary labours immediately after his conversion.
Such is our view when we recall the procedure followed by
other great figures in history who were converted and later
exercised a great influence on the world. St. Augustine comes
to mind here. They all needed an interval of time for study and
meditation, time to assimilate their new impressions and
coordinate new blocks of thought. They needed time to master
the tumult of their emotions.

A shy, retiring man does not speak freely of the things that
happen in his inmost soul. It was hard to induce St. Ignatius to
tell what had happened within his soul; and even when he
spoke, he was sparing of words. St. Luke seems to have passed
over this period in Paul's life; perhaps he was ignorant of what
had happened, or Paul had told him in the strictest confidence.
The "many days" mentioned in the Acts (9:23) seems to refer to
the "three years" of the Epistle to the Galatians (1:18). Fortunately for us, Paul was later forced to lift the veil somewhat by the
attacks of his enemies. "Immediately I condescended not to flesh
and blood," he writes to the Galatians (1:16), meaning that he
was not influenced by any natural consideration or by his
friends. "Neither went I to Jerusalem"; what business had he in
Jerusalem? The memory of his recent fury there was still fresh in
his mind. Besides, his position with regard to the Twelve was
exceedingly delicate, and the attitude of the Sanhedrin would
certainly not be benevolent.

"But I went into Arabia." Arabia at that time included a
large territory: all the present Arabian peninsula as far north as
Damascus and the Euphrates. Properly speaking, however,
Arabia consisted of Arabia Petraea, that stony Arabia with its
famous caravan centres: Petra, high in the romantic mountains
of Arabia, Gerasa, the modern Jerash whose ruins date back to

the Greek and Roman eras, Amman Philadelphia, the modern capital of Transjordan, Bosra on the Hauran, and Emesa, the modern Homs. Just at this time, the Arabian sheikh Aretas was at enmity with Herod Antipas, the tetrarch, because Herod had dismissed the sheikh's daughter and sent her home because he was infatuated with Herodias. Here in Arabia, Paul felt safe from the investigations of the agents of the Sanhedrin.

Laden with the memories of these tremendous experiences in and around Damascus, with his Bible under his arm, the lonely pilgrim picked his way through the treeless, mountain wilderness that would later attract so many Anchorites and Stylites. He wore the Oriental Bedouin dress, the long full garment with the leather girdle and the brightly coloured turban. Had not the desert been the foster-mother of many prophets and preachers? Even afterward it received to itself men like Gregory of Nazianzus and John Chrysostom. Paul would not need to be fed by the ravens like Elias; he would find it easy to earn his bread. For here, if anywhere in the Orient, the guild of tentmakers flourished, supplying tents for the thousands of nomads traversing this and the neighbouring deserts. Here in the mountains the Bedouins sold black goats' hair to the carders who made the heavy ropes and cords which were equally impervious to sun and rains. Out of this material the nomads of the desert have for thousands of years made their movable homes. The weaver's loom is erected at the edge of the desert; the cords are fastened to pegs in the loom. The weaver arranges the black lacings between which he will send his swift shuttle back and forth. Only once while travelling through these treeless wilds did I come upon the pleasant sight of a gigantic terebinth. We rested in the shade of its spreading branches, and soon a number of roving Bedouins joined us under the tree.

As he strode wearily through the inhospitable desert, Paul must have rested under one of these century-old patriarchs of the wild. He sat deep in meditation, but when the roving sons of the desert joined him, no doubt he talked to them of some of those things that weighed so heavily on his soul. These three years, spent in retreat in the Arabian desert were the most quiet, the most contemplative and, no doubt, the happiest of his stormy life. Now that process of complete transmutation of his soul began under the influence of the sacred pneuma, the spirit of Jesus, to which he refers in the Epistle to the Philippians (3:8): "I count all things to be but loss for the excellent knowledge of Jesus Christ my Lord; for whom I have suffered the loss of all things." This inner change must have been twofold to correspond to the two divisions of the soul: an emotional and an intellectual change.

The changes in his emotional life were those that he called "putting on the Lord Jesus Christ" and "this mind... which was also in Christ Jesus" (Rom. 13:14; Phil. 2:5). His buoyed-up state of mind seemed to make religious truths crystal-clear. More and more he was confirmed in the certainty of what he held because of his supernatural faith and the approbation he had received from Ananias. Besides this, as the days went by in the desert he found peace and a certain mildness of temper, quite different from the old harsh exclusiveness of the Pharisees. He lost none of his old gifts and talents. He retained his former prophetic insight, his keen intellect, the excellent training of his will. His old interest in worldly things was obliterated by the glory of his new ideal which demanded nothing less than the total surrender of his being to God. In a word, his emotional being was now aflame with the love of God.

Together with this emotional change, his whole mental structure underwent a change. Out of the process came the outlines of that doctrine which professional theologians somewhat academically call Paulinism or Pauline theology, but which he himself called "my gospel," which "is not according to man. For neither did I receive it of man; nor did I learn it" (Gal. 1:12), which was "my knowledge in the mystery of Christ" (Eph. 3:4), and his insight into the universal plan of salvation. Not as though he had a gospel essentially different from that of the other apostles, for then he would have been cast out from the

Church. But he preached that gospel with a greater insistence, with a more powerful persuasion, with rhetorical force unlike any other, and he imprinted on that gospel his own' distinct personality and carried it far out to the Hellenistic world.

In that process of the transmutation of his religious consciousness two things more important than all the others emerged: a new concept of Christ and a new concept of faith.

The Apostle's new concept of Christ goes back to that occurrence on the road to Damascus. But before that, when he was a Pharisee, Paul had a fairly accurate idea of Christ's course of life and of his personality. On the road Jesus had said, "I am Jesus whom you persecute." How can a man persecute a person or a cause that he does not know? Our Lord went on to say, "It is hard for you to kick against the goad." The goad was certainly not the heavenly vision, for at that moment all his resistance had collapsed. He must have been carrying the goad about with him for a long time. How long? Hatred has a way of collecting and hoarding all kinds of things for its own purposes, just as the Pharisees had been doing during Jesus' lifetime, and we cannot attribute ignorance of these matters to Paul.

One of the modern scholars'[3] of Pauline history declares that Paul was present at the Crucifixion together with the Jewish priests and that he had carried away with him an unforgettable impression of Christ's death. Then it was that Paul had first felt the goad in his heart, just as the pagan centurion received the impression that Christ's death was the death of a son of the gods. The point is, of course, open to question, but those who propose it say that this is the only explanation for the passage in the Epistle to the Galatians (3:1): "O senseless Galatians, who has bewitched you that you should not obey the truth: before whose eyes Jesus Christ has been set forth, crucified among you?"

The goad which our Lord speaks of is in this instance a good figure of disposing grace. Besides this disposing grace, a number of historical and Old Testament elements were present

---

[3] P. Feine, *Der Apostel Paulus, 1937.*

in the background of Paul's mind which would afterwards be of use. But all such material would be of little avail unless some bond would unite them or some factor would coordinate them. The factor that reconciled all opposing elements and put order into the chaos of his mind was the creative power of grace, a new principle of life which Paul himself spoke of when he said: "The old things are passed away. Behold all things are made new" (2 Cor. 5:17). This is that sacred pneuma which shed on his soul the glorious light of Christ's countenance (2 Cor. 4:6).

He did not need to go to Jerusalem to learn from the apostles the historical details for his concept of Christ. He knew enough for the present, and after all Christ himself could alone give him a deeper insight into the person of Christ. Peter's confession of the Son of God at Caesarea Philippi was attributed by the Saviour himself to a direct revelation from above: "Flesh and blood has not revealed it to you, but my Father who is in heaven" (Matt. 16:17). The new idea of Christ that now began to take form in Paul's mind was not the product of his own thought processes or of some spurious fiction of the imagination with which, as his enemies said, he distorted and falsified the idea presented by the Gospels. Dr Feine, one of the most eminent students of St. Paul, remarks: "It would have been the first and the only instance of its kind if St. Paul had been able by his own powers, and with the help of his own imagination alone, to change himself so completely and fashion a new life to which for thousands of years so many souls who were thirsting for Christ turned for guidance."

How did Christ appear to the newly converted apostle? For an answer to this question we must rely on whatever we can conclude or surmise from the Epistles. The fundamental thing that he learned at Damascus was, however, that Jesus had intervened in the course of history with all his power in order to effect the salvation of men. He learned that Jesus was the ambassador sent by God with all powers, that he was the Messias. With the redeeming death of Jesus on the Cross a new aeon had dawned. His Resurrection was the seal for the statement that he was the Son of God, not in some applied sense in which the Jews used the expression, but in the real sense in which Jesus used it before Caiphas.

Now this heavenly Jesus intervened most mercifully in Paul's life. He applied to Paul that grace which he had merited for all mankind, and Paul had been permitted to behold the glory of his divinity in his countenance. From what he recalled of the prophets, he began to understand more and more clearly that Jesus was the Saviour of sinners, the Saviour of the world. Even now he began to be conscious that according to Christ's will all the barriers which the Jews had erected between themselves and other peoples must be torn down. If the sins of all mankind had been the cause for which God had permitted his Son to die on the Cross as the lamb of sacrifice, then it was clear that the Gentiles had an equal right to benefit from this sacrifice.

His idea of Christ even contained some earthly features, although he had not yet learned the wealth of detail that tradition offered. More than any other detail of Christ's earthly life, the cross impressed him as the masterpiece of divine love, which he later described for the Galatians and preached to the Corinthians: "For I judged not myself to know anything among you, but Jesus Christ, and him crucified" (1 Cor. 2:2). After that he was deeply moved by Jesus' poverty, his selflessness, his love of mankind, and his fulfilment of his Father's will (Phil. 2:6-10). He was already enthralled by the love of Christ and he would nevermore be able to escape from its bonds, "for the charity of Christ presses us" (2 Cor. 5:14). Now he has begun to understand what it means to be a Christian: a man whose whole heart has been taken captive by Christ. A man who has risen like the Saviour above all that is narrow, all that is national, even above the whole earthly sphere, who bears within himself "the image of the heavenly" (1 Cor. 15:49).

Paul knew something of Jesus as a historical personality, he knew his earthly circumstances, his earthly descent, the details of his birth, his relatives, and all that was included in his human environment. He refers to these things occasionally in his epistles, but he was not concerned with them; he mentions them only in passing as mere factual details. All these things were the earthly vessel containing something infinitely more precious. A vessel like Mary of Bethany's alabaster box which had to be broken in order that "the odour of his knowledge" might be released (2 Cor. 2:14). Now that Jesus was dead, he had stripped all these earthly things from himself and lived a heavenly life. The historical Christ, one might say, is a clearly diaphanous veil through which we discern the Pauline portrait of Christ.

It is hard to say how long it was until Paul attained this knowledge of Christ. The portrait was certainly not complete at the end of these years in which his spirit wrestled with itself; details were being added as the years went by until he attained "the knowledge of the Son of God, a perfect man, the measure of the age of the fullness of Christ" (Eph. 4:13). But he did possess the essential traits of the portrait. Some of Paul's critics have said that during these years in the desert Paul evolved an idealistic picture of Christ with gigantic exaggerations and that even many of his contemporaries did not understand him, and that it was for this reason that he stands out above his fellows in solitary greatness. But today sincere students of St. Paul of various faiths realize that his concept of Christ was not essentially different from that of the other apostles, and that everything Paul and St. John have to say in their mystic teaching about Christ was contained in what Jesus said about himself. It was Christ himself, who founded Christianity, and not the solitary thinker in the Arabian desert. The complete picture of Christ existed of course only in the mind of Christ himself, and each of his disciples presented this picture and preached the same gospel according to his own personal gifts.

Paul looked at the picture of Christ with all its implications of salvation and justification; he viewed Christ as the Saviour of all men and he referred to Him as the second Adam, the spiritual head of the race. Paul looked at Christ from the soteriological viewpoint. St. John looked at Christ from the standpoint of the eternal, pre-existing Logos, and that interpretation presupposed Paul's viewpoint. It is quite unthinkable that any opposition should exist between the teaching of St. Paul and that of St. John. Their teaching was not the result of religious speculation; it was something produced in them by the Spirit (1 Cor. 2:10-16). In the presence of this revelation Paul knew but one response: an unconditional assent to the concept of salvation contained in the idea of Christ. He called that assent, that surrender of his spirit – faith, a word that was to play such an important part in the destiny of Western civilization.

Paul had travelled a long way from the Temple and its courts and the smoke of the sacrifices that ascended from its altars. He began to realize that until now he had never really prayed, that he had never got any farther than the anterooms of religion. What he used to refer to as "being more abundantly zealous for the traditions of my fathers" (Gal. 1:14) and being concerned for the honour of Java, was only a sterile, empty service of the letter of the law, a blind, fanatical surrender to an abstract law which was the apotheosis of an alien, transcendental will. But now he began to feel coursing through all the fibres of his being the warmth and power of faith, a force that allayed all the restlessness of his soul, that banished all uncertainty and dispelled every doubt, that tenderly drew out the goad in his conscience and flooded his soul with light and warmth. This was something different from that old subtle, dissecting dialectic he had learned in Gamaliel's school. It was not that cold and calculating analysis of the divine will to which his people were so prone. It was not the old arid intellectual acceptance of some dry and dusty dogmatic proposition violently torn from the whole law. This new spirit that sent life into every nerve and fibre was an exultant, joyous assent to the concrete reality of the way of salvation which God had manifested through his Son. Our expression, "to hold as true," is woefully deficient in expressing the depth and fullness of what faith meant to St. Paul. This expression can easily limit the meaning to a simple act of the mind, while Paul's act of faith was something that required the whole man. Faith is not the act of philosophizing about the contents of revelation. It is not the realization of the elemental needs of the religious man, it is not some inner intuition. And it is not that searching out of the hidden riches of the knowledge of God that Paul calls *gnosis* and *epignosis,* knowledge and understanding. Paul's faith is, above all things, something that is within the capabilities of the simple and the poor to whom Jesus referred in his prayer of thanksgiving: "I confess to you, O Father, Lord of heaven and earth, because You have hid these things from the wise and prudent and have revealed them to little ones" (Matt. 11:25). By this faith invisible things become real and visible, they take on substance, they are drawn from their metaphysical distance and brought into the immediate concrete reality (Heb. 11:1).

Faith is not an excursion into some fairyland, nor is it a pitiful collapse of strained and overburdened nerves. It is rather "the power of great souls and the light that burns in faithful hearts" as St. Leo the Great says (*Sermo 2 de Ascens).* Because his soul and mind remained balanced and healthy, Paul never allowed himself to indulge in emotional excesses or spurious visions during these lonely years in the desert. He was saved from such aberrations, as he himself knew, by the spirit of Jesus. Was it not the spirit of Jesus that had been poured out upon him and that had flooded his whole being? (Rom, 5:5) Filled with that spirit and the joy of that new faith, he was impelled to call out God's sweet name, "Abba, Father" (Rom. 8:15). His soul was filled with a light, he breathed this luminous atmosphere, he spoke of it as being "in Christ Jesus." Within him a dynamic warmth drew forth all that was noble and good and lifted him up to high prayer and worship.

Can anyone explain how this faith is produced within us?

How the divine and the human are intertwined and interlaced? Paul knew only this: that it was God's gift, a calling "from my mother's womb ... by His grace" (Gal. 1:15). If anyone would have confronted him as he returned from his three-year sojourn in the desert and asked him about these things, he might have said: "If then any be in Christ a new creature, the old things are passed away. Behold all things are made new" (2 Cor. 5:17).

While Paul was thus elaborating his idea of Christ, he possessed within himself the embryo of the whole Christian teaching; the unfolding and development of the details would be the work of the following years. Already he felt the obligation "to carry My name before the Gentiles and kings and the children of Israel" (Acts 9:15), and to announce how he had been "apprehended by Christ Jesus" (Phil. 3:12). Already he felt the hand of God resting on his shoulder: "A necessity lies upon me. For woe to me if I preach not the gospel" (1 Cor. 9:16).

Suddenly he appeared again in Damascus. His features had an ascetic cast, his high forehead was the brow of the thinker, and his eyes seemed to have looked long on the mysteries of God. Things had changed in Damascus. The city was no longer under Roman rule; the rigid government of Tiberius' reign had ceased. The first years of Caligula's reign were marked by a general decline in the imperial authority in Syria because it had been Caligula's express policy, during the early part of his reign before he became insane, to re-establish the authority of the native rulers of the Orient. Thus he established the kingdom of Herod Agrippa, and "gave away large territories and rich cities without reason." [4] Only a short time before, Vitellius, the imperial legate, had given up the city of Damascus to Aretas of Petra, the Bedouin king, without a struggle. When Paul arrived, one of Aretas' sheikhs with his turbulent Bedouins was holding forth in the city as ethnarch and commandant. The Jews in the city were enjoying greater freedom and they made the most of their opportunities to proselytize, especially among the women.

---

[4] Theo. van Tichelen, *Paulus, der groesste Christusjuenger*, 1926.

To obtain the support of the Jews for the new regime, certain
concessions were made to them, and each new concession was
a further licence to new acts of religious violence.

Paul went to stay in the house of his old friend Judas, the
innkeeper. In that house he had experienced the greatest good
fortune of his life, and there he wished to begin his apostolic
career. On the next Sabbath he went to the synagogue and
signified his intention of speaking to the congregation. When he
began to show from the words of the prophets that Jesus was the
Messias, his hearers voiced their resentment, and a hundred fists
reached out to attack him. Some of them shouted: "Is this not he
who persecuted those that called upon this name in Jerusalem
and came forth for the intent, that he might carry them bound to
the chief priests?" (Acts 9:21) Others shrieked: "Take him away!
He is an apostate!" Paul barely escaped with his life.

Soon a group among the Jews decided to take action
against the apostate. They met and swore to lure him to some
dark corner of the city and murder him. The Arabian ethnarch,
won over to the plan by a gift of money, ordered the gates of the
city to be watched lest the fugitive escape. But Paul had a plan of
his own. He must escape, for how else was the word of the Lord
to be fulfilled? His plan was not without its romantic aspects,
and Paul may have smiled as he discussed it with his brethren.
By the dim light of the swinging lamp above them, Paul
celebrated the Eucharistic meal. How poignant were the words,
"... the same night in which He was betrayed ..." He wished to
fortify himself once more with this holy food. Then he bade
them all farewell and embraced them as they came forward,
these good people who had shown him such great kindness.
Some of the men disguised themselves as farmers and camel
drivers and about midnight they started out with Paul in a small
cart through the narrow streets. They stopped at a house which
adjoined the city wall. Through a window of the house that
opened through the wall Paul was to escape. Laboriously he
climbed into a basket which was let down along the wall by

heavy ropes sliding through the hands of his friends. He made his way through yards, gardens, fields, and cemeteries until he reached the highway that connected with the *via maris* to the south. And when in the dark of night he came to that place in the road where the Lord had appeared to him, he may have fallen down on his knees to give thanks from the fullness of his heart.

CHAPTER NINE

THE MOTHER CHURCH IN JERUSALEM

"And when he was come into Jerusalem, he essayed to join himself
to the disciples; and they all were afraid of him,
not believing that he was a disciple" (Acts 9:26).
"And it came to pass, when I came again to Jerusalem, and was praying in
the temple, that I was in a trance, and saw Him saying to me:
Make haste and get yourself quickly out of Jerusalem;
because they will not receive your testimony concerning Me" (Acts 22:17).

Back in Damascus the brethren were undoubtedly relieved to see Paul go. Even the best among them must have felt a certain discomfort in the presence of a fiery personality like Paul's. But Paul was debating within himself which direction he should take. Danger did not unsettle his mind; in fact, it seemed to inspire him to new activity. He could choose between two roads: one went north to his home in Tarsus. If he went home to Tarsus he would miss making contact with the original apostles in Jerusalem, and people would say that he had been too proud and independent to learn what he could from those who had witnessed Christ's life. Others would accuse him of trying to be above the sacred traditions of the mother Church in Jerusalem.

He felt, therefore, that he ought to go and visit Peter and associate himself with the primitive Church. He knew all that was essential about Christ's earthly sojourn, but he could learn more about the details, about such things as the exact words that Christ used and the intimate circumstances of His life. Besides this, he lacked the necessary knowledge of the order of services observed by the Jerusalem community; he must be informed about the rites observed in baptism, the instruction of catechumens, and the celebration of the Last Supper. He needed to learn those things that the Master had told His disciples after He had risen from the dead, and whatever He had told them while they lived intimately with Him during His public life. He realized that he could not establish his own sacramental ordinances if Christian unity were to persist. Thus it was that the spirit of Jesus which he had learned to follow most submissively led him south to Jerusalem.

How different was his mood from that of the other journey some three years before. Then his fanatical hatred had made him blind to everything about him; now he looked about at the country in which the Lord had lived with tender remembrances. Perhaps he turned aside from the road to visit Caesarea Philippi where once the Master had talked about the rock and the Church that he would build on that rock. Perhaps he went into the synagogue at Capharnaum, and then walked along the shores of Lake Genesareth, passing by Mount Thabor. Soon he was able to look down on the city where Gamaliel was even now sitting with his circle of pupils who would speak of him as a despicable renegade. What were his thoughts as he passed the place where Stephen had been stoned? "Stephen, I have come to make atonement for this deed." He had gone forth from the city as the grim persecutor; he was coming back now a fugitive.

Things had also changed in Jerusalem during the last three years. The Sanhedrin had waited then for his return from Damascus to continue with the persecution; but they had waited in vain. Somehow the persecution died out, and gradually the whole countryside was being covered with a net of

Christian communities.

Paul found himself in an uncomfortable position with regard both to the Christians and to the Jews. The Christians did not trust him. Some thought this story about his conversion was a trick. Only one man among the Christians understood him and was able to vouch for him as a newly converted Hellenist and former school companion. That man was Barnabas. Barnabas who, because of his extraordinary mildness and gentleness and because of his special gift of being able to sympathize with others, was called the "Son of consolation." It was Barnabas, perhaps the most lovable of all the persons of the early Church, who had looked kindly on this lonely brother and discerned beneath this dejected and embarrassed exterior the soul of a great apostle. It was Barnabas who here for the first time stretched forth his friendly hand into Paul's life. Taking Paul by the hand, he presented him to Peter and James, the most venerated of the apostles.

Thus Paul was admitted into the company of the disciples and, from this kindly act of Barnabas, came one of the most beautiful and fruitful friendships in the history of the Church. Paul did not meet the other apostles at this time; they were probably away at their various mission posts. But Paul had come principally to visit Cephas, as he preferred to call Peter, so that he might know him better and be initiated by him into the living tradition of the primitive Church. For fourteen days they conferred with each other. Peter, always kind and wholesomely natural as we know him from the Gospels, probably invited the newcomer to live with him in the house of Mary, the mother of Mark, who in turn was the nephew of Barnabas.

The Bible is often a remarkably unsatisfactory book that puts our curiosity to a severe test. Frequently it passes over in silence what we think might be the most interesting details. How dramatic, for instance, were these talks between Christ's most eminent and fiery apostles? From the two opposite poles of the world of culture, Christ's love had brought them together, the uneducated, simple fisherman from Galilee and the educated cosmopolitan and academician.

Like Nicodemus, Paul sat listening avidly until late into the night to Peter as he told of those three wonderful years of his life. Paul was never satisfied. He wanted to know about every small detail. He often interrupts the narrative with pre-emptory questions and fervent exclamations. Then one night he revealed his most secret feelings to his friend: "Cephas, the most amazing thing about all this is the miracle of His love. That the Master should love me, that he should forgive me, reveal himself to me, to me who persecuted him, who attacked the members of his mystical body, loaded them with chains and put them to death, that is incomprehensible." "But, brother Saul," Peter may have answered, "that is the way he always was. But you do not know my story. Oh, I treated him more shame-fully than you did." And as Paul began to remonstrate, Peter went on: "No, brother Saul, at least you were not a coward. But I, whom he had chosen from among all the rest as his closest friend, whom he favoured and preferred on every occasion, I who lived with him day and night for three years, who ate and drank with him, I who saw his glory on the holy mount (2 Pet. 1:17-18), I was the only one who turned against him on the night of his suffering. I swore that I did not know him, that I had never known him, and I left him helpless and defenceless in the hands of His enemies. For three terribly dark days I was deep in grief and remorse, while the Master, who had loved me so much, lay in the cold sepulchre, and the last words that he heard me say were the words with which I blasphemed and denied Him. Then came Easter. The Lord rose from the dead. And all the time he was in the grave I felt he was thinking of me. On Easter morning he left a message with the women, a message for me in particular: 'Go, tell his disciples and Peter' (Mark 16:7). Tell Peter, tell me, and even then I did not dare call myself an apostle. Brother Saul, now you know why I love him. Do you wonder that I wish nothing more than to die for him?"

Thus they talked with each other, and so fourteen days sped by. From the first moment these two souls were drawn close together in a sacred friendship. Nothing is more beautiful in the Church than this deep love between two men, than their high regard for each other, as here between Peter and Paul. This particular friendship lasted, even in spite of occasional misunderstandings, to their common martyrdom.

Now Paul began to gather a new series of impressions and experiences when he went with Peter to make a pilgrimage to the holy places in Jerusalem. Or can anyone think that Paul had no desire to see these places? That he did not wish to see the room where Christ had instituted the everlasting monument of His love? That he did not ask to receive the Holy Eucharist in the upper room from the hands of Peter? And as they stood together, Peter recalled what he had seen here: "Here, brother Paul, is where he reclined that night at supper and here is where he knelt to wash my feet." Where else would Paul have learned the words of the institution that he afterward repeated for the Corinthians? He desired to know everything in detail and he was not content until Peter had explained exactly how all these things had happened. This is certainly what he meant when he wrote later on: "For I have received of the Lord that which also I delivered to you..." (1 Cor. 11:23).

Perhaps one evening the two apostles walked out under the pale moon to Gethsemane, retracing the steps of the Master and his disciples on a fateful night. The Epistle to the Hebrews, which is written in St. Paul's spirit and style and certainly contains his thought, refers to our Lord's prayer in the garden: "Who in the days of his flesh, with a strong cry and tears, offering up prayers and supplications to him that was able to save him from death, was heard for his reverence" (Heb. 5:7).

On that stony, skull-like elevation near the northwest corner of the city wall, Peter knelt down and touched the ground, feeling around as if for something he had lost. Suddenly he whispered, "Here it is," and Paul too put his hand into the cleft in which the foot of the Cross had been allowed to fall. Together they went down through the gardens and then through the narrow opening of the sepulchre. "Here," said Peter, "we found the cloths folded together and the grave empty."

Thus the vision of Christ which he had received from the Master himself, was filled out with a traditional background during this fourteen-day visit with Peter. No man had a better opportunity to learn all the details of our Lord's earthly life. Even after these fourteen days, Paul was in continual communication with Barnabas his co-worker for many years, with Silas his travelling companion, with Mark the Master's biographer, and with the apostles James, and John, and Philip the deacon. From Paul's letters we can conclude something about the manner in which Paul made inquiries in Jerusalem. In the first letter to the Corinthians (chap. 15), he indicates quite clearly that he made careful inquiry about the Resurrection and about Christ's appearances after the Resurrection. Again he uses the expression, "which I also received" (1 Cor. 15:3), as indicative of an established tradition.

If we assemble the details that Paul refers to in his letters and those he spoke of in his oral instructions, we will have a sketch of Christ's life which implies an exact knowledge of the circumstances of Jesus' earthly life, from an account of his coming to his Ascension. Paul knew Jesus as his model and teacher, as his friend and master. More than all other details, the Cross and the things that took place on Golgotha hold a central place in Paul's mind.

Almost every article of the Apostles' Creed can be found in Paul's letters. He also reproduces many of Jesus' words with great fidelity. He is perhaps even more exact in quoting the words of the institution than Matthew or Mark. He quotes Christ's words for the sending of His disciples (1 Tim. 5:18 ff.). He gives Christ's teaching on the indissolubility of marriage; and he snatched from oblivion the Lord's saying: "It is a more blessed thing to give, rather than to receive" (Acts 20:35), which is not mentioned in the Gospels. When he wrote his letters it was not necessary for him to give a colourful description of the various scenes in Jesus' life; his hearers knew most of the details. His frequent direct and indirect references to our Lord's earthly career are more numerous than in the other New Testament writings except the Gospels, and the fact that he made such references presupposes that his hearers were in possession of the details. Thus he was in communication with the primitive Church and the earliest tradition, and therefore he was able to say: "I think that I also have the spirit of God" (1 Cor. 7:40).

Later Paul often emphasized the point that his message and doctrine were independent and autonomous (Gal., chap 1). But by this he meant that he had obtained by personal revelation a deep insight into the mystery of the divine economy of salvation. He did not intend to imply that his teaching had come entirely and exclusively from heaven. Even his interpretation of the significance of our Lord's death, burial, and Resurrection, which is such a distinctive part of the Pauline doctrine, was not unknown to the other apostles. Otherwise he could not have supposed that his hearers would understand when he was writing to the Romans and Colossians explaining the symbolism of the mystical burial of baptism, since these communities had been instructed by other apostles (Rom. 6:4; Col. 2:12).

It would be almost impossible to understand St. Paul's letters, with their extreme succinctness of expression and their frequent hidden references, unless we remembered continually that he was addressing people who had already been instructed, converts who had learned the elements of the Christian faith from him orally.

Naturally Paul did not spend all his time in Jerusalem with Peter. His was aggressive by nature; he kept pushing on to give testimony about his new religious discovery. In the synagogue of the Libertines he frequently found himself in bitter debate with his former colleagues. Was there any desire on his part to atone for the past by a martyr's death? He was not far from sharing Stephen's fate. All this time the disciples in Jerusalem trembled, for him and for themselves. Until now they had sedulously avoided any clash with the Pharisees, and some Pharisees had come over to them. Gradually the Church became a kind of Jewish Christian community in which the question about the validity of the Mosaic law was taboo. And now this reckless fire-eater comes along. Without any consideration for others, without caution, he must expose the sorest spot where every nerve ached. Another Stephen had come, and they were all threatened again with the consequences that came after Stephen's death.

The days were full of confusion. Every religious controversy was settled with the knife and the dagger. For such critical circumstances, Paul had not yet learned the proper missionary method; his temper was still too uncompromising. His missionary effort ended in failure, worse perhaps than his failure at Damascus. Peter and James felt obliged to talk to him. "Brother Paul," they said, "it is all in vain. You are merely causing confusion." He was deeply pained. Years later, when he was defending himself after being taken prisoner (Acts 22:17), he told how on this occasion he had gone to the Temple and poured out his heart in prayer: "They will, none of them, listen to me; they know too much about me." He and the brethren were saved from another catastrophe only by the Lord's preemptory command: "Make haste and get yourself quickly out of Jerusalem ... Go, to the Gentiles afar off will I send you" (Acts 22:18, 21).

Everywhere hired murderers lurked, ready to take his life. The brethren arranged for his secret departure to Caesarea, outside the jurisdiction of the Jews, where many ship lines took on passengers. He was not permitted to stop on the way or visit any other Church communities. And so "I was unknown by face to the Churches of Judea" (Gal. 1:22). From Caesarea he sailed past Tyre and Sidon to Seleucia; then he traversed "the regions of Syria and Cilicia" (Gal. 1:21), and thus after many detours he came home to Tarsus.

The more timid brethren in Jerusalem probably breathed more freely after their dangerous brother had departed. St. Paul and the community at Jerusalem were destined never to understand each other, and the blame for this unfortunate condition must probably be shared by both parties. The disciples at Jerusalem were too suspicious of the newcomer, and they were too attached to their old way of life. On the other hand, Paul offended others by a congenital aristocratic exclusiveness, and also by a speculative manner of talking and preaching that was a radical departure from the old method. Frequently Paul introduced some of his old rabbinical teachings attired in Christian dress into the argument, and such speculative reasoning was obscure and unintelligible to simple folk.

At the same time, Paul's eagerness to attack new problems could lead only to further conflicts. But has any great thing ever been accomplished without this conflict between the old and the new? Did not the Saviour himself say: "I came not to send peace, but the sword"? (Matt. 10:34.) But the times were not yet ready for Paul, and Paul himself was not ready for his work. The great sword of the Messias about which the boy had dreamt at Tarsus must first be forged on the anvil of new humiliations and sufferings.

CHAPTER TEN

QUIET IN TARSUS

*"They brought him down to Caesarea
and sent him away to Tarsus"* (Acts 9:30).

It was about A.D. 39, and Paul was once more back home in Tarsus. We do not know whether he went there directly or whether he stopped in Syria or Cilicia to preach the gospel. No historical evidence exists that Paul laboured in Syria, and the Churches there may have been founded from Antioch. The Cilician Churches referred to in Acts 15:41 seem to date from this period, but the origin of all these Christian communities is shrouded in obscurity.

The intrinsic evidence of his writings seems to indicate strongly that Paul spent the next three or four years in quiet and silence waiting for the divine call. God often permits those whom He has chosen for some work to wait a long time. Like his Master in Nazareth, so Paul was to hold himself in readiness for that moment when he would hear the call. His programme for the next few years was contained in the words of the prophet: "It is good to wait with silence for the salvation of God" (Lam. 3:26).

For a will as untamed as his, and a heart eaten up with a consuming fire, this period of waiting was no easy matter for

Paul. Now, when the whole world seemed to be rushing to its doom in the last years of the imperial lunatic Caligula, it was a severe test for his faith in God and for his scant patience. In a moment like this a man needed faith like Abraham's.

But God is a great King, and kings often expect others to wait for them. The Scripture is full of this waiting in the Lord. Indeed that whole period before Christ was nothing so much as a period of waiting; and from the standpoint of eternity all created time is the period of waiting for the coming of the Lord, the great judge of the world.

Waiting for the Lord requires a strong soul. The small, fidgety, nervous man cannot wait, but is either too early or too late. The man of God, however, the saint, who has acquired some self-discipline, knows how to wait for God. For him the moment of time that God has preordained is the precise and opportune moment to act, the instant that the Holy Scriptures call *kairos* and which the Greeks pictured as a boy with a forelock running swiftly by. It is good for us to remember that such times of testing came in the lives of the saints, that there were times of apparent inactivity when the saints seemed to be searching and groping for the will of God. Thus the saints seem to come a little closer to us, a little closer to our own concrete world.

If we had any reason to believe that Paul's parents were still alive and that they had become Christians, it would be natural to suppose that this tired and disillusioned traveller from Jerusalem went home to his parents to rest and refresh himself. But apparently Paul had no such good fortune. We do not even know whether the kinsmen who had been converted before him (Rom. 16:7) were close relatives or not. It is much more likely that, if his father was still alive, he was broken-hearted when he heard of his son's apostasy, and learned how Paul had disgraced the proud name of this Pharisee family to follow that low sect of Nazarenes. Perhaps then his father treat-ed him as a renegade and disowned him and sent him away from his parental home. That may have been the reason why

Paul was poor all his life, and why at the same time he was so sensitive and proud that he would accept support from no one, not even from his compatriots.

Twenty-five years before, as a carefree and ambitious student, Paul had left his native city; in the meantime he had returned only for short visits to his home. Now, as he returned again, everything seemed strange; he felt like a foreigner in his own country. But actually the world about him had not changed as much as he had.

He was like St. Francis of Assisi after he recovered from a serious illness and found his old world changed, changed indeed to such an extent that he was unable to find a place in it. One of the hardest things that can happen to a man is for him to discover in his most fruitful years that he is superfluous and that his activity is of no value. No phase of self-discipline is quite so difficult as to keep one's abilities and talents alert and active in some work that God seems to be rejecting.

Paul had to disappear from the scene, and it seems that things went better as soon as he was gone. The Acts seem to imply that after Paul had gone the Church began to prosper: "Now, the Church had peace throughout all Judea ... and was filled with the consolation of the Holy Spirit" (Acts 9:31). Long ago he had renounced his connection with the rabbis, he had given up those youthful dreams about fame and a great career. But every bulwark behind which his ego might still be entrenched must be razed to the ground before God could make use of him for the gigantic task he had in mind. Only when Paul's submission to God's will was complete, only when he humbly took the lowest place in the Church, would he hear the command: "Friend, go up higher."

On the outskirts of Tarsus is a rocky cavern in which, according to an ancient tradition, Paul lived these years as a hermit. But it is much more probable that we would find Paul somewhere along the tentmakers' street in the Jewish quarter of Tarsus; as later in the Middle Ages when the guilds flourished, each trade and craft had its own street and its separate bazaar. The "Well of St. Paul," pointed out now to the tourist, is more probably on the site of his parental home or of one of his temporary abodes. It was now fortunate that as the son of a Pharisee he had been obliged to learn a craft when he was a boy. As recently in the deserts of Arabia and later on his missionary journeys, so now he was independent of outside help.

In his free time he often walked through the city; sometimes he went through the agora or along the shore of the Cydnus and paused to listen to the wandering Greek orators who were displaying a smattering of the wisdom of the great philosophers. "The Greeks seek after wisdom," he wrote later (1 Cor. 1:22); but what he heard here was no longer that wisdom which was the daughter of Zeus, who in a brilliant and sublime hour had permitted the Stagirite to forge ahead until at the foot of the divine mountain he was able to look up and discern the proof for the existence of the "unmoved mover." But as he listened and observed, he was learning the methods of popular disputation among the Greeks, and his ear was being tuned to a greater facility in the use of the Greek language.

Paul was no lover of profane writings; the Bible was his book, and it is doubtful whether he read any other book. He was the Christian Socrates in the sense that men were his books. From his oral intercourse with the Greeks he retained many a winged and apt expression that served his purposes so well later in his letters and addresses. Thus in his speech in the Areopagus in Athens he quotes a passage from one of his countrymen that is found also in Cleanthes' famous prayers to Zeus: "For we are also his offspring" (Acts 17:28), and another passage from Epimenides: "For in him we live and move and are". In the first letter to the Corinthians (15:32) he quotes two passages from Menander: "Let us eat and drink, for tomorrow we shall die," and the proverb: "Evil communications corrupt good manners," and in the letter to Titus (1:12) he quotes from Epimenides again: "The Cretians are always liars, evil beasts, slothful bellies." In view of his coming missionary labours it was most fortunate that he could spend these quiet years of study and introspection unnoticed and undisturbed in one of the most brilliant cities of Greek culture.

In another respect these hidden years were valuable for St. Paul, or shall we say that the long winter during which the seed of wheat lies buried beneath the blanket of snow is wasted? That period when a mysterious death is occurring in the invisible cells of the seed? "Amen, amen, I say to you, unless the grain of wheat falling into the ground die, itself remains alone" (John 12:24). Much bread is produced during the long winter night. When we read Paul's letters we wonder how, amid his ceaseless activity, he was able to develop such profound mystical thoughts, thoughts that require a period of deep reflection. That period of meditation and reflection occurred in these years at Tarsus after he returned dejected and alone from his retreat in Arabia. That period in Arabia and these years at Tarsus were profoundly important and decisive years in Paul's life, for it was at this time that he developed and perfected his great system of theology. In his letters he speaks with determination and emphasis of his own gospel, and that gospel was formulated and thought out here in Tarsus.

As the years went by, the life and person of Jesus, his Passion, his Resurrection, his preaching, and his act of redemption were the object of the continual reflection and meditation of the other apostles. All these events began to recede into a dreamlike, misty distance, and now as they thought of those blessed days when they lived with Christ it seemed more and more as if their eyes had been veiled then. Now they were asking themselves, who was this whom we looked at so often, whom we touched, whose voice was heard so often in our ears? For them, too, he was God the Saviour, the Lord of life, the Lamb of God, their peace and reconciliation, their life and resurrection, the Lord whose name is above all names. They too lived by this mystery of Christ; they too were aware of the universal significance of his redemption. But beyond all this, deep down and far away were ramifications and conclusions and thoughts and connections that they knew not yet; that lay undeveloped in their believing consciousness. But the former rabbi of Tarsus was driven on by his quick and urgent mind to search out the deepest recesses of the mystery on which "the angels desire to look" (1 Pet. 1:12).

We know some of the sources of Paul's concept of Christ and the component parts of his supernatural faith. His experience at Damascus was the primal spark, the creative source that coursed through his whole life in undiminished force. Alongside this source flowed the stream of tradition which bound him to the primitive Church. Another source was his intensive study of the Old Testament. In its light he elaborated these new events, and its obscure passages, on the other hand, were illumined by the light of the gospel.

What he had learned from the Old Testament about the creation of the world and about the call of Abraham fitted in with the new revelation about Jesus and formed a wonderfully harmonious whole that filled him with adoring astonishment. Ever more frequently he was granted private revelations and visions to which he often refers (2 Cor. 12:1). These revelations came when his own thought processes were at the end of their resources or when he was in danger of straying into error. They came as mental inspirations and suggestions, and we should not think of them as violent interventions on the part of God. When the Lord comes into our lives he does not come as the boisterous wind in a storm but rather as the soft rustling of the zephyrs and we will not know when or where he blows.

Paul's gospel did not come full-fledged from heaven; it was the result of divine illumination and of much prayerful contemplation and deep immersion in the Scriptures. We can discern this twofold character of his thinking in his letters and we can clearly follow the development of his doctrine if we read his letters in their chronological order: first the seed and the first blade in the two Epistles to the Thessalonians; the growing plant in the four great Pauline Epistles (Galatians, the First and Second Corinthians, and Romans); lastly the mature fruit in the captivity letters and the gleanings in the pastoral letters.

How did these revelations occur? The question is like asking where lightning goes or what is the course of divine inspiration? Revelations may come in two ways: the symbolic way through religious phantasms, and the intuitive way through the intellect. With the prophets of the Old Testament, revelation generally took place through symbols whose inner meaning was sometimes revealed by an inner illumination and sometimes was left obscure. The colourful and picturesque language of the prophets shows the path which revelation took: the way of the symbol impressed on the imagination. With St. Paul these revelations came more often by way of an inner intuition, as the comprehension of a great complex of truths and conclusions with many branchings, together with some evidence of the divine origin of the revelation. We have examples of such revelations in the lives of the saints. Thus, for instance, St. Ignatius Loyola tells us that after his conversion at Manresa he was permitted to see the mystery of the Trinity in a globe of light so clearly and convincingly that, even if he would not have had the teaching of the Church, he would have been convinced of the truth of the Christian religion by this experience.

The knowledge that Paul obtained from these revelations was ordered by the mighty power of his great constructive mind which elaborated and coordinated everything under one grand viewpoint. In his letter to the Romans, Paul presents his own system of religious philosophy, and that system was thought out during these years at Tarsus when he had sufficient time to meditate on the condition of the world and the significance of the death and Resurrection of Christ. In the light of his new knowledge he travelled again over the tortuous paths over which mankind had gone from the beginning. As a Christian he was now in a position to take a more sympathetic view of the

Gentile world than formerly as a Pharisee. However deep his sympathy may have been for the Gentiles, his judgment was nevertheless impartial. In the days before Christ, mankind lived under the anger of God. God had not left the Gentiles without some manifestation of His existence, but the pagans did not draw the right conclusions; instead they deified the world which should have been the reflection of God for them, and thus they made themselves guilty. All pagan worship provokes God's anger because it is nothing but the worship of demons.

The religious condition of the Jews was not much better than that of the pagans. Besides the gift of reason they had revelation, the law, the prophets, and the sacred books, but all these advantages only served to increase their guilt. As the pagans deified and worshipped nature, so the Jews deified and worshipped the letter of the Law. Before his conversion, Paul struggled with all his might to attain justification through a most meticulous observance of the Law. But this superhuman effort to subject the will to the Law resulted in two attitudes of mind that themselves were antagonistic to each other: an exaggerated feeling of justification expressed in the words: "O Lord, I thank you that I am not as the rest of men," and a feeling of utter dejection and depression of spirit in which he cried out: "Unhappy man that I am, who shall deliver me from the body of this death?" (Rom. 7:24.)

How does the transformation from the unchristian state into that of a true Christian take place? Paul offers us the benefit of his own experience, and in his explanation he gives us an insight into the nature of Christianity that we do not obtain from any of the Synoptic writers. His thought is akin to that of St. John, who describes it by the figures of the seed of wheat and the vine and its branches. By a creative act of God a change took place in Paul; a change that went to the roots of his being. It was no mere development of religious potencies, but a complete break with his past. A change took place that meant an entirely new view of his existence; a change that could be expressed only by the contrast between life and death. Indeed, he suffered a kind of death, he was drawn into Christ's death, burial, and Resurrection (Rom. 6:2-8; Gal. 2:20; 6:14; Col. 3:3). A new man arose with Christ to live united in a supernatural way with Christ, retaining all his individual characteristics, but drawing life from the Holy Spirit, who is the bond that unites the faithful to Christ.

What happened to Paul, happens to every Christian even though he may not have such a drastic experience. For every Christian the barriers of time and space are bridged over by faith and baptism so that he may have a new existence in Christ. The Christian's life is buried with Christ, and he is removed from the world and sin (Eph. 2:13). This removal into Christ is the effect of Christ's redemptive act on the Cross. It is not merely a declaration by God, but is something real, although it is a mysterious process within the soul. The Christian puts on Christ as a garment, not as an actor attires himself for his role, but like the priest at the altar who in a sense becomes Christ and speaks for Him. For Paul these things were not simply metaphors; they were realities, things more real than the concrete things of life. But like all mystic processes these changes within the soul elude the language of the people; they can be expressed only in paradoxes that sound like the "foolishness of the Cross."

In the presence of this Christian state of life, the ordinary everyday existence paled into something casual, passing, insignificant; he knew this earthly life as something that, at times, sprang into view with a voluptuous brilliance, as the arena on which the issue for the great moral battle is waged. Paul cast aside the external habiliments of this earthly existence and penetrated into the "hidden man of the heart in the incorruptibility of a quiet and a meek spirit" (1 Pet. 3:4).

During these lonely years at Tarsus, Paul struggled to find words that would express the fundamental facts of this new spiritual life. Again and again he coined expressions like "suffering with Christ," "dying with Christ," "being buried with him," "live with him," "be conformable to him," "be incorporated in him." In most instances, however, he expressed these ideas by the brief phrase, "in Christ Jesus."

This union with Christ is the vital core of St. Paul's theology and ethics. If we disregard this thought, his doctrine will remain a fairy castle to which we have no access. From this viewpoint of union with Christ, we must consider Paul's doctrinal structure, for it is this that gives his teaching unity and cohesion. A work of art must be viewed from a certain advantageous angle, and for Paul's teaching that point is Christ; Christ is the beginning and the end. Everything is in him, through him, and for him. Paul does not isolate the historical figure of Jesus, but he thinks of Jesus as the eternally pre-existing Word in the bosom of the Trinity and the transfigured and glorified Christ of our redemption. That core of Paul's teaching is expressed in his words to the Galatians: "With Christ I am nailed to the cross. And I live, now not I; but Christ lives in me" (2:19 f.).

This teaching of St. Paul is not only a new doctrine, a new cult, or a new system of ethics; it is a new life given to men by the Spirit through Christ's mystic death. This is the absolutely new and surprising thing about Christianity that no merely human religion was able to attain. And today we cannot stress too much this central point of our religion, because in the course of centuries the essential thing may have been covered over by practices, ceremonies, interpretations, and mere incidentals. Many years ago Harnack, in his famous lectures in Berlin, said that the essence of Christianity consisted in the teaching of the Father and the infinite value of the human soul. But that liberal explanation showed that Harnack had missed the essential thing in Christianity. Today our religious literature seldom penetrates to the actual core of Christianity, and in order to become true Christians we should concentrate our attention on that essential point. These were important years at Tarsus. Here Paul completed the whole structure of his teaching. When he actually began his missionary journeys, no signs of development can be discerned; everything is complete and mature. Here in some humble workshop he conceived those magnificent thoughts which later he wrote down in his letters and addressed to the world. We cannot overestimate the importance of revelations that were given him here in Tarsus and earlier in the Arabian desert. Later, when he was compelled to defend himself against a boasting foe, he lifted the veil from the sublime religious experiences of these hidden years. "I know a man in Christ: more than fourteen years ago (whether in the body, I know not, or out of the body, I know not; God knows), such a one caught up to the third heaven. And I know such a man . . . was caught up into paradise and heard secret words which it is not granted to man to utter" (2 Cor. 12:2-4).

During all these years he was tortured by the thought that beyond the Taurus and the Amanus mountains lay vast territories that should be opened up and conquered for Christ. It seems that he sometimes broke his seclusion and made short journeys into Cilicia and Syria, impatient for the hour to come.

CHAPTER ELEVEN

THE CHURCH IN ANTIOCH

Antioch was the third largest city of the Roman Empire, with over half a million inhabitants, surpassed only by Rome and Alexandria. It was the metropolis of the Orient, the residence of the imperial legate of Syria, and the most beautiful city of the East. The story of Paul's life takes us again and again to large cities, to centres of population. After Jerusalem, Antioch became the second mother of the infant Church. The development of the early Church went from Jerusalem to Antioch to Rome. For twenty years Antioch was Paul's home and the headquarters from which he set out on his great undertakings.

Where the coast of Syria forms a right angle with the coast of Asia Minor, about thirty miles inland, on the south bank of the broad Orontes as it sweeps on to the sea, Antioch lies at the foothills of the Amanus to the north and the Casius to the south. It had contact with all the important places in the Empire; it was famed as the city of the Seleucides and of Alexander the Great, and was ideal as the central point for a new Church that was to spread out to the pagan world. What Tarsus was for the hinterland of Asia Minor, that Antioch was for Mesopotamia and Arabia.

When a native of Antioch spoke of his city, his eyes sparkled with pride and enthusiasm. He hastened to describe for the stranger the great colonnaded avenue that Herod the Great had given the city with royal munificence. The four rows of marble columns formed three lanes in this great Corso, the middle lane for heavy traffic, the outside lanes for pedestrians and the smart equipages of the rich. The great avenue divided the city for several miles from west to east and reached the foot of a mountain. From the summit of this mountain a mammoth statue of Jupiter overlooked the Corso and the city. From the island in the river at the north another colonnaded avenue extended from north to south. This avenue together with the other formed a vast marble cross, thus dividing the city into four parts. The colonnades were further ornamented with exquisite sculptures such as succeeding ages were not able to reproduce. To the north of the city the Orontes embraced an island on which had been built the royal palace of the Seleucides. There the imperial legate and governor with his cabinet and general staff resided. The north shore of the Orontes was dotted with the country houses of the rich. The city itself was enclosed in a great wall that had over three hundred fortified towers, a masterpiece of Hellenic military architecture.

Antioch also boasted one of the finest water systems of all ancient cities. It was proud of the many public and private baths, the fountains, and the great network of canals fed by the clear waters of the Orontes pouring a lavish supply of water into the palaces of the rich as well as the hovels of the poor. Only Tarsus and Damascus had water systems to compare with that of Antioch. Antioch was also the Paris of the Orient, the city of lights because of its excellent illumination. Libanius, the panegyrist of the city, wrote: "In Antioch at night other lights replace the light of the sun. Day and night are distinguished only by the manner of the illumination. Busy hands scarcely notice the difference when night comes and men go on working undisturbed by the darkness. And, if anyone desires, he may go on dancing and singing through the night, so that Hephaestus and Aphrodite share the night." Libanius' reference to Hephaestus speaks of the highly developed arms industry, while Aphrodite, of course, recalls the worship of the goddess of love which perhaps nowhere else was so diligently cultivated as here in Antioch. Here, too, was the mint that coined the Roman money bearing the imprint of Caesar. When Jesus asked the Pharisees, "Whose image and inscription is this?" He probably held in his hand a coin minted in Antioch.

The social picture of Antioch, like that of all large cities of antiquity, was deeply lined with shadows. Every citizen owned at least two slaves, and the wealthy factory owners, the rich merchants, the landed gentry, and the leaders in the army and government had everything they desired. Interesting proof of their full enjoyment of life is found in the well-preserved ruins of the many villas and country homes that stretched for ten miles back along the Orontes to the ancient Apamea. The favourite spot of the Antiochians was the famous Daphne, the modern desolate Bet-el-Ma, then an entrancing paradise with inviting groves shaded by great laurel trees, formal gardens, and playing fountains. Here the happy crowds promenaded in holiday attire, while from the deep shadows of the groves they heard the enticing music of the flute and harp.

Antioch marked the border line between two worlds, the East and the West, and here the soft indulgence of Syria, the fakirism of India and Egypt, and the Orient's love of deception mingled to make the city a pool of every kind of wickedness. Once when Juvenal wanted to condemn Rome, he said that the waters of the Orontes had been poured into the Tiber and deposited their scum near Rome. From the descriptions of Libanius, Pausanias, Philostratus, and Lucian, and the references of St. John Chrysostom, Renan evolved the following moral picture of Antioch: "Never before had there been such a gathering of jugglers, mountebanks, travelling players, buffoons, magicians, wandering priests, ballet dancers, and circus people. The city was agog with races, gladiatorial and athletic contests, dances, parades, and bacchanalia. Everywhere was wanton indulgence, all the folly and treachery of the Orient, the most shameful superstition, and the unreasoned fanaticism of the pagan orgies. The whole scene was like the dream of an opium eater, like the drunken revelries of Sardanapalus."

The worst feature of this condition was the fact that the mysticism of the Orient was able somehow to envelop all evil with an aura of glory. The Oriental religions of the time were mere glorifications of natural urges. Their deities were principally the gods of vegetation and growth, and they were generally represented in couples, as the goddess mother, Cybele and the savage Attis of the Phrygians, the twin gods of Isis and Osiris in Egypt, the Asiatic Dionysius and Sabacius, and the Sandan and Heracles of Tarsus, whose cult resulted in such crude orgiastic excesses.

The lowest cult of the Orient was that of the Syrians and the Phoenicians, the neighbours of the Israelites. What the Bible tells of Moloch and the human sacrifices offered to him is only too true. The Syrians' worship of the gods was nothing more than an elevation of murder and debauchery to divine worship. Particularly the worship of Adonis and Astarte was an apotheosis of vice, and their temples continued to be places of professional vice until the end of the pagan era. In the spring the festival of vegetation and the complete emotional intoxication with which it was celebrated often resulted in sexual excesses and sometimes in self-mutilation. In this international den of vice, Christianity was about to make its entrance. If ever a city stood in need of the glad tidings of Jesus Christ, it was this city of Antioch.

The population of Antioch was a colourful collection from all peoples of the Orient, but we can distinguish among them four separate types. First the silent, haughty Roman, arrogant and overbearing because of his conquest of the world. Second, the Greek and half-Greek, generally a devotee of sensualism who long since had lost any belief in the gods. Third, the native

Syrian, degenerate, effeminate, cowed, who belonged to a lower caste banished to the suburbs. Fourth, holding himself aloof from all these, the Jew, always conscious of his proud claim to be the favourite of the Almighty. The Jews formed a considerable colony under their own ethnarch and they engaged in an active programme of proselytizing.[5] If anyone thought seriously about religion, he went on the Sabbath to the Jewish synagogue, where the copper vessels and silver lamps stolen by Antiochus Epiphanes from the Temple in Jerusalem still hung from the ceiling. The numerous proselytes from paganism were divided into two classes: the full proselyte or "proselyte of the sanctuary," who submitted to the entire Mosaic law and to circumcision, and the half-proselyte or the "proselyte of the gate," who was friendly to the Jewish religion and frequently attended its services. We have, therefore, four distinct groups: the Jews, the full proselytes, the half-proselytes, and the pagans.

During these years when Paul was deep in meditation on the mysterious ways of Christ, the seed of the new religion was being sown in many places. In the port cities of Joppe (Jaffa) and Caesarea, from there to the green island of Cyprus, to the fabulous Nile country, down to Ethiopia by the treasurer of Queen Candace, to Cyrene in North Africa, yes, even as far as Puteoli near Naples and to Rome in the very shadow of the imperial palace. The first progress of Christianity from its native land was not a result of missionary journeys. It was principally the storm of persecution that dispersed the first believers from Jerusalem, that sent Judaeo-Christian merchants and craftsmen out into the world, and these sowed the first seeds of the gospel. The honest workmanship and the thorough business methods of these so-called Hellenistic Jews won them a welcome wherever they went, and their happy, good-natured disposition made friends for them in strange lands. Their missionary activity, however, was one-sided since they announced their message only to the Jews, not because they wished to exclude the Gentiles but

---

[5] Josephus, *Antiquities*, XII, 3.

because they believed that such was the will of God.

They took it amiss that Peter had baptized the pagan officer Cornelius and his family and had received him without further ado into the Church. Peter justified his action by a vision that had been granted him and by the corroboration of the Holy Spirit, who had descended upon these pagans even before their baptism. Against that position none of them was able to argue, but they maintained that this case was an exception, and Peter himself did not venture to draw the obvious practical conclusions from his position because of that wing in the Church that remained faithful to the law.

Causes do not move forward merely by the force of theoretical argument. They need to be propelled by action, and now in Antioch things began to happen. A courageous group of lay apostles from Cyprus, the home of Barnabas, others from Cyrene, including perhaps Lucius and the two sons of Simon of Cyrene, were the pioneers of missionary activity among the Gentiles. Here in Antioch, this great metropolis of the world, where the difference between Jew and Gentile was not thrown in such bold relief, the first Church with a mixed membership was founded. A Church for both Jew and Gentile. A Church emancipated from the yoke of the Mosaic law, the second cradle of Christianity. Besides this, another event had taken place: the earthquake of A.D. 37 had turned men's minds to the supernatural and even now they continued their interest in religious subjects. Finally, in every city, no matter how degenerate, some men of noble character will be found. The Christian Hellenists met such men in the bazaars, in the market place, and in the public baths, and engaged them in conversation. Their faces were lighted with enthusiasm when they told how they had found real happiness by knowing Jesus. Men listened, and soon the talk spread through the bazaars.

All this happened, of course, without any special intent or plan. That fact contains a lesson. The Church did not receive from her Founder a detailed plan or programme to be used for future problems and cases. Outside the realm of revelation, the Church would recognize the will of God in the course of facts and circumstances. Thus the spirit of God moves through history where it wills.

Because of the frequent traffic of caravans, the news of the Church was not long in getting to Jerusalem. The Church in Jerusalem decided to send a representative to Antioch to observe things, and Barnabas was chosen to head the mission. A better man could hardly have been found for this delicate task. Barnabas was a man of calm, even temperament, a man who inspired confidence, especially because of his great sympathy and his deep, simple religion.

Barnabas looked with wonderment at the great city of Antioch, at its spacious avenues and colonnades, and at the great statue of Zeus erected at the end of the colonnaded avenue. But his greatest interest was in a certain side street in the quarter called Epiphania where the Christians were living. Unfortunately every vestige of this neighbourhood has disappeared in modern Antioch. The basilica mentioned by some of the Greek Fathers, as St. Athanasius, St. John Chrysostom, and Theodoret, in the fourth century was already called ancient and apostolic. According to an old tradition,[6] it was situated on Singon Street near the Pantheon. Barnabas saw at once how favourable were the prospects for the faith here in Antioch. He was not concerned about the argument that was being waged; he had his eye on the essential thing, he was the practical missioner. He saw that here was the finger of God when he heard of the many charismatic gifts, of the prophecies and miracles, that had been granted to the Church in Antioch. On his first appearance in their assembly, Barnabas made a fervent speech to the Christians, a speech that reached its climax in his exhortation: "Be faithful to the Lord, adhere to the Lord." That was Barnabas' religion. He did not desire to win men for himself or for some party in the Church, he wanted them for Christ. Afterward he wrote a calm report to

---

[6] *Cf. Chronikon* of Joannes Malalas.

Jerusalem, to which he appended the counsel to accept things in Antioch as they were.

But Barnabas felt vaguely that this did not settle the argument. The problem remained, and at any time it might demand a solution. Jesus himself had not expressly answered the question about the future validity of the Mosaic law. His own observance of the law might have been interpreted in several ways, and now the question of the law must be solved according to the mind of Christ. It was indeed a thorny problem that the Master had bequeathed to his Church, and Barnabas was not the man who would be able to take hold of the difficulty and settle it once and for all. But he did know a man who could attack the problem, and it was a happy hour when he remembered the name of Paul of Tarsus.

CHAPTER TWELVE

ANTIOCH

"And Barnabas went to Tarsus to seek Saul: whom, when he had found, he brought to Antioch. And they conversed there in the Church a whole year; and they taught a great multitude, so that at Antioch the disciples were first named Christians" (Acts 11: 25).

It may have been a spring day in 42 when Paul was sitting at his loom and his friend Barnabas came, put his hand on his shoulder, and said: "Brother Paul, the Master needs you now. The Master is here and he is calling you. Come with me to Antioch." What glorious evenings these two friends spent together, sitting on the housetop, telling each other of their experiences since they had parted years ago! Barnabas noticed how mature and reflective Paul was now, and Paul was glad to hear that Christ's cause was prospering among the Gentiles.

If Barnabas had not come, Paul would have worn himself down between the upper and lower millstones of his own solitary thinking. Solitude and separation from the world are good things, but they should be only transition periods in a man's life. A man will know his ability and his strength only when he tries them out in action. The invitation to action was another of the great benefits that Paul derived from his friendship with Barnabas. No matter how great a genius may be, he needs a friend and he also needs the community, for without it even the greatest man can do nothing worth while. The Church has acknowledged Barnabas' services by granting him the title of apostle, because he really belongs to the founders of the Church among the Gentiles.

Paul's hour had come at last; now he knew what his life's work would be. For years he had waited for this moment, and now it had come, so simply, without the sound of trumpets. Such are God's ways, often hidden to our eyes, but always wonderful and majestic in themselves. Was it not that way with St. Teresa of Avila when she groped for years in spiritual darkness? St. Francis of Assisi began by dragging bricks and mortar together to repair a poor little chapel until he realized his vocation when he heard a plain sermon by a simple village priest. Was not St. Ignatius Loyola completely in the dark about the needs of his time when he went off to Palestine? Only when he was repulsed there did he come to know his mission in life. St. Camillus of Lellis changed orders three times before he found his life's work. We ourselves do not determine our life's work. It is not we who choose God. "You have not chosen me: but I have chosen you" (John 15:16).

Most likely Paul and Barnabas soon went down to the sea at the mouth of the Cydnus to embark on some ship that would take them the day's voyage to Seleucia. Hurriedly they climbed the heights, looking back across the distance once more to where they saw the snow-capped crown of the Taurus range. For twenty miles the road went through hilly country, passing laurel groves, oleander clumps, then the vineyards, the famous orchards, orange and citron groves, and they found the pungent, clean smells pleasant in their nostrils. On the last hill Paul stopped to gaze down on the wonderful sight of the Orontes valley. Stretched out before him was the silver ribbon of the broad-breasted stream, ornamented with the pearls of the glistening marble villas of the city's rich. Poised on the waters were the ships of the pleasure seekers, and far beyond he heard the rumbling undertone of the busy city.

Together they said a prayer to Christ, that he might bless their entrance into the city. Glancing up they saw the gigantic statue of Charon, ferryman of the shadow world, the symbol of death came face to face with the apostles of life.

They trudged on past the royal palace. They saw the caravans that had just come from China by the ancient "Silk Route" over East Turkestan. Swarthy-skinned men stood beside their camels, and here were groups of slaves; for Antioch was always a good slave market. Barnabas took his friend straight to Singon Street where the elders generally met. They greeted him with awe and reverence, for had he not seen the Lord? But there were already other notables in Antioch. Barnabas was accorded the first place as the legate of the apostles, and the Acts of the Apostles gives us a list of the prelates in Antioch. In this list Paul is mentioned in the last place: "Now, there were in the Church which was at Antioch prophets and doctors, among whom was Barnabas and Simon who was called Niger, and Lucius of Cyrene and Manahen who was the foster brother of Herod the tetrarch, and Saul" (Acts 13:1).

Paul now began to enjoy what was perhaps the happiest time of his life, these beautiful days in Antioch. For one full year the two friends worked together peacefully in this new Church of Antioch on which the early dew of grace still lay. It was like the idealistic first year of a priest's ministry. As yet routine had not hardened and chilled their enthusiasm, as yet narrowness and meanness had not hampered and cramped generosity of spirit. Everything was free and magnanimous. The breath of the Holy Spirit blew steadily on the sails of the little ship. It was inspiring to see how these pagan souls, so despised by the Jews, were ennobled by the preaching of the Cross, how quickly they reached out for the treasures of Christ's grace, how generous they were with Christ, while the Jews always stopped to drive a bargain with Jehovah.

Paul was now in the full powers of manhood. But even

before he came to Antioch "a great number believing, were converted to the Lord" through the ministry of Barnabas, and now that Paul had come we may well suppose that more converts were being made. In the evening, while the fine young gentlemen of Antioch and their fashionable ladies went strolling out to Daphne to celebrate the orgies of Adonis and Atargatis, brave little people like the merchants, labourers, and slaves who had never before heard of such a thing as a selfless love, came to catechism instruction and the teaching service of the Church. Sometimes they met in another's house, or they sat on a roof top, climbing the outside stairs from the street, or they sat round a splashing fountain in some inner court. Sometimes Paul gave instructions in an orange grove along the Orontes, or beneath the colonnade of the great avenue, and there he breathed for the first time the sacred name of Christ.

For long these people had been the captives of pagan culture; now their ancient longing for a higher life was being satisfied. Light was in their eyes as they heard Paul tell of the Son of God who became a slave, how He offered his life in atonement to give new nobility to their souls, and a new freedom. Sometimes the instruction was halted by the din of passing groups of drunken revellers, by the cymbals and castanets of passing Isis priests and Bacchus priestesses. On Saturday evening they came together to celebrate the Lord's Supper. According to an old tradition that came from Christ Himself, the service began with the agape or love banquet. After Christ's death the apostles had boasted that for three years they had eaten with Jesus (Acts 10: 41), thereby indicating their intimate friendship with him. Christ gave his most precious gift after such a love banquet. The agape showed that the Christians were united to one another, while the Lord's Supper gave expression to their union with Christ.

This weekly service supported the Christians for the week; into each workday the words of the service echoed: "Maranatha, come Lord Jesus" (1 Cor. 16:22; Rev. 22:20). Paul

was conscious of a new and glorious freedom, and his spirit of
freedom spread to others. Many of the Christians had gone to
the synagogue and lived according to the law of Moses, but
they soon saw that the law was an insupportable burden.
Incessantly they heard, "Don't do that. Don't touch that."
Everything was either "clean" or "unclean." A man could never
accept an invitation to dinner because he could never be certain
that pork or an Orontes eel would not be served. It was wrong
to buy meat in the market because it might come from the
pagan sacrifices, and poultry was suspect because it might not
have been bled properly. They had been instructed about all
these observances by the disciples that had come from Jerusalem, but Paul and Barnabas never talked about these things.
Indeed, Paul used to say that the death of Christ had freed them
from the old law of Moses.

Under the guidance of Paul and Barnabas the Antiochian
Church was the first to recede from the position of the mother
Church in Jerusalem. Paul and Barnabas did not know how it
came about; often they were amazed at the tremendous vitality
of the "seed" of the gospel in this pagan soil. It seemed that this
was just the right soil for it, prepared by the hand of God.

The important thing about events is that they often drive
ideas to the surface, hidden thoughts and concepts are brought
out into the light where they can further develop. And so it was
in Antioch. Everything that was happening built up a situation
in which the world-wide culture of Hellenism was contrasted
with the concept of a world-wide Church. Gradually the
Church began to fill in the forms of the Hellenistic world. The
new development was marked by the new name given to the
members of the Church. Here in Antioch they were for the first
time called Christians. The Jews had called them Nazarenes, as
Semitic peoples still do. The brethren referred to themselves as
"disciples," "saints," "friends," and "faithful." We know how
keen the sense of the ordinary people is for the essential
element, and how pupils in school often express in one apt

word the outstanding trait of their teacher. Somebody uses an expression, and at once it is adopted by all others because it has hit on the essential thing. The ordinary people are gifted in this respect, and the people of Antioch especially were known for their sharp wit. Once the Emperor Severus asked: "Do they have anything but clowns in Antioch?"

When the Antiochians gave the name Christians to the members of the new Church, they were unerringly touching upon the essential thing. Just as later the term Catholic was used to express the universal quality of the Church. The point was that whether a man was a slave or freeman, black or white, Roman or Jew, Greek or Scythian, in the Church the only mark that counted was that they were slaves of Christ. The fact that the brethren were always singing hymns about Christ at home and at their services, as we read in Paul's Epistles, was probably the proximate occasion for forming the new name. At any rate they used the name of Christ more often than the name of Jesus, otherwise the good Antiochians would have called the members of the new religion Jesuits, and the Fathers of the Society of Jesus would today have to be content with the name Christians. Since the meaning of the word Christian, disciples of the anointed, is Hebraic, whereas the root word is Greek, and the termination is Latin, one student points out that the name Christian expresses the universal character of Christianity.

This Hebraic, Greek, and Latin term is a striking counterpiece to the inscription which Pilate wrote for the Cross in these three languages as the unwitting herald of the universality of the Church.[7] "It is a solemn moment when a new creation receives a name, for it is by the name that a person or a community becomes a being distinct from all others."[8] Here, at Antioch, Christianity thus stripped off its Aramaic garment, it began to speak Greek and it definitely entered into the Graeco-Roman cultural world, and the influence of those ancient

---

[7] H. F. B. Mackay, *The Adventures of Paul of Tarsus*. London, 1931.

[8] E. Renan, *Paulus*.

cultures reached deep into its own cultural, dogmatic, and auth-
oritarian structure, leaving an imprint that stands out clearly
today alongside the later imprint of Western civilization.

The Church at Antioch was in an exalted mood; "there was
great rejoicing," according to an old manuscript (Codex D).
Barnabas' glowing reports to the mother Church at Jerusalem
soon brought a large number of wandering preachers, called
prophets, just as in a later century St. Boniface's favourable
report about the missions in Germany brought many missioners
from his homeland, England, to Germany. These preachers,
highly favoured by the Holy Spirit, were esteemed and honoured
by the people. They stayed for some time in a local Church and
kept the first fervour of the faithful alive, and they formed a
liberal party in the Church. Among these preachers were also
several erratic and eccentric spirits that wandered from Church to
Church. Sometimes they claimed to speak in the name of the
Spirit when they were patently not in communion with the Spirit.
It required much patience to overlook these embarrassments and
to keep order in the community.

One of these wandering brethren, Agabus, brought disturbing news from Jerusalem. The common ownership of property
was not working out well. The whole idea was contrary to human
nature, because people wanted to make some little provision for
the future. It was a keen disappointment to many to see this
primitive practice disappear. Prompted by the Holy Spirit,
Agabus also foretold a great famine that actually occurred A.D.
44 during the reign of Emperor Claudius.

Because of the sharp decrease in the number of pilgrims
going to Jerusalem, the Church suffered greatly there. At
Antioch, when the brethren came together to discuss the plight
of the mother Church, no one dared to criticize the saints in
Jerusalem because they had been so improvident for the future.
At this point in the Acts of the Apostles (according to Codex D),
the author begins the use of the pronoun "we," indicating that
Luke, a native of Antioch, was present at this assembly. The

faith had come from Jerusalem; there the apostles still resided. What was more natural than to repay the spiritual gifts with temporal gifts? Everyone contributed as much as he could. The bond of faith uniting them to the brethren in Jerusalem became a bond of charity, because their faith was enlivened by charity. And yet, with all their religious enthusiasm, these early Christians were practical people. The elders chose Paul and Barnabas to take their offerings to Jerusalem. They wrapped the money in a leather pouch, and the two friends were soon on their way.

The earlier dislike and mistrust that Paul had found in Jerusalem seems to have disappeared. Poverty and persecution have a way of softening tempers. Indeed, Paul and Barnabas found the Church in Jerusalem in the midst of great sorrow. James the Greater, John's brother, that "son of thunder," as our Lord had called him when he wished to call down fire from heaven on the inhospitable Samaritan city, this great leader of the Church had only a few days before been put to death under King Herod Agrippa I. Once again, and this would be the last time in the history of the Jewish people, the kingdom of the Herods was resuscitated for three years.

The ruling Herod was a nephew of that Herod who had murdered the children at Bethlehem. He had spent his youth in Rome, and at the court of Tiberius received his education together with the imperial princes. Thus he became a friend of Caligula. He had become the royal man about town, who knew how to cover up a life of indulgence with the appearance of strict morality and adherence to the Jewish law. To conciliate the people, he began his reign with a persecution of the Christians. This time, however, the persecution was to reach out for the leaders of the Church, and so James was condemned without trial or hearing, merely at the royal whim, to be beheaded, just as John the Baptist had been beheaded by Herod Antipas. At the instigation of their mother, the brothers John and James had once asked our Lord for the two positions of honour, at his right and left, in the coming Messianic kingdom. The gentle

Master, seeing deep into their minds, smiled and said, "You know not what you ask" (Matt. 20:22). But beneath this childish ambition, he also saw the stuff from which heroes are made. "Can you drink the chalice that I shall drink?" He asked; and they answered proudly, "We can."

That boyish dream was now scarcely remembered. Jesus' death and the events of Pentecost had taught them the bloody seriousness of their calling and the spiritual nature of the Messianic kingdom. They had become silent and modest men; they had also become braver men. Now James had drunk that chalice. He had hardly begun to work, and then he was called away. Such, humanly speaking, is the tragedy of facts, such also is their divine comedy: The Bible is a terribly unsentimental book. With but a few words about the death of James, it goes on as if the shedding of blood in witness of the truth was an ordinary thing; and so it was. Martyrdom, or at least the continual prospect of martyrdom, would be the normal status of the apostolic life.

The second blow was meant for Peter, but it missed. God does not permit his eternal designs to be thwarted. He carries them out even if it is necessary to send an angel. How else would his prophecies come true? It was A.D. 44, sometime after Easter. News travelled slowly in those days, and in Antioch they had not yet heard of these happenings. Paul and Barnabas were now entering the city with their little caravan laden with foodstuffs and money. In the city they found none of the apostles except James, the "brother" of the Lord, whom even Herod dared not touch because of his great reputation for holiness.

Paul and Barnabas lodged in the house of Mary the mother of Mark. Here they heard from young Mark, Barnabas' nephew, and from Rhode the servant of the Marks, how Peter had been saved during that night of terrors. They told how Peter had fled and that now when anyone asked them where Peter was, they told them that he was in "another place" (Acts 12:17). Peter probably left the kingdom of Herod and stayed with the Churches in Syria. The story that he went to Rome at this time is a fabrication of a later date.[9] The whole prison watch, sixteen men, were put to death by Herod when he learned that Peter had escaped, a sign of how cheap he regarded human life and also how highly he valued the prisoner (Acts 12: 4, 6, 19). All this must have weighed heavily on Peter and the Church. Such problems as these cannot be mastered by our finite minds even with the help of the most elaborate theodicy. In the face of these obscurities and riddles in God's world, we can only bow our heads in submission.

Now the centre of the Church was shifted from Jerusalem to Antioch; Jerusalem became merely an episcopal see. The leading position went to Antioch and later to Rome. Thus the royal fool, who had imagined himself a god (Acts 12:22) and was punished by a sudden death, had been the instrument that set afoot an important development in the life of the Church. Paul makes no mention of this journey to Jerusalem in his letter to the Galatians (chap. 1), probably because he had not been able to consult Peter and also because the practical purpose of their mission had failed. This may be the simplest and best explanation for the difference between the Acts of the Apostles and the Epistle to the Galatians with regard to his journeys.

Leaving Jerusalem, Paul and Barnabas took young Mark with them to Antioch, where he later joined a foreign mission band. His home in Jerusalem could have served as the model of the true Christian home. His father was dead. His mother was one of the wealthy Jewesses who believed in our Lord. She apparently maintained a large house to which the apostles always had access. The upper room that she placed at the disposal of the apostles was probably the first Christian church. Some students surmise that the Garden of Gethsemane belonged to her. In that way young Mark grew up in an atmosphere consecrated by the presence of our Lord. He knew everything that the Master had done. He knew his miracles; he knew many of his sayings by heart. Besides this he wrote Greek and spoke

---

[9] Eusebius, *Hist. eccl.*, II, 14.

it fluently, though with a slight Aramaic accent. It was perhaps
Mark who, because of his anxiety about Jesus and the apostles,
had gone into the Garden of Olives on the night of the Passion
with merely a cloak over his shoulders, and when the soldiers
tried to hold him left them with the cloak in their hands. He
was singularly fitted to write the Gospel of Jesus as Peter had
preached it. Barnabas had great hopes for his young nephew.

As they went on to Antioch he was thinking how the
people of Antioch would listen with awe as Mark spoke about
Jesus and the apostles.

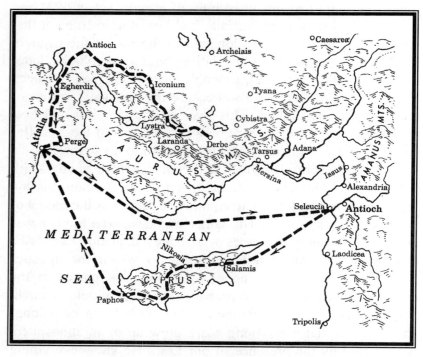

St Paul's First Missionary Journey

CHAPTER THIRTEEN

THE MISSION TO CYPRUS

*"The Holy Spirit said to them: Separate for me Saul and Barnabas,
for the work to which I have called them"* (Acts 13:2).

Since their return from Jerusalem to Antioch, Paul and Barnabas had become more conscious of the difference between the two cities. Antioch was the city of feverish activity and enterprise, and Jerusalem gratefully acknowledged the work that the Holy Spirit was doing in the younger community. More and more Antioch was becoming the outpost of Christian mission activity. Only fifteen years had passed since the death of the Lord, and already a string of missions and Churches stretched down the Orontes valley and along the Syrian and Phoenician coast. In contrast, Jerusalem remained the city of the most ancient tradition, surrounded by an aureole of its high privileges and unique associations. Antioch looked out upon the world, while Jerusalem became a city of cloistered exclusiveness with a peculiar Jewish aristocracy.

A year has passed; it is now spring of A.D. 45. For some time an unusual activity could have been noticed in the Church of Antioch, something like the activity in the hive before the bees swarm. Recently Paul had been referring more frequently to Jesus' command to preach the gospel. "For a necessity lies upon me," he exclaimed. "For woe to me if I preach not the gospel" (1 Cor. 9:16). Just as St. Gregory the Great, when he saw the young English slaves, was impelled to send missioners to England, so Paul when he saw the ships and men from all parts of the world, from Illyria, Gaul, and Spain, in the ports of Syria, felt an inner compulsion for the foreign missions. Now and then prophetic voices spoke of the same thing in the assembly. Finally, the congregation of the church on Singon Street in Antioch was assembled for an unusual observance, the first missionary service of which we have any knowledge.

After considering the matter, the council of the elders had decreed a fast for everybody in the Church in order to discover the will of the Lord. Now five of the most respected men, some prophets and teachers, stood in the middle of the congregation, and a more cosmopolitan group was scarcely ever brought together in such a small church. They were three white men and two dark-skinned men from Africa. It was a miniature of the Church's mission to the world. First in the group was the kindly, gentle Barnabas from Cyprus. Next to him stood Simon called Niger. This does not mean a Negro in our modern sense; the North Africans were a different race although they also had dark skins. Today we might have called them Moors. Was this Simon of Cyrene? If it was, we can easily understand his enthusiasm for the Christian missions. Next to him was his compatriot, Lucius of Cyrene. The fourth man was Manahen, the foster brother and youthful companion of the tetrarch Herod Antipas who had put John the Baptist to death. The two boys were brought up by the same mother; they had received the same education. One became a terrible tyrant, an adulterer, a murderer; the other an apostle of the Lord. How different the paths that men follow! The fifth man of the group was Paul of Tarsus. Thus we behold the most interesting group of missioners ever assembled.

The Eucharistic meal is over, and the election urn is brought forward. Everyone lies prostrate on the floor in prayer.

Suddenly a voice is raised, solemnly, earnestly; as from another world the voice of one of the brethren who has the gift of prophecy calls out: "Separate for me Saul and Barnabas, for the work to which I have called them." A second voice, and a third join in the cry, and then the whole assembly joins in shouting with southern exuberance the names, "Saul, Barnabas." An election is not needed. Paul and Barnabas stand forth before the council of the elders, while the elders, prophets, and teachers impose hands. This ceremony is not the conferring of the epis-copate, for Paul had been made a bishop by the Lord Himself. This imposition of hands was the formal acknowledgment of their mission, the external recognition of the calling that they had received from the Holy Spirit.

We cannot help but admire the venturesome spirit of the little Church in Antioch. Only a short time before, it had itself been founded, and now it had plans for conquering the whole world, and it was ready to send forth its best talent for the ven-ture. Some members of the assembly may have remarked that the very best of the preachers were being sent away, but the Holy Spirit has no time for such human considerations. The Church of Antioch bowed before the divine will, and "imposing their hands upon them, sent them away" (Acts 13:3).

Among those present at the service in the church on Sing-on Street was a fifteen-year-old boy who watched the sacred function intently, and even then his eyes must have revealed the great devotion he had for St. Paul which he speaks of so often in his letters. Later he sat at the feet of St. John, and thirty years after this scene he himself was consecrated bishop of Antioch, and again thirty years after that date he was thrown to the lions in the Roman amphitheatre under the Emperor Trajan. The boy was the future Bishop Ignatius, who died about the year 107. Like Paul, Ignatius was a Roman citizen, and like him he went to Rome to die. While his ship lay for a long time at anchor at Smyrna, the aged Bishop called Polycarp the bishop of Smyrna, another disciple of John, and the bishops of

Ephesus and Magnesia and their priests, to give them his
farewell blessing. It was there at Smyrna that he wrote his
seven famous letters to the Romans and the Churches of Asia
Minor. Even after all the years since then these letters express
the spirit of Paul. Like Paul before him, Ignatius styled himself
"a prisoner of Christ," calling his chains "my pearls." The most
striking thing about these letters is their strong emphasis on the
Catholic principle of authority and on the monarchical character
of the episcopate. Very early Antioch became one of the support-
ers of the organization of the Church. When we read in Ignatius'
letter to the Church at Smyrna, "When I am close to the sword,
I am close to God," we seem to hear the words of Paul.

At Antioch, Paul began the great adventure of his mission
journeys, his Alexandrian campaign in reverse, from the Orient
to the pillars of Hercules, "to the uttermost boundaries of the
West," in the words of Clement of Rome. Here we turn a new
page in the history of the mission activity of the Church. Until
now the Church had spread only along the coasts and the banks
of rivers; now she was to strike out into the heart of foreign
lands. For the present Barnabas was the superior of the mission
band. Perhaps it was another beautiful spring morning when
Paul and Barnabas, accompanied by the priests and people,
went down the great avenue of pillars, through the gardens
outside the city, to the harbour of Seleucia. On a clear day even
now the two great arms of the breakwaters of the harbour can
be seen beneath the surface of the water; they were named for
Paul and Barnabas. The little group knelt by the water for a last
prayer: "How beautiful are the feet of them that preach the
gospel of peace, of them that bring glad tidings of good
things!" (Rom. 10:15) The passengers and the sailors aboard
the ships had never seen anything like this before. The brethren
embraced each other once more, and then the ship slid out into
the dark blue waters.

They were happy as they began this great adventure.
They were still young, they were intimate friends, and the un-

known world into which they were going had a great attraction for their youthful minds. More than any natural attraction, they had the knowledge of their divine calling for this mission. Barnabas was especially pleased that they had been able to take along his nephew, the young John Mark, as an assistant on the mission. Many a brave expedition started out from that harbour, both before and after. Great kings, generals, and immense armies of crusaders in days to come. History has forgotten most of them; they have left no mark in the world. But the work of these three poor missioners to conquer the world for Christ has remained. Someone has called the missionary journeys of Paul a Christian Odyssey, and certainly since Homer's time no ship sailed on a bolder venture. The name of that Cyprian vessel deserved to be immortalized much more than Columbus' ship, for this voyage was of far greater importance than that of the courageous Genoese.

Barnabas proposed that they make the isle of Cyprus, his homeland, their first stop. If it had been left to Paul the ship would have taken another course. Cyprus was not a traffic point where the great sea lanes crossed, and Paul knew that the gospel seed must be sown in the great centres of world commerce. But for the present he yielded, especially since John Mark also wished to go to Cyprus. The east coast of Cyprus rises in a blinding white glare straight up from the water like the cliffs of Dover in England. Modern steamers stop at Larnica, but the apostles landed some thirty miles to the north at Salamis, which was at that time the largest port of Cyprus. Only an extensive area of ruins near the modern Famagusta marks the site of the ancient Salamis. Salamis was Barnabas' native city. Friends and relatives came out to greet him, and Paul also was given a warm welcome for Barnabas' sake, even though it had been Paul's persecution of the Christians that had sent refugees from Jerusalem here with the seed of the gospel (Acts 11:19). Once a beautiful city, Salamis had been the home of a Greek colony with a considerable number of Phoenicians and Jews.'[10] We know of the large Jewish colony in Salamis from the terrible pogrom ordered by the Emperor Trajan to exterminate the Jews.

Weeks passed while Paul and Barnabas went from synagogue to synagogue to preach. It seems that here, in Salamis, the Jews of the Diaspora were quite patient; at least, we hear of no disturbance. Since Barnabas was the leader of the mission band, every occasion for unpleasantness would be carefully avoided. When they preached to the Jews it was always necessary to show the historical basis for Christianity; it was necessary to show that the Messias was the fulfilment of the Jews' expectations, of the highest Jewish traditions. The Resurrection of Christ offered no great difficulties for the Pharisees; their principal problem was the relationship of this religion to the Mosaic law.

The seed was being sown; the people now had something to think about. When the apostles came back on their return journey, they hoped to gather in the harvest. They went on into the mountainous country along the Pedaeus River to which the Cyprians owed their good crops. In these mountains, Herod the Great had settled many Jews to work the copper mines that he had leased from Emperor Augustus. From the eastern end of Cyprus to the western tip is about sixty miles in a straight line. If Paul and his companions visited each of the fifteen important cities that Pliny mentions, preaching only once in each city, the crossing of the island would have taken at least four months. As they went from town to town they saw the big groves of fruit trees, oranges, lemons, figs, mulberries, peaches, and apricots. Even today, after the destructive occupation of the island by the Turks, we can judge how bountiful must have been the supply of fruit in ancient days.

Everywhere little Christian groups were being formed. The leaven was at work; the movement had begun. Later Barnabas would return to complete the organization of the Church, but now the missioners were trudging down the old Roman road to

---

[10] Cf. Flavius Josephus, *Antiquities*, XIII, x, 4; cf. also Philo, *Ad Gaium*, 36

Paphos. Now the road went down from the old settlement to the new city below. Up in the heights of Amathus, the modern Limasol, was the famous sanctuary of Aphrodite, who according to the legend had appeared to men in this place for the first time as Venus Amathusia, the ancient queen of the world. This was not the Aphrodite of Plato, that goddess of grace and beauty, but the lustful goddess Astarte of the Phoenicians, the goddess of the sons of Cham, with all her shameful mysteries, her worship of fertility, her brutal glorification of the lower urges, who not only drew to her temple the people of Paphos but lured large groups of pilgrims from distant lands. Here in her temple, children served as priestesses in her sorry trade. This was the wanton and abominable perversion of the worship of Baal and Astarte that had conquered Greece and from Carthage threatened to poison the whole West with its pestilential breath if Rome had not succeeded in its providential task of destroying Carthage.

The Roman governor of the island, Sergius Paulus, lived in New Paphos. He belonged to the Roman nobility, and according to Pliny he was a man of considerable culture and education. He was an authority in matters of natural science, a member of the imperial commission to regulate the Tiber, a man with an open mind, a searcher after truth, not a blase sceptic like Pontius Pilate. Luke said he was a man of great insight because he was sincerely looking for knowledge about the supernatural. His official duties left him much time for study. Like other proconsuls in the Empire he had about him in his court a group of young men, sons of Roman patricians, who were to learn the science of government in preparation for their later careers. To dispel the monotony of life in the provinces, Sergius Paulus seems to have surrounded himself with a kind of court of the muses, by encouraging scholars, poets, and theosophists among whom the most prominent was a learned Jew named Bar Jesus. Bar Jesus was one of a number of Jewish magicians, or Elymas, who travelled about like the cynical Greek philosophers. Elymas is the Hellenic version of the Arabian Ulema, i.e., wise man. An Elymas was not an ignorant and uneducated magician or medicine man. Such a man would never have had access to the court of Sergius. He was generally an educated theosophist who had studied the secret teachings of Egypt, Babylonia, and Persia. Jewish magic, at that time, was held in high esteem, claiming to derive its knowledge from the hierophants of Egypt, and even from Moses himself.

This dabbling in secret knowledge should not detract from our opinion of Sergius' education, since no less a scholar than St. Augustine gave nine years of his life to the study of the occult teachings of the Manichaeans. This was the period of transition when philosophers were deteriorating into sophists, and sophists became magicians. A certain amount of Oriental occultism was fashionable in the houses of the great. Paganism exhausted itself in three stages: the ancient mythology, under-mining the simple faith of the common man; then philosophy degenerated into sophistry and finally pagan culture descended to magic. Some of the clearer thinkers as, for instance, the Stoics, went back to the original idea that the world had an origin, and therefore that it had a cause, and that human life demanded something like a moral unity. A careful student of this age writes: 'This Elymas at the court of Sergius Paulus represented that powerful influence which occult teachings have over the mind and will; he represented that strange way of life of occultism which Christianity had come to destroy." [11] It was precisely against this kind of Oriental mysticism that Paul was fighting in his old age when he wrote the Epistle to the Colossians and his pastoral letters.

The preaching of the two missioners had become the talk of the town, and the governor invited them to his house for a religious discussion. This was the first time that the gospel made contact with aristocratic Roman society. It was natural that for this occasion Paul and Barnabas exchanged places;

---

[11] Cf. W. M. Ramsay, *Cities of St. Paul*

here it was the Roman citizen who counted, not the Cypriot.

From Paul's appearances in Lystra, Thessalonica (1 Thess. 1:9), and Athens, we know the method he used when he addressed pagans. When he spoke to a pagan audience, he began with man's natural knowledge of God, from monotheism, the teaching of the immanence of God. He spoke of the God that is within us in order to speak of the God who is above us, of the supramundane Creator and God. Then he spoke of our relationship to God and of the practical conclusion of worshipping God.

Up to this point he spoke with philosophic calm. Now as he proceeded to speak of the gospel of Christ, a new enthusiasm lit his features, and there was fire and spirit in his oratory as he told of the Resurrection and of his experience on the Damascus road. He was all aflame when he spoke of the Lord in whom was the salvation of the whole world. Paul's spirited address and his undoubted sincerity must have deeply impressed the governor, but, as a prudent man and as a Roman jurist, Sergius, wishing to hear the other side, invited the Elymas to speak. Now swords were crossed by the kingdom of light and the kingdom of darkness. As a Jew of some education, the Elymas knew the Scriptures, but Paul had not disputed with Stephen for nothing; he had spent long years in study and meditation. Paul noted that his speech had impressed the governor, and he was determined now to show that the religion of Jesus was not a pale system of thought, but that it possessed the power of God, power to lay all magic in the dust.

He looked piercingly into the eyes of the magician, who began to stagger from the midst of the gathering, groping his way out as if he had been suddenly blinded. The pitiful behaviour of the magician under the piercing gaze of Paul convinced the governor that magic was no longer tenable, that it was a delusion and a snare. The conversion of Sergius Paulus was Christianity's first conquest in the upper strata of Roman society.

For the second time since the fall of Simon Magus, Christianity had come into conflict with the magic of the Orient and had come off victorious. Paul's unmasking of the magician was a telling argument for the governor. Indeed it was the most effective way of showing him the truth of Christianity. The gospel would never have conquered the ancient culture of paganism if it had not been able to show its superiority over the magic and mysticism of the East. Therefore Christianity adopted an approach different from that of today to reach men's minds. At that time nothing was considered true and divine unless it was guaranteed by an accompanying miracle. Hence, the story of the New Testament is so frequently interwoven with the miraculous.

In a sense it was also a personal triumph for Paul. From now on it is Paul and not Barnabas who is the leader of the expedition. Now Paul's name is mentioned first, and Barnabas recedes more and more and finally disappears from the story. According to tradition, Barnabas continued to the end in the mission of Cyprus.

From now on also St. Luke refers to Paul only by his civil name, Paul. That was probably the name he gave when the governor asked him. He now adopted this name since in the Greek world the Hebrew name would have told of too close a connection with the people of Israel. The name Paul was a Roman name, it sounded better in the Roman world, in that vast Roman *imperium* of which he was so often thinking, it was more in accord with his calling as the Apostle of the Gentiles.

Paul appealed to the Graeco-Roman world as a free-born member. He was no alien, he was not the herald of some strange Oriental cult. He had just defeated the magic of the East in order to show that the gospel had nothing in common with the magic religions of the East.

The Elymas did not forget his defeat. According to tradition, he was able eventually to stir up the Jews against Barnabas and beat him to death.'[12] Mark buried the body in a Roman grave near Salamis. In the reign of the Emperor Zeno (489) the body of the gentle saint was discovered with a copy

---

[12] Migne, P.G., LXXXVI, 189.

of the Gospel of St. Matthew on his breast.[13]

Was Sergius baptized then, as is generally supposed? The Acts of the Apostles say nothing about it. Perhaps Elymas, because of his large following, was able to hasten the departure of the apostles. It seems more probable, however, that Paul and Barnabas left soon because it was now late in the season, so that they could get a ship to Asia Minor in order to cross the Taurus range before winter set in. Paul never came back to Cyprus; he looked on the island as Barnabas' territory and he had no desire to build on another man's foundation.

---

[13] Cf. H. V. Morton, *In the Steps of St. Paul*, London, 1936.

CHAPTER FOURTEEN

THE COUNTRY OF THE GALATIANS

"Now when Paul and they that were with him had sailed from Paphos,
they came to Perge in Pamphylia.
And John departing from them, returned to Jerusalem" (Acts 13: 13).

Since he had unmasked the magician before Sergius Paulus, Paul's authority was growing, and now he insisted on his plan of going to Asia Minor. He would rather have gone immediately to Ephesus, because he preferred the great commercial centres. But he was not able to find a ship going to Ephesus; ships were going only to the southern coast, to the port of Attalia. That probably determined his route. He had no definite route mapped out in his pocket. Often he was guided by the circumstances of the road, accepting the obstacles and difficulties as indications of God's will. The route over malaria-infested Pamphylia into Asia Minor was extremely dangerous and time-consuming, and no one went that way unless he had an urgent reason. In the case of a merchant that urgent reason was the desire for profit, for the soldier it was duty, and for the missioners it was the call of God. Paul was never deterred by anything difficult or dangerous.

Years ago when he was a boy he had a sympathetic feeling for the coarse people who lived on the other side of the mountains. Many Jews had gone into the interior following the Roman colonizers as crows follow the sower in the field. Cyprus kept up a lively trade with Asia Minor and it may have been that the new Christian Churches on Cyprus had suggested to the apostles that they bring the message of the gospel to their brethren on the mainland. Unconsciously, too, Paul was carrying out an adventure of his boyhood dreams. Often as a boy he had dreamed of going over the mountains to explore the region beyond.

It was late autumn of A.D. 45, when the three companions sailed from Paphos to Asia Minor. We can understand why Paul did not go to Cilicia: a prophet has little standing in his native land. As they sailed across the sea, they saw to the north the jagged skyline of the mountains like a forbidding wall. Paul was a good companion and a good narrator. He once advised his followers not to omit the salt from their speech, and certainly he did not fail in this respect.

"Look, Mark," he said, "over there, at the foot of those snow-capped mountains, is my own city Tarsus, and beyond the white wall of those mountains is Antioch in Pisidia. That was where my father got the goats' hair for making tents. They are good-natured people, not nearly as hard as they appear to be.

"Over there is the Pamphylian plain. It is an unhealthy place. People die there like flies. They say an angel of Satan eats up their energies and turns them yellow and green, and I almost believe it. In my homeland, Cilicia, we also have that angel of Satan. He rises from the swamps in the evening clothed in the flowing robes of the fog. Once when I was a boy his hand touched me. His hand is like fire, and when he touches you your blood boils in your veins and your eyes are like balls of fire. But the Lord will protect us against this destroying angel and we will hurry across this land."

But Mark had not had a good day. He seldom said anything. He seemed to resent it that his uncle Barnabas had given over the reins to this stormy man, filled with boldness and

recklessness. Now he was talking about crossing over that forbidding wall of snow and ice to see the barbarians on the other
side. He had heard something about these Isaurian robbers,
how they attacked the traveller, robbed him, and disposed off
his body in the icy mountain lakes. Mark could not understand
the high courage of the Apostle now, but the day would come
when he would (Col. 4: 10).

Asia Minor at that time was a mosaic of many native
princelings, tribes, provinces, dialects, superstitious practices,
and strange cults. Even though Hellenism had made some
progress, every town still had its own god whose Latin or
Greek name did not hide his Asiatic origin. The whole coast
was filled with holy places, esoteric priesthoods who engaged
in unheard-of mysteries. Pamphylia was an imperial military
province governed by a propraetor, or commanding general.
Like every other province, it had its contingent of the imperial
priesthood, a temple to the emperor and to the divine Roma, all
of which possessed rich endowments.

An outstanding characteristic of the population of Asia
Minor was their natural disposition to religion and their inclination to superstition and the most primitive forms of secret
cults. About this time a certain Apollonius of Tyana flourished
as a wonder-worker. Shortly after him the vogue was for a
Peregrinus Proteus and Alexander of Abonoteichos who led the
gullible people into all kinds of folly.

The apostolic travellers landed in the bay of Attalia, the
modern Adalia, at the mouth of the Kestros river. From over its
staunch bastions, erected against the pirates of the sea, the city
of Attalia looked proudly out to sea, sunning itself in the
golden glow of its orange and lemon groves. They started
immediately up the river to get to Perge several miles north of
Attalia. Here they would find the beginning of the road that led
to the pass across the ravines and precipices of the Taurus
mountains. Here in the foothills the path was bordered by wild
cactus hedges and prickly pears as high as a house, but as they

ascended they saw pines, fir trees, and gigantic broomcorn, and when they lifted their eyes to the heights they saw great cedars swaying majestically in the wind.

The road got rougher and harder to travel. The wind blowing from the mountains was more piercingly cold. Barnabas pushed on, fired by Paul's enthusiasm, but Mark began to object. Why were they going up into these high mountains? They wouldn't find a synagogue there, or the protection of a ghetto. All they had seen were almost impassable mountain trails leading the traveller to the very edge of breath-taking precipices, over bridges that had been tumbled aside by the raging torrents. This was not the kind of missionary work he had pictured to himself. He was a city boy, and now his courage evaporated when he came to grips with wild nature.

The reckless impetuosity of a leader like Paul was too much for Mark. He felt that he was not equal to the demands and dangers of this journey. What he had heard from the inn-keeper back in Perge had frightened him. He told his uncle that he wished to turn back and get the first ship that would take him to Caesarea, but Barnabas did not approve of Mark's decision. He realized that he had to decide between deserting Paul and the mission and allowing his nephew to go home alone. With a heavy heart he decided to allow Mark to go back alone. That seemed to be what his apostolic duty demanded.

Mark's desertion at the beginning of the campaign wounded Paul deeply; even after many years he still remembered the smart of that disappointment. He thought that Mark was timid and he recalled the words: "No man putting his hand to the plough and looking back is fit for the kingdom of God" (Luke 9: 62). But Mark turned back for another reason, a reason that was more fundamental, something that he could not very well disclose, and that Luke also preferred to pass over. In cases like this Luke would rather have us read between the lines. Back in Jerusalem Mark had grown up in the midst of the original apostles; he had been surrounded by the old Jewish tradition that still bound the young Church to the synagogue. Paul, it was evident now, was determined to tear the Church from the synagogue. Mark had been one of Peter's favourite disciples, his Greek interpreter, and that was where he would rather have remained. Indeed, once Peter called him "my son, Mark" (1 Pet. 5:13).

Here in the wild mountain passes appeared the shadow of the great problem that would haunt Paul all through his life. It was the great cause for which he would have to offer everything, even the tender feelings of friendship. The divine call to some great undertaking means much happiness and a rich blessing because it is a sign of God's confidence in a man; but it also means a heavy burden and often a world of sorrow. God's friendship is at the same time God's burden; "for the word of God is . . . more piercing than any two-edged sword and reaching the division of the soul and the spirit, of the joint also and the marrow" (Heb. 4: 12).

Paul's greatness as an apostle consists in no small degree in these inner sacrifices which he made for the cause. Many years later Mark conquered this youthful weakness and, when Paul was a prisoner in Rome, he became a valuable fellow worker.

The two friends continued on their way without Mark. Soon they found themselves surrounded by an Alpine world, a country that even today has not been thoroughly explored. The journey made great demands on their physical strength because of the bad roads and the sudden severe changes in climate. Crossing the Taurus range, they found a sudden change in climate. Today the traveller may pass blooming peach trees; tomorrow he may be battling a snow storm in one of the Phrygian passes. While Tarsus lies only 240 feet above sea level, Antioch in Pisidia is 3,600 feet above the sea, Iconium 3,081 feet, and Lystra 3,690 feet. Furthermore, the apostles could have had only the most frugal provisions: some hard bread which they softened in a wayside stream, a handful of olives, and anything that the rocky country might have provided them.

The region around the Cilician Gate was extremely wild. Often the path went along the Kestros river which had worn a steep canyon into a solid rock mountain. High above, the stone walls reached to the sky where sometimes a lonely pine tree swayed against the blue. Sometimes the path wound round the mountain with the heights on one side, and at their feet the precipice fell down with breath-taking suddenness to the river as it poured angrily over the granite blocks that disputed its way. In these desolate places the frightened traveller was often met by a roving robber band from Isauria, dark men with forbidding faces, black beards, piercing eyes. Paul had seen them years ago racing across the Arabian desert with their lances poised high. Sometimes an arrow whistled by the traveller to halt his steps until the robber could discover what wealth he could take. Often the travellers came to a crossing of the mountain stream where the bridge had been washed away. And, like the Turks today, the apostles had to swim across, holding their clothes and poor belongings above their heads.

For three days now they had followed the Kestros, reaching the pass itself. From there they would descend on the north side of the range to the Pisidian plateau, through pine forests and mountain meadows where sheep, goats and buffalo herds were grazing. As night came on they hurried to find whatever shelter some camel-driver could offer them in his dirty hovel. Sometimes wild dogs might attack the traveller, or some inhospitable shepherd block his path; or the demons of his rising fever torture his brain in the chilly night air that rises from the cold valleys on each side. Often the miserable traveller stretches his weary body on a stony ledge and thinks himself fortunate if he can climb beneath an overhanging cliff.

The difficulties of the hard journey brought these two friends close together. Nothing unites us more than sharing the same experiences and the same dangers and sorrows. Often, when they stopped to look at some great riven block of stone, at the rushing of some waterfall, they thought of God's close presence, of how He had revealed himself on the rock of Sinai. They thought of the rock that was Jahve, that rock of which David sang in his psalms about nature and the mountains. Later the rock symbolized Christ for Paul: "They drank of the spiritual rock that followed them: and the rock was Christ" (1 Cor. 10:4).

They were glad on the fourth day when they began to emerge from this mountainous terrain and saw below a beautiful mountain lake and beyond the massive Sultan Dagh, the modern Egerdir Gol. This beautiful lake, some 2,800 feet above sea level, seems to transport us to the enchanting shores of Lake Maggiore in Italy. The blue waters of the lake were covered with sailing ships that plied between the shore cities. On the opposite shore they saw the site of the modern city of Egerdir that now gives its name to the lake.

Since Paul and Barnabas did not prefer the route across the lake, they had to climb the heights on the east side of the lake where again and again they had a view of the beautiful lake, as they travelled the Roman road that went from Ephesus by way of Antioch to Tarsus. Today a spur of the main railway line from Smyrna to Tarsus reaches out to Egerdir.

On the fifth day they passed Egerdir; on the sixth day they were in sight of the goal of their journey, Antioch in Pisidia at the foot of the majestic Sultan Dagh. They passed the great arches of a Roman aqueduct as they approached the city. The province of Pisidia was the southernmost part of the old kingdom of the Galatian King Amyntas, but now it belonged to the Roman province of Galatia. To exterminate the robber bands infesting the countryside, the emperors Augustus and Claudius had found an effective means. Throughout the province they founded colonies of Roman veterans. The city of Antioch was originally such a Roman colony with certain rights and privileges. The principal colonists of Antioch were veterans of that

Celtic legion that Caesar had raised in Gaul, above whose regimental banner was the symbol of the lark. Everywhere in Antioch the travellers smelt the pungent odour of the tanneries. The Jews had many privileges in Antioch granted them by their greatest friend, Julius Caesar, at whose bier it was said they lay prostrate every night in mourning.

Antioch was also a holy city, dedicated to the worship of the moon god, called Men or Lunus by the Romans. Above the city gate Paul saw a picture of this god, the head covered with the Phrygian cap, two horns growing from the shoulders, his hands resting on a lance.

This god, Men, was no other than the ancient Persian god Mithras of the Mazda religion, who was worshipped in Babylonia as the sun god Shamash, in Syria as Baal, in Phrygia and Thrace as Attis or Sabazius, in Greece as Helios. He had been merged here with the old moon god. The worship of Mithra or Men was fundamentally a world religion which the fickle Galatians, after they had come here from the banks of the Rhine, adapted to their own druid worship. The Phrygian cult of the goddess mother Cybele was also acceptable to the Galatians because at home they had also had mother gods.

About all this religious history the two ambassadors of Christ entering the city of Antioch in the fall of A.D. 45 knew nothing. They did not realize that the hideous effigy above the gate represented Christianity's worst enemy in the East. Here, as also in Tarsus, the night was often illuminated by the flames of orgiastic observances, by the worship of the sun, the moon, and the planets. Writing to the Galatians later, Paul referred to these excesses by which the name religion was defiled: "But then indeed, not knowing God, you served them who, by nature, are not gods . . . How turn you again to the weak and needy elements, which you desire to serve again?" (Gal. 4:8) Near the modern Turkish village of Yalovach may be seen immense blocks of marble and fluted columns of great architectural perfection that are the ruins of the old acropolis of Antioch in

Pisidia. Today the Turks will be found lounging along the banks of the mountain stream that hurries through the village, lying on their mats, sipping coffee, and smoking their water pipes, and perhaps in much the same way the Galatians may have been idling about and gazing curiously as these newcomers entered the town. Paul and Barnabas asked where they would find their fellow countrymen. In the Jewish quarter they found lodging with some weaver's family or some tentmaker.

Entering a town such as this, Paul did not have with him a set plan for conducting his mission, but he did follow a certain method. Two things are to be noted about his method: he generally followed the furrow that had been traced by Jewish emigration for many years. That is, he went to those places where Hellenistic Jews had spread their net of synagogues in the Roman Empire. Besides this, Paul generally chose a place where he could find employment at his trade. While he was engaged in his trade, a great amount of time was consumed, it is true, but it gave him the opportunity of getting to know people and of being financially independent of the congregation. Even though he proclaimed the evangelical principle that the preacher of the gospel had the right to live by the gospel, he was proud to be able to say that he had been no burden on the Church. Barnabas was of the same opinion.

These things gave Paul's missionary method a certain pattern. When he came to a town, he sought the Jewish quarter and employment with some tentmaker or weaver. Having found employment, he became a member of his employer's family community according to the Oriental custom and began to work at the loom. On the following Sabbath he went to the synagogue and introduced himself there as a man learned in the law. The usher assigns him a special place and, when the Scripture reading is over, the hazzan comes to him with the presiding officer's message to address the assembly.

In fact, hardly any other way was left for Paul to preach a new religion, since any religion different from the state religion was proscribed as unlawful religion. Only the synagogue had a legal right to make proselytes. For decades the pagans were unable to distinguish between Judaism and Christianity and on account of this confusion both religions had to suffer because of each other (Acts 18:2; 19:33).

Everything was at hand, therefore, to gather in the harvest that stood white in the field. The Roman Empire offered its world-wide commerce, Hellenism had united the world with its language and culture and instilled in the minds of men a desire for a saviour, and Judaism, without willing it, had by its monotheism and moral law educated many for Christ and had become the anteroom of Christianity.

Such was the beginning of Paul's campaign in Asia Minor, an adventure which in many respects excelled the march of the ten thousand Greeks to the Black Sea. What a great ado Xenophon would have made about the adventure, while Luke passes it all over in silence. Paul himself seems to have told his friends very little about it. What we know was forced from Paul by the attacks of his enemies (2 Cor. 6: 5; 11:26).

CHAPTER FIFTEEN

IN ANTIOCH OF PISIDIA

*"But they, passing through Perge, came to Antioch in Pisidia: and entering
into the synagogue on the Sabbath day, they sat down"* (Acts 13:14).
*"Persecutions, afflictions: such as came upon me at Antioch, at Iconium,
and at Lystra: what persecutions I endured.
And out of them all the Lord delivered me"* (2 Tim. 3:11).

There was an air of holiday in Antioch. The bazaars were
closed; groups of people in holiday attire walked through the
streets, Jews and those who "feared the Lord" went to the synagogue. The synagogue had been built on the shore of the Anthios
river so that water would be easily available for the purifications.
Above the door of the synagogue two olive branches were
carved in the stone with the inscription: "Temple of the Hebrews." In the basement were the rooms for the purifications.
Anyone who had eaten forbidden meat or touched a corpse or a
grave had to wash himself. In the front, a broad flight of stone
steps led to the prayer room. Within, a green curtain hung
before the cupboard where the Bible rolls were kept, before the
curtain was the seven-branched candlestick, while many lamps
hung from the ceiling. In the centre of the platform was the
reader's dais. The women sat to one side behind a wooden grill.
   The news had gone out that two men learned in the law

had arrived. When Paul and Barnabas came to the synagogue this Sabbath morning, they wore the broad, white-and-brown striped scarf, the tallith, which distinguished them from the proselytes. Everybody watched as they were presented to the people, Paul as a learned scribe, Barnabas as a Levite. They declined the places of honour near the rabbis, remembering what our Lord had said: "Beware of the scribes, who love to walk in long robes . . . and to sit in the first chairs in the synagogues" (Mark 12:38 f.). After the prayer had been said, the servant of the synagogue reached for one of the Scripture rolls, took off the richly embroidered cover, and unrolled it to the place where the reading had stopped on the last Sabbath. After the reading, the president of the synagogue sent an invitation to Paul to speak. Paul went to the front and stretched out his arm, the customary gesture of the orator of ancient times to command attention.

Paul's missionary sermons followed one style, the matter being adapted to the occasion. His line of argument was two-fold, one for the Jews, the other for the pagans. St. Luke gives us a sketch of the sermon for a synagogue audience (in Acts 13:15). It has three parts, each introduced by the address: "Men, brethren."

The Jews were a proud race with traditions older than those of any other people on earth. They knew they had a message for the world. That message was threefold: the doctrine of mono-theism, a sublime moral law, and the expectation of the Messias. They knew that they stood in a world of gross polytheism and degradation, as the only sober people among those who were intoxicated. Their whole history was the recollection of the great deeds, the wonderful and terrible things of God (Ps. 105). In an address to the people of this race, that history could not be ignored. Therefore Paul began with a review of God's leadership of the race in the Old Testament, which was directed toward the Messias. Immediately his hearers smiled with pleasure because they were to hear a Messianic sermon. Step by step, Paul explain-ed the prophecies, all of which pointed to the Christ. When he

came to speak of David, he gave his line of thought an un-
noticeable turn to speak of Jesus, without leaving the prophetic
theme. He passed over the unfortunate story of Judaism since
the Babylonian captivity, and went on to speak of the great
event that began fifteen years before in Palestine: the Baptist
movement by the Jordan. That movement had reached as far as
Asia Minor.

In his second part Paul marched on with mighty sentences. The whole purpose of this history was not Abraham or his
posterity. It was the establishment of the kingdom of God. Now,
God had actually sent that One in whom all the prophecies
unite as the streams and rivers flow into the ocean, Jesus. He
had spoken that great word, his name, that name that stood like
some continental divide between the old and the new. He went
on to show how the atoning death of the Messias had come to
fulfilment through the blindness and malice of the fathers of
Israel. Just at that time, the Jews were accustomed to recite
every Sabbath that prophetic psalm written by David describing
the passion. Some of the words of this psalm were repeated by
Jesus himself on the Cross.

"O God, my God, look upon me,
Why have you forsaken me? But I am a worm, and no man:
The reproach of men, and the outcast of the people.
They parted my garments amongst them:
And upon my vesture they cast lots."

Official Judaism, in its vain dream of national glory, had
interpreted these words as describing the affliction of the enslaved and dismembered race and the travail out of which the
national hero was to be born. But Paul showed his hearers how
the people of Jerusalem and their leaders had not recognized
the Messias and had delivered him up to the pagan Pilate as an
enemy of the state. He described how Pilate in his bloody irony
had given expression to their blindness in the inscription he
wrote for the Cross, and how all this malice and ignorance had
served the fulfilment of the divine decree of man's salvation.

He may also have described to his audience the details he had read in the official record of the trial before the Sanhedrin, how the Jewish priests had mocked the dying Messias: "If you be the Son of God, come down from the cross" (Matt. 27:40), and Jesus had answered in the words of this twenty-first psalm. The Jewish people had forsaken their Messias and now they would wander about the earth, forsaken by God until the end of the world.

Not long ago Paul himself had misunderstood these Messianic prophecies, but at Damascus he had seen things in a new light. His mission was to open the eyes of all the people of the world to God's salvation. Paul stood before them as a witness of the Resurrection, and tomorrow he would be in Macedonia, in Greece, and then in Rome, and last of all in Spain, and he would not rest until he had brought the message to every people.

In the third part of his sermon, Paul referred to a personal experience they had all had. "You all know that the law of Moses never brought justification. In Jesus you will find that for which you are seeking: forgiveness of sins, peace, and reconciliation with God." Here for the first time he expresses the contrast between grace and the law. The Judaic system has now been replaced by a higher message.

The leaders of the synagogue stared silently at the floor; they were uneasy about this new preacher. A buzz of voices rose in the audience; men were arguing about these proofs from the Scripture. The proselytes and those who "feared God" were encouraged. They were pleased to hear that no difference existed between them and the others.

Paul had not made a bad beginning. Outside, many surrounded him, asking him and Barnabas to stay and speak again on the next Sabbath. The sermon became something of a sensation in the town. During the week Paul had many callers at his lodging. Was it really true what he had said about Jesus? Had he really seen him? They told the whole story of what had happened in Jerusalem, clearing up the strange rumours that had come this far.

On the next Sabbath the synagogue was filled long before the time for the service to begin. The leaders of the synagogue were disappointed to see that the pagans were in the majority; they felt that they were being replaced and that they were being dislodged in their possession of the hope of the Messias. Unwillingly they made room for the two strangers at the speaker's desk, but they had resolved to make strenuous objections today.

Barnabas, with his winning, gentle manner, was the first to speak. No one could be angry with him; he was so conciliatory and kind. He emphasized the things they all believed in, not where they were at variance.

Then Paul spoke. From the Acts we may conclude that his text was the forty-ninth chapter of Isaias in which Israel speaks of its great mission to bring the knowledge of the revelation to the rest of the world: "Give ear, you islands, and hearken, you people from afar . . . And he said: It is a small thing that you should be my servant, to raise up the tribes of Jacob and to convert the dregs of Israel. Behold, I have given you to be the light of the Gentiles, that you may be my salvation even to the farthest part of the earth" (Is. 49:1, 6). But how could this be fulfilled now? The people were conquered, the house of David had been brought low, the Temple was filled with pagan abominations. Paul pointed out the contrast between the prophecy and the tragic present, but it was this very destruction of the nation that was the first ray of light announcing the morning. Without the dispersal of the Jews among the Gentiles, the burning hope for the Saviour would never have been spread. As strangers all over the world, the Jews would be the heralds of the Messias, the light among the Gentiles.

Then Paul began to speak openly about Christ. Israel had lost all its privileges; the thing that counted was not blood relationship to a race, but faith in Jesus. And Jesus had come to break down the wall between Jew and Gentile. "In Christ," he said, "there is no difference between Jew and Gentile, between master and slave, between man and wife. In Christ we are all at once one." The leaders of the synagogue saw how that wall of separation on which they had laboured for centuries was falling in ruins, and in wild anger they rose from their seats. The speaker could not go on because of the shouting and screaming. "Take him away. He's a heretic. We'll have no such Messias." National pride and national jealousy stood in the path of truth. Even good people will not listen to the truth when it goes against their national prejudices.

But the pagans were applauding the missioners. The synagogue rang with their cheers, and outside those who could not get in began to applaud what they heard Paul stood on the platform, as if cast in bronze. His eyes seemed to be looking inward, as if he were in communion with some invisible person. He knew that another moment of decision had come in his life.

It did not take long: just a moment, while the angry contradictions struck from below, he made a decision that affected his future, a decision that reshaped the future Church. Did the Lord lift the veil for an instant to show him how he would be condemned as an apostate, how the undying hatred of his people would relentlessly follow him wherever he would go? And he knew how terrible his people could be in hatred. Paul assented to his fate. Slowly he came back to the present; slowly he was able to get a hearing again; slowly in measured sentences, laden with meaning and emotion and resolution, he said: "It was necessary that the word of God should be spoken first to you: but because you reject it and judge yourselves unworthy of eternal life, behold we turn to the Gentiles" (Acts 13:46). The die was cast. Like an ocean the waves of sorrow would from now on pour over him. Barnabas stood steadfastly at his side, and together they reproached the leaders of the synagogue with the words of the prophet: "I have set you to be the light of the Gentiles," but now that day was passed.

On that day Paul hoisted his flag high on the mast of the

Church's ship. From that day on, the Church would bear Paul's imprint, because he had explored better than others the universal spirit of the Master. The Church of Christ is a world Church; it receives all nations within itself, it is bound to none. For us today that is a plain truth, but for the Jews it spelled a spiritual revolution.

The two apostles were forbidden to speak in the synagogue. They gave instructions in their rented lodgings, in private homes, in the open, on the streets. Everywhere they were forming living cells of the mystical body of Christ. In the evening the faithful gathered round Paul and Barnabas, and later they came to hear the teachers and presbyters trained by the apostles. In his letter to the Galatians, Paul mentions these teachers expressly, according them the right to support from those whom they instruct: "And let him that is instructed in the word communicate to him that instructs him, in all good things" (Gal. 6:6).

It was a fine field of labour, like the other Antioch in Syria. Now they could preach the crucified Christ, unhampered by the narrowness of the Jews. When they told these pagans of Christ's Passion and death, tears were often seen to course down their cheeks. They need not speak now of those innumerable petty Jewish laws about eating, washing of hands, new moons, the miserable observance of "days and months and times and years" (Gal. 4:10). The God of Paul and Barnabas was not the reckoning merchant, counting pennies and fractions, but a great king who made all sinners happy by the grace of His royal word.

When they heard Paul speak, the stories about Zeus seemed foolish. Zeus was always bent on some romantic adventure, and Cybele was in mourning about her beloved Attis. The rite in which Cybele's picture was washed in the river and then carried about the town, in a wagon drawn by two donkeys, seemed so childish now. How stupid the old moon-god Men looked, and no one could say whether these gods had really ever lived or not. The closer you examined these gods, the more incredible they seemed.

But they knew that this glorious Christ actually lived only about fifteen years ago. His friends were still alive, and he himself had appeared to Paul. How happy they were when Paul freed them from all their old fears of ghosts and demons. Today we can have no understanding of how great a weight the ancient superstitions were on men's minds. It was really the devil's tyranny, something like the medieval belief in spooks and witches which was nothing but a relapse into paganism. The bond between the apostles and the congregation came to be ever closer. Their spiritual exaltation was unlimited. As Paul later wrote to the Galatians: You "would have plucked out your own eyes and would have given them to me" (Gal. 4:15). What a happy occasion it was when a new group of disciples was received into the Church! The whole congregation, attired in white, went to the ceremony on the banks of the swift Anthios that rushed down from Sultan Dagh.

The new Christian movement caught hold throughout the land. The farmers, when they came to market, heard of the good fortune of their relatives and friends in town, and they went to the apostles to ask them to come out into the country. So Paul and Barnabas toured the villages and hamlets of Sultan Dagh and also places along the seashore.

We have good reasons to believe that Paul addressed his letter to the Galatians primarily to the southern Galatians. If this conclusion is correct, then it seems to be certain that the sickness (to which he refers in Gal. 4:13) must have attacked him here in Antioch for the first time. It is not at all surprising that Paul may have contracted malaria in the swamps of Pamphylia when he came through them, and then here, in Antioch, the disease was running its course. One day he would be forced to lie in his lodgings burning with a raging fever, and then came days of physical exhaustion. Three times Paul had experienced these attacks when he was writing the second letter to the Corinthians, and three times he had asked the Lord to take away from him this "sting of the flesh."[14] Now in Antioch as he lay stricken by the fever when the work was so pressing, he prayed to the Lord, but within himself he heard a voice: "My grace is sufficient for you: for power is made perfect in infirmity" (2 Cor. 12:9).

Even from his sickbed, blessing went forth to the people. Afterwards Paul did not regret these painful days. While he was sick he learned how attached and grateful his converts were to him. Those who are sick with malaria have a great disgust for themselves and they think that others are also disgusted, and so the patient seeks to hide in some lonely place, away from the eyes of visitors. But as things were in the Orient, no such thing as a private room could be found for Paul. He lay in the common workroom and living-room, which had neither a door nor a full wall on the street side.

According to Hogarth, the English archaeologist, malaria was believed by the ancients to be one of those diseases inflicted by the gods on human beings because they had entered a holy place while they were unclean. In the presence of any person so stricken by the gods, the superstitious Oriental would expectorate in order to drive off the demon of malaria. Paul was probably referring to these customs when he said in the letter to the Galatians: "Your temptation in my flesh you despised not, nor rejected: but received me as an angel of God, even as Christ Jesus" (Gal. 4:14). At first these naïve people peered cautiously into the house, but soon they came every day filled with pity for their great apostle, who lay with glassy eyes and feverish pulse on his bed. When they were sick they cried and tossed, and talked wildly in their hysteria and imagined they saw demons. But even in his fever Paul was speaking about Christ; he spoke to Him, and chanted the psalms. The Galatians now began to realize that being a Christian was something unusual, that even in sickness the Christian was different from other men. When

---

[14] Tertullian explained the expression "sting of the flesh" as meaning a severe headache, according to an old tradition.

they came to see Paul, they did not spit to ward off a demon; instead they would have plucked out their own eyes to give to him when they saw his glassy stare. They understood how a Christian accepts suffering and death.

Paul's sickness was a blessing in another respect. It was the reason why he cancelled his plan of going to the Ionian coast. He resolved now to devote himself further to the southern Galatian territory. He always followed his own rule of the "open door," that is, he always went where the door was opened for the gospel.[15] Such was the beginning of the Galatian Churches. Galatia (for "Gaul") was an extensive term. Originally it stood for Gauls and Celts, but at this time it comprised the many tribes – Celts, Phrygians, Pisidians, Lycaonians – that were united under the Galatian king Amyntas. The real Galatians were the veterans of the Celtic Legion.

More than a year had passed and the first Galatian Church had been formed, mostly of pagan converts. Soon the first signs of persecution could be noticed. The Jews had a definite plan in oppressing their Christian opponents. Because of their money holdings and shrewd business deals, they obtained considerable influence over the higher classes of society. Many rich Jewesses married Greek and Roman officials, and cultivated friendships among the women of the ruling class. Thus the leaders of the synagogue were able to win over to their cause the police force of the city through the influence exercised by their women.

The Jews represented to the police authorities that the apostles were importing an alien, forbidden cult; that they were setting up a certain Christ as the king of the East; and that this Christ had been executed by Roman authority in Pilate's time. This was, of course, nothing less than high treason.

An uprising of the people can easily be incited by any

---

[15] According to some students the expression "the open door," originated with St. Paul (1 Cor. 16:9) and was adopted by the English, who in turn made it a diplomatic term in modern international affairs.

mob or rabble. Then the police declare that they can be no longer held responsible for the peace of the city unless certain strangers leave. If the Jews could not win over the public authorities to do their work for them, they themselves inflicted the punishment of scourging in the lower chambers of the synagogue. That method seems to have been used repeatedly in St. Paul's life.

What a long life of martyrdom! Old manuscripts have an added note to the effect that Paul had much sorrow and tribulation here in Antioch. Probably one of the scourgings by the synagogue or one of the floggings by the Roman lictor, mentioned by Paul in his canticle of suffering (2 Cor. 6:4-10; 11:23-25), took place here in Antioch. Magistrates in cities of the hinterland cared little about the rights of Roman citizenship. Many years later, when as an old man he lay in prison in Rome, Paul recalled these sufferings in Antioch in his second letter to Timothy (3: 11).

Today the ruins of Antioch make a desolate scene. Tumbled blocks of marble and broken arches of the old Roman aqueduct mark the place where Paul first gave witness to the divinity of Christ with his blood.

CHAPTER SIXTEEN

ICONIUM

*"And it came to pass in Iconium that they entered together into the
synagogue of the Jews and so spoke that a very great multitude
both of the Jews and of the Greeks did believe"* (Acts 14:1).

When Paul and Barnabas left Antioch with the bloody
stripes of the scourging still fresh on their backs, they had a
choice of going either east or west. To the west the road would
take them into the mountain country of Pamphylia via Apamea
to Ephesus. To the east lay Iconium beyond a salt steppe and an
almost impassable swamp. The two friends were probably
impelled to go east because they considered this country a part
of the southern Galatian district, and also because these
Galatians had won their hearts.

They came on a high mountain plateau which was
surrounded by snow-capped volcanoes: to the north the Sultan
Dagh, in the south the Taurus range, southeast the Kara Dagh,
and in the distant east the Karadja Dagh. It was a desolate
region, like the steppes and deserts of central Asia. In the summer this plateau is a terrifying desert from which clouds of dust
rise into the stinging heat. In the winter it is covered for months
with deep snow. In the spring, when the winter rains are over,
the region is an undrained swamp into which a rider's horse

often sinks to his withers.

Let us suppose that Paul and Barnabas spent a year in Antioch. Then it would have been the autumn of A.D. 46 when they came to the place where now we find the ruins of some great castle. Here it was that Frederick Barbarossa, after an extremely difficult march across the top of Sultan Dagh, with his forces substantially reduced, was lured into a trap by Kilijj Arslan, the supreme lord of the Turks. Finally on 18 May 1190, shouting their battle cry, "Christ conquers, Christ rules," his forces were able to breach their way into Iconium. At the solemn service which the Emperor ordered in thanksgiving for the victory and which was attended by the entire crusading army, he commanded the Bishop of Mainz to preach on the text take from the Acts of the Apostles (13:51): "But they, shaking off the dust of their feet against them, came to Iconium." Even today the city of Iconium lies like a charmed city in its flowering oasis, sur-rounded by the ocean of the sand of the desert, some 3,000 feet above the sea, at the crossroads of the traffic of ancient times.

The Iconians were proud of the history of their city. It had existed before the Deluge and had been rebuilt after it. Prometheus had made other men out of clay to replace those that had drowned. In their native pride the Iconians derived their city's name from this incident, from *ikon,* a picture. Emperor Claudius had settled a colony of veterans here, and after that they liked to call the city Claudiconium. Roman officials ruled the city, and Poppaea, Nero's wife, was represented on their coins as a goddess. The population consisted chiefly of Hellenistic Galatians, Roman officials and veterans, and Jews. Since then, as now, Iconium was noted for its weaving of wool, Paul probably found employment and shelter easily.

It was here in Iconium that the famous Thecla episode took place. All we know about this young pagan convert comes from the apocryphal acts of the apostles, *Acta Pauli et Theclae,* and from a marginal note made on a manuscript of the Second Epistle to Timothy (3:11).

According to Tertullian,[16] a certain priest in Asia Minor, out of devotion to St. Paul and his disciple Thecla, wrote a novel about Thecla in which he intermingled a great deal of falsehood with the facts. Because of this liberty with the facts of St. Paul's life, the priest was suspended from his office. Some of the Eastern Fathers of the Church, as, for instance, St. John Chrysostom, accepted the essential parts of the story, and some indeed had a fervent devotion to Thecla, just as many of the Western Fathers had a deep devotion to the thirteen year-old Roman St. Agnes. Harnack was of the opinion that the story was not a complete invention, that a girl by the name of Thecla actually existed and assisted Paul in his mission. Even in the liturgy today her name and the three torments she suffered are mentioned in the prayers for the dying. The story reminds us somewhat of the story of St. Francis and St. Clara of Assisi.

According to Ramsay the main outline of the legend is as follows: After they were driven from Antioch, the two apostles took the Via Sebaste, the King's highway, to Lystra. At the Carelian Sea the road branches off to the left to Iconium, and at the fork of the road a certain Onesiphorus (2 Tim. 1:16), who had been informed of their coming in a dream, was waiting for them. He examined the two men as they were passing him on the road and recognized Paul by his appearance – a small man, with eyebrows joining over his rather prominent nose, a thin growth of hair, bowed legs, a face full of light and charm. Onesiphorus led the apostles to Iconium, sheltered them in his house, which became the first meeting place for the Church in Iconium. The *Acts of Thecla* remarkably mention that the Christians genuflected in adoration of the Blessed Sacrament.

Onesiphorus had a wealthy neighbour, whose house was much more spacious than his, and from a window of the house the neighbour's daughter was able to hear everything that Paul said. Among other things she heard the Apostle praise virginity,

---

[16] Tertullian, *De baptismo* 17

and she was so impressed by what she heard that she immediately broke off her plan of marrying the son of a wealthy family.
Both families were greatly puzzled by her behaviour and caused
Paul to be watched, because a large number of young people
came to Paul's lodging. Some of them misunderstood what he
said about virginity as a prohibition against marriage. Paul was
soon imprisoned, accused of mingling in the private affairs of
the citizens and of practising magic.

Thecla bribed the doorman of her father's house so he
would allow her to go out at night, and she gave the turnkey at
the prison a silver mirror so that he would let her in to see Paul.
All night Paul instructed her in the Christian faith, and the
instruction was still going on when Thecla's mother and her
lover found her in the morning at the feet of the Apostle. The
sufferings and ultimate fate of Thecla, which are pictured in
true Oriental fashion in the novel, are of no further interest to
us. Now the city was divided into two parties: one for Paul and
the other against him. The mob had been won over by bribery,
and Paul was flogged by the lictor with rods, and afterwards the
missioners had to flee the city.

St. Luke mentions the great success of Paul's preaching
in Iconium, the uprising of the mob, and the fact that the
apostles had to leave hurriedly after labouring there for some
time. His silence about the legend of Thecla is, of course, no
proof to the contrary. Luke was at all times a prudent writer
and he was careful not to give rise to any misconceptions. He
says simply: "They . . . fled to Lystra, and Derbe, cities of
Lycaonia, and to the whole country round about" (Acts 14:6).

In this passage the Acts mention that Paul and Barnabas
worked signs and wonders. This was a region where pagan
wonder-workers and fakirs like Paul's contemporary Apollonius
of Tyana, had turned the heads of the gullible population. In
such a place it was necessary for the apostles to show by their
charismatic gifts that the gospel was superior to all pagan
witchcraft and magic.

We may well suppose that the apostles laboured in Iconium for over a year and that they made trips into the surrounding country, into the numerous villages on the slopes of Ala Dagh and Loras Dagh where they founded little country Churches which later would be attached to the principal Church in Iconium. Alongside Antioch, Iconium remained for a long time one of the focal points of Christianity in inner Asia Minor and comprised a patriarchate with fourteen cities.

It was not to remain so always. The time came when Iconium became the residence of the sultans and the central city for the dancing dervishes in Turkish Asia Minor. Before the first World War, Iconium had a population of 60,000 and began again to have a world significance because of the Baghdad railway. The Armenian Christians remained loyal to their faith to the last, until they were massacred most brutally by the Turks during the war. Thus Paul's inheritance, the fruit of his efforts and sufferings, the beloved Galatian Church, was completely obliterated. But that is all in accord with the great tragedy of Paul's life and his place in history.

CHAPTER SEVENTEEN

LYSTRA AND DERBE

"Calling to mind that faith which is in you unfeigned,
which also dwelt first in your grandmother Lois and in your mother Eunice,
and I am certain that in you also" (2 Tim. 1: 5).

For the second time the apostles had to leave their work in a town and flee. This time the road took them into the inhospitable region of Lycaonia. As soon as they had left behind them the gardens of Iconium, the land began to look like the forbidding steppes. Here and there a few pastures for sheep, goats, and donkeys, but nowhere anything to attract the Jews. The country had a reputation for lawlessness, and Claudius had tried to put some order into it by establishing Roman colonies. In the mountains round about, especially in the valleys of the Kara Dagh, the Black Mountain, which raised a frightening peak sheer into the sky, robbers had had their dens for many decades. Cicero, when he was proconsul of Cilicia, had once campaigned against these robbers. Near here he was once encamped on 3 August 51 B.C. as we know from the letter written to Atticus: "I came to Laodicea on July 31, and that date should mark the beginning of a new calendar. Today I am going to the camp at Lycaonia and from there we will march toward the Taurus Mountains where I will try to engage the robber chieftain

Moragenes in battle and settle this issue."

For hundreds of years during the Turkish dominion of Asia Minor the site of the Galatian Churches founded by Paul and Barnabas, except Iconium, was unknown. It was only in 1833 that the site of Antioch became known through the explorations of the English clergyman Arundell. In 1885 and 1888 an American, Sitlington Sterret, discovered the sites of Lystra and Derbe. The distance from Iconium is only about twenty miles as the crow flies. The road, however, presents considerable hazards for the modern traveller. The road is poor, sometimes no more than a cattle path, sometimes it is lost in a swamp. By this road our travellers came to Kilisse, the modern Binbir-Kilisse. The ruins of some fifty Byzantine churches and monasteries, which once gave the place the name of "a thousand and one churches," are the pitiful monument of what was one of those flourishing Galatian Churches whose origins go back to the days of Paul and Barnabas. A few miles from here, at the village of Khatyn Serai, Sterret found an altar stone bearing the inscription "Lystra," definitely marking the site of the old military colony of that name.

The Lycaonians were a good-natured, superstitious, ignorant people. They spoke an Anatolian dialect that Aristotle and Cicero had ridiculed. Only a few people spoke or understood Greek. The Greeks who had settled here had brought with them their Phrygian legends about Zeus and Hermes and adapted them to the local Lycaonian saga. Often these legends were connected with some unusual natural phenomena. At the entrance to the town were two old linden trees whose trunks and branches were intertwined. The Greeks, always ready for some fantastic story, said that these two trees were really Philemon and Baucis, two people who had once received a visit from the gods, Zeus and his companion Hermes. The gods had been unable to find shelter anywhere until they came to the poor hut of Philemon, who took them in and served them. The next day, after revealing themselves, the gods told them to ask for some favour. The little couple said that they would like to enjoy good health until their old age and then die on the same day. Their wish was granted, and besides this Zeus decreed that they should be changed into these two trees and thus remain united for all time.'[17] This beautiful legend expresses humanity's ancient longing for intercourse with God, an obscure longing for the incarnation and the epiphany of God and his Logos, since Hermes was the divine messenger and spokesman. This longing for the divine is a relic of man's earliest experiences, a longing that breaks forth everywhere, in the popular myths of the pagans as well as with the Jews, as in God's visit to Abraham under the oak. With the Greeks, however, the legend of God's descent to man was soon travestied. Zeus disguised himself and fell in love with the beautiful children of men and became an adulterer, as in the legend of Amphytrion.

Now the messengers of Him who had sent his Son to satisfy man's longing for the divine stood at the gate of Lystra. "The goodness and kindness of God our Saviour appeared" (Titus 3:4). The people of Lystra had dedicated their city to Zeus and built a small sanctuary at the city gate served by a pagan priest. Paul's ignorance of local custom and this Zeus legend almost cost him his life.

Very likely the apostles brought with them a recommend- ation from the brethren in Iconium to some Jewish family in this almost entirely pagan city. That family, with whom they lodged, consisted of three persons: the Jewish grandmother Lois, her daughter Eunice, whose pagan husband had died, and her son, a young man called Timothy, gifted with almost feminine feeling and tenderness (2 Tim. 1:7), as we often find in youths who are brought up in the company of women exclusively. Timothy's father was probably a Roman official. Such mixed marriages were not infrequent in the Diaspora. The mother and grand- mother of this family evidently lived in expectation of the coming of the consolation of Israel, and they had thoroughly

---

[17] Ovid, *Metam.* 8, 611

instructed the youth in the Scriptures.

The women confided to Paul that the boy had not yet been circumcised, but Paul did not seem to consider circumcision of much importance. Baptism, he said, would take care of everything. He conceived a great liking for Timothy. He did not know that some day he would impose hands on him to ordain him a priest and a bishop. The pleasant companionship in this Jewish family was a welcome change from the Jewish fanaticism he had encountered in Iconium, and he realized that the ancient religion of the Old Testament was different from that arid system in which he had been reared. This family became the focal point for the Christians in Lystra.

St. Luke implies that the apostles extended their activity to the neighbourhood about Lystra, and that young Timothy went along as guide and companion. It was a fine prelude to those journeys that Timothy would make at the side of the Apostle. Everything seemed to go well until one day their work came to a sudden end.

The gate of an Oriental city is the public meeting place for markets, for judicial trials, and for the casual social gatherings of the people. One day, a feast day of Zeus and also a market day, the city was filled with farmers from the vicinity. A number of beggars appeared as usual, just as today beggars seem to have a preference for the steps leading to temples and courthouses. The apostles made use of the opportunity to preach to such a large gathering of people. Among those who listened was a poor cripple who had never walked. His thoughtful eyes looked longingly up to the apostles as if they were a heavenly manifestation. Perhaps, at the moment, Paul was speaking of Jesus the divine physician, the helper in every human need, of the Messianic prophecies foretelling that when the Messias came the blind would see, the dumb speak, and the lame would walk. The flame of hope seemed to leap up in the eyes of the cripple, and he waited now for the word of his healing. His steady gaze and his pitiful appearance disturbed Paul in his preaching.

Suddenly Paul felt within him the sacred fire. He stopped
preaching, he concentrated his eyes and all the power of his
soul on the cripple and with an imperious gesture commanded:
"Stand upright on your feet." As if driven by some higher
force, the lame man stood up and walked about.

This is a striking parallel of the healing of the lame man
by Peter. The radiation of dynamic power and the confident
surrender to that power by the cripple unite for the miracle. But
the phenomenon cannot be explained merely as the effect of the
power of suggestion. In a miracle, it is true, God makes use of
natural forces as far as they go. What that limit is, we do not
know, but the divine spark leaps to bridge the distance between
the limit of natural powers and the ultimate supernatural effect.

A confusion of shrieking voices rises above the crowd;
the cripple is standing, swinging his crutches high in the air. It
is a mark of St. Luke's historical accuracy when he records that
the people lapsed into their dialect as they shouted to each
other: "The gods are come down to us in the likeness of men."
They knew immediately which gods they were: Zeus, the
eternal wanderer, with his messenger Hermes had come to visit
them. Was not the taller, dignified Barnabas, with his dark
beard, like Zeus whose statue stood at the city gate? He was the
silent god, and that expressed his calm and dignity. And the
smaller, talkative, volatile god was none other than Hermes.

The priests of Zeus were already being told about the
divine appearance, and the procession with flute players and
two sacrificial steers was on the way to the shrine of Zeus at the
city gate. While the crowd was shouting in its dialect and making
these preparations, Paul and Barnabas understood nothing, but
now they began to sense the meaning of this activity. Excitedly
they rushed into the crowd, to clear up this fatal mistake. "You
men," they said, "why do you do these things? Did we not tell
you that these gods of yours do not really exist? We also are
mortals, men like you."

Today a modern missionary might have handled the

situation differently. He might smilingly explain to the good people that it was a case of mistaken identity, instead of preaching a sermon about the spiritual nature of the concept of God. But Paul and Barnabas as Jews had a congenital horror for anything like idolatry. Just at this time, Apollonius of Tyana was going about the country, apparently working miracles and allowing the people to worship him as a god. And Tyana was not far from here. Had not Christ come to destroy this deceit and mockery? Paul's extemporaneous sermon, however, failed of its intended effect. He and Barnabas were no more able to understand the primitive psychology of this primitive people than we might be able to forecast the reactions of a tribe of cannibals on some South Sea island.

To take a toy from people who have not advanced beyond their childhood, or to destroy some pet idea that fascinates them, is always dangerous. Natural people, untouched by civilization, are generally harmless until some misunderstanding awakens a hidden instinct and rouses their fury. To call their pet delusions folly, to make them look ridiculous when they want to adore a human being, is exceedingly dangerous. Their attitude may make a complete change: "If these men are not gods, then they are magicians." These people knew no other explanation. All that was needed now to stir the fire into a conflagration was that some Jews should come from Iconium. And they came, as if they had sensed the situation. "Beware of these men," they said. "They are dangerous deceivers, magicians, and criminals. Every town has had to stone them and throw them out of the city. If you allow them to stay, you will bring down on yourselves the anger of Zeus." And the gullible people of Lystra were ready to believe the calumny of the Jews.

Some days later when Paul was trying to make another address, he felt a different attitude in his audience. He sensed something antagonistic in the air. Soon he heard derisive calls and shouting. The crowd was moving in closer about him; a sharp stone was thrown and struck him on the forehead. Blood

flowed down his face in a strong stream; he fell to the ground.
More stones were thrown, sandaled feet reached out to kick the
prostrate form. Paul's eyes closed, and in the darkness
suddenly he had a vivid picture of another stoning, a stoning in
which he had taken part. He saw an angelic face, bending down
to him. He saw Stephen. If he could only atone for that deed,
for the memory of that cruelty was the hidden sorrow of his life.
He heard a voice: "I will show him how great things he must
suffer for my name's sake." A large stone was thrown, another
kick, and the picture vanished. It was dark, the darkness of
unconsciousness. Horny hands took hold of his tattered garments
and dragged the body out the city gate and threw it into a ditch
by the road.

That day Barnabas had preached in a different part of the
town. In the evening, when Paul did not return, a dark premonition haunted Barnabas and the good people of Timothy's
family. Soon they learned from some frightened Christians what
had happened. They could not go out immediately because of
the anger of the mob which might sill be cruising about the
town. But late that night (as we read in the Beza text), Barnabas, Timothy, the two women, and perhaps some other
disciples, went out to mourn the dead. Stricken by grief, the
gentle Barnabas bent low over the silent form in the ditch to
look once more into that blood-streaked face. What would he
do now without that good friend?

The disciples lift the body, the women wash the blood
from the face. But, he is alive, he moves, his eyes open. Paul is
not dead. The Lord had saved him, his work was not yet finished. Ten years earlier Paul himself had been the chief witness at
the stoning of Stephen, and the chief result of that stoning for
the Church was the gain of one of her bravest defenders. A
timid youth, young Timothy, is the witness of this night scene
at the gate of Lystra. The chief result of this stoning will be that
Paul will gain one of his most faithful disciples. A son who
would be the consolation of his declining years. Perhaps that

night Timothy began to understand what it meant to be an apostle, to suffer for Christ. Twenty years later, when Timothy was a bishop, Paul wrote him a letter and reminded him of this night: "But you have fully known my . . . persecutions, afflictions: such as came upon me . . . at Lystra" (2 Tim. 3:10 f.).

A superficial observer might have said then that the miracle worked for the cripple was useless, just as Peter's miracle when he healed the lame man at the Temple door, which had only brought him a jail sentence. But to conclude from the momentary effect is too short-sighted. God's plans look into the long future. Often a thing must first undergo misunderstanding, often it must go down to apparent failure, before the essential thing is gained.

They could not stay in the city. Paul would have to be brought safely away from the Jews who were still there. He could not be given any rest or care. They found a small farm wagon and on it they laid him tenderly, and Barnabas and Timothy went along to Derbe, some thirty miles away. Paul bore the scars of that stoning all his life; they were his stigmata. Later he referred to them when he wrote to his beloved Galatians: "Henceforth let no man be troublesome to me; for I bear the marks of the Lord Jesus in my body" (6:17).

In view of this bloody incident at Lystra we might be inclined to ask whether Paul may not have been somewhat imprudent and hasty in his quick condemnation of the people's mistake. He should perhaps have exploited the occasion for the benefit of the gospel. But if we reason thus, we have not read history correctly, nor do we understand Paul's character. Paul would have rejected with vehemence any suggestion of mental reservation or double-dealing.

And the evil against which Paul inveighed was precisely the chief evil of paganism, the degradation of the divine to the human level and the exaltation of the human above the divine. Paganism wished to erase the distinction between the human and the divine, it wished to destroy the infinite abyss between the Creator and the creature. Ultimately this movement led to the destruction of all that was human, as may be seen in the principal examples of the system, Caligula and Nero. The apotheosis of the Roman emperor was in its heyday at that time, and it took hold in Asia Minor more than in other parts of the Empire. This fundamental error of paganism could not be overcome unless the doctrine of the *majestas divina* would be preached without modification.

Like Jesus, Paul had no greater motive than to defend the honour of God and to preserve intact that abyss between himself and his heavenly Lord. St. Luke seems to suggest a parallel between Paul who here rejects the offer of divine honours, and Herod Agrippa who in his insufferable pride accepted divine honours, and even demanded them. Herod was quickly punished by an angel, and Paul was convinced that he would likewise have been punished if he had usurped the honour due to God.

In the same consciousness of his own lowliness, in the same spirit of humility especially with regard to Christ, Paul protested against being made a hero by some of his followers in Corinth: "Is Christ divided? Was Paul then crucified for you? Or were you baptized in the name of Paul?" (1 Cor. 1: 13.)

Paul's physical endurance, his ability to bear so much suffering, is amazing. After the loss of so much blood at the hands of the mob in Lystra he was taken in a clumsy wagon over a rough road through a salt steppe for over thirty miles. Their destination was the little mountain village of Derbe on the boundary line of Galatia. Until recently it had been a robbers' den, but here Claudius had now settled a colony of veterans.

Paul's Jewish enemies, who were sure he was dead, naturally did not follow him to Derbe, and so the two missioners were able to found a congregation of Christians in peace, undisturbed by the Jews. Later we shall meet a certain Gaius of Derbe (Acts 20:4), and it is possible that Paul and Barnabas may have lodged in his house when they came to Derbe. Paul was no doubt obliged to remain in bed for some time after his arrival to recover from his wounds and his weakened condition. Paul's sickbed here in Derbe was the occasion of a fruitful apostolic activity. Like the three other Christian Churches in Galatia, Derbe was also born in pain, and Paul probably referred to this thought later in his letter to the Galatians when the Jewish element again threatened their faith: "My little children, with whom I am again in travail, until Christ be formed in you" (Gal. 4:19).

It was a work that required toil, to emancipate these children from their spiritual slavery, from the miserable elements of their superstition, their service of the moon and the skies, to the liberty of the children of God. If anyone is inclined to say that Paul was a fanatical, unfeeling zealot, all he need do is read the Epistle to the Galatians to see that Paul was consumed by his love and his willingness to spend himself, wrestling for other men's souls. He will understand the profound sorrow that Paul expresses in that letter, the sorrow of a mother who fears the loss of the child at her bosom.

In Derbe, too, the apostles must have remained somewhat over a year, extending their ministry into the neighbouring valleys to the Sea Ak-gol and the ancient town of Heraclea, the modern Eregli. Paul kept up his communications with Lystra, Iconium, and Antioch, and Timothy was probably the ever-ready messenger, so that when he made his return journey all these Churches were able to give a good account of themselves. When we remember that the neighbouring provinces of Cappadocia and Isauria also received the light of the gospel from Paul, we will appreciate the tremendous value of Paul's labour and suffering for the gospel. He himself thought his sufferings important for the Church, since he considered them a complement to the sufferings of Christ (Col. 1:24).

The tragic fate of these Churches of Asia Minor sounds a fearful warning for us today. Founded at the cost of so much effort and suffering, where are they now? What has caused the disappearance of all the glorious religious foundations in Asia

Minor, Armenia, and North Africa? Was it not that the people
forsook the spirit of Jesus and his great apostle? That they did
not heed the warnings in the Epistle to the Galatians and the
threats of the Apocalypse? That they became petrified in the
service of the letter and the observance of externals? That they
wasted their energies debating fine distinctions and personal
jealousies? Finally that they separated from the fountain of
spiritual renewal that flows from the rock of Peter? "But if the
salt shall lose its taste, how shall its saltiness be restored ?"
(Luke 14:34) And so the apocalyptic riders with the green
banner of the Prophet rode over the salt steppes that were once a
Christian people. It is a warning for other times and other
people.

    Four years have passed since Paul and Barnabas left their
mother Church in Antioch. Often they had been seized with
longing to see the brethren with whom they had been able to
correspond only through the caravans and travelling merchants
they met. Paul may also have looked longingly to the south
from his sickbed. Only 125 miles beyond the Taurus was his
beloved Tarsus. When he was a boy back in Tarsus and wond-
ered what was on the other side of the mountains, did he ever
dream of such adventures as he was having?

    The missioners might have returned by way of the Cilic-
ian Gate and the Syrian Gate and thus have reached Antioch in
a few days, but their apostolic responsibility for the newly
founded Churches caused them to return as they had come.
Changes in the officials during these years made the journey
less dangerous. Now they began that finishing organizational
work. Everywhere they ordained priests and teachers. In many
places they had to compose the differences between the liberty-
loving spirit of the Greeks and the narrowness of the Jews.

    After the last farewell service in Antioch of Pisidia, they
ventured into the wild ravines and canyons of the Taurus down
to Perge. Here they founded the last of the Churches. With
trophies of seven battlements conquered for Christ – Salamis,

Paphos, Antioch, Iconium, Lystra, Derbe, and Perge – they went home. Paul brought back from this journey something that no one could take from him. He had learned to harness his fiery temperament, he had learned to bear the yoke of Christ's meekness, his stormy spirit was transformed into a strong, enduring patience.

CHAPTER EIGHTEEN

MOSES OR CHRIST

"And some, coming down from Judea, taught the brethren:
That, unless you are circumcised according to the custom of Moses,
you cannot be saved" (Acts 15:1).

With the thundering of the mountain waterfalls still sounding in their ears, Paul and Barnabas returned to the proud city on the Orontes like two victorious generals coming back from the wars. They were received with honour by the elders and brethren as pioneers of the faith. It seemed to them as if they had come out of a wilderness into civilization. Everything appeared so well tended and beautiful in contrast to the savage roughness of the Lycaonian countryside. To their friends they seemed to have aged somewhat, as if they had undergone exhausting experiences. They asked: "Paul, where did you get those scars on your face?"

The kindliness and understanding that the brethren show-ed them were good to hear. It was an unusual missionary cele-bration when the two apostles addressed the congregation in the church on Singon Street and told of the new foundations, of their preaching, and of their sufferings and hardships. With the congregation Paul and Barnabas intoned a solemn prayer of thanksgiving for "the great things God had done with them and how he had opened the door of faith to the Gentiles" (Acts 14: 26).

Afterwards the apostles sat with the elders and inquired about the status of the work in Antioch. The priests were able to report that they had not been idle. A series of Churches up into the Amanus Mountains and as far up as Cilicia was being established. "And what," asked Paul, "have been your experiences with the Jewish Christians?" The priests looked troubled, wondering whether they should speak of the matter. "If things continue as they have been going," they said, "we fear that we are rushing into a crisis. The brethren in Jerusalem do not seem to understand our circumstances. They have never got beyond the limits of Jerusalem. They deny Christianity to our converts from paganism, and they say that they should not have been baptized unless they had first accepted the Mosaic law. Unless something is done about it, the Church will be divided into two parts."

It was hard to have these bitter drops of wormwood fall into their cup of joys on the first night of their return. Paul saw immediately that all he had so far accomplished was threatened. If this movement won out in the end, his work would be nullified, or there would be a schism.

Now the whole problem was isolated in all its magnitude. He had long feared the day when it would demand attention. No difficulty arose from the full proselytes, but the majority of the converts from paganism were half-proselytes or those who "feared God," who had only a casual connection with Judaism. To make their reception into the Church depend on their circumcision and acceptance of the Mosaic law would narrow the Church down to a synagogue and deny the universality of the redemption. To receive them into the Church as half-Christians, alongside the full Christians consisting of the Jews and full proselytes, would mean the creation of an inner and outer circle in the Church, it would mean the erection of the old barrier in the midst of the Church. It would mean making Christianity a race religion, whose validity depended on Jewish blood.

To take these pagans into the Church and then avoid their company at table would make them Christian pariahs. It was, therefore, a religious and a sociological problem alike. Paul recognized the problem, more than any other, in all its implications, and it was he who brought it to an issue. Such was the problem as it was viewed in Antioch.

In Jerusalem, however, many brethren were still alive who were witnesses to the fact that the Lord had been born under the law, that he had observed the law, and they had heard him say that he had not come to destroy the law, and that no iota of the law would pass away. These disciples valued the prescriptions about eating, about the Sabbath, and circumcision as a most beautiful inheritance from the fathers, which separated them from the uncleanness of the Gentiles. Was this noble race, that had given so much to the world, to die out now?

The Acts of the Apostles clearly indicate that the original apostles did not take the particularizing and narrow view. Even the religion of the Old Testament prophets was not a national religion, and Jesus himself had proclaimed the universality of his religion and the universal apostolate of the Twelve. Certainly the mother Church in Jerusalem had not forgotten all this. Pentecost was recognized as an event that signalled the universality of the Church. But Jesus had come to save the world and he had come into certain historical circumstances. He had come as the completer of the Old Testament, and his Church was to carry the message of salvation to all mankind.

But the difficulty was this: Christ had nowhere given any direction about the conditions under which the pagans should be received into the Church. The method of carrying out his mission was obscure. Was Peter's vision at Joppe meant for all cases, or only for the case in point? In Jerusalem they accepted the narrower view. We must not judge the apostles in Jerusalem too harshly. They wished to decide each case on its own merits, as to which pagans were to be admitted into full communion in the Messianic community.

Personally the apostles observed the law, as they had seen Jesus do, but they knew that salvation came from Jesus alone. A period such as this, when a new religion must find its forms of expression and its own distinctive cult, is an exceedingly difficult one. The pious practices of Judaism were highly developed, and for the present the Christians observed them. With regard to the fundamental problem, they hoped the decision could be put off and, like Peter, they kept silence.

Many of the Pharisees who had been converted did not accept this view. When they were baptized they may have put aside the robes of the Pharisee but they did not put off their Pharisaical spirit. Under the influence of these people Christianity in Jerusalem was gradually being re-formed into Judaism. They tyrannized over the whole congregation and intimidated the apostles. On one score, however, these Jews cannot be condemned: no matter how great their error they never went so far as to degrade the God of the Old Testament to a Jewish or racial god. That would have been a denial of everything the prophets had said.

Their fundamental mistake was this: they admitted that God is also the God of the pagans and that his Messias is the King of all men. The pagans may participate in his kingdom, but not on the same footing with the Jews. They were willing to share their monotheism and their moral law with the pagans, but the Messianic expectation had been a family heirloom of their race. A man could become a full-fledged citizen of the kingdom only as a descendant of Abraham or by being circumcised and thus being incorporated into the Jewish race. Salvation was to be transmitted through the law and circumcision as through another sacrament. Christ's merits were to be transmitted through Jewish blood and the ceremonial law, and Christianity was to be the culmination and fulfilment of Judaism. And so the real substance of Christianity, as salvation exclusively through Christ, was put in serious danger.

This school of thought received much encouragement

from the highly venerated person of James the Less, our Lord's closest relative. The undisputed leader and head, we might say the bishop – the word was not yet in use – of Jerusalem. Hegesippus says[18] that James was one of those four "brethren" of the Lord who in the beginning had been without understanding of his mission (Matt. 13:56; Mark 3: 21). A long time later his eyes were opened.

James united a meticulous fidelity to the law and a stern ascetic life to his love of Jesus. No scissors had ever reached his head, and no oil had ever touched his body. Even while he was still living he had become a myth. All his life he had been a Nazarene. We can hardly imagine the holy awe this man inspired in all his contemporaries, Jew and Gentile, if only half of what tradition tells us is true. He wore no sandals, no woollen clothing; because he wore only linen he was the only layman who was allowed to enter the Holy of Holies. He was unmarried (although this seems to conflict with 1 Cor. 9:5); he was a vegetarian, he drank no intoxicating drink, and it was his custom to pray for hours on his knees in the Temple. People said that he was doing penance for others as Jeremias had done and that his desire was to avert the threatened judgment of the Jews. They called him "The Just" and "The Guardian of the People." He needed only to raise his hands in prayer and a miracle would happen since; if a really pious man desired it, he could create a world. In a word, James was a patriarch of the Old and New Testaments.

The Pharisees and Sadducees dared not attack him; even Herod feared him. When the other apostles were driven from the city, he remained. On his account many Pharisees had become Christians, and also priests of various classes who, it seems, continued to function as Jewish priests. Externally the Church appeared no different from a pious Jewish sect. Nothing was known outwardly of her inner mystery, of her Eucharistic life. The liberal movement inaugurated by Stephen seemed to have

---

[18] Cf. Eusebius, *Hist. eccl.*, II, z25

died down entirely. But Paul was his spiritual heir.

With James as the central point, a conservative party had formed in the Church at Jerusalem. Presuming to use James' name, this party sent some of its extreme members to Antioch as soon as they heard that Paul and Barnabas had returned from Asia Minor, had formed a large Church with many pagan converts, and were now about to inculcate their ideas in Antioch. The messengers were received respectfully by the elders in Antioch, because they were representatives of a great personage in the mother Church. But the faithful were chilled in their devotion because every time the men from Jerusalem had occasion to touch a convert from paganism they hastened to wash themselves. They refused all invitations to dine in a Christian home; they were not permitted to sit at table with anyone uncircumcised, much less could they eat from the same dish as was the custom then in the Orient.

These men seemed never to have heard of the Spirit that came on Pentecost. Everywhere they sensed danger and uncleanness. But when they sat separately at their own tables, away from the rest, on the Sabbath at the love banquet, and when they openly declared in the assembly to the Antiochians, "Unless you are circumcised according to the custom of Moses, you cannot be saved," the storm broke loose. It must have been a violent affair; St. Luke speaks of "no small contest" (Acts 15:2). Until now St. Paul had called the converts from paganism "saints, the elect, children of God, citizens and familiars of God," but now these pious men from Jerusalem called them "unclean, sinners, strangers, aliens," and denied that they were Christians at all.

Paul and Barnabas protested that this tyrannical interference with the smallest details of life – with what a man ate – would alienate these freedom-loving Greeks. They reminded the envoys from Jerusalem that this insistence on circumcision would drive the men away since the pagans had always found it repulsive and had long ridiculed it. Besides this, circumcision for an adult was an operation not without some element of risk. If a man were circumcised he could no longer frequent the public baths, and for that reason, as St. Paul says (1 Cor. 7:18), many Jews tried to hide the sign of their descent by surgical means, they tried to "procure uncircumcision."

The law of Moses looked on mixed marriages as adultery, so that if a converted Jew had married a convert of Greek descent, he was subjected to the abuse of having his marriage called unlawful. The laws about eating brought a whole cluster of knotty problems to weigh on men's minds. If a man wanted to live kosher, he would have to buy his meat at a Jewish shop and ask if the animal had been properly killed. In short, if a convert had to observe the Mosaic law he would be cut off socially from the rest of the world. Then Christianity would become a small sect, but not a world religion.

The most serious thing about the controversy was that these men from Jerusalem not only created a social division, they also differed dogmatically. For ultimately the question was whether a man was saved by the law or by the grace of Christ. Yet all Paul's arguing was in vain. It was impossible to overcome Jewish prejudice and Jewish training.

But the Holy Spirit would breathe in the Church, and the barrier between the parties would disappear. God gave the apostles wisdom and fortitude, and by His grace Paul became the chosen warrior to complete the work so that the Church would be truly catholic, universal. A fundamental decision must be obtained as soon as possible from the highest authority in Jerusalem. Paul was moved to make the trip to Jerusalem by a special revelation (Gal. 2:1). He was concerned about two things in this journey to Jerusalem: the triumph of Christian liberty and the recognition of his status as an apostle by the mother Church. He accomplished both purposes.

CHAPTER NINETEEN

THE APOSTOLIC COUNCIL

"And the apostles and elders assembled to consider this matter." (Acts 15: 6)

Accompanying Paul to Jerusalem was a young man whom Paul had recently won over to Christianity, Titus, for whom he had great hopes. This young man of exceptional gifts was to become Paul's most faithful disciple and his ablest helper, whom he sent on the most difficult missions in years to come. Writing to him, he called him "Titus, my beloved son according to the common faith" (Titus 1:4). Paul took this splendid youth to Jerusalem as a trophy of his conquest of the pagans, as a living proof of those excellent fruits that were growing on the tree of the Gentile Church. He thought that Titus' personal charm and his faith would win over the brethren in Jerusalem; but Paul would be disillusioned.

The journey to Jerusalem in the autumn of A.D. 48 was like a triumphal tour. They landed on the Phoenician coast, visited the Churches at Sidon, Tyre, Ptolemy, and Caesarea, and then went inland through Samaria and Judea. Everywhere the faithful listened with satisfaction to Paul's story of how Christ had been received by the pagans. Finally, after some weeks, Paul arrived with his companions in Jerusalem. If we recall the description of the delegates to the Council of Constance as they arrived for the first session, the picture of Paul and his group entering Jerusalem would suffer by comparison. Yet no council of later years was to make a decision of greater importance than this Council of the Apostles. In a sense this council was the model of all other councils in the Church, and without this Council no other council would have been held.

The Church at Jerusalem was composed of three groups: the apostles, the council of the elders, and the faithful. Among the apostles three stood out as "pillars" of the Church: Peter, James the Less, and John. As they met together, the atmosphere told of a coming storm. The session was preceded by a religious celebration. Probably a love banquet and the Eucharist were celebrated.

The congregation listened in a breathless silence to the report of the missioners. When they finished, general applause rang through the hall. The conversion of the pagans was accepted as one of the surest signs that this was the Messianic kingdom. But some of those who applauded were carried on by the enthusiasm of the others; they applauded with poor spirit. The influential group of Judaizers and Pharisees did not approve. Immediately they proposed objections, manifesting clearly the wide rift that divided the assembly. The fact that the Holy Spirit had already decided in favour of the pagans, did not affect these stubborn and hard men. They simply shouted: "Everyone must be circumcised and be made subject to the law of Moses."

Paul's temerity in bringing Titus into the assembly of the saints was a challenge, and they demanded that the bloody rite be performed on him immediately. Titus found himself in an exceedingly painful position. Some of the brethren said that the matter needed more prayer and reflection, and the meeting that began so solemnly broke up in a stormy scene. Once more a decision had been postponed.

In the Epistle to the Galatians, in an involved and tortured sentence, Paul says that not for one instant had he yielded to the demand that Titus be circumcised. From the strained grammatical structure of the sentence, it is evident that even after many years Paul still felt the pain and embarrassment of that scene. Some students are inclined to the opinion that, when he wrote that part of the letter, Paul was prostrated by the feeling of defeat and so lost command of the grammar of the passage. It is not surprising that Luke, because of the conciliatory nature of his book and his desire not to wound anyone, does not mention the incident.

For Paul the matter was as follows: The fundamental question whether circumcision was necessary for salvation, and whether his missionary method was right, had to be settled. This question was only part of a still greater question: whether salvation came exclusively through the grace of Christ. If this question were once decided, he would be able to yield to the demand for circumcision in special instances without compromising himself or the gospel, in order to maintain peace or for some other higher reason. One of the darkest mysteries in God's providential guidance of the Church is the amount of liberty it allows for human narrowness.

In the meantime Paul was busy with private conferences with the three "pillar" apostles. His use of the term "pillars" seems to carry with it a slight suggestion of Pauline irony for those who doubted his apostleship. But he was determined that the original apostles should be convinced that he, like they, stood firmly on the ground of the gospel, and he wrested from them the official designation Apostle of the Gentiles. Now his vocation at Damascus was considered equally valid with the calling of the other apostles.

During these private conferences with the apostles, Paul probably reached that agreement in which the missionary territory was divided as expressed in the classic formula: "that we should go to the Gentiles, and they to the circumcision" (Gal. 2:9). They were now fully in agreement that salvation was only through the grace of Christ. On that day the three "pillar" apostles gave Paul their hands in fellowship and sealed the pact of the division of their missionary fields. That division was not, of course, to be exclusive, since each of the apostles had received a universal commission from the Lord. If these three men had not come to an agreement with Paul, what would have been the consequences for the Church? But their love for Jesus overcame every difference.

At last the day came for the handing down of the decision. After all the parties had an opportunity to express themselves, Peter rose to speak. His address is a masterpiece. He does not refer to Paul. He recounts his own experiences and announces his own understanding of the divine decree. He isolates the problem clearly in three stages:

1. God had already taken the initiative in this matter when he commanded Peter to baptize the pagan Cornelius.

2. The moral law of the Old Testament is impossible of fulfilment in view of man's weakness.

3. Salvation comes only through the grace of God freely given. This prudent address paved the way for Paul and Barnabas and prepared the hearers for a favourable reception of Paul's viewpoint.

Prudently Paul allowed Barnabas to speak first since he had a warm place in the affections of the congregation in Jerusalem. Barnabas preferred to let the facts speak for them. The Holy Spirit had made no distinction in the distribution of the gifts of grace, of miracles, and of prophecy. Why then, if God had opened the door, should any man close it?

Peter's address was a severe blow to the Judaizing party, but they still had a trump to play, a card in which they put all their hopes, the support of their "secret emperor" James. Paul had seen little of the great man, and had spoken to him only in passing. All during the session James sat silently without revealing by any movement what his inner thoughts were. Both sides waited breathlessly to hear his voice. Then the great man, simply and humbly acknowledged his support of Peter's view, that God's decree of salvation was for all men without exception. But, in contrast to Peter, as a true follower of David and of the Old Testament, he called on the authority of the Old Law, on the witness of the prophets, especially Amos who had foretold a Messianic kingdom for all peoples. The justification, he said, for the conversion of the Gentiles was simply the will of God.

This did not mean, James went on to explain, that the Mosaic law, of which circumcision was the sign, was now invalid or outlawed. He calmed the Judaizers somewhat by saying that the law was not in jeopardy since there would always be a sacred tribe of people who would read the law of Moses in the synagogue and try to realize its ideals. 1. To cement a brotherly feeling between both parties, James proposed that the Antiochians regard the feelings of the Jewish Christians. They should avoid any participation in pagan sacrificial meals for which social intercourse with pagan relatives and friends was often the occasion. 2. The pagan converts should remain aloof from that sexual immorality which was customary in pagan temples and was often sanctioned by the religion of the pagans. This referred not only to marriages contracted in the forbidden degrees of relationship but also to the pagan institution of prostitution and the Greeks' national vice of pederasty. 3. The pagan converts should observe the food laws, i.e., the exclusive use of kosher meat in the common meals. That meant that they should not eat meat that was not properly butchered or meat that had not been bled. For thousands of years the Semites had had a horror of eating bloody meat, meat that had not been bled out. It was a racial characteristic based on the idea that some mysterious power, such as the soul itself, resided in the blood. Many Jews believed that the demons had a particular appetite for blood and they feared that if they ate bloody meat they might swallow a demon.[19] Many peoples had a revulsion against the flesh of certain animals. It is remarkable that a man

---

[19] Origen, *Contra Celsum*, VIII, 30.

with as much strength of character as St. Boniface had not overcome the feelings and prejudices that dated from this Jewish-Christian era. Although he was himself of Germanic blood, he had serious doubts whether his German converts could be permitted to eat the flesh of horses, crows, or storks; to settle the matter he appealed to Rome.

This food regulation was not a slight requirement. By it the pagan convert was prohibited from purchasing meat except from a Jewish butcher; if the latter would not sell to the Christian, he would have to do his own butchering. If you went to the public market you could not distinguish between *macellum,* the meat of sacrificial animals, and other meat. In itself the prohibition was not injurious and for the sake of those who were "weak" (Rom. 14:2), as Paul said, it should be observed. As for himself, Paul would have been willing to become a vegetarian if he could thereby gain a soul or avoid scandal, because all this formalism was now as nothing to him. After much discussion the compromise measure was accepted. Whether Paul agreed to it is not clear, and it is noteworthy that in his letters he never refers to the apostolic decree, not even when he discusses the doctrine of sacrificial meat (1 Cor. 8).

The apostles tried to lift the discussion from the lower plane of human narrowness to the higher plane where the Holy Spirit would guide them. The consciousness of divine guidance was felt by the apostles, and when they wrote to the Church at Antioch they mentioned it: "For it has seemed good to the Holy Spirit and to us" (Acts 15:28). At this first council the four classical marks of the Church were clearly in evidence: by the unconditional acceptance of the pagan converts under the authority of the apostles the Church professed herself to be both catholic and apostolic, and by holding herself aloof from the worship of idols and by the ideal of sexual morality in the midst of a degenerate culture the Church appears with the shining crown of holiness on her brow. The bond of unity was to be maintained by contributions of the wealthier brethren in the younger Churches. These were to be sent to the impoverished mother Church in Jerusalem.

Paul was glad to have this opportunity of making reparation to the Church of Jerusalem for the financial ruin to which he had contributed by his persecution years ago. For that reason the collection for Jerusalem has such an important role in his letters.

The whole procedure of the synod at Jerusalem is an example of the interrelationship of the human and the divine. By the dynamism of men the Church is always being propelled to further development. The static of the divine element preserves her organic unity and her continuity beginning with her divine origin.

The conclusions of the synod were written down in an apostolic encyclical which was delivered to the Church at Antioch by two delegates who were accompanied by a large retinue, including Paul, Barnabas, and Titus. The newly cemented unity of the Church is expressed in the choice of the delegates: Judas Barsabas of Jerusalem, a Christian from the very beginning, and probably a brother of the Apostle Matthias; and Silas, or Silvanus, a Hellenist like Paul with two names, Jewish and Latin, born in the Diaspora as a Roman citizen. Both delegates had the gift of prophecy. As impartial representatives of the Church of Jerusalem, they were to explain the decree. When the letter was delivered, read, and explained to the assembly at Antioch, great rejoicing broke out: Again and again Judas and Silas had to tell about the great influence that Paul and Barnabas had on the original apostles and how great a victory they had won. Judas returned to Jerusalem, but Silas, like Barnabas many years before, was attracted by the wonderful spirit of the Church in Antioch and remained.

CHAPTER TWENTY

PETER AND PAUL IN ANTIOCH

"But when Cephas came to Antioch, I withstood him to the face,
because he was to be blamed." (Gal. 2:11)

Some people look at past events in a glorified light, as if
none of the crudeness and smallness of our times ever appeared
to disturb the idyllic picture. In that naive outlook some people
believe that friendships, like that between Peter and Paul, were
never tried by difficulties. But the day came when that friendship
between the princes of the Apostles was put to a severe test.

The apostolic decree with its compromise, intended to reconcile both opposing parties, did not fully clarify the situation.
Soon it was seen that it was only a temporary solution. In their
concern for practical unity, they had neglected the theological
and religious viewpoint. The truth that salvation is owing exclusively to grace, without the works of the law, was not
emphasized enough. Even that sociological problem about con-
sorting and eating with pagans had not been settled. Did
Christian liberty free only the pagan converts from the law, and
were the Jews still bound to carry the whole burden? If so,
there would again be two classes of Christians, those who were
loyal to the law, the clean and the perfect, and on the other side
those who were free of the law, the unclean, the imperfect.

Even though the pagan converts observed the food regulations decreed by the council, many Jewish Christians of the stricter observance did not believe that they should consort with them or consider them equal to themselves. They still thought that the ancient abyss continued to divide the unclean offspring of some pagan tribe from the true son of Abraham. The Jews' racial pride was a monstrous thing, and a universal Church could never be built on it. None of these practical matters had been decided in Jerusalem because of the unpropitious atmosphere that prevailed there.

Some time earlier Peter had come to Antioch to make a visitation of the Church there. He brought with him his favourite disciple, John Mark. He was delighted to see the fine Christian spirit of unity here in Antioch, and without further thought he joined in the life and customs of his hosts. The Antiochians were proud to have the most venerable head of the Church in their midst. Peter visited families and accepted invitations to eat. He joined in the love banquets on the eve of the Sabbath by which the brethren prepared themselves for the celebration of the Lord's Supper.

He never asked whether the food was clean or unclean or according to the Jewish law. He did not reject the food whether it was rabbit stew, pork, or an eel caught in the Orontes. The Judaizers in Jerusalem were anxious about Peter, and soon after, some of the people who were close to James sent men to Antioch to spy on Peter. These men did not dare to attack the decrees of the council, but by their behaviour toward the Gentile Christians they robbed the community of its earlier congeniality. They had resolved to bring matters to a head.

Paul was pained to see how his friend Peter was now not sure of himself. How he was being intimidated, how he gradually withdrew from the society of the Gentiles, and finally how he refused to sit at table with them. Even at the love banquet he sat at a separate table with the Jerusalem party. What pained Paul even more was that Barnabas, his chief ally, imitated the ambiguous conduct of Peter. The members of the congregation felt affronted by Peter's peculiar conduct, that they were degraded to the rank of a lower class of Christians. Paul's greatest concern was with the dogmatic issue. Since ecclesiastical discipline grows out of the inner conviction of the Church, this dubious behaviour would obscure the teachings of the faith in an essential point, and the hard won victory at Jerusalem was threatened with nullification.

Faith cannot be separated from life, and therefore it was the faith that was in danger, and with it the whole redemption. Basically Peter and Paul were agreed in their determination that the Church must not be allowed to disintegrate. But as to method, Paul was by far the better student of human nature. He knew his former Pharasaical brethren too well to believe that they had been sincere in their assent in Jerusalem. He knew how insatiable they were in their demands, and he knew that by indirection and devious tricks they would attempt to reverse the decrees of the council.

And so the old spectre rose up before him, threatening to destroy all he had worked for. What could he do? Peter could not be persuaded to go back to his earlier practice. He continued to refuse every invitation from the Gentiles. At long last, after he had prayed a long time, Paul determined to adopt extreme measures even at the risk of wounding his best friends. He had always acted without regard to flesh and blood when Christ's cause was in question. Only Paul could resolve to take this step, and even he must have felt within himself the prompting of a higher voice. He felt that he was acting at Christ's behest.

Paul's enemies believed they had won the fight, but the battle really broke out in the open assembly. Heated remarks were directed at Peter for his manner of acting, and Peter still tried to justify himself. Then the time came for Paul to speak. The expression, "I withstood him to the face," has no unfriendly or insulting implications in the Greek. It means simply that he spoke openly, not behind Peter's back. Paul's clear reasoning and sincerity once more won the day.

The two most prominent apostles in opposition: it was a terrifying thought. We cannot minimize the scene and say it was a mere difference of opinion or a temperamental outburst. Paul called Peter's attention to his dubious conduct, charging that he was not walking the straight path of the truth of the gospel. That, while he appeared to yield to some, he was actually injuring others and endangering the faith. What Peter and Barnabas were doing was not heretical, but their weakness might be the occasion for others falling into serious error in a matter of belief that was of the essence of Christianity.

In his letter to the Galatians, Paul gave a sketch of the address he made to the Judaizers on that occasion. Even in this summary of the speech, with its ungrammatical sentences that are so difficult to translate and understand, we sense the hot breath of his holy passion and zeal.

His arguments were three:

1. All of us, he said, you and I, Barnabas and all the rest who are Jews by blood, are accustomed to look on the Gentiles as sinful by nature. But deep in the conviction of our Christian faith we know that no man can stand before God pleasing to him, neither by the most perfect fulfilment of the natural law nor by the works of the law. Because we believed this we came to be Christians, and we have forsaken the law. To turn back to the law, and draw others with us, would be a denial of our faith.

2. We have been relying on the abundant graces of Christ's redemption and we have freed ourselves from the law, and so we have been acting until now. If that would be a sin, then the sin would be that of Christ, who is the author of our faith. If giving up the law makes us sinners, then your complaint against me would be supported: that I made Christ cooperate in sin. On the contrary, it is you who make Christ the servant of sin by re-erecting the structure of the law which Christ repealed. The matter is like this: if I build up again what I formerly tore down, I show that I made a mistake. By accept-

ing the gospel I showed that the law was insufficient and that it was an unsafe building. But if I set up that unsafe building again I show that I acted hastily and sinfully, and I say that the grace of Christ alone is not enough.

3. The law is dead, abrogated, outlawed. It has been deprived of binding power by the death of Christ. By the Mosaic law Christ was condemned to the Cross. By that act the law dissolved itself; it showed how absurd it was; it brought about its own destruction because it was senseless and unworkable. Since the Christian is united to Christ in life and death, he also is dead as far as the law is concerned; for him the law does not exist. By dying with Christ the Christian begins a new life, Christ is the new life. This argument contained much mysticism, but apparently Paul's mysticism was not unknown to his hearers or to, the Galatians to whom he was writing. The law and its observance are no longer the formative principle for the Christian personality. Now it is Christ himself, that mysterious indwelling of Christ by the grace of the Spirit that breathed on Pentecost.

These were weighty arguments. But the most powerful argument was Paul himself in his complete surrender to Christ as he revealed himself to the assembly: "With Christ I am nailed to the cross. And I live, now not I, but Christ lives in me. And that I live now in the flesh: I live in the faith of the Son of God, who loved me and delivered himself for me" (Gal. 2:20). He breaks forth to express his mystical love of Jesus, the love that was kindled on the Damascus road. And now we know why Paul, more than any other apostle, understood the contrast between the law and grace. It was because no other apostle had had the experience of his conversion.

It is to Paul's everlasting credit that he searched out the problem to its ultimate foundation and its last conclusion. His fight was another battle in his war against the apotheosis of the Jewish race, making itself the only vehicle of salvation. Peter and Barnabas were big enough to see their error, and so the day was saved. Feelings were bruised for a while, and a bitter taste may have remained. For even holy people cannot accept a public rebuke without some pain. Later all the unpleasantness disappeared, and the union of Peter and Paul in martyrdom wiped away any remembrance of this bitterness. And on it all, history has shed its glory and light and placed the two apostles together as brothers.

Sometimes the scene at Antioch is imagined as a painful situation in which the authority of Peter was attacked. Such a view is based on an incorrect idea of authority, different from that in the Gospels. In times to come, those in authority were much more sensitive about their authority and more apprehensive about safeguarding it than in apostolic times. The Master had said: "He that will be first among you shall be your servant" (Matt. 20:27), and "Neither be called masters: for one is your master, Christ" (Matt. 23:10). What happened was simply that two men, both of them beloved by the people, open and honest in their convictions, settled a difference before the congregation. Would to God that no greater scandal besmirched the Church. Peter's humility, the way he took Paul's hand, disarmed those who had been critical of his conduct. Peter felt that Jesus had again spoken to him, this time through Paul, and tears again moistened his eyes as once before on that Good Friday.

Similar scenes would recur in the history of the Church. Providence allowed this one to occur so early in the Church's life for the comfort and guidance of later times. Someone has said that one of the most useful books in hagiography would be a book not about the virtues of the saints but about their failings. For one period we have, such a book: Holy Scripture pictures, with uncompromising candour, the weakness of her human heroes alongside their greatness. It may be a comfort to know that divine grace found obstacles even in the great ones of God's kingdom. But in one respect the saints were all alike: in their boundless love and complete surrender to Christ. When the time came, Peter could be as determined as Paul or the two sons of thunder, and that time came when he died for Christ. If someone had congratulated Paul on his victory that day, he might have replied that in Christ there was neither winner nor loser.

After this episode, Peter disappears from the New Testament narrative. This is the last scene of his life recorded by the sacred book. We have two letters, it is true, that bear his name, but their contents incline greatly to Paul's doctrine. It is not an ignominious departure from the stage. Peter in the end manifests his finest qualities, his humility, his honesty, his willingness to hear the truth from a brother without cavil, purely out of love for Jesus.

At times the supernatural direction of the Church is more evident than at others. In the beginning Christianity contained some violent contrasts, and without the Spirit the young organism might have been rent asunder. On the surface it seemed that Peter and James stood for the law while Paul stood for Christian liberty. Once Paul exclaimed: "Extinguish not the spirit" (1 Thess. 5:19). The law easily becomes as inflexible as stone unless it is imbued with the Pauline spirit. Sometimes the Pauline freedom is endangered, and then Paul must speak. At other times the Petrine tradition is attacked, and then Peter must speak. But in the exclusive sense there is no such thing as a Pauline Church or a Petrine Church, or the Johannine Church that overcame both, for Peter and Paul and John are all equally disciples of the Lord, and the Spirit of God contains them all.

Why is the Acts of the Apostles silent about this occurrence at Antioch? Luke certainly knew of it, since he was a native of Antioch. It is probably another of those problems presented by the Scriptures, whose solution is not important for salvation. We should keep in mind that St. Luke is not only a historian, he is also a responsible churchman. He had Tacitus' gift of delineating character and describing circumstances with a minimum of words. He knew where to highlight and where to put the accent. When he passes over an incident in silence, that is significant. As an inspired writer he was writing primarily for his own time and not for the satisfaction of ages to come. His book was written fifteen years after these events, and in the interval everything had changed and the old bitterness had disappeared. The old antagonisms were forgotten. Why, then, should he open old wounds? And so Luke, with his accustomed nobility and regard for the feelings of others, silently passed over these stormy scenes.

CHAPTER TWENTY-ONE

THE PARTING OF FRIENDS

"And there arose a dissension so that they departed one from another.
And Barnabas indeed, taking Mark, sailed to Cyprus.
But Paul, choosing Silas, departed" (Acts 15: 39).

After the rejoicing at the victory of Christian freedom, the Acts goes on to say: "And Paul and Barnabas continued at Antioch, teaching and preaching, with many others, the word of the Lord." It seemed that nothing was ever to happen that would disturb the harmony between these two men who for years now had fought and suffered together for Christ. Little did they suspect that before the year would come to an end something would occur to shatter their friendship, and that they would separate without ever joining in the work of the missions again. The service of the gospel requires many sacrifices, but sometimes these sacrifices are somewhat the result of personal whims and feelings.

Not long after the great day of Antioch, Paul began to feel the urgings of his missionary wanderlust. He felt that he ought to visit his new Churches in Asia Minor and then go farther afield. He invited Barnabas to go with him – apparently he bore no resentment for Barnabas' conduct in the late controversy – so that together they might relive the joys and sorrows in the founding of the Churches. Barnabas was glad to go, but he had a request: he wished to take his nephew Mark along. Mark had long regretted his desertion at Perge, and his uncle desired to give him an opportunity to wipe out that blot on his record. But Paul, as the responsible head of the mission band, felt obliged to refuse the request. He had an extremely high ideal of the responsibility of an apostle and he set no limit to the devotion and self-oblation an apostle ought to have. He did not think that Mark was ready to make that act of self-surrender. Besides this, he may also have been afraid that Mark might have an influence on Barnabas that would impede his plans.

The life of a missioner is a serious business, and it cannot be endangered by considerations of relationship and friendship. In that respect Paul was adamant. Perhaps Paul's judgment of Mark was unfair; Barnabas took a much milder view of his fault. But who can judge human character adequately? Only the all-wise God can judge correctly; we see only through the prism of our weak minds and our distorting sympathies. Barnabas insisted on taking Mark, and the difference between the two apostles – the Acts uses the expression *paroxysmus*, an embitterment – became so serious that they separated, taking different fields to work in and going their separate ways. Barnabas took his native island of Cyprus and immediately sailed with Mark. Thus a great missionary friendship broke on the rock of a personal difference, and with this separation Barnabas disappears from the scene. From the light that radiated from Paul he receded into the obscurity of legend.

From the human viewpoint, Barnabas certainly acted more sympathetically. Paul may have been too severe a judge in Mark's case. For afterwards Mark proved himself an able worker, especially as the author of the Second Gospel. Paul seems to have been harsh to Barnabas. This was the Barnabas who had so often brought light and courage into Paul's life, and it seems that Paul owed Barnabas some gratitude. But as man goes on step by step in knowledge, so Paul was only gradually growing into the likeness of Christ. He was not always able to suppress the quick and violent movements of his heart. After all, there was only One who walked in this world without being marked with Adam's weaknesses.

The Bible is remarkably frank about the faults of its heroes, and therefore it is a book that will edify, teach, and educate men. It also gives this comfort, that God can make use of these failings of men to benefit His kingdom. While Barnabas appears in this incident as the more humane and amiable, Paul's action was not devoid of greatness. He was completely dedicated to his work. He was the man of action, and he shared the fate of those men who sometimes must act against the dictates of their hearts, who must act heartlessly for their cause. We must not be quick to judge. Would that the discords in our lives always served such a noble purpose as Paul's! We cannot believe that Paul made his decision without pain, as if he were hard as a diamond. In years to come he must often have looked back to the day when no one believed in him except Barnabas, especially that unforgettable day when Barnabas came to Tarsus and invited him to come to Antioch, or that tragic day when he lay in the ditch bruised and wounded and he saw the kind face of Barnabas bend low over him to hear his heartbeat. Such bonds of friendship are not severed without leaving bleeding hearts.

In the course of years all the differences were composed. They corresponded and told each other of their missionary experiences. Paul stops to praise Barnabas and defend him (1 Cor. 9:6). Only Barnabas like himself had never taken a female helper on his journeys, and Barnabas too had lived from the labour of his hands so as not to be a burden to the Church. As events turned out, Barnabas was right about Mark. Mark became a courageous, unselfish worker, a valuable assistant to both Peter and Paul. But even a saint and a genius can be in error. Paul was quick to make reparation for his unfair judgment. Writing to the Colossians from prison in Rome, he said: "Mark, the cousin german of Barnabas, touching whom you have received commandments. If he comes to you, receive him" (Col. 4:10).

And during his last imprisonment he was again thinking of Mark when he wrote to Timothy: "Take Mark and bring him with you: for he is profitable to me for the ministry" (2 Tim. 4:11). The cloud between them had been dispersed; they were united now in mutual understanding, and also in prison (Philem. 24).

Looking at the matter from a loftier viewpoint, we can see that a higher power is here at work. Barnabas could not have remained indefinitely as Paul's assistant. He was too important to remain always at Paul's side. If this break had not occurred, they would have had to separate anyway to give Barnabas' gifts of leadership an opportunity to unfold.

Barnabas had earned his own missionary territory. No man had been a truer, nobler, more unselfish friend than he. He was no flaming spirit, no fiery orator, he did not put forth original ideas as Paul did, but his gentle seriousness, his paternal tone, his special charisma of prophetical admonition, gave men comfort and courage, and endeared him to his followers. His was a clinging nature; he could not forget his native land, and there he wished to be buried. His grave is pointed out to the traveller about eight miles north of Famagusta.

In his method of explanation and preaching, Barnabas showed always that he belonged to Paul's school of thought. The theory, first proposed by Tertullian, that Barnabas was the author of the Epistle to the Hebrews, is probably only a guess. Origen, too, admired the elegant literary construction of this anonymous work among the canonical books, the polished and even flow of its Greek, which might well be a reflection of the serenity of Barnabas' soul. As a native of Cyprus, Barnabas might have imbibed some of the refinement of Alexandrian culture which seems to reveal itself in the Epistle to the Hebrews. At any rate, the Epistle to the Hebrews reflects the spirit and character of Barnabas much better than the so-called Epistle of Barnabas, which is the concoction of some mediocre writer who appended Barnabas' name.

CHAPTER TWENTY-TWO

TIMOTHY

"There was a certain disciple there named Timothy, the son of a Jewish woman that believed; but his father was a Gentile" (Acts 16: 1).

March of A.D. 49 had come. That time of the year had arrived when kings go forth to war and when merchants and missioners go out to foreign lands. Again Paul felt within himself the urge that drove him westward, always westward: to Ephesus, to Rome, to Spain. Rome was the secret, never-spoken goal of all his planning. Only in that wide Roman world would this royal eagle have room to spread his wings. Barnabas and Mark had already sailed for Cyprus. The time had come for Paul also to start out.

He did not like to travel alone because of his frequent attacks of malaria and also because the Lord had sent his disciples out in pairs. Silas would be the right companion for him. He was faithful, ready for hardship and sacrifice, and he was free from the Jews' narrowness and prejudice. Paul was glad to have a companion who had been a member of the Jerusalem congregation and especially one who had been close to Peter (1 Pet. 5:12). Since Peter permitted Silas to go with Paul, evidently no resentment remained from their recent difference. Silas would be valuable to Paul because his presence was a kind of approval from the Church at Jerusalem. With regard to the civil authority, Silas was also the right man because he was a Roman citizen. Evidently Silas had been won for the mission by Paul's determination to go as far as the great cities of Greek culture in Ionia and along the Aegean Sea. And eventually Silas' whole life was bound up in Paul. It seems that when a man once came under Paul's influence, he could never extricate himself. In speaking of his new companion, Paul preferred the Roman name, Silvanus, because it was more in tune with that Roman world into which he hoped to go.

This time Paul went by land that they might be able to visit the new Churches in North Syria and Cilicia. So they went north from Antioch, then they ascended into the Amanus range on an excellent Roman road through territory green with laurel and myrtle, and in the higher regions with oaks and pines. Arriving at the romantic Roman castle of Pagra which guarded the pass over the Amanus, they stopped to get their breath and look back once more on the lovely plain of Antioch. In another hour of walking they were swallowed up by the ancient Syrian Gate, the modern Beilan Pass.

The basalt surfacing of the old Roman road can still be seen in places as the traveller descends to the Gulf of Alexandretta, the modern Iskanderun. The port city of Alexandretta was beautifully located with a half circle of mountains behind it. From here they went into the plains, past the famous battlefield of Issus where in 333 B.C. the great Macedonian had conquered Darius and decided the fate of Europe and Asia. Ever since that time this battle of Alexander has intrigued the imagination of men. In that battle Hellenism was born. It was the beginning of that worldwide orientalized Greek culture. Then the two streams of Eastern and Western culture began to flow together so that Alexander may be called a precursor of the gospel. If the Greek language had not been established as a world language, and if the Roman state had not been extended to the Orient, Paul's great march across the Roman Empire would not have been possible.

On the other side of the gulf the missioners passed through a city that became well known in later Church history, the ancient Mopsuestia, the modern Misis. Then by way of Adana (Seihan) they came to Paul's boyhood home of Tarsus. In every town they stopped to visit the brethren and publish the decrees of the Council of Jerusalem, which permitted Jews and Gentiles to eat the same bread and drink from the same cup in the friendship of Christ.

At Tarsus, Paul and Silas provided themselves with a tent and with some provisions, probably some hard bread, olives, and some dried fruit. Then they said farewell. Tarsus was a terminus for the caravan routes over the Taurus to Lycaonia and Cappadocia. Writing to Atticus, Cicero remarked once that, until the beginning of June, the Taurus is impassable because of the deep snow. Thus the apostles could not have left before the end of May.

The first day they passed the summer villas of the rich citizens of Cilicia through country as beautiful as an Alpine valley. The second day the journey began to be more strenuous. The Taurus in Pamphylia does not compare in savagery with the forbidding wildness of the Taurus here in Cilicia. The Cilician Gate, sometimes called the Devil's ravine, is so narrow that in time of war it could be barricaded. Today in crossing this mountain, the Baghdad railway winds through seventy tunnels, and the modern traveller in his comfortable coach may see here and there the ruins of the old road built by Assyrian, Persian, and Roman engineers.

The old military road up which Paul and Silas were climbing was a little west of the present Chakyt ravine and crosses through a dangerous defile. Here the limestone walls rise dizzily to a height of a thousand feet or more, and sometimes they are only twelve paces apart. A mountain stream roars through this narrow pass leaving only a narrow footpath between the stone wall and the wild water. At places the stream must be crossed over a fallen tree trunk. At the narrowest part of the defile are the ruins of a stone altar and two votive tablets with inscriptions that have been wiped out by time. Through this pass came the swords of Damascus and balsam from Jericho. Through this defile passed the Logos, once made man but now become a spirit again for the whole world.

The first messengers of the Logos to go this way were these two lonely wanderers, their garments tied about their waists, their mantles in a roll on their backs; they had the light luggage of poverty but they were armed with the sword of the spirit. Little did they think they were going the way that once a Christian posterity was to march to free the birthplace and the tomb of the Lord. Did they suspect that some day the seed they were now sowing would be ruthlessly uprooted by the fanatical hordes of Mohammedans, that thousands of Armenian Christians would be victims of their murderous bands, and that some day the bodies of the dead would be taken down to the sea by the Cydnus and the Sarus, that this Cilician soil would thirstily drink up the blood of martyrs?

Even Paul would have been stricken dumb at the thought of this tragedy of mankind's history; graciously God limits man's vision of things within a narrow consciousness and draws the veil over the future. Only One was able to look triumphantly on the Gorgonian face of sin and the devil, and even he when he saw it in Gethsemane felt drops of bloody sweat being forced from his pores.

The ancient road clings precariously to the mountainside. Sometimes being merely a narrow path and sometimes going over trestles built alongside the wall. Paul and Silas stood at the Cilician Gate, that narrow defile at the top of the mountain. Through this pass had gone many of the world's great conquerors: the Pharaohs, the Assyrians, the great Persian monarchs Xerxes and Darius; then came Alexander, Harun al-Rashid, and Godfrey of Bouillon. Emerging on the northern slope, the ravine widened out to a magnificent valley only to narrow again up to Bulgar Pass some 10,000 feet above sea level.

It took a man on horse four days to travel this mountain road. Since, as even today, the bridges were often washed away, the traveller must swim these raging streams. Occasionally a Roman military guardhouse would offer shelter from the elements and protection against robbers. Paul was thinking of these dangers when he wrote: "In journeying often, in perils of waters, in perils of robbers . . . in perils in the wilderness . . . in hunger and thirst" (2 Cor. 11:26). Nowhere do we have any indication that Paul ever enjoyed the comfort of a riding animal on his travels. But even if he had one here, the descent into the Cappadocian plain would not have been pleasant. After the rainy season the whole country is a vast swamp. Without a guide both man and beast might sink miserably into the morass. This was the old land of the Hittites. Here and there a rough figure holding some wheat and grapes was hewn in the rock, the ancient Hittite god Sandan. Paul had heard of Sandan back in Tarsus.

After a seven-day march, the two travellers reached Kybistra and Heraclea where they probably found a Christian community, and then they came to friendly Derbe.

The people came running out to meet them and welcome them back. Their first question: Where is Barnabas? That night Gaius and the presbyters met with Paul to consult him about their problems because they had been only partly instructed and they had no written Gospel to turn to.

One family especially waited for Paul's return as that of a spiritual father, the family of Lois and Eunice, and Timothy. Timothy was growing up to be a fine specimen of manhood. His youthful enthusiasm, his piety, and his natural prudence pleased the great Apostle. In some men's eyes we seem to be able to read that they are children of God, and Paul evidently perceived special gifts in Timothy's character. For the first time, Paul was experiencing the joys of one of those idealistic friendships which resulted so often in the Church from the common love and friendship of Christ. Paul was also beginning to realize that, like his divine Master before him, he needed to form a group of disciples about himself who would continue his work when he could carry on no longer.

Paul told Timothy of his plans, and he also confided to Eunice and Lois his desire to consecrate Timothy to the Lord. No doubt it had long been the secret ambition of these good women to see Timothy enrolled as one of Paul's helpers. Timothy knew the Scriptures by heart. Since his earliest youth his grandmother and mother had read to him from the sacred book. He spoke and wrote Greek like a native Greek, and so he could be of great service to the Apostle as his secretary.

Paul began preparing Timothy for the priesthood. He inquired of the elders of Iconium and Lystra about Timothy's character, and these men were enthusiastic in their praise of the young man. They told Paul how he had been of help to them and how he had often acted as the reader in their services. Together with Paul and Silas, the elders imposed hands on the young Timothy. During this rite of ordination it seems that Paul and the elders made addresses or "prophecies," and that Timothy also "confessed a good confession before many witnesses" (1 Tim. 1:18; 6:12; 2 Tim. 2:2). Most absorbed in these sacred ceremonies were Eunice and Lois because they were in a sense making their oblation to God's kingdom on earth.

Evidently Timothy's father had died when Timothy was quite young. But out of deference to the father, Timothy's mother had not insisted on his circumcision. That fact became a difficulty because of the prejudices of certain Jews and Jewish Christians. According to the law the child was to follow the religion of the mother. Since the rite had been omitted in Timothy's case, this lack might well be the occasion of argument, prejudice, and antagonism toward their missionary enterprise. Paul would never have been able to take Timothy into a synagogue without grievously insulting the brethren he wished to win over.

Many people in the community were apprehensive about what the results would be. Paul decided quickly to settle the matter. In Titus' case he had refused circumcision because Titus was of pagan parentage and also because circumcision was being demanded on principle. Timothy's was a different case. Now the rite of circumcision became merely a question of expediency, and Paul was never a stickler about secondary matters. He had only the one great goal in mind. The means might change from day to day. As it was, however, his enemies refused to see his ultimate goal; they accused him of inconsistency. They said he had no principles and that he only wanted to please men (Gal. 1:10).

Timothy's happiness on his ordination day soon was replaced by the sorrow of parting. He was to accompany Paul, perhaps he would never see his home again. Paul's great courage and the high level of his aims soon influenced the young priest and inspired him with the strength to make the surrender of himself to a supernatural purpose. On his side, Paul was pleased to see how Timothy had become attached to him, he was touched by Timothy's grateful appreciation of his leadership, for even such hardy souls as Paul's need these human attachments lest they lose themselves in the clouds. In his frequent sicknesses, in those lonely nights, in his care for all the Churches, Timothy was to be beside him in sympathetic understanding. Timothy follows him to Corinth, to Ephesus, to Jerusalem, and finally to Rome. He was his indefatigable secretary; in him Paul confided his thoughts. Timothy became so much a part of Paul that Paul's pastoral epistles betray the pen of another secretary when Timothy is absent.

Paul was full of gratitude for these invaluable services. While he was in prison in Rome he wrote: "For I have no man so of the same mind, who with sincere affection is solicitous for you . . . Now know the proof of him: that as a son with the father, so has he served with me in the gospel" (Phil. 2:20, 22).

With genuine pride he calls him my "beloved son in faith" (1 Tim. 1:2). It is interesting to note the problem of succeeding generations even in the Church. How an original, independent, creative generation of men is succeeded by a generation that lacks these qualities, but with great fidelity and docility receives the impressions and teachings of the older men. The second generation of apostolic Fathers in the Church were the docile pupils of the first original generation. We should not criticize them because they lacked originality and creativeness. In the plan of Providence they could not be otherwise than obedient.

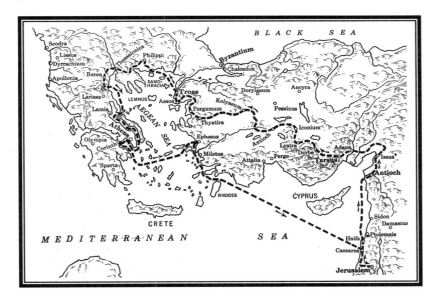

St Paul's Second Missionary Journey

CHAPTER TWENTY-THREE

LUKE THE PHYSICIAN

*"And a vision was showed to Paul in the night, which was a man of
Macedonia standing and beseeching him and saying:
Pass over into Macedonia and help us"* (Acts 16:9).

The Churches of southern Galatia had been strengthened
and confirmed. Now Paul was again being drawn westward,
always to the west. He still cherished his old plan that had been
thwarted by his spell of sickness. Should he go now through the
Meander valley to the Ionian coast? By way of Apamea the
Roman road went directly from Metropolis to Ephesus, but
"they were forbidden by the Holy Spirit." The Oriental was
guided by signs and omens in his important decisions much
more than we imagine today. He lived more in a supernatural
atmosphere, as can be seen from Homer and the institution of
oracles. He felt that he was being led by higher powers, whose
will could be discerned from dreams and constellations. Even
though much of this led to superstition, it indicated a deep
belief in the existence of unknown powers that shape man's
destiny.

Paul and his companions consulted God about their plans.
It is noteworthy how Paul relied completely on God in his
missionary itinerary. In Apamea the road forked, and here the

Holy Spirit "vetoed" Paul's cherished plan of going to Ephesus. In Ephesus it seemed that almost unlimited possibilities for expanding the faith were offered. But Paul did not complain; his decision was quickly made. If the spirit of God barred one road, other roads would be open. If he should not go to Ephesus, he could consider Mysia, Bithynia, and northern Galatia. So it was northward that he must go. They probably went by way of Synnada and Cotyaeum to Dorylaeum (Eskisehir), an important road junction in northern Phrygia on the western border of Galatia. But Paul was not attracted to the hinterland; he wished to go to the sea. Hence he decided to go to Bithynia because it offered the rich commercial centres and ports of Nicaea (Iznik), Brusa (Bursa), Nicomedia (Izmit), and Chalcedon (Kadikoy). But on the road north, the great mass of Mount Olympus rose before them as if to stretch out a warning hand; again heaven seemed to veto their plan but in no positive way. They simply found no thoroughfare north to the sea.

It may have been the autumn of 49 when the missionary group stayed aimlessly on the border of Phrygia, Mysia, Bithynia, and Galatia. They might have considered going east into northern Galatia, to Gordium and Ancyra, to the land of the Tektosages and Tolistobogii. Paul had come to know members of these nomadic tribes in southern Galatia, and some scholars think that he visited this country and was detained there by an attack of sickness. Luke, however, makes no report of such an important foundation as that of a northern Galatian Church, and he was writing missionary history. This excursion into northern Galatia would have taken at least a year, and that long period cannot be found since by March 51 Paul is already in Athens. But if Paul actually turned eastward here, he found an interesting people.

It is more historically sound to conclude that from Dorylaeum Paul turned west. He wished to go to the sea. The road went through Aezani, with its pretentious temples to Zeus and Cybele, across the great Roman bridge that spanned the Rhyndaccus, along the southern border of Mysia to Thyatira

(Akhisar) the home of Lydia, dealer in purple. At Pergamum (Bergama) Paul may have stopped to view the enormous temple to Zeus, high on its many terraces, that "seat of Satan" (Rev. 2: 13). Pictured on that monument was the battle of the gods in which Paul's beloved Galatians were subjugated by Hellenic culture. How much more beneficent than the victory of the kings of Pergamum was the victory of the apostles! From Adramyttium (Edremit) they walked through the thinly populated province of Mysia, passed the southern slope of Mount Ida, from whose peak, according to Homer, the gods were permitted to watch the battle of Troy. Finally the historic plain of Troy, watered by the Scamander and the Simmers, lay before the missioners.

Thus, without planning to do so, Paul had gone diagonally across Asia Minor, from the southeast to the northwest. Here he would learn what the Spirit had in mind when he twice vetoed Paul's plans: Paul was to begin the campaign for Europe. The Homer for this new Odyssey, his biographer Luke, was already waiting for him. Here for the first time Paul looked on the European mainland, he saw his first European island, Samothrace, rising in the foggy distance from the sea. To the north he saw the fields of ruins that marked the site of the old city of Priam. Aeneas, carrying the old man on his shoulders, had started out from here, and after many vicissitudes they had come at last to the shores of Italy. Vergil, the court poet, made Aeneas the founder of the Augustan dynasty, veiling it with the nimbus of many ancient traditions.

The ruins at Troy were, therefore, a sanctuary for the Romans, and they had marked them with several temples. Once Alexander the Great, because of his devotion to Achilles, had leaped in full armour from his ship to offer an oblation here to the hero of Troy. And after Alexander's death his generals built on these shores, opposite the island of Tenedos (Bozcaada), the beautiful harbour and city of Alexandria Troas. Caesar, it is said, entertained the thought of transferring the seat of the

Empire to this place sanctified as the origin of his house. Augustus made the city a colony of Italian veterans. Here Greece and Rome joined hands, and the monuments of that union are the massive ruins of aqueducts, arches, architraves, pillars, and beams that once spoke of the mighty power of Rome.

Even if Paul had not read the Greek poets, whom he sometimes quotes, he must have known the poems of Homer because they were part of every schoolboy's reading matter. Paul, too, was sensible to all these human accomplishments and he did not pass through these regions without admiration for what the ancients had achieved. Perhaps the old legend of that Greek who for ten years had suffered unspeakable things for a woman's love did not impress him. For he had come not to proclaim a legend but reality and a sacred message. Paul was a man of one idea: to win the world for Christ. The runner of Marathon who carried the message of the Greek victory to Athens allowed nothing to delay him until, after crying out the news of the victory, he fell exhausted and died. Paul may have felt that he also was a runner carrying the message of an exciting victory: that the Son of God had come, that He had conquered the gods of Olympus and opened up for men a magnificent future. Compared with his message, what was Troy, what was Ilium?

Paul was glad to behold the sea again. In his mind the world-embracing sea and the worldwide Church were somehow associated. He was again thinking of the greatness of the Roman Empire. He could not help admiring its spirit of adventure, its love of liberty, its sense of order and discipline, its genius for lawmaking, its ceaseless striving for progress united with a perduring patience. He felt a kinship to the Roman spirit. To take the gospel to Rome was his secret ambition. Perhaps that desire appeared to assume reality here at the doorstep of Europe. Many years later he wrote to the Romans: "having a great desire these many years past to come to you" (Rom. 15:23). But that longing was always thwarted by the Spirit, for Rome was to be Peter's domain.

After a few days' rest the travellers went down to Troas. Evidently Troas had but few of the brethren and no synagogue, but Paul probably struck up a conversation about religion with everybody he met.

On the wharves you could always find someone to talk to, especially Macedonians and Greeks. Ships were docking every day from Europe, and he could not decide what to do. Which ship should he take? Then the Lord took a hand in the matter, and led Luke, whom Paul had known in Antioch, across the Apostle's path. We conclude that the meeting between Paul and Luke took place here, since Luke, by his use of the pronoun "we," indicates that from here on he is one of the party.

Paul's meeting with Luke gave his plans a decided turn. Luke had been a proselyte – perhaps Paul had even baptized him back in Antioch. His unusual knowledge of the sea and sailing indicates that he was born in some port city and had travelled a great deal. Greek physicians were found travelling all over the world, and it seems probable that Luke was practising his profession here in Troas, and also that Paul may have called for his ministrations in one of his attacks of malaria. This happy meeting between these two developed into one of the most fruitful friendships in the history of Christianity. Except for that period between Paul's first and second stay at Philippi, Luke was his constant companion from now on. He shared the Apostle's first and second imprisonment in Rome. Paul speaks of him three times in his letters written in prison: the first time in the Epistle to the Colossians: "Luke, the most dear physician, salutes you" (4: 14). These words seem to express Paul's gratitude for Luke's services. As he sends Luke's greetings to the Colossians, Luke must have been known to them. In the letter to Philemon, Paul mentions Luke as one of his co-workers.

In his second imprisonment, Paul wrote somewhat pathetically to Timothy: "Only Luke is with me" (2 Tim. 4: 11). According to an old prologue to the Gospel of St. Luke, written in the second century, Luke remained unmarried, and after

Paul's death he continued to labour in Achaia, died in Boeotia at the age of eighty-four, and was buried in Thebes. After exhaustive scholarly research, it was found that Luke must have studied the current Greek works about the art of healing, because of his knowledge of technical terms both in his Gospel and in the Acts of the Apostles. "The study of medicine was considered as important as the study of philosophy in the Greek schools of the time, and Luke's position in the social world was comparable to the physician's position today."[20]

Luke had three genuinely Greek traits. First, his love of travel, especially on the sea, which must have endeared him to Paul immediately. His precise knowledge about ships' sailings and ships' lines indicates that he practised in seaports and perhaps even on board ship. In ancient times nobody took a voyage for pleasure; there was always some business reason. The second trait was his ability to write. His excellent education is indicated by his ability to express himself with ease and elegance. He was an accurate observer and a conscientious chronicler. On sheets of papyrus he made notes of the information he was able to collect from eyewitnesses about the life of Jesus. His Greek was purer than that of any other New Testament writer. And of the three most famous schools for higher learning, Athens, Alexandria, and Tarsus, Luke probably attended the last. Perhaps it was in Tarsus that he met Paul for the first time. Carefully adhering to the etiquette observed by ancient writers, he never speaks of himself, but always remains modestly in the background except for one instance (Luke 1:3).

The third trait is his undying loyalty and tender devotion to another. Although he profoundly admired the Apostle, he always measured his words. He looked calmly on the scene; unmoved by it, he drew the picture of the Orient with its quick emotional changes and its sudden outbreaks of passion and feeling. He was an artist who painted with words; calm and factual. He became

---

[20] H. B. F. Mackay, *The Adventures of Paul of Tarsus,* London, 1931.

the biographer of one of the most passionate of men. Sometimes friendships, such as this between Paul and Luke, are valuable not only for the individuals concerned but also for the Church.

The brilliant light radiating from Paul's personality illumined Luke and brought him to the attention of the world and made his work important for posterity. Thus divine providence has given us two pictures of the early Church. The one sketched by Paul's hand in his letters that seem to pulsate with his zeal and fighting spirit. The other drawn by the calm, sure hand of the surgeon who mastered the scalpel and the quill with equal ease. Two fine qualities of Roman and Grecian culture were joined in Paul and Luke: the calm, cool light of reason in Luke, and the glowing fire of Paul's prophetic spirit.

Unquestionably it was Luke who first directed Paul's thoughts to Macedonia, because he had connections there. One evening Paul and his friends were standing on the seashore looking over to where Europe and Asia seemed to join hands. They were talking to Macedonian sailors as they saw the peaks of Samothrace's mountains floating in the golden mists of the setting sun. Paul felt himself torn by apostolic longing, as once Gregory the Great felt a longing when he saw the young English slaves in the streets of Rome. And the desires of the day became visions at night, and one night these longings took on a definite meaning during a vision in a dream. Over beyond the waters, above the mountains of Samothrace, he saw a Macedonian, beckoning to him with outstretched arms and calling out to him: "Pass over into Macedonia, and help us."

It was Europe calling for Christianity. Once a youth of twenty-two years had come from Macedonia to bring the gifts of the West, the Greek language and Greek philosophy, to the Orient. Now the West was spiritually bankrupt and it was calling desperately for the East's greatest gift.

The course of Western culture was changed by this vision. The next morning Paul told his friends of the vision, and they all agreed that it came from the Lord. As an educated Greek,

Luke recalled the famous dream of Agamemnon which Zeus had sent to deceive the King (Iliad 2, 1-75). As a Christian he knew that God did not deceive men, and "we sought to go into Macedonia: being assured that God had called us to preach the gospel to them" (Acts 16:10).

"Pass over to us," he had said. It was not far; the passage could be made in two days, but spiritually and culturally it was very far indeed. The Jew felt comparatively close to the ways of Syria, Phrygia, and Galatia, but the culture of Rome was still far away. Paul would have to remake himself to become a Greek for the Greeks and still more to become a Roman to the Romans.

"Pass over to us." The Church has heard that call again and again. Often she has had to adapt herself to the thinking, the emotions, the strange ways of alien peoples and races, because she cannot suppress the natural and wholesome characteristics that come from nature's God. To pass over means to speak the language of the people whom she wishes to convert, to live their lives, to share their fortunes.

CHAPTER TWENTY-FOUR

LYDIA, A SELLER OF PURPLE

*"And sailing from Troas, we came with a straight course to Samothracia
and the day following to Neapolis. And from thence to Philippi,
which is the chief city of part of Macedonia, a colony"* (Acts 16: 11).

When Paul and his three companions landed in Macedonia
it was Christianity's entrance into Europe. Once a brave and
wholesome people lived here and became not only world
famous through the leadership of a young monarch but in the
plans of divine providence it played an important role in preparing the way for the gospel. Solemnly and yet simply the
Scriptures tell the story: "Now it came to pass after that
Alexander the son of Philip the Macedonian ... had overthrown
Darius king of the Persians and Medes: he fought many battles
and took the strongholds of all, and slew the kings of the earth
... And the earth was quiet before him ... And after these
things, he fell down upon his bed and knew that he should die"
(1 Mach. 1:1 ff.).

Of all ancient peoples, the Macedonians were most like
the Romans, but since 167 B.C. the Romans had been the rulers
of the land, dividing it into four districts, Thessalonica and
Philippi being the host important.

Even in the distance they saw the temple of Diana,

perched somewhat precariously on a high cliff that jutted out over the water near the port city of Neapolis. On the pavement of the Church of St. Nicholas in Neapolis, a circle marks the supposed spot where Paul and his companions landed. The travellers passed by the city, climbing the heights on the celebrated Roman road, the Via Egnatia, and soon they were high in the coastal mountains of Pangaeus. Reaching the pass, they had a wonderful view to the north. They looked down on a well-watered plain, and farther to the north the hills around Philippi could be made out. It was a bucolic landscape from which may have come all the inspiration for the ancient shepherd poetry. From these colourful fields of asphodel, legend had it that Proserpine was taken down to Hades to be the queen of the infernal regions.

This legend seemed to express the tragic atmosphere that lingered over the land of Hellas and accentuated the longing for the message of immortality and the resurrection that Paul and his companions brought with them. Down below, near the little river Gangas, Brutus and Cassius had fallen in battle against Mark Antony and Octavius for the freedom of Rome (42 B.C.). Here now were messengers of a new freedom, heralds of a new world conqueror, who had achieved more for man's freedom without the sword than all other champions of freedom. Here on this battlefield had been hammered out the imperial crown for the house of Augustus. Therefore Augustus had raised up Philippi to be a Roman military colony with the rights of the city of Rome and exemption from taxes.

The veterans living here considered themselves true Romans, and together with their deities (Minerva, Diana, Mercury, and Hercules), they brought with them Roman speech and culture. They felt that they were in direct communication with Rome and Jupiter Capitolinus because of the Roman road that crossed Macedonia from east to west, and by way of Brundisium went to Rome. Thus Philippi had become a typical Roman provincial town. A miniature Rome with a forum, a theatre, a castle, and a military wall. The people were proud of their franchise, and each year they elected two mayors, like the two Roman consuls, whom they called *archontes* or strategists. When these officials went to the forum to hand down a sentence, they were preceded by two lictors carrying the bundle of rods and the executioner's axe.

Some of the original settlers still lived among these Roman colonists. King Philip had brought them to Philippi from Thrace and Macedonia to mine gold from the Pangaeus mountains. They had always been a difficult people, blunt in speech, proud, sullen, loud, and always ready to join in some political disturbance. The women seemed to exercise considerable influence. If they could be won for the gospel they would be a great help.

During his first days in Philippi, Paul studied his prospects and the best way for him to announce the gospel. Soon it was the Sabbath. However, the town had no synagogue because not enough scribes lived here to permit the formation of a council. But even though they had no synagogue, the Jews had an enclosed place of prayer, probably a grove with a fence or wall about it, called a *proseuche*. The rabbis knew that if the people had no public religious exercises they would soon succumb to indifference and atheism.

Luke knew his way about and led his companions through the city gate to the banks of the Gangas, and soon they came upon the place of prayer, surrounded by a low garden wall. They were agreeably surprised to find some Jewesses and God-fearing pagan women at their morning devotions. Behind them rose the snow-capped Pangaeus and beside them the brook sang its melody. These women had little religious knowledge, but a lively and sincere interest made up for what they lacked. When a person has that lively interest, God will do the rest. With these good women listening, Paul gave his heart free rein to speak, and perhaps never did he have a more grateful audience. Among these women one stands out for her special interest in religion. She was well dressed, not a citizen of Philippi, but a stranger from Thyatira in Lydia, and for that reason was called Lydia. She was a wealthy business woman, who had probably taken over her deceased husband's trade in purple. Ever since Homer's day, Thyatira had been known for its purple. Since this was such a costly product, a large capital was required for the business.

Lydia was one of those souls that might be said to be naturally Christian, and as soon as she heard of Jesus she knew that he was the way, the truth, and the life. We should like to suppose that besides Lydia, those two other women, Evodia and Syntiche, whom Paul admonishes in the letter to the Philippians, were also among those present at this early service by the banks of the Gangas.

Luke reveals his artistry and his understanding of the workings of grace when he describes the conversion of Lydia, "whose heart the Lord opened to attend to those things which were said by Paul" (Acts 16:14). Lydia was a prudent woman, knowing the need for reflection. But in this instance she did not hesitate. She immediately decided to be baptized. Perhaps it was the same day, or on the following Saturday night, that Paul and his companions went down to the Gangas with the newly converted women for the baptismal ceremony. Soon Lydia's influence had prevailed in her household and they, too, were converted. Indeed, we might suppose that she became an apostle not only in her home but also in Thyatira and that she shared in the praise which John expresses in the name of Jesus to the angel of the Church of Thyatira: "I know your works and your faith and your charity and your ministry and your patience" (Rev. 2: 19).

Her second act as a Christian was to invite the apostles to leave their lodgings and live in her large business place. "If you have judged me to be faithful to the Lord, come into my house," she said. She was speaking prudently as a business woman. There were reasons for the move: her house was perhaps the only suitable place for the services of the future Church. No doubt, Lydia also felt honoured to be able to make the offer. She felt that motherly concern for the apostles and the first Church.

Luke adds, "She constrained us." He may have smiled at the thought, since the apostles probably needed little urging. But when Paul accepted her invitation, she could not have been insensible to the honour. Lydia became one of the pillars of the primitive Church. She was the maternal friend of the Apostle and of all the messengers of the gospel. Later Paul writes to these people of Philippi: "And you also know, O Philippians, that in the beginning of the gospel, when I departed from Macedonia, no Church communicated with me as concerning giving and receiving, but you only. For to Thessalonica also you sent once and again for my use" (4:15). These gifts to which he refers passed, no doubt, through Lydia's capable hands.

Who would have thought that the gospel would make such a quiet and unassuming entrance into Europe? It did not come solemnly as before the philosophers on the Areopagus, nor dramatically as then on Cyprus before the statesman. It came in an idyllic scene, one summer morning when the sky was red in the east. When the gospel came to Europe it spoke first to the women, because the men were not present, just as with the Samaritans it was a woman to whom Jesus spoke about the mystery of the kingdom of God. The women were the last ones to remain by the cross, and they were the first at the empty tomb. The gospels have a sad story of hypocrisy, hatred, persecution, calumny, treason, and cowardly flight to tell, but these things are never told about women.

The men are in the spotlight as the heralds of the gospel, as the great missioners and the representatives of religion. But where would Christianity be today without the Christian woman in her role as mother, wife, sister, and as the dispenser of charity in a thousand different kinds of misery? Paul had a deep appreciation of the services that a woman gives, and he was the first to employ women actively on the missions. He had a high regard for such intellectual women as Priscilla, who instructed the learned Apollo. He acknowledged the services of Chloe in Corinth, of Phebe in Cenchrae, and of the mother of Rufus, "his mother and mine." When he wrote to Philemon, the rich merchant, he did not neglect to send his greetings to Philemon's wife Appia.

He had special praise for woman's work in the home and in the rearing of children. He esteemed the prophetic gifts of the daughters of Philip in Caesarea, and he was concerned about those brave widows who engaged in the charity activities of the Church. He desired them to be supported by the Church (1 Tim. 5:3-16). These noble women stand at Europe's portals to receive the messengers of the gospel and to admonish the women of other days that they, too, have a sacred mission in the Church, that they are the priestesses to whom the sacred fire was first entrusted in the West.

But we cannot pass over such noble men as Epaphroditus, whom Paul called his "brother, and fellow labourer, and fellow soldier," who looked him up when he was a prisoner in Rome and brought him gifts. We know also Clement and many others who took their places beside the women, and served so faithfully that Paul declared that their "names are in the book of life" (Phil. 4:3). No other Church was ever so dear to Paul as this Church of Philippi. It was his first love on European soil, his joy and his crown (Phil. 4:3). He says: "God is my witness how I long after you all in the bowels of Jesus Christ" (Phil. 1: 8).

CHAPTER TWENTY-FIVE

THE FORTUNE-TELLER

"And it came to pass, as we went to prayer,
a certain girl having a pythonical spirit met us,
who brought to her masters much gain by divining" (Acts 16:16).

The founding of the Church in Philippi is one of the most interesting and instructive episodes of the primitive Church. It is the foundation of a Christian Church in a community that was overwhelmingly pagan, and we can observe the spiritual bankruptcy and intellectual helplessness of paganism. In a short time Paul and Silas had made a considerable number of converts in the city and soon they were gathering for services on the banks of the Gangas or in Lydia's house. In the evening after a hard day's work the brethren spent a pleasant hour together, speaking of their work, their successes and problems. But the Acts tells us nothing of these lighter moments in the life of the apostles. It leaves these things to be laboriously pieced together from what we read between the lines.

The Acts of the Apostles is a book about heroes, an epic, a stern account of missionary events. It prefers to picture the great days of decision and combat; the idyllic days that intervened it passes over. Its theme is to show that everywhere the first apostolic successes were owing to suffering, that wherever they went the apostles had to water the new territory with sweat and blood.

Once again it was a woman who set the apostles on a different course, but this time it was not a prudent and understanding woman like Lydia. It was a highly hysterical girl, a spiritistic medium. Along the street that the apostles took to reach the place of prayer, where they went frequently to instruct converts, lived a young slave who was in communication with the spirit world. She was said to have a pythonic spirit, or she was a *"pythia,"* one of those oracles that were under the protection of Apollo, who was the god of divination. The girl was also a ventriloquist; and in her seances she was able to speak in voices not at all like her own voice, hence supposed to be voices from the world of spirits. Such fortune-tellers had great vogue at the time, and since she was a slave she brought a handsome income to her master. A high price would have to be paid for such a slave. In this instance the girl was the property of a group of priests who exploited her gifts.

Whenever Paul passed this house, his great spiritual gifts seemed to irritate the poor creature. She always ran after him, shouting: "These men are servants of the Most High God, who preach to you the way of salvation." That did not mean that the girl had any idea of the truth of Christianity. Under the dominion of the demons she had to give testimony of the higher power that she sensed in Paul and Silas.

The word "Most High," was originally a Jewish name for God, which had been adopted by the pagan cults of Asia Minor, especially in Pontus, and it was applied to Zeus, Attis, and Sabazius. The use of this word by the girl may indicate the origin of her religion. The idea that certain men belonged to a definite deity and were their messengers came from the Orphic and Dyonisian mysteries, which also taught that men should enter into some magic and redemptive relationship with certain gods.

But the revealed religion of Christianity, which is the complete opposite of the dark realm of paganism, needed no support from the demons. Jesus had accepted no testimony of the devils that seemed to be shouting everywhere from the bodies and souls of the possessed. Paul was immediately aware of the hostile nature of this testimony and he could not, even for a moment, allow the gospel to be compromised. He had to repel any suspicion that the religion of Jesus had any connection with the powers of magic. Paul knew that now he had to show the superiority of Christianity over the kingdom of the devil. Even if that brought down on him the fury of Acheron and all its demons.

The girl herself deserved sympathy and protection, for, after all, she was not fighting the truth like Elymas on Cyprus. Paul commanded the devils in the name of Jesus to go out of the girl. The frozen expression of her features, the paralysis that had seized her soul seemed to dissolve. The girl felt the beneficent return of reason and her own free will. The sweet power of Christ entered her soul and the grace of the Holy Spirit filled her eyes with grateful tears for her deliverer. She felt freed from some monstrous power. She returned to herself, and we can certainly suppose that she entered the service of Christ as did that possessed man whom Christ had freed, and as Mary Magdalen did after he had driven seven devils out of her.

Here Paul again had come into contact with that fearful power which tyrannized over the ancient world and which had become the sign and emblem of that world. The powers of hell were making war in the human sphere.

If that girl belonged to an association of priests who were thirsting for the profits of her trade, we may well suppose that now her owners would arouse the whole pagan population against the apostles. Until now Paul's enemies had mostly been Jews, who attacked him when he endangered their religion. But the pagans fought him when he endangered their money. He would find that out later in Ephesus.

Fortune-telling was not protected by law, and the priests had little hope of successfully suing Paul in the courts. So they had to make some kind of political or national accusation. "These men," they decided to say, "disturb our city, being Jews; and preach a fashion which it is not lawful for us to receive nor observe, being Romans" (Acts 16:20). The charge had a great deal of truth in it; Paul and Silas were really preaching a religion that would make important changes in the morals and customs of this Roman colony. True Christianity always arouses people from their thoughtless lethargy and carelessness. Christianity is not a system of thought without obligations, it is a programme of life. Even then in Philippi it may have come between man and wife, between parents and sons and daughters.

The praetors cannot be blamed for not keeping cool heads in the midst of the tumult that surrounded them. It was impossible to conduct an orderly hearing or to give the accused a chance to speak. Since the case concerned only two wandering Jews, the judges did not ask much about their status, but sentenced them summarily to be "beaten with rods." The metallic voice of the Roman officer went ringing down the hall, *Lictor, expedi virgas, ad verbera!* ("Untie the rods, flog the prisoners!"). That famous justice of Rome was not taken seriously out here in a provincial town. Cicero had ample reason for his passionate complaint against Governor Verres *(In Verrem,* 2, 1, 9).

We wonder why Paul and Silas, as Roman citizens, made no objection to the sentence. We know that in towns like this, petty officials often disregarded the rights of Roman citizens. But why did not Paul and Silas make an attempt to secure their rights? It may have been that they could not make themselves heard in the din and confusion. It seems that they had not been given an opportunity of defending themselves (Acts 16:37). It could not have been that they were insensible to this indignity. Who could say that of Paul, who was too proud to accept even an alms?

Perhaps it was that Paul claimed the rights of his citizenship only when it would profit the gospel, and in this instance it might have been for the advancement of the gospel to make this bloody sacrifice, for by this illegal procedure the authorities made themselves guilty of a grave crime according to the *Lex Valeria*. Now the authorities would be at Paul's mercy and he could then demand consideration for his followers. And the next day the authorities were really alarmed.

It was a brutal world in which Paul lived. In the letter to the Romans he speaks of the heartlessness that was a characteristic of paganism. The ancient world went down to destruction because there was no love in it, and it could be saved only by the supreme love of martyrdom. Paul was not the man to toy with the idea of martyrdom as does the average man on the street, and then when there is any possibility of making a sacrifice most men ride post-haste away or try to move heaven and earth to escape. Here Paul was a stark realist. He had steeled himself for every hardship and suffering. "In many more labours, in prisons mare frequently, in stripes above measure, in deaths often ... Thrice was I beaten with rods" (2 Cor. 11:23, 25). He looked on his life as a contest in the arena, and he shunned no effort to be perfectly trained: "but though our outward man is corrupted, yet the inward man is renewed day by day" (2 Cor. 4:16). With that spirit a man can conquer the world.

CHAPTER TWENTY-SIX

IN PRISON AT PHILIPPI

"And when they had laid many stripes upon them,
they cast them into prison, charging the gaoler to keep them diligently.
Who having received such a charge, thrust them into the inner prison
and fastened their feet in the stocks" (Acts 16:23).

In the ruins of the lower city of Philippi we can still see sections of the great pillars which were once the silent witnesses of Paul's martyrdom. Timothy and Luke, as mere helpers of the mission band, were not harmed. Perhaps they were absent and learned of Paul's fate only later. But the suffering of Paul and Silas was not yet over. They were placed in a dark evil-smelling cell of the prison which was high on the mountain side, and the cells were partly dug in the rocky side of the mountain. The prisoners' feet were secured in wooden stocks, iron rings were fastened to their wrists and necks, and the rings were attached by means of chains to other rings fitted into the stone walls. The prisoners were forced to sit erect; their backs ached and burned from the open gashes and welts from the flogging. From the other cells came curses, screams, groans, and unearthly yelling.

The guards, when relieved at the third watch of the night, seemed to hear a voice singing. A jubilant voice such as these desolate walls of Philippi had never heard before. The cursing died away, the brutal men in the cells paused to listen:

"When the Lord brought back the captivity of Sion,
We became like men comforted.
Then was our mouth filled with gladness:
And our tongue with joy.
Then shall they say among the Gentiles:
The Lord hath done great things for them" (Ps. 125).

It was unbelievable that prisoners should be singing instead of howling; chanting pious hymns instead of mouthing curses. What kind of God is it that gives such endurance? These men must be the messengers of some new God. This is a melody that was never heard before. Yes, indeed, it is the melody that Christianity brought to the world. It is the melody of true joy sung by St. Francis of Assisi in the canticle of the sun.

Paul and Silas were confident. The Lord who freed Peter when he was in prison would not forget them. And just as the faithful were praying for Peter that night in the house of Mary, Mark's mother, so they were praying this night with Timothy and Luke in Lydia's house. Sometimes God makes the storm his messenger, or an angel, or fire, but this night an earthquake was the herald of his will. In the Mediterranean area and especially in Macedonia and the Aegean Islands earthquakes were not an unusual occurrence; but the coincidence of an earthquake with the apostles' prayer was certainly an act of God's special providence. After the earthquake happened, everything else was quite natural. One who has had some knowledge of Turkish prisons wrote: "If you had ever seen a Turkish prison you would not be surprised to hear that the doors burst open. The doors to each cell were fastened by one bolt and when the earthquake came the door posts fell apart, the bolts slid from the locks and the doors fell open. The chains and stocks were torn loose from the walls because clefts appeared in the shaken walls, letting the iron rings fall to the ground."[21] Things have not changed a

---

[21] Cf. W. M. Ramsay, *St. Paul the Traveller,* London, 1898

great deal in the Balkans even after two thousand years.

We know the emotional reaction to an earthquake. At first people are as if paralyzed, they lie helpless waiting for the next blow. Accepting the earthquake as an answer to their prayers, Paul and Silas stood up and went into the outer cell where the other prisoners were freeing one another from chains and stocks. The apostles calmed their fellow prisoners and urged them not to escape. In the meantime the warden of the prison came running from his house. When he saw the gaping holes where the cells were, he thought all his prisoners had escaped. In true Roman style he preferred suicide to death by execution, which would have been the penalty for neglecting to guard the prisoners. As he drew his sword, he heard a voice calling from the darkness, "Do yourself no harm, for we all are here."

From the extreme of utter despair, the warden went to the other extreme of joy and gratitude toward the men who had saved his life. According to the Beza MS, the other prisoners were again locked in their cells, while Paul and Silas were taken into the courtyard. In the eyes of the warden these two men were messengers of some great God, like the fortune-teller who shouted in the streets. Yesterday he noticed how they had courageously suffered the flogging without making an outcry. He had heard them singing hymns to their God, and now that God had come to their aid. He shuddered to think of how he had put the ambassadors of such a great God in irons.

Paganism gave a man no principles to judge by; it gave him no solid ground to stand on. Everything was a matter of sentiment and emotion, and the pagans were always being tossed about between unreasoning fear and superstitious hope. A man threw his life away in a moment of despair; he knew of no reasonable relationship to any god. The gods had eyes and ears, it is true, but saw and heard nothing and they cared nothing about man's plight. But the God of these men, thought the warden, was entirely different. He made his followers free. He made them strong and joyful. If only he could belong to such a following! And from the depths of his pagan soul he cried, "Masters, what must I do, that I may be saved?" "Tell me what I have to do to win the favour of your God."

Paul and Silas were regarded as superior beings. Had they not brought on the earthquake? The warden's family and household stood around in the courtyard by the fountain. And here occurred the most remarkable lecture on religion in the Church's history; this was the most abridged catechism course of all time. Recall the condition of the two apostles: yesterday they had undergone the horrors of the flogging, then had come the sufferings of the prison and the excitement of the earthquake and the prison break. They were weak from loss of blood, they were weak from hunger. But now they had a duty to perform. Immediately they pitied these ignorant people and forgot all about their own comfort.

Paul and Silas were not men who baptized without preparation of the candidates. They adhered to a strict routine. If time pressed, they omitted a long dogmatic instruction, which could be supplied later. Above all things they demanded that complete contrition of the soul, its complete unsettling, an unreserved willingness to surrender to grace, and the implicit faith of the naturally Christian soul. All that had happened during the night had done more to produce these effects than a long course of instruction. In their religion, the pagans regarded external things as most important, and now when Paul began to speak about baptism, the keeper of the prison, like the Ethiopian eunuch, probably asked impatiently, "Why cannot we be baptized immediately?" When Paul saw how these people desired salvation, he concluded his address with the words: "Believe in the Lord Jesus, and you shall be saved, and your house." And so without further ado, as the sun was rising, the whole family was baptized at the fountain in the prison courtyard.

The keeper's wife was the first to realize that the two prisoners had nothing to eat since the day before. She brought them into her house, and prepared a bed for them. The warden himself reverently washed their wounds. Then they had a love banquet to celebrate their baptism. During that unforgettable morning an unbreakable band was forged between the Apostle and his new converts. Whenever Paul came back to Philippi, he never failed to visit his friend the warden, and in his letters to Philippi he sent his greetings to him. When he looked back on such successes for the gospel, Paul must have thought within himself that it was worth the suffering he had undergone.

The authorities of the town were not left in ignorance of the events of the night. The earthquake had shaken the whole town; it had also unsettled their bad consciences about the sentence that had made a mockery of the Roman law. Early in the morning messengers came to the warden from the judges and said: "Let these men go." But this was the moment Paul had been waiting for; now he had the authorities in his power. Luke is clearly satisfied about the turn of events as he tells how his master checkmated the judges and how he suddenly hurled the fact of his Roman citizenship at their feet like a bomb. He could afford to be exigent now. He refused to leave the city without receiving the honours of the town and being solemnly escorted by the city fathers.

He was a disciple of Christ and he had shown that he knew how to bear dishonour and shame for Christ, but he also had a certain amount of self-respect that kept him from submitting to treatment like a tramp. The lordly gentlemen of the city hurried to him now and with all the magistrates and their friends (according to the Beza text) stuttered their apologies and begged the apostles to leave the city for the sake of peace, because there might be an uprising. Paul may have had some difficulty to suppress his amusement, but he remained master of the situation. By acceding to their request, he could put them under obligations to himself. After all, it would always be to their interests that he keep silent about the whole affair. As Luke relates the details of the scene, we cannot help but notice that his Greek nature thoroughly enjoyed the comedy of the situation.

Paul and Silas were in no hurry to leave the city. First they permitted the magistrates to escort them to Lydia's house where the faithful had gathered. Then Paul ordained presbyters and elders and gave directions for the management of the Church. Luke, who had not been involved in the incident, remained to supervise the development of the new Church. We know he remained, because from this point until the twentieth chapter he replaces "we" with "they." It may have been that Philippi was his second home and that he was practising his profession here. Through Luke, Paul kept in touch with the brethren at Philippi. Philippi was the only Church he never had occasion to censure, and Philippi was also the only Church that was permitted to relieve Paul's poverty by an offering of money.

Whenever Paul recalled his stay in Philippi he seemed to remember also the ignominy he had suffered there. He wrote later to the neighbouring Thessalonians: "But having suffered many things before and been shamefully treated (as you know) at Philippi" (1 Thess. 2:2). Such was Europe's first payment for the gift of the gospel, but Paul's spirit could not be brought low by any feeling of resentment or bitterness. On the contrary, like a mother, he loved that child most for which he had suffered most.

For Paul, suffering was an important means in the care of souls. Like any other establishment, the Church of Christ can be maintained only by those means by which it was established. According to Paul's understanding of the mysticism of the Passion, the trials of the Messianic era fall upon different groups and individuals because Christ desires co-sufferers in his Passion. To every true member of the mystical body of Christ a certain amount of these sufferings will be meted out. The closer a man is to Christ the greater the degree of his suffering. Thus the greatest suffering came to the apostles and the founders of the Churches. The apostles are gladiators destined for death, they are the paladins of Christ, "a spectacle to the world and to angels and to men ... We are made as the refuse of this world, the off-scouring of all, even until now" (1 Cor. 4:9, 13).

CHAPTER TWENTY-SEVEN

In Thessalonica

"And when they had passed through Amphipolis and Apollonia, they came to Thessalonica, where there was a synagogue of the Jews" (Acts 17:1).

Philippi was the only city from which Paul departed at peace with the local authorities. Here indeed he got an escort of honour. He never seemed to be quite settled in a place, when he had to move on. His apostolic wandering was a continual going and coming; he was always being ejected from some city, always being driven off. Yet this excessive activity, this restless movement hither and thither, was not incompatible with the greatest recollection of spirit. External necessities, untoward circumstances, drove him onward; but he was able to concentrate more than most men. It is almost inconceivable how Paul's spirit, tortured by restlessness, was able to create that compact system of religious thought proclaimed in his Epistles.

It was probably in the spring of A.D. 50 when Paul, Silas, and Timothy started out on the Via Egnatia for the two-day march of some twenty miles westward to Amphipolis. A few days before their backs had felt the lictors' lash. The gashes, though tended by Lydia's hands, still burned, as did their feet bruised by the stocks in prison, but these stalwart apostles marched bravely on. The road was good. Sometimes it led them past lovely meadows and fields of flax, sometimes it took them beneath the refreshing shade of the plane tree. A cool breeze came down from the snowy peaks of the Pangaeus range, and crystal streams tumbled down from the heights and hurried on to the Struma river and then to the Bay of Strymon. Sometimes the travellers stopped to drink the cooling waters and rest by the road; and in the evening they left the mountain region behind and entered the valley of the Struma. Amphipolis lay a few miles inland from the sea, with a fine view out to the Aegean. Here they lodged for the night. The next morning a walk through the town convinced them that it was too small to become the central point in their missionary work in this territory. Their destination was Thessalonica. Paul always preferred to work out from the greater cities. The outlying villages could be easily evangelized from the cities.

So, on the third and fourth days they made the forty miles between the Strymonian Gulf and the coastal range. Now they walked through thick forests; now they had an enchanting view of the sea, then they passed two lovely mountain lakes in the peninsula of Chalcidice. Many groves of oaks, plane trees, and pines invited them to rest. They passed the tomb of Euripides, the Ibsen of antiquity, where a soul torn by doubt and storm now was at rest. And as the thick shades of chestnut woods came down on the evening of the fourth day they came to Apollonia. Now the last lap of the journey lay before them: only fifty miles more to Thessalonica.

After an exhilarating walk through the lake region of Mygdonia they came, late in the afternoon of the sixth day, to the eastern shore of the gulf of Thessalonica. Down below they saw the blue waters of the eternally moving sea, and far in the distance the setting sun was painting purple shadows on the everlasting snows on the many-peaked Thessalonian Olympus, the sacred mountain of the gods. There was the throne of the "cloud-compelling Zeus," and every pious Greek spoke of that mountain with the same holy awe that the Israelite had for

Mount Sinai.

"That," said Paul to his companions, "is where the Greeks believe their gods dwell. Let us tell them about the Father in heaven; let us tell them that these mountains are merely his footstool." It was only the simple man of the people that believed the gods lived on Olympus. Educated men knew better. Below them, they saw the marble buildings of Thessalonica in the gathering dusk. The ancient city of Therma, now called Thessalonica in honour of Alexander the Great's sister, was the undisputed metropolis of Macedonia, possessing one of the safest and largest harbours of the Aegean. The Via Egnatia, really a continuation of the Appian Way, extending from Dyrrachium to Byzantium, united the city to Rome and Asia. Today portions of the old road, twelve feet below the present highway, have been exposed.

The travellers entered their first European metropolis. The city rose in semicircular terraces from the shoreline, broken by cross streets and ornamented with the green of the gardens and the darker green of cypress trees. The ruins of Roman temples and triumphal arches today attest the age of the city. In ancient times, Thessalonica's hot springs, its theatre, arenas, shipping accommodations, lured merchants, travellers, officials, and legionaries. Ships docked from all parts of the world. Men were coming and going from everywhere with all sorts of ideas and news. If the gospel were once established here, it would quickly spread all over the Mediterranean territory. And so it happened. Scarcely a year had passed when Paul wrote from Corinth to Thessalonica: "For from you was spread abroad the word of the Lord not only in Macedonia and in Achaia but also in every place: your faith which is towards God is gone forth" (1 Thess. 1:8).

Thessalonica was a free city under home rule. While Philippi as a veteran colony bore the Roman imprint, Thessalonica bore the mark of the pleasure-loving Greek. Like all Greek cities it had distinctly democratic ideas. Every year a council of six "politarchs" was elected. In order to bridle the city's passion for liberty, the Roman governor resided here with his lictors.

Morally the population did not have the best of reputations. The people were overreaching in business, they were always quick to seize an unfair advantage. They lounged about the streets and in the hippodrome, they were often lazy and over-curious, and preferred to be supported by others rather than by their own efforts. In marriage they were often unfaithful; they were given to sensual pleasures, and the houses of joy had a fair clientele. Strangers got this impression when they came to this port city. Even in his first letter to them Paul had to warn his converts of these dangers (1 Thess. 4:1-12).

For the rest, Thessalonica was a quiet city of workmen. The carpet and tent-weaving industry flourished; excellent examples of the Oriental weaver's art were spread out in the bazaars together with excellent tooled leather articles. The population was a cosmopolitan mixture: Macedonians, Greeks, Syrians, Egyptians, Jews, Roman officials, and legionaries.

Our travellers inquired for the Jewish quarter. Paul had a recommendation from friends in Philippi introducing him to a fellow tribesman whose name in Greek was Jason. Jason, it seems, had a small textile factory and a rather large salesroom for his wares. Paul and his two companions received a warm welcome and were given shelter, food, and employment. The next morning Paul had on his leather apron ready for work at the loom. His companions also made themselves useful to their host because they did not wish to be a burden to him, especially since they planned to remain for some time. Writing to them, Paul said: "For you remember, brethren, our labour and toil; working night and day, lest we should be chargeable to any of you" (1 Thess. 2:9).

If Paul were to come back to Thessalonica today, he would not be surprised to see so many Jewish newspapers sold on the street. Even in his time the Jewish population was very large. The Jews had a large synagogue which through the support of the great merchant princes and bankers had become the religious centre for Jews all over Macedonia. Paul went to the synagogue on the first three Sabbaths after his arrival. He found a mixed congregation, but one that was sincerely interested in religion. As was customary, he and Silas were received with respect as scribes from Jerusalem and they were asked to make an address. From the scant indications in the Acts, we may conclude that Paul took as his text and theme the famous fifty-third chapter of Isaias. That chapter is one of the most important and decisive chapters in the Old Testament; it is the prophecy of the vicarious suffering of the Messias for sinful mankind:

"A man of sorrows and acquainted with infirmity:
And his look was as it were hidden and despised . . . .
He was wounded for our iniquities:
He was bruised for our sins.
The chastisement of our peace was upon him:
And by his bruises we are healed . . . .
He was offered because it was his own will,
And he opened not his mouth.
He shall be led as a sheep to the slaughter
And shall be dumb as a lamb before his shearer."

This was the passage that had disturbed the Ethiopian proselyte, the treasurer of Queen Candace, the passage that Philip explained as referring to Jesus' suffering. According to the teaching of the primitive Church, that passage found its fulfilment in Christ. And now Paul insisted on touching this sorest of all spots, he insisted on taking the veil from their eyes and making them look full on the painful truth. "Your hopes," he told them, "for a Messias crowned with victory is a fantastic dream, a figment of your feverish imagination. The real Messias wears a crown of thorns." Here again was that great disillusionment, that great scandal, that stumbling block, on which the Jewish people broke.

For three Sabbaths Paul told them of the cross of Christ,

how Christ had to suffer, not by some inevitable fate of the
pagan gods, but because of the loving decree of God. He showed
them that the Cross was the point where all contradictions
agreed. That it was the reconciliation of all disagreements, the
solution of all difficulties. Jesus hung on the Cross as the head
of all humanity to atone for our ancient fault.

Thus for the first time the Cross of Golgotha was casting
its shadow on Thessalonica. These three sermons of Paul's
were like thunderclaps that unsettled men's souls; people talked
about them the next day in the streets. Fortunately he found
some among the Jews who believed, but for the greater part he
had to turn to the pagans; they were better disposed.

Christianity has always demanded a certain preparation
of mind and heart. As the first preparation Paul required a profound study of the Scriptures. He himself introduced his
converts to the Bible. He wished them to study it humbly and
simply, especially the prophets.

He always began with the Scriptures; he "opened up the
Scriptures." The key to the Scriptures was the great central
thought of Christ's atoning death.

Whenever the Church was in danger of becoming too involved in externals or excessive activity, or when it seemed to
become tied up in legalism, or when political interests seemed
to sap its strength, it was always the Scriptures that were the
rejuvenating fountain.

The second disposition of the soul required by Paul was a
sincere desire for the truth. The third requirement was a certain
holy awe and reverence for divine things, the beginning of the
fear of the Lord, even though at the outset it was somewhat
primitive and mingled with superstition, as in the case of the
warden at Philippi. When these three dispositions were present,
Paul had little difficulty in destroying the errors of paganism or
Judaism and opening his hearers' minds to receive the crucified
Redeemer.

CHAPTER TWENTY-EIGHT

FROM THESSALONICA TO BEROEA

"But the Jews, moved with envy and taking some wicked men of the vulgar sort and making a tumult, set the city in an uproar; and besetting Jason's house, sought to bring them out to the people" (Acts 17:5).

Paul was not only a missioner, he was also a pastor of souls. He was not only able to conquer for the Lord, but he knew how to confirm and preserve what he had gained. He was not interested in quick, brilliant successes. As a missioner he calls himself a "wise architect" (1 Cor 3:10), and as a pastor he compares himself to a father, "as a father does his children" (1 Thess. 2:11).

According to the First Epistle to the Thessalonians, these three sermons in the synagogue were really only the upbeat, the beginning of more intensive pastoral work among those who were won over. Luke does not mention this follow-up work because his purpose was to tell about the expansion of the gospel and he was always hurrying on to new theatres of action. After Paul had won over the best elements in the synagogue, it became necessary here, as everywhere else, to separate from the synagogue. Then he began the really intensive instruction in Jason's house, in the workshops, in the street, in the cells of the slaves, in the reception rooms of the upper classes (Acts 17:4).

His pastoral care was extremely personal, he talked face to face, man to man, and he went from house to house.

You could see Paul and Silas going down the streets looking up their converts, knocking at door after door, up and down steps. Paul had a personal interest in every individual. He listened to a man's doubts and difficulties. He put himself in the man's place, and then he poured out his great powers of persuasion together with his enchanting amiability. He kept them all in mind: the hesitating, the weak ones, the doubters, the fearful ones, the critics, the enthusiasts. He lost sight of none. It was a wonderful course in pastoral theology for Timothy to see his master's spirit and method.

In the first letter to the Thessalonians, Paul describes his method. He tells how he sat within the circle of his pupils and disciples, and spoke to them as a father, teaching, encouraging, admonishing them to walk worthy of God. The tenderest emotional touch, the full gamut of feelings, were at his disposal. He always tried to knit a close bond of personal friendship between himself and his converts. This idea of personal friendship as a missionary method is something peculiar to St. Paul. In that friendship there was no thought of personal gratification or self-glorification. For Paul it was simply a means of establishing a friendship between the convert and Christ. Christianity was not an abstract thing for Paul, it was not an airy mental relationship. It was rather a tender, intimate union with God, it was something real and alive, something for which anyone would be ready to suffer and die. "I do all things for the gospel's sake," he said (1 Cor. 9:23).

Sometimes it was hard for Paul to penetrate through the layers of ideas that environment, temperament, and education often pile on men's minds. But he was generally able to bore through to a man's real personality. "And I became to the Jews a Jew, that I might gain the Jews: to them that are under the law, as if I were under the law, (whereas myself was not under the law), that I might gain them that were under the law. To them that were without the law, as if I were without the law (whereas I was not without the law of God, but was in the law of Christ), that I might gain them that were without the law. To the weak I became weak, that I might gain the weak. I became all things to all men, that I might save all" (1 Cor. 9:20 ff.).

But the strict regimen of amiability was not mere cold calculation in which the heart played no heart: "Whereas we might have been burdensome to you, as the apostles of Christ: but we became little ones in the midst of you, as if a nurse should cherish her children. So desirous of you, we would gladly impart to you not only the gospel of God but also our own souls: because you were become most dear to us" (1 Thess. 2:7). That is not the language of cool calculation. Never before had anyone been so prodigal in self-surrender, never before had anyone fought so passionately for souls as the Son of man in the form of the Good Shepherd, and now when the Good Shepherd reappeared in the form of His greatest Apostle.

In the early days Christianity in Thessalonica had a strong charismatic trend. The Holy Spirit poured Himself out upon the newly converted and lifted them up into ecstasy. Paul also experienced times when his charismatic gifts were especially powerful. A few months later he reminded the Thessalonians: "Our gospel has not been to you in word only, but in power also; and in the Holy Spirit and in much fullness" (1 Thess. 1: 5). In such moments he spoke with the flaming language of the prophets, moving his hearers to tears about their past lives or at the sufferings of the Crucified. Sometimes while he was talking they cried out in gratitude for the joy and comfort they had found. Sometimes a lame man leaped up cured, or one who had been possessed rose calmly and walked away free. When he talked they felt how the light of his mind shone into the dark places of their souls. How he dispelled their doubts, how he untied the ugly knots made by the double law of the flesh and the spirit. They felt his hand as the hand of a great surgeon, healing and soothing: "For the word of God is living and effectual and more piercing than any two-edged sword and reaching the division of the soul and the spirit, of the joints also and the marrow: and is a discerner of the thoughts and intents of the heart" (Heb. 4:12).

But these ecstatic moments were only the introduction to a long period of reform and sanctification. After the great moment of baptism when the waters of the stream came over them like a heavenly garment, then the Apostle undertook the detailed work of instruction. Gradually the converts were weaned away from the bland pabulum of the beginner and they were given more solid food. Paul was far from condemning their first enthusiasm as silly emotionalism; he had had experience in these things himself. But he warned his converts that it was not this flood of emotion but "this is the will of God, your sanctification" (1 Thess. 4:3).

Soon the Church at Thessalonica was rivalling the Church at Philippi in its spirit of faith and sacrificing love. Everyone of Paul's Churches had its distinctive mark, and in Thessalonica it was an extraordinary consciousness of Paul's eschatological teaching. One thing seemed to make a deep impression on these excitable Thessalonians: the imminent destruction of the world. At that time the whole Empire had an uneasy feeling that the end was at hand. Paul himself was much occupied with the thought of the end of the world and he expresses hopes for the Parousia without, however, determining the time for the world catastrophe. When they heard Paul talking about the end of the world, the last judgment, and the things that would precede these events, the Thessalonians were able to envision the red sky of the day of doom.

Caligula, with his insane pretensions, robbed the Empire of the high place it held in men's minds under Augustus and Tiberius. Under Claudius a group of unscrupulous women like Messalina and Agrippina played fast and loose with the dignity of the imperial throne. Strange things were happening, so went the reports: comets in the sky, bloody rains, miscarriages, pestilences, floods, and the lightning that struck the statue of the Emperor and the temple. All this foreboded some great evil. Everywhere men were asking: "Who will be emperor? Will it be Messalina's son, Britannicus, or will it be Nero, Agrippina's son?"

Perhaps some of the Christians misunderstood Paul when he told them: "Do not worry about these things. We Christians have our own state and government. The children of the world call the Emperor their lord and god, but we have a greater Lord and God to whom the Father himself has given a kingdom. Jesus is our Lord and King." Those were dangerous words in the hands of the Jews, and they knew well how to use them. At that time the sword of Damocles was hanging over the Jews. Claudius had recently by decree expelled the Jews from Rome, and any day the decree might be extended to the provinces. In the meantime the Jews were trying to be exceedingly loyal to the Emperor, and they looked for ways to direct the imperial anger to other victims. Paul and the Christians would serve the purpose well.

Jewish money was used to bribe a mob, "wicked men of the vulgar sort," as Luke says, to go down the streets shouting: "Paul is a traitor." As the mob went through the streets, it gathered recruits from every bazaar and wine-room until it came to Jason's house. When his friends saw the mob coming, they hid Paul and his companions. Angered and disappointed because its prey had given it the slip, the mob seized Jason and some of the brethren as hostages and dragged them before the city authorities in the agora. They were accused of high treason. "These men are turning the whole world upside down, and now they have come here too, and Jason has been harbouring them in his house. They all oppose the decrees of the Emperor and they talk about another king, Jesus."

Here in Thessalonica, under the eye of the Roman governor, the city fathers acted more circumspectly. They knew, of course, the brand of the patriotism of the mob and of its masters. They knew that Jason was a decent, honest citizen, and so they merely required bail of him that he should see to it that these strangers left quickly and quietly.

The same night Paul called the elders of the Church for a conference in Jason's house to give them directions about the conduct of the Church. Then he bade them all farewell and thanked Jason, that noble man, for his loyalty and generosity. It was hard for Paul to leave this Church now, when it began to give such fine promise. His earlier premonitions that difficult days would come for his converts and especially for Jason had not been unfounded. Later whenever we hear of the Church in Thessalonica we hear of their persecutions and tribulations (1 Thess. 2:14; 2 Thess. 1:4).

At that time Paul thought that his absence from Thessalonica would be only for a short time. But he was wrong. It was eight long years before he saw his friends in Thessalonica again. And then, when he returned, he was not allowed to rest anywhere, but was forced to flee from house to house. "Our flesh," he said later, "had no rest: but we suffered all tribulation. Combats without; fears within" (2 Cor. 7:5). But these continual trials welded the congregation together and kept their zeal alight. No other Church merited Paul's praise for its patience and constancy and its fraternal charity as did Thessalonica (2 Thess. 1:4). And besides, Thessalonica gave him two faithful co-workers: Secundus, the companion of his last journey, and Aristarchus, who shared his imprisonment in Rome (Acts 20:4; 27:2; Col. 4:10; Philem. 24).

It was near the beginning of A.D. 51. Under cover of the night Paul and his companions left the city. They wandered along the gulf shore, guiding their steps by the light of ships' masts at sea. After a while they left the Egnatian highway and turned into a country road which took them, after a twelve hours' march, to the quiet town of Beroea (the modern Verria) in the third Macedonian district. Beroea was a picturesque town, off the road, at the foot of Mount Olympus. The people were engaged in the cultivation of their vineyards and olive groves, some too were carpenters, quarrymen, and tradesmen. They cared little about what went on in the big cities and what people there were talking about.

It was Paul's intention to wait here until the storm died down in Thessalonica. Twice he tried to go back, but he could not stay because of the devilish hatred of the Jews there. So he made use of the opportunity to found a Church in Beroea. Even little Beroea had a Jewish colony and a synagogue, but the Jews here "were more noble than those in Thessalonica, who received the word with all eagerness" (Acts 17:11). Paul started a biblical movement. Jews and proselytes were studying their Greek Bibles and looking up the passages that Paul was quoting to prove the non-political character of the Messias. Here in Beroea the educated classes were joining the Church, a proof that the early Church was not made up exclusively of the proletariat. And Beroea, too, contributed a valuable co-worker of Paul's, Sopater, the son of Pyrrhus (Acts 20:4) who often travelled with Paul.

Paul's joy in Beroea did not last long. The troublemakers from Thessalonica came to Beroea, but they were not accepted so readily. Nevertheless the peace was disturbed, and there was always the mob that could be bought. In Beroea again, the brethren decided to take steps for Paul's security, and again his activity in a city was terminated in flight. Paul now decided to leave Macedonia altogether and go to a country where the hatred of his fellow Jews could not so easily reach him. He went by sea this time. The Beza text says: "He avoided Thessaly, because he was prevented from preaching there." According to a tradition still alive in Verria, Paul went by Aiginion to the port of Methoni (Eleutherochori).

Some students surmise that Paul had another attack of illness in Beroea or on the road to Methoni. In view of all these vicissitudes it would not be surprising. Perhaps that was the reason why his escort did not turn back at the seaport but continued with him to Athens. Paul left a part of his heart in Beroea: Silas and Timothy. He was willing to go without them because the Church in Beroea needed them so greatly. But when he reached Athens and was saying farewell to the brethren from Beroea, he sent an urgent message to Silas and Timothy that "they should come with all speed." He must have been suffering a great deal.

CHAPTER TWENTY-NINE

AT ATHENS ALONE

"Now while Paul waited for them at Athens, his spirit was stirred within him, seeing the city wholly given to idolatry" (Acts 17:16).

For a man who has been under severe mental strain and worry, nothing is so refreshing and beneficial as a sea voyage. Paul probably realized that during his four-day voyage along the coast of Thessaly, with the high Olympus, and Ossa and Pelion gliding slowly by. His ship passed through the straits of Euripus; then he had a fleeting glimpse of the plains of Marathon, and soon he sailed round Cape Sunium to reach the fabulous capital of Greece.

It was perhaps the fourth day of the voyage when they rounded Cape Sunium (the modern Cape Colona), the extreme point of the Attic mainland. Sailing north the voyager is greeted from the heights of the temple by the sea god Poseidon and the land goddess Athena. Even today the white of the marble temple shimmers in the sunlight. It was Greece's first greeting to Paul. Now the ship's sails were full blown as the wind sent the ship skimming through the Saronic Gulf, past the world-famous Aigina and Salamis into the harbour of Peiraeus filled with a forest of ships' masts.

Now he looked on that great city of Theseus and Pallas

Athena, the goddess of wisdom. Attired in her glistening armour and helmet, holding the golden lance, Athena seemed to say that power and beauty, these two earthly ideals of man's dreaming, were an inseparable gift of the gods. But if ever they are separated from each other or from the gods they will bring a nation to its ruin.

Only once in the history of the race had this ineffable miracle occurred: that a tiny nation within the space of hardly a hundred years had scaled the heights of the human spirit, in science, art, philosophy, political knowledge, and physical culture, and the name of that miracle is Athens. Today we stand in admiration at the everlasting youth of the Athenian spirit that rises from its ruins. And though its body may have gone down to dust, Athens great name lives still, and not only its name but its ideal and its law of noble proportion and beauty.

The Apostle's heart may have beat a little faster when he saw the sun's rays reflected back from shaft and spearhead of Athena's lance. Or when he heard the ship's boy in the crow's nest call "Athenai." Paul was no barbarian, he was not insensible to all that Athens meant in culture, education, in art, in its elevation and worship of the human ideal. Did he not write to the Philippians: "For the rest, brethren, whatsoever things are true ... whatsoever lovely, whatsoever of good fame, if there be any virtue, if any praise of discipline: think on these things" (Phil. 4:8)?

But the Greece to which Paul was now coming was not that proud, freedom-loving Hellas of the Persian Wars, not the Greece of Pericles, not even the Greece of the Macedonian kings that shared in the glory of Alexander. Since the fall of Corinth (146 B.C.) it had sunk to the condition of the Roman province of Achaia. It had been depopulated and plundered and despoiled by hordes of greedy Roman prefects. Here on Greek soil, on the battlefields of Actium and Philippi, the imperial crown of Rome had been beaten out of the hard metal of the Roman character and ornamented with the jewels of Greek art and culture. Since that day Greece had been only a shadow of its former self. Its cities and countryside were laid waste, sheep and cattle grazed in the market places of towns and cities. In the Peloponnesus, Sparta and Argos alone retained importance. Olympia had fallen from its heights. In Thebes, the city of Pindar, only the ancient castle was still inhabited; all of Boeotia was a desert land.

The old noble families had died out; their sons had hearkened in their zeal for republicanism to the call of Brutus and were left to die near Philippi. Only Athens and Corinth had survived the collapse. Athens owed its preservation to the fame of its ancestors. Corinth was allowed to rise again from the dust of its ruins by the grace of Rome. Now Greece was only a vast art museum for the tourists of the time, and the Greeks themselves had become the custodians and cicerones of their former achievements. Thousands of Greeks were homeless wanderers in the western provinces. The world had become their fatherland. A striking parallel to the fate of the Jews: to have fallen from such heights to such depths. And Hellas did not have a prophet, as Israel had, to sing her misfortune in immortal lamentations.

Yet Athens in its ruins exercised such influence that no Roman was considered educated if he had not studied in Athens. It was part of the making of the Roman nobility of mind and of the sword to have sojourned in Athens. Here in Athens men like Cicero, Ovid, Horace, and Virgil received their greatest inspirations. Statesmen and political leaders like Caesar, Antony, Pompey, and Augustus paid their homage to the beauty of Greece. As today every Christian nation has a national sanctuary in Jerusalem or Rome, so every nation of ancient times considered it an honour to erect and endow some monument, some temple or statue or colonnade in Athens.

As Paul walked up from Peiraeus to Athens, he passed the graves of many famous men, and all the while above him he had a view of the miracle of the Acropolis. Entering the city

through the double door, the Dipylon, he now stood on the soil
of Athens. He walked down the Dromos, the great colonnaded
avenue, to the Cerameicos, the market place, and inquired for
the Jewish quarter, where he found shelter with a fellow Jew.
He had seen many beautiful cities, but the overwhelming riches
and beauty of this city must have confused him. Perhaps he felt
somewhat as Peter did, when that simple man beheld the Rome
of the Caesars for the first time.

He felt lonely and forsaken in the midst of this cold, soul-
less heap, of marble which spoke of the downfall of paganism.
Perhaps he felt as we would feel if we were transported and left
alone in a city like Mecca or Benares. He had no one to whom
he could open his soul. His thoughts were with his beloved
Thessalonians. He says somewhat pathetically: "I remained at
Athens alone." Therefore he told his companions before they
went back to Thessalonica, "Tell Silas and Timothy that they
should come with all speed."

For days Paul wandered about the city to study the
character of these remarkable people. He had never seen a city
of pure Greek culture before. This was not the most favourable
moment in Greece's history. Athens was no longer the city of
Pericles and Plato, and not even the city of Hadrian. With the
exception of Plutarch and Ammonius of Alexandria, it had no
outstanding personality. The city seemed to be at a standstill in
its history, as if it had paused to hear what this messenger of a
strange God had to say.

On one of his first days in Athens, Paul climbed the hill
to the citadel which was formerly the residence of the kings but
which was now relinquished to the gods. What he saw there
was the most perfect reflection of the zenith of classical art.
The Acropolis still stood above the city like a royal diadem,
and the most beautiful jewel in that crown was the Parthenon,
the temple of Pallas Athena with the gold and ivory statue of
the virgin goddess sculptured by the great Phidias. For the
Greeks, Pallas Athena was a divine revelation because she

sprang full-armed from the head of Zeus. She was considered the highest incorporation of divine wisdom, a pure and radiant apparition high above the more sensuous cults of Aphrodite and Dionysus. Perhaps Paul also stopped to gaze on that other Athena who sat deep in thought as if meditating on the future of Greece. It would have been a significant meeting. The artist pictured what Homer had said centuries ago, that Athena was the personification of divine guidance inasmuch as she watched over young Telemachus, preserved Odysseus in the greatest dangers, and tamed Achilles' anger when he had already drawn his sword to run Agamemnon through.

A few steps farther brought Paul to the Erechtheum. There that sacred olive tree still flourished which was said to have sprung forth at the goddess' command. A lamp fed by the purest olive oil burned day and night before the shrine of the divine benefactress. Here, too, Paul saw that the Athenians had erected an altar to Sympathy, because of some obscure longing in their darkened minds for the great mercy of the redemption. The altar to Sympathy was erected at a time when the Greeks were a nation of free men. Now they had succumbed to a slavish spirit that prompted them to pay extravagant honours to their Roman masters. If Paul went a few steps farther, he would have found the temple erected to the genius of Rome and Augustus. Since the days of Caesar and Mark Antony, the apotheosis of the emperors had become a national religion in Greece. As once they had erected an altar to Sympathy, so now they might have erected one to flattery and sycophancy.

Scarcely eighty years after Paul's day, Hadrian would come to Athens for the dedication of the temple he had rebuilt in honour of Zeus Olympus, and on that occasion he himself would receive the honours of Panhellenius and Soter. He became an Olympian god and his wife Sabina was worshiped as the goddess Demeter. When a people is enslaved it knows no other way to honour its masters than by their apotheosis. Here is a classical instance of how the enslavement of man and the

worship of man go together, while the worship of God makes
man free. And yet Athens had not fallen as low as Corinth and
other cities which as Roman colonies had introduced the bloody
gladiatorial games. When Athens, in the second century,
wished to follow Corinth's example, Demonax, the philosopher,
arose and cried: "Then, first destroy the altar to Sympathy"
(Lucian).

As he came down from the Acropolis, Paul passed
through the propylaea, those magnificent examples of classical
architecture. All this beauty and elegance was made to serve
the ideal of the fatherland. Every four years the great national
feast of the Panathenaea was celebrated here with elaborate
musical, declamatory and dramatic performances. The feast
culminated in the ascent of the people to the shrine of Pallas
Athena. Then a young woman offered a rich saffron robe to the
goddess and received from her hand the laurel wreath. That
feast was celebrated for six hundred years, during which time
the Parthenon remained dedicated to the virginal goddess, until
it entered the service of the virginal Mother of God.

Only the crudest barbarian would be able to stand unmoved before these monuments so redolent of humanity. Paul
paused on his way at the temple to Nike. Here he had a view of
the beautiful landscape of Attica. Even today it is a view that
fills the soul with satisfaction. In the blue distance he could see
the cupola-like heights of Acrocorinth across the Saronic bay,
and below lay the city of Corinth: the scene of his greatest joys
and his most poignant sorrows.

Farther down the hill he passed Socrates' prison, that
noblest of all Greeks who had conversed about immortality as
he waited for the return of the sacred ship from Delphi. Once
the Delphic oracle had called him the wisest of all men because
he knew the limits of his knowledge, because he knew his own
ignorance, that *docta ignorantia* which Nicholas of Cusa
praised as a form of humility. During the seventy years of his
life, Socrates turned his mind more and more to that Being who

is all spirit and power and goodness. He had silently become a member of the invisible Church which receives into her bosom all those who sincerely seek the truth and who cannot belong to the visible Church of Christ, which Paul had come to establish now on Grecian soil. Socrates was proud to call himself the slave of that perfect, invisible Being, from whom he derived courage in that terrible hour when he felt the poison rising to his heart.

Socrates' attitude in the face of death was something new for paganism. It was a kind of prelude to Christianity. We do not know, of course, whether Paul was conscious of these things as he went by Socrates' death cell, but there is an objective intellectual relationship between Socrates and Paul. From Pythagoras a great tradition of thought goes through Socrates, Plato, Aristotle, and Cleanthes to Paul. They were all seeking, as Plato once said, that certain knowledge whose properties are: "one and the same species in all places, complete and whole, unity with relation to all, through all, and over all properties – catholic." Thus it was Plato and Aristotle *(Eth. Nic.,* 2, 7) after him who for the first time coined the word "catholic." These words of Plato seem to adumbrate the famous definition of St. Vincent of Lerins: *Quod semper, quod ubique, quod ab omnibus.*

But besides these consoling reflections which seemed to tell of a believing past were others not so encouraging. Athens was filled with temples, altars, statues, colonnades, pictures, some simple, some coloured, made of wood, bronze, marble, gold, silver, and ivory. Every time he left his lodgings, he did not go into the street but he entered a temple. According to Petronius, it was easier to meet a god than a man in Athens. We are accustomed to believe that before Christ came, Jerusalem was the religious capital of the world. But that was true only in the sense that Jerusalem contained the seed of the religion of the future. For the people of the time, Jerusalem was about as significant as Mecca is for us today. The real religious capital of the world was Athens, just as it was the artistic and cultural centre. The sight of these innumerable altars and shrines was unbearable to a man with Paul's monotheistic and biblical training. The Acts of the Apostles says that "his spirit was stirred within him" at what he saw.

Renan, in his life of St. Paul, accuses Paul of being blind to the beauty around him because of his Jewish iconoclastic prejudices. In his French dramatic pathos he cries out: "Tremble, you beautiful and chaste images of the true gods and goddesses, for there stands the man who will swing the hammer against you. He will say the fateful word, 'You are idols,' and the error of this ugly, little Jew will be your death sentence." Paul did not, of course, hurry from statue to statue, to drink in its beauty. There are times when we cannot be concerned about beauty for beauty's sake and art for art's sake. Such was the moment when Jesus stood before the marble magnificence of the Temple and said, "There shall not be left here a stone upon a stone that shall not be destroyed." Such was also the moment when Paul saw the flashes of God's anger over the ancient world.

The Greek loved the pleasures of sense; he worshipped the pleasing lines of the human form. But Paul was looking for the soul, and ancient art had no concept of the soul. In the primitive art of the catacombs the God-loving soul opened its eyes, and therefore that art is not decadent but the beginning of a new art. If pagan art had not decayed, perhaps no Christian art would have been born to give the soul a chance to speak. Then we would not have had a Giotto and a Fra Angelico. Now we know why Paul felt so lonely in this city without a soul. Tired and exhausted by the impact of so many hostile impressions, he fell on the cot of his poor lodgings in a prayerful dialogue with Christ.

CHAPTER THIRTY

"THE UNKNOWN GOD"

"Now while Paul waited for there at Athens, his spirit was stirred within him, seeing the city wholly given to idolatry" (Acts 17:16).

Paul had been in Athens for some time. Following his old custom, he went first to his fellow Jews, who were numerous in Athens at that time. On the first few Sabbaths he went to the synagogue and talked to the Jews and those who were God-fearing. He seems, however, to have had little success, probably because the Jews in Athens had been secularized by the culture of Athens and neglected the synagogue services. He had to turn, therefore, to the pagans. He knew he would have to study the religious views of the philosophers. Day after day he strolled through the city, looking for an opportunity to talk to some one about the message that burned in his heart.

The more he saw of Athens, the more that first exalted impression of the Acropolis receded and was replaced by the picture of Athens' religious degeneration. Once walking through a street, he stopped suddenly before an altar with the inscription: "To some unknown god." We know from several sources that at that time, in Athens as well as in other places such as Pergamum, altars were erected to some indefinite, unknown god. Down near the port of Phalerum was another such altar, on which, according to St. Jerome, the inscription was, "*Diis Asiae et Europiae et Africae, diis ignotis et pere-grinis.*"[22] The Greeks wished to pay honour to any gods besides their own native gods and they wished to forestall any interference by these unknown deities. They tried to mention the name of every god, but the unknown gods also had to be propitiated. Paul read the inscription in another sense, as an agnostic expression, something like, "Who is God? Who can know him?"

In a sense Paul rightly read the Greek mind, for since the time of Socrates and the Orphics, the Greeks became more and more convinced that the well-known popular gods were only partial expressions for some great, unknown, nameless Being. Plato had proved the existence of this great Unknown from the inner experiences of the spirit. Aristotle had demonstrated Him from the external world. But they were succeeded by the Academy with its passion for scepticism, and the Unknown receded again into the clouds. Since, now, the God of revelation was nameless for the pagans, and his name was not to be spoken by the Jews, Paul took this indefinite inscription as the expression of a longing for something higher and better– as a groping in the dark for the true God. Paul was no student of comparative theology. He heard the cry of proud Greece for the hidden God, the *Deus absconditus,* just as he had heard the Macedonian's cry at Troas.

Athens was the centre for Greek mythology, that elaborate fiction of mind and imagination which so greatly influenced the culture of the world, that classic story of the history of the gods. The underlying thought of Greek mythology was that the universe was one great unity, comprising a hierarchy of personal powers, all of which sprang from the head of Zeus, the father and chief of all the gods. Man, too, in some way came from the seed of the gods. Man, too, had a divine origin. When a great man died, he joined the ranks of the gods and became an

---

[22] *In Tit.,* I, 12

example and inspiration for other men. The masses accepted all this teaching about the gods in a literal sense, but the philosophers knew that these gods were poetic expressions, symbols, various aspects and attributes of one Deity.

That ancient faith of the Greeks had deteriorated at the time when Paul came to Athens. Aristotle, who represents the highest point in Greek thought, was not fortunate enough to have a worthy disciple to carry on after him, until St. Thomas Aquinas came. And so his spiritual bequest to his people was wasted away by mediocre men. The Sophists threw religion aside and thought to see the divine origin of all things in the interplay of atoms or in the inevitable force of natural law. The old ideals and models now became empty forms, abstract concepts of virtue and vice. The old Greek spirit drooped its wings and was no longer able to rise again.

Paul found no one of Plato's or Aristotle's stature. He merely heard the meaningless repetition of their sayings. With few exceptions, all of Greece's philosophers tottered about, leaning on the beggar's staff. The Stoics and the Epicureans mentioned in the Acts had themselves become that derisive thing, "word sowers." Deftly they draped the philosopher's cloak about their shoulders, but the prophet was not to be found under the cloak. Strangers coming to Athens were shown the academy of Plato. Or the plane trees in the valley of Ilyssos where Socrates had reclined with his followers, or Aristotle's lyceum, the Stoa of Zeno, and the garden of Epicurus. They liked to promenade in the agora, carrying little canes, their hands washed in perfumed water. Here in the government buildings, in the bazaars and temples, they stopped to talk with their acquaintances and exchange some literary saying. They heard the news about any new mode in philosophy or politics or religion.

Everywhere Paul received the same impression; the ancient culture of the Greeks was completely emptied of all its former worth. Now religion served only to glorify this earthly life. It was the canonization of patriotism. For a man like Paul, all of whose old ideals had gone down to ruin and who now saw but one essential thing, the sweating dock worker was far more interesting than Zeus on high Olympus. A little prayer-meeting made up of slaves, sailors, and workmen, was more important than a whole university of professors. You may call it fanaticism; but, then, Jesus also was a fanatic. Or has there ever been a great radical in thought or action who did not view the manifold details of life from one exclusive viewpoint? Jesus had but one thought, to which he related everything else: the "one thing necessary." For St. Francis of Assisi it was to follow Jesus in poverty and humility; for Ignatius Loyola it was loyalty to Jesus, the royal captain. Paul was also a man of one thought: the new man, the new life in Christ. It is no wonder that this purely pagan environment made him uncomfortable.

At last Timothy and Silas arrived from Beroea with good news about the Church there. Paul was encouraged again, and began to visit the agora, trying to engage men in a conversation about religion. The agora was the social and scientific centre of Athens. When Paul went there, he immediately attracted attention because of his external appearance. His threadbare cloak that made him look like one of the Cynic wandering preachers, and his alien nasal twang about which the people of Tarsus were frequently derided.

Young philosophy students went back to tell their teachers about the new arrival and his quaint philosophy, which seemed not to fit in any of the known schools. His little speeches, they said, were a topsy-turvy of Oriental nonsense. Some Attic wit nicknamed him the "word sower," a man who gathers unrelated things together into a speech. But somehow the fellow was interesting, and some believed he really was "a setter forth of new gods." This expression requires explanation. According to Plato, the Stoics, the Cynics, Seneca, and Epictetus, the highest type of man is that which has a deeper and more sacred knowledge of the gods. These men are the messengers of Zeus on some special mission to the rest of men. Examples of this type were Pythagoras, Empedocles, Socrates, and Chrysippos. Beside the genuine examples of *theioi,* imitations were found, such as those charlatans and magicians after whom the people always ran. Paul had met such an impostor at the court of the Governor Sergius. Both in the Orient and in Greece men seemed to be impressed by the thought that something divine was to be found in certain men. Such "divine" men appeared occasionally in Greece and Asia Minor. They practised voluntary poverty, they renounced earthly comforts and possessions. All of which impressed the Stoics and the Cynics as special signs of close relationship to the gods.

When Paul went to the agora he must have made an unusual appearance to be taken as one of these "divine" men, and as a "setter forth of new gods." He probably made no objection when they understood that he was preaching a new religion. His hearers got very little from his address; they caught up a few words and phrases:

Jesus and Anastasis. Soon they thought they had grasped the whole of the new teaching. This religion of Paul's announced a new divine couple, a male and female divinity, Jesus and Anastasis. They had no inkling that this prattle would some day obliterate their philosophy and overturn their chairs of learning. But it took four and a half centuries until in 529 Emperor Justinian closed the school of philosophy in Athens by one stroke of the pen.

Because of this curious misunderstanding Paul was invited to appear before the Areopagus, the most learned and venerable senate of Athens. The Areopagus was a conservative association of noblemen. It was the classical tribunal for all questions in religion, morality, culture, and education, and its authority was recognized the world over. The old men making up the tribunal were surrounded by traditions and legends of the greatest antiquity. At this time the Areopagus met in the royal hall of the Stoa where Demosthenes had made his speeches. Here it

was that Paul, before a large audience, consisting of the great
lights of Athens, professors and students, delivered his trial
lecture. It was in no way a judicial procedure. The Apostle was
not speaking as if accused, he was merely giving information
about his teaching to the city's highest board of education. The
fact that Cicero asked the Areopagus to call the philosopher
Cratippus indicates that the tribunal exercised some state
control.

Paul was no cultural barbarian. He was not an iconoclast.
But his ideal was higher than the artistic ideal of beauty. His
ideal was the beauty of the soul. He desired to form Christians
out of living men, to make warm-hearted men out of cold
egotists, to form Christ in men's souls. In place of that beautiful
myth of Pallas Athena coming from the head of Zeus, he wished
to tell about the reality of the eternal Logos, the incarnate
wisdom of God. His was a far higher art than chiselling lifeless
statues out of cold marble.

CHAPTER THIRTY-ONE

THE AREOPAGUS

"But Paul, standing in the midst of the Areopagus, said: You men of Athens, I perceive that in all things you are too superstitious" (Acts 17:22).

Four hundred years before, the same eternal stars of Hellas were shining above this same tribunal while the wisest of all the Greeks stood there. Socrates, the most religious thinker of Greece, was defending himself against the charge of godlessness and of introducing new gods, because he had hearkened to the voice of God within him and had taught his disciples in this manner. Though the verdict against Socrates was most unjust, we must admire the earnestness with which those judges watched over the traditions of the past.

Paul was now standing before the weak successors of those great thinkers. He was talking to a frivolous generation for whom religion was no longer a serious thing but merely an interesting topic of light conversation.

Until now Paul had always stood on ground that was somewhat prepared when he talked to Jews or proselytes. Here in Athens there was a complete change of stage and scenery. He was standing now on purely pagan ground. Therefore he changed his accustomed technique. His address makes us conscious of the pagan atmosphere. He had to find another starting point to lead up to Christ. When talking to the Jews, he had always appealed to the word of God. Now, talking to the pagans, he appealed to God's work in nature. When speaking to the Jews, he referred to divine revelation as found in the story of salvation. Here, with the pagans, he referred to God's revelation in man's consciousness, to that inner longing for God expressed in the desire for religion.

He found no common ground where he could meet the philosophers. There was no inner relationship between the ideas of Christianity and the concepts of paganism. He found only a remote resemblance inasmuch as the human soul naturally adapts itself to Christianity and every soul feels some need for salvation.

Paul did not find any schools of Platonic or Aristotelian thought in Athens, although some of their ideas continued in some form in other philosophical schools. His hearers on the Areopagus belonged to one of two schools: the Stoics and the Epicureans.

He began his address with a play on words. The word *deisidaimonesteros* originally, at least in the days of Xenophon and Aristotle, meant someone who feared God. But now it had taken on another meaning: someone who was superstitious and feared the demons. Thus the Greek's passion for the miraculous and the divine is expressed in this term, which could be taken to mean normal religious piety or an abnormal superstition. His hearers accepted the word as meaning the normal religious feeling, as Paul intended they should. It was a word of conciliation and enlisted his hearers' sympathy. They were still more attentive when he proposed to solve a difficulty for them: the puzzle about the unknown god.

"You say that I set forth new gods among you. On the contrary, while I was going about your city I found an altar dedicated to an unknown god, and therefore you seem to be worshipping something that you do not know. In a way you are right, for this unknown god and the true hidden God, whom I announce to you, have this in common, that they are both surrounded by mystery.

"But this mysterious God ought not to he unknown to you for he has shown himself to you by his creation, in nature, the heavens and the earth. All of which are the work of his hands. I need not prove to you the existence of the highest God, because you know this as citizens of the city that produced Plato. You know that there is a God infinitely superior to those poor gods on Olympus. You enclose these gods in the rooms of your temple, but the true God is the Lord of the earth. He fills the universe and cannot be shut up in temples made with hands.

"You surround your gods with many servants, you give them food, you invite them to a sacrificial meal, you pour out good wines for them as if they needed these things. But God does not need our gifts; we need his gifts. He gives us food and drink, our life, our breath. You say that the gods live above us in blessed quietude and do not care about men who are only atoms accidentally thrown together in this universe. No. God takes pleasure in his handiwork and he does not despise what he has made. He has a plan for mankind. The whole human race came from one man and spread over the earth. He is not the God of one people like Zeus or Pallas Athena who love the Greeks alone. He has placed the spark of his spirit in every man and commanded every man to seek him. Thus all men are seekers after God, but especially you Greeks.

"Your great men, Homer, Pythagoras, and Pindar sought him in mysterious myths. Your artists sought him in the eternal laws of beauty; Plato and Aristotle sought him by philosophic thought. Your mystagogues are seeking him now in mystery cults, your officials are seeking him in the person of the Emperor or the genius of Rome. You go too far afield to find him; he is easy to find. Enter within yourselves. God is in us and we are in him. Did not one of your poets, Epimenides, say: 'In him we live, and move, and are? That is why he is so close to us, that is why He is so easy to know.'"

Paul went on to explain their natural desire to know God. He recalled a phrase from the poet's hymn to Zeus, "For we are also his offspring." God not only made us, but he is also the model of our being. The artist is not less than his product. If we are sparks of God's spirit, we can partake in his life. Paul did not yet speak the name of him through whom this participation is to take place, although that name burned his lips.

As long as Paul talked about philosophical matters, his audience followed him attentively. They recalled having read something like this in Plato's works. These ideas were not objectionable to the Stoics, although they preferred to lose themselves in pantheistic speculations. Nor were the Epicureans disaffected, because they had come to have a certain Platonic tendency. But all that Paul had said was the bait to lead them on to the real theme. Now the charm was to be broken. He spoke but a few more sentences, but into them he put the quintessence of his sermon to the pagans. Four thoughts, he enunciated and they were unpalatable to his proud hearers.

He chides the Greeks for their religious backwardness; he speaks of their ignorance. "These puerile religious ideas that are popular around the country are fit for children. We are beyond that now. God was patient with that infantile thinking, but now the time for groping and uncertainty is over." The people were becoming restless. This was unheard of. This barbarian telling the most cultured people of the world that they are ignorant children.

Paul went on calmly. "God has come forth from his obscurity and he demands that every man make a decision. Will he go on in his uncertain groping, will he continue in this emotional longing for redemption, or will he change and acknowledge the reality of God's existence and of the redemption in the God-man." What was this? A change of heart? Or, did he mean something like contrition?

Paul was not unaware of the growing unrest, but he went on. "God has taken a hand in man's destiny, by the man whom

he has appointed, who will judge the world in equity."
'Judgment of the world?" This was too much.

Paul heard their outcries, but he still went on, now all
afire. "Yes, you Athenians, what I am saying is the truth. I who
stand before you, I saw that man appointed by God. His own
people persecuted him, and condemned him to a painful death,
just as your ancestors condemned the noble Socrates. But God
confirmed his mission by 'raising him up from the dead'. "

Now he had spoken the fateful words: crucifixion and
resurrection. They had come out of his mouth bluntly. Someone laughed in the crowd, and when men laughed Paul could
not go on. He stopped without speaking the name of Jesus. He
could not expose that sacred name to the ridicule of these fools.
It was a painful situation for the president of the assembly and
the other philosophers. They concealed their disillusionment
with polite phrases: "It was very interesting. We will hear you
again concerning this matter."

Paul knew he had failed. "So he went out from among
them," saddened and disillusioned. More to himself than to
Timothy, he said: "I have made a sorry failure of it. Had I only
kept quiet about the resurrection and told the story of Jesus
first. I have had enough of these educated people. It is better
that I go to the simple working classes. In the future I will not
talk about the wisdom of the Greeks. I will talk only about
Christ and the foolishness of the Cross."

As Paul went back to his lodgings, he noticed that some
people were following him. Turning around he saw a dignified,
friendly man who introduced himself as Dionysius, a member
of the Areopagus. He saw also a woman whose penetrating
gaze pierced her heavy black veil. It was Damaris. There were
others; not many, but they formed his little congregation in
Athens. "Areopagite," was a title that was sought after and
respected throughout the ancient world. Many legends have
formed themselves about the person of Dionysius, and the
greatest theologian of the sixth century hid himself under that

name. No doubt, Dionysius became the pillar of the Athenian Church and perhaps he was its first bishop. While the Sophists stood about on the steps of the Areopagus, ridiculing this unusual Jew from Tarsus, Paul sat with his new disciples in his lodgings and talked long into the night about Jesus.

Some have attacked the genuineness of Paul's address on the Areopagus, because the ancient historical writer generally invented such an address from his own reaction to the situation in which his hero was placed. But the fact that Paul's speech was a failure is, in a way, a proof to the contrary. If the speech were invented, it would probably have been successful. Ernst Curtius, one of the greatest students of antiquity, said that whoever attacks the reliability of this report about Paul tears one of the most important pages from the history of mankind. And Gregorovius said: "In all the history of Athens, no event was more remarkable than the appearance of Paul. In all the annals of the Christian missions no action was more daring than Paul's sermon in Athens, the Acropolis of paganism, surrounded by all the brilliance of its arts and literature. From the meagre report in the Acts we can guess what the inspired Apostle told the philosophers of Athens: that this beautiful Hellenic world was going down to inescapable death because it was too narrow and loveless. Because it rested on the privileges of one race and the slavery of the barbarian races." Who would have thought then that this new religion announced by Paul in Athens would be the one palladium to which the Greeks would owe the preservation of their nation, their literature, and their language?

When Paul went to rest that night in his poor lodgings, what disturbing pictures raced across his mind? Perhaps he was in a mood like that of Elias when the prophet sat beneath the juniper tree and prayed, "It is enough for me, Lord, take away my soul." Perhaps some figure rose beyond the Saronic Gulf and stood on Acrocorinth, saying: "You have still a far way to go, Paul."

He was not able to found a large Church at Athens. He

never referred to the Church at Athens in his letters. He wrote no Epistle to the Athenians, and on his third missionary journey he did not stop at Athens. Even in the second century the Church at Athens was not flourishing. Athens was one of the last cities to be converted. It was one of the last bulwarks of pagan philosophy against Christianity. The same year, 529, that St. Benedict transformed the ruins of Apollo's temple on Monte Cassino into a monastery the last seven Athenian philosophers, expelled by an edict of Justinian, wandered out of Athens to Persia to find refuge at the court of King Chosroes.

CHAPTER THIRTY-TWO

THE CHURCH AT CORINTH

"After these things, departing from Athens, he came to Corinth" (Acts 18:1).

Paul never felt at home in Athens. He was too much an Asiatic. He felt that this proud cultured spirit of Athens could never harbour the universal spirit of Christianity. Often his thoughts turned to his beloved Churches in Macedonia. Again and again he was at the point of returning there. The last picture of Thessalonica in his mind was that of an infuriated mob set upon him by the Jews. Since he left he had received only fragmentary news about the trials suffered by the Church at Thessalonica. He had to have some news from Thessalonica and he wished to send them his message of encouragement. He was willing to make the sacrifice of the company of his dearest friend in order to settle this uncertainty about his children.

Therefore, before he left Athens, he sent Timothy by the first ship to Thessalonica, and went alone to Corinth. Paul went purposely into the large cities, knowing that here the great intellectual battles are fought. "Whoever controls Corinth, controls Greece." If the knowledge of Jesus would but reach the port of Corinth, it would be only a matter of time until all the islands roundabout would hear of him. In Corinth, he knew, he would find a cosmopolitan population without that cramping national pride of Athens. Every opinion had a right to be heard in Corinth, and in such soil the seed of the gospel would easily take root.

We do not know whether Paul travelled the forty-mile highway through Eleusis and Megara, or the shorter way by sea to the harbour of Cenchrae which would have taken him between the islands of Salamis and Aigina to the Isthmus itself. Here the sea is like a mountain lake, hemmed in by high rock walls. To the left he saw the mountains of Aigina crowned by the sanctuary of Aphaia. On the right were the heights of Salamis, the steep cliffs of Megara, and the pine-covered hills of Argolis. As he sailed on to Corinth he had time to collect his thoughts. Never before had he realized how great an obstacle the false wisdom of the world is in the renewal of mankind. In the Epistle to the Romans, which Paul wrote some years later from Corinth, he warned his readers against that attitude of Greek philosophy which keeps men away from the truth: "They became vain in their thoughts. And their foolish heart was darkened. For, professing to be wise, they became fools" (Rom. 1:21).

The Acropolis was receding in the distance, and another picture moved into focus. At first he saw it only vaguely in the bluish misty distance, but gradually it took clearer form, the high mountain that ranged up behind the city of Corinth. From Cenchrae, Corinth's eastern port, Paul walked through meadows. Then the pine woods of Poseidon, the pleasant valley of Hexamilia, and after a gentle rise the city itself. Paul stopped after the three-hour walk to look about himself. It was a magnificent view: the purplish waters of two seas, one on either side. Corinth enjoyed an unusual site, between two gulfs, the Isthmian and the Corinthian.

Paul crossed the bridge over the Leuka river into the suburb of Kraneion. Here he passed the monument to Diogenes, who would have been glad to blow out his lantern if he had met Paul. Perhaps no two cities differed as much from each other as Corinth and Athens. The latter was like a medieval university

city, resounding with the song and noise of students. Corinth
was like a busy anthill or beehive, full of colourful peoples of
every land. Corinth's hegemony over Greece was now only a
memory. In 146 B.C. the Roman general Mummius had laid
the place in ruins.

But that excellent site between two seas, on the bridge
from the East to the West, the key position for the Peloponnesus,
could not remain unoccupied. A hundred years before, Caesar
had settled a colony of Roman veterans and freedmen on the
ruins of the ancient city. Thus, under the protection of the
Roman eagle, an ancient Port Said was established. A slide was
built over the Isthmus so that the smaller ships could be taken
over the land to avoid the long trip around the Peloponnesus.

Now the old Roman colonists were disappearing before
the increasing number of Greeks, Africans, Syrians, and Jews
who settled in Corinth. The old culture and civilization of
Greece was gone. Instead, the Syrian Levant brought the shameful practices of its Astarte and Melkart cults, Rome brought its
brutality and the bloody games of the arena, the Phrygians
brought their worship of Attis and Cybele, the Egyptians brought
their strange cult of Isis and Serapis, and from Thrace came the
mysteries of Dionysus. Once Corinth had been the city of
Poseidon with his dolphin and trident, but now it was dedicated
to Aphrodite Pandemos, a degenerate Astarte.

Aphrodite's temple was erected on Acrocorinth. About the
temple thousands of prostitutes lived in quaint little houses behind
rose gardens where they robbed foreigners, tourists, soldiers,
sailors, merchants, and officers, of their health and money and
spread the Corinthian disease over the whole Empire. Their
symbol was the statue of Lais, the most famous temple slave, in
the form of a lioness tearing its victim apart with its claws. Like
the Vestals in Rome, these Corinthian hierodules were given
special places in the theatre, according to an ancient inscription.

"Corinthian girl" seemed to be synonymous with
"prostitute." The Corinthian drunkard and *bon vivant* were the

accepted comic figures of the stage. Down below in both harbours the scum of the seafaring world gathered in the sailors' taverns and public houses. When Paul wrote his Epistle to the Romans here in Corinth and described the desolate picture of paganism, he must have had this city in mind. Yet he loved Corinth more than Athens, because the worst obstacle that stands in the way of the gospel is not the weakness of sinful flesh but the pride of the spirit. "And where sin abounded, grace did more abound" (Rom. 5:20).

From the First Epistle to the Corinthians we learn that Paul was discouraged and depressed when he came to Corinth. The failure at Athens was like a thorn in his side. Like all men, Paul was dependent on temperament and moods. Even the Son of God, in his human nature, was subject to feelings of depression and exaltation. Since Paul had found this new life in Christ he was the happiest of all men. Even in prison he was able to sing psalms and hymns, but at intervals, like all the saints, he was cast down into deep depression.

No one, seeing this stranger trudging down the street in the Jewish quarter, would have surmised that in ages to come the historical significance of this city would be bound up with the fact that this poor tentmaker had come to Corinth. Nor did Aquila and Priscilla, realize that their meeting with Paul, here in Corinth, meant that their names would be recorded in the annals of the Church, or in the book of life for that matter. Paul met Aquila and Priscilla while he was looking for lodging and employment. With customary oriental hospitality, Aquila opened the door for Paul, bade him enter and introduced him to Prisca, his wife. They considered it an honour to give shelter to a teacher of the law. This was the beginning of one of the most fruitful and beautiful friendships in the early Church.

This new friendship was a blessing for Paul in many ways. For one thing, it directed his eyes toward the West and to Rome. His hosts had led an unusually adventurous and active life. Aquila was born in Pontus on the Black Sea; he went to

Rome where he established himself as a tentmaker. There he probably came to know his wife. Paul prefers to call her Prisca, while Luke calls her Priscilla. Her name appears in the mausoleum of the Gens Acilia in the catacombs of St. Priscilla, indicating that Priscilla was probably a freed woman of that noble family. Ramsay, however, thinks that Priscilla was of nobler status than her husband, and that she was a highly respected Roman and a proselyte when she married Aquila the prosperous Jewish merchant. Both Aquila and Priscilla seem to have enjoyed more than the usual education as is indicated by their close relationship to Paul and the learned Apollo.

Priscilla was evidently the moving spirit in the family. In four out of six instances her name comes before Aquila's. She became one of the greatest female figures of the early Church, and none of the women who supported Paul in his missionary endeavours received such high praise as she (Rom. 16:3).

In the evenings when his work at the loom was done, Paul made Aquila and Priscilla tell him about Rome. They told him their story. Only a short while before, they had been forced to leave Rome by a decree of the Emperor Claudius, occasioned by a pogrom which had broken out in the ghetto in Rome, instigated, Suetonius says, by a certain Chrestos. The wanderings of Aquila and Priscilla indicate how unsettled was the condition of the Jews of the Diaspora at that time. Some time after this we shall meet them in Ephesus, then again in Rome, and finally in Ephesus again. Wandering about from place to place, they were obviously unable to come by much of this world's goods, although during their second stay at Rome they seem to have been in better circumstances, since they were able to donate their house on the Aventine for the use of the brethren.

Besides being bound to Aquila by this Christian friendship, Paul was united to him by their common trade at the loom and by their common labours for the kingdom of God. Aquila's workshop, like most others, was a room that opened on the street of the carpet bazaars. Here Paul sat day after day with his hosts weaving into the woof and warp of the loom thoughts that were divine. Sometimes, with tent-cloth folded on his knee and needle poised in the air, Paul told the apprentices and visitors about all those things that burned in his soul. If Cicero had been present at some of these sacred discussions he would have changed his opinion that no man could be an intelligent being in a workshop.

According to our view of manual labour today, we might be inclined to think that Paul's unselfish manner of life would have gained an easier entrance for the gospel into men's hearts. But in ancient times, and here at Corinth as well, the old aristocratic notion still held sway and denied all labourers, including even sculptors and artists, the rights of citizenship because this preoccupation with physical labour debased a man's psyche and dulled his appreciation for high ideals. Even Plutarch spoke with little regard for such artists as Phidias and Archilochos. At a time when manual labour imprinted a stigma of disgrace and social debasement on a man, Paul's example was something new. A long time was to pass before the Christian view of labour would gain the ascendancy.

Paul's sociological views were partly derived from his Jewish past. As Judaism had permitted slavery only in the mildest form, so it had surrounded the worker with an atmosphere of respect. Paul's regard for the worker was also based on the religious reason that every man is the temple of the Holy Spirit and has a spiritual, supernatural relationship with Christ. "He who despises a brother, despises not a man, but God."

Corinth had a large and wealthy Jewish colony which had recently received an addition on account of the troubles in Rome. In excavations at Corinth an inscription has been unearthed which may have been placed over a synagogue, probably the successor to the one in which Paul preached. Here he found not only strict Jews, but also some Jewish Christians who had been expelled from Rome, and some pagan Greeks who had fled the vices of the city to find refuge in the holy religion of Israel.

Still remembering his failure in Athens, Paul was

somewhat reserved at first in this pagan milieu. In his early addresses he sought to prepare the ground by developing from the prophets the idea of a suffering redeemer and then casually mentioning the name of Jesus. Like a builder, he carefully tested how much the foundations would bear, "as a wise architect, I have laid the foundation" (1 Cor. 3:10).

One day the loom was quiet. Silas and Timothy had come from Macedonia, bringing good news and an offering of money. We know who contributed the greater part: Jason of Thessalonica and Lydia of Philippi. Paul was a man of vehement emotions. With all his soul he shared the fate of his Churches. He lived with them, suffered with them, he was mystically bound up with them. And now he was wonderfully revived and refreshed when the burden of uncertainty and care fell from him. Now his enthusiasm, his strength, and his courage knew no bounds. The renewal of his spirit was noticed on the next Sabbath when he preached in the synagogue. After the preparatory sermons, he went boldly on to the full gospel of Christ, speaking fearlessly of the Crucifixion and the Resurrection, and of the Messias who would come to judge the world.

After the synagogue services some important Jews came to his lodgings and began a course of instructions. Paul's first great success was Stephanas, a rich proselyte, who came over with his whole family. Paul liked to speak of Stephanas as the "first-fruits of Achaia" (1 Cor. 16:15). By that expression Paul meant that this congregation in the capital city had the obligation of spreading the gospel of Christ throughout the whole country of Achaia, for he expected a great harvest now in this province.

Two other important men, Fortunatus and Achaicus, soon followed Stephanas' example. Paul made an exception here, and he himself baptized these men. It must have been a solemn occasion when Paul, together with Silas, Timothy, Aquila, Priscilla, and the baptismal candidates stood on the bank of the Leuka river to begin the sacred ceremonies. There beneath the pine trees, Paul made an address, the candidates made a profession of faith, psalms were sung, and lastly the sacrament was conferred. The next convert was Titus Justus, who owned the large house next to the synagogue. Titus was a member of the Roman colony, a *colonus*, and through him Paul made contact with the upper Roman class. Titus may have been a member of the famous pottery family whose ceramic products were famous throughout the world.

By this time the jealousy of the synagogue was awakened. The rich Jewish merchants and financiers had too much national pride to permit this upstart to disturb the religious peace with such compromising statements as that all the hopes and the thousand-year-old privileges of their nation ended in a Messias who had died shamefully on the Cross. On the next Sabbath the storm broke lose. It was a repetition of the scenes that had taken place in Pisidian Antioch and in Thessalonica. Paul stood unmoved on the platform. When his opponents had shouted themselves tired, he made a grand gesture which was not without its effect on those Oriental minds. He shook out the dust from his garments as if he were casting off all responsibility for them, and said: "Your blood be upon your own heads; I am clean. From henceforth I will go to the Gentiles" (Acts 18:6). It was a kind of excommunication, the first that Paul ever invoked, and by it he forestalled the ban of the synagogue.

Calmly, as once his Master had done before him, Paul strode with his friends through the threatening crowd. Outside Titus Justus stood in his path and offered him his house as a meeting place for the congregation. Paul accepted gladly. And now the division of minds, the schism of the Jewish congregation, had taken place. Some went back into the synagogue, some went with Paul into Titus' house next door. Some were still hesitant and came stealthily later on. But the separation had been made; the first Gentile Christian Church had been founded in Corinth.

CHAPTER THIRTY-THREE

MARANATHA!

Sunday was the busiest and most inspiring day for Paul at Corinth. Here in Corinth we have the first indication of the observance of the Christian Sunday (1 Cor. 16:2). The beginnings of the religious services in the early Church are shrouded in darkness, but Paul's account of the charismatic life of the Church in Corinth and the candour with which he assailed certain abuses lift the veil that hangs over this interesting feature of the life of the early Christians. Besides this, we have the account of the Sunday service in Troas, the indications in the Didache, written in the first generation after Paul, and a letter written by Pliny from Bithynia to Emperor Trajan about the beginning of the second century. The religious services developed slowly and thus we can attribute many details of a later time to the apostolic era.

According to Pliny's report, two kinds of services were to be distinguished on the *stato die,* i.e., Sunday. One was celebrated at daybreak, the other was observed later, perhaps during the evening of the same day. At the first service, a hymn to Christ as God was chanted, alternately by two choirs. At the second service the Christians ate two kinds of food, one the common food, the other an innocent food. A twofold meal seems to be indicated: the Christian *agape* and the Eucharistic sacrificial meal. We also hear that at the early service the Christians bound themselves by the *Sacramento* to a strict observance of Christian morality. It is not certain that this was the baptismal vows. Perhaps it was a public confession of sins, such as the Didache speaks of in the fourteenth chapter. "On the day of the Lord come together, break bread, and give thanks, after you have made known your faults." Whether these two services were held in Corinth in Paul's day, we do not know.

We need not go to the pagan services with their acclamations and litanies for the models of the Christian service: the synagogue service is entirely sufficient to serve as a model. In the synagogue there was a strictly determined order of prayers, chants, readings, and addresses. Paul probably restricted the readings to the Messianic texts of the prophets. Gradually certain narratives about Jesus, and some of his sayings and sermons came to take the central place in these readings. About this time, too, Paul started to imitate the custom of the Sanhedrin, which had its own couriers and letter service throughout the world. Paul began to write to his Churches in order to unite them closer to himself and to establish a bond between the Churches as well. These letters travelled from Church to Church. They were copied, read in the Sunday service, preserved in the archives of each Church, and soon came to be regarded as part of the Scriptures.

After the reading, Paul talked to the people. From the depth of his religious experiences, he brought forth this point and sometimes another. At first he limited himself to the most elementary questions of the Christian life. He avoided all vain oratorical polish and ornament. He had learned that these people were surfeited with philosophical and oratorical tricks. That they had to be shown the Cross in its fearful reality (1 Cor. 2:2). In Paul's mind the death of Christ was inseparable from his Resurrection, without which it was an incomplete work. He presented the Resurrection as an act of salvation, as the culmination of Christ's redemption. For Paul the Church was not the mere custodian of a historical truth; then the gospel of Christianity would be no more than a lesson in history. In his mind the acts of the redemption were a flaming portal through which we must all go with Christ into glory.

Because of the powerful personality that stood behind it, his unornamented speech radiated a compelling and attractive force on his hearers' minds. But when he was caught up by enthusiasm for Christ, he reached the greatest heights attained by human oratory. Recall his canticle on charity in the thirteenth chapter of the first Epistle to the Corinthians. He pictures the sublimation and glorification of the human heart in words whose equal cannot be found in all the pages of ancient literature.

Paul's services in Corinth must have been an inspiring and touching experience. His hearers must have felt the palpable presence of the Holy Spirit. Those things that occur only rarely in the lives of the saints today, were frequent experiences. Sudden illuminations of the mind, inspirations, ecstasies, the gift of prophecies, the discernment of hearts, the gift of tongues, and the healing of the sick. Mark concludes his Gospel with the remark that Jesus had promised his followers great signs and wonders.

The Corinthian religious services, therefore, were not stiff assemblies without the spirited participation of every individual. The Greeks were an unusually musical people with a highly developed sense for rhythm. For those joyous apostolic days Paul had offered a programme: "Speaking to yourselves in psalms and hymns and spiritual canticles, singing and making melody in your hearts to the Lord" (Eph. 5:19); he added "in your hearts" to prevent that purely aesthetic pleasure of the Greek. Paul speaks of a special gift of psalms and of hymns and canticles. By these he probably means those poetic effusions composed in special times of religious enthusiasm, like the Old Testament canticles. Except for the canticles recorded in the Gospels, the canticle of the Blessed Virgin, of Zachary, of Simeon, and of the Church at Jerusalem during Peter's imprisonment, we have only fragments in the Pauline Epistles (Eph. 5:14; 1 Tim. 3:16; 2 Tim. 2:11).

These songs, perhaps first composed and sung in the family circle, were gradually incorporated into the liturgy. We must not be surprised to find lyrical passages in the Gospels and Epistles, because the ancient orator and poet generally composed music for his words. The text was composed and recited with musical rhythm to the accompaniment of flutes, zithers, lyres, harps, and other stringed instruments. Ancient music was always the servant of the text. Even prose was presented in chant form, somewhat like our Gregorian chant. We have little understanding of the rhythmic sense of the Greek, a quality that was later adopted by Roman oratory. It may be recalled how Gracchus, when he made his political speeches, made use of the services of a flutist who occasionally gave him the proper pitch and even accompanied him during the more moving passages of the address.

Ancient writers, the pictures on reliefs and vases, tell us how important music was in the worship of the gods. Music was supposed to have the magic power to make the gods present and to disperse the demons. In the Christian view, however, music was to awaken and deepen religious feeling and devotion. For that reason Christ is so often pictured in the art of the catacombs as Orpheus. We may very well suppose, therefore, that the lyric passages in the Epistles and in the Gospels, as for instance our Lord's canticle to his Father at the Last Supper, were not recited in our present-day toneless manner, but somewhat like Gregorian chant. Augustine tells us that he was deeply moved, even to tears, by the chant of the Church in Milan. That could not have been a monotonous, toneless sound. In the early Church the choir was not a voluntary group of people such as we have in our churches today. It represented a definite personality: sometimes it sang for the Christian soul in love with God, sometimes it was the voice of Christ himself, sometimes it was the voice of Christ's bride, the Church. Men and women joined in the rhythm and cadence, but with a fullness of tone and melody, with a joyous outpouring of their souls. And the mystic tone of their praying and singing was all in accord with the grateful confidence that was reflected in their happy faces.

Nor was the Scripture reading like ours today. In ancient times man never read silently with his eyes alone. He always read aloud, that is, he observed the modulations, swells, changes of pitch and tempo, that so rejoiced the ancient world. For the Greek the spoken word was a powerful thing. Our matter-of-fact age cannot understand this. Prizes were awarded for good reading in public contests. Among its offices, the Church had the office of reader.

A new thing happened in the Church at Corinth: woman came to the forefront. Among the Jews women were kept in the background. In the synagogue they occupied the balcony or a room close by the main auditorium. No one bothered to teach the women the law. It is not surprising to see the grateful homage the women offered Jesus. They were drawn to him especially since he seemed to be interested in their souls. Mary at Jesus' feet in Bethany, Mary washing the Saviour's feet, the woman at Jacob's well: these are all pictures of woman's new position in Christianity. In the Orient there had been no woman problem. But here in Greece the women were not content with their harem existence. In Rome women attained their greatest freedom during the reign of the emperors, and even in religion they began to make their influence felt.

Ever since Paul began his second missionary journey, we see how women appear ever more prominently. We saw it first in Philippi. In Thessalonica patrician women were the principal support of the Church, and in Athens Damaris worked with the

Areopagite. But the women of Corinth were particularly active. The outstanding characteristic of the women in Corinth was their attachment to the Church and the daring with which they undertook to exercise important functions at divine services. Some of them had the gift of prophecy, and Paul did not silence them, in keeping with what he said to the Thessalonians, "Extinguish not the spirit. Despise not prophecies" (1 Thess. 5:19). Only when some of them no longer wore their veils, the symbol of their subjection, did Paul utter a rebuke.

After the reading service, the congregation sat down to a common meal, called the agape or love banquet. These agapae were the result of the intense community feeling of the early Church. We do not know whence they were derived, whether it was the Jewish Sabbath meal, or the Greek friendship meals. Nor do we know the exact liturgical or religious significance of the agape.

After the agape the unbaptized left, while the others went to the upper room for the Eucharistic meal. The upper room in Oriental houses was a special chamber for the reception of guests. It was high and airy, with many windows. Many lights were lit; the faithful began by making a confession of sins to the Apostle, and then went in an orderly procession to the sacrificial table, bringing their baskets with wheaten flour, grapes, incense, oil for the lamps, pure wheat bread and wine from the fields of Isthmus and Argos, while the *Kyrie eleison* was repeated by alternate choirs. Paul took parts of the bread and wine and proceeded to the consecration of those two elements which have ever been the simplest, the noblest, and the purest food of mankind. In inspired tones an acclamation developed into a solemn dialogue between Paul and the congregation. "Lift up your hearts." "We have lifted them up to the Lord." "Let us give praise to the Lord our God." "It is right and just." Then in solemn cadences Paul repeated the narrative of the Last Supper, as he had received it from the mother Church in Jerusalem: "The Lord Jesus, the same night in which he was betrayed, took bread ... (1 Cor. 11:23). The congregation responded with, "We thank you, holy Father, for your holy vine David, your servant whom you have revealed through your Son, Jesus Christ."[23]

Now the faithful approached the Apostle to receive from his hand a particle of the consecrated bread and to drink from the chalice, and after a gentle embrace and the kiss of peace they returned to their places. While some of the sacred meal was now carried to the sick, the sacred ceremony reached a climax in the hymn of thanksgiving, from which the rite took its name, Eucharist. The conclusion of the service consisted in a prayer:

"Look down upon your Church, O Lord, and preserve it from all evil and perfect it in love. Gather your saints from the four parts of the world into your kingdom which you have prepared for them. For yours is the power and the glory for all eternity. May your grace come to us, and may the world depart. Hosanna to the God of David. Whoever is holy, let him approach; whoever is not holy, let him do penance. Maranatha. Amen" *(Didache,* chap. 10). "Maranatha" could be taken in one of two senses: "The Lord has come," or, as it is translated in the Apocalypse, "Come, Lord."

Thus the congregation assembled as one "body" about the Lord as its "head." It was thus Paul envisioned the congregation when he prayed for it, when he wrote to it, when he talked about the building up of the house of the Lord. In this united service the faithful became more and more conscious of their union in one body. During the day they were dispersed by their daily occupations, in the slave quarters, at the bakers' trough, in the bazaars, in an alien world, sometimes exposed to ridicule. But in the evening they gathered for this common service of dedication. Here they experienced the miracle of the community. The glowing enthusiasm of a common faith and a common hope.

---

[23] *Didache,* chap. 9

CHAPTER THIRTY-FOUR

THE FIRST EPISTLE TO THE THESSALONIANS

*"Paul and Sylvanus and Timothy to the Church of the Thessalonians:
in God the Father and in the Lord Jesus Christ"* (1 Thess. 1:1).

It was a happy day for Paul when Silas and Timothy came to Corinth. Paul disliked working alone on the missions. He was no pale ascetic, but rather a red-blooded person who needed sympathy, cooperation, and human consolation. When the two travellers from Thessalonica stood in the doorway of the shop, a bright ray of joy leaped up in Paul's face. They embraced one another warmly. That day the shuttle hung idle on its chain, and it seemed as if there would be no end of talking. Even after nightfall, when the oil lamp had been lighted, Paul and his friends sat talking until far into the night.

"Now, Timothy," Paul asked, "tell me, how are things in Thessalonica?"

Timothy was able to give an excellent report.

"Their faith," he said, "remains undisturbed. Things happened as you said they would, but through all the persecution they remained faithful. Their fidelity to one another and their brotherly love have made a deep impression on the pagans throughout Macedonia. They hold you in the highest esteem. They are entirely devoted to you and are looking for your return. They do not believe the calumnies they have heard about you: that you were a flatterer, that you were covetous, looking for their money". Paul was glad.

"But," Timothy went on to say, "there are some shadows in the picture. Death came to reap his harvest in the congregation. During a storm recently, some fishermen were drowned. The families of the deceased are disturbed. They are asking, 'What has become of these dead?' They were hoping for the great day of the return of the Lord and for his triumph over the enemies of God. The people are especially worried about the day of the Parousia. Some are trying to calculate the exact day and hour when it will occur. They are looking everywhere for signs. They go from house to house and say that it is useless to work or start a new business or repair a house. And many people, because of that talk, are becoming poor and soon they will be a burden on others. They misunderstood your sermon about the last things."

The people of Thessalonica did not doubt the resurrection. Otherwise Paul would have used another tone in his reply. They were not concerned about the fact itself, but only about the time of the resurrection of those who are asleep in the Lord.

Paul gave the matter thought. "Timothy," he said, "I wish I could go to Thessalonica tomorrow. But, that will not do; I cannot leave this Church. Tomorrow morning go out and buy writing material. We will write a letter to Thessalonica."

It was a happy moment when Paul decided to write that letter, for it was the beginning of one of the most important achievements of his life. An important moment in the world's history as well. Paul had no inkling that after thousands of years men would think gratefully of that little workshop in Corinth where his first letter was written. This was the beginning of the New Testament, and the first page of the book was a letter born of the need of the moment. It was A.D. 51, some twenty years after the Lord's Resurrection.

We would very probably have begun the New Testament

with some solemn announcement and much ceremony. We would probably have begun with such solemn words as, "In the beginning was the Word." But God generally does the opposite of what we would do. Sometimes he announces his works in solemn fashion, as when he said, "Let us make man," or when he addressed the universe, "Hear, O you heavens, and give ear, O earth, for the Lord has spoken" (Is. 1:2). Sometimes he sends an archangel, as when he announced the incarnation of his Son. At other times he allows the work to come into being like a seed of wheat cast aside at the edge of the field. No man knows it is there until it begins to grow. Such was the beginning of the New Testament in the weaver's shop at Corinth. This is like the God of the Incarnation, who permitted his Son to assume human nature in a poor house in Nazareth, and to take on the form of a servant in a stable in Bethlehem.

Until far into the night Paul talked with his two friends about the difficulties of the Thessalonians, and during the discussion he made notes on his wax tablet. He spent the rest of the night in thought and prayer. When we read the letter it is clear that it was the result of prayer and meditation. Indeed, all of Paul's letters are really prayers, written in God's presence.

The next morning, Timothy went out and bought the writing material: some papyrus sheets, ink, pumice for smoothing rough places and for sharpening the quills, a sponge for erasing, paste to attach the sheets together, and some sealing material and cords to tie the roll. Pliny tells of the nine kinds of paper available then. If he had enough money, Timothy probably bought some paper of the *hierarica* brand, which was about ten inches wide. Egyptian paper was very expensive at the time, and when a shipment failed to arrive from Egypt, the officials rationed it to the consumer. It is not likely that Paul used parchment, such as the Jews used for the Sacred Scriptures.

And so the three missioners went to work. The physical labour of writing the letter was never done by the one who composed it. Besides, Paul's fingers were too stiff and rough to write well. Therefore, according to the old custom, he dictated the letter. We may suppose that Timothy and Silas took turns writing the letter. Years later Silas served in the same capacity for Peter (1 Pet. 5:12). That fact may account for the considerable amount of Pauline thought that found its way into Peter's two letters. The writer sat cross-legged on the floor, like the Egyptian village scribe. The oriental had no solid support when he wrote but, incredible as it may seem, he wrote on the flat of his hand. An expert writer could write continuously for two hours, and therefore pauses were required in the dictation. In Paul's letter, these pauses probably occurred during the transition passages from one point to another. The change in mood in Paul's letters is accounted for by the fact that his letters were often the work of several days.

Timothy is cutting the quill with a knife and sharpening the point with pumice stone. Paul is leaning against the loom, head in hand, or sometimes he walks back and forth. He begins to dictate:

"Paul and Sylvanus and Timothy to the Church of the Thessalonians, in God the Father, and in the Lord Jesus Christ. Grace be to you and peace."

'But Paul," Silas interrupts, "this is your letter. Our names should not be mentioned here."

"No, Sylvanus," Paul may have said, "it is our letter, for we all have the same interest in our friends in Thessalonica."

The inclusion of the names of his young co-workers was a gesture characteristic of Paul. His nature was too modest and generous to exclude them. Throughout the letter he uses the pronoun "we," indeed sixty-five times, to show that Timothy and Silas were cofounders of the Church at Thessalonica.

Here at the beginning of the New Testament we hear that threefold expression: faith, hope, and charity. The old Platonic eros, that painful, unsatisfied longing of the soul for the unattainable, eternal beauty, and the sensuous eros of the Gnostics were to be transformed by Christianity into the Christian agape.

The tone of the letter throughout is tender and intimate. It tells of Paul's unreserved desire to understand their joys and sorrows. The First Epistle to the Thessalonians is not a polemic letter like the Epistles of the third missionary journey. It is not a systematic exposition of logical thought. It tries to reflect the feelings and emotions of those who were disturbed by Paul's sermon on eschatology. For this reason, the first two letters to the Thessalonians are dominated by eschatological considerations. It would be foolish to conclude, as some critics have done, that the teaching about the last things was the central point of Christian instruction, or that Christian dogma developed from the idea of the last judgment.

Paul reminds the Thessalonians of that eternal decree by which God knew them from all eternity and had chosen them to become members of Christ's Church. The Church, therefore, has roots in eternity. It is founded on a supra-historical act of God which Paul calls election. The gospel declares an injection of a higher world into this earthly existence, a new world in the midst of this old, passing world. A man who openly became a Christian was often looked upon as a disturber of the peace, as politically dangerous. Paul found that out in Philippi. But in Paul's mind, suffering was something that belonged to the idea of a Christian. Sometimes the greatest suffering for the convert is that inflicted by his own people. Therefore Paul was concerned about the Jewish problem; it left him no rest. All his life he was fighting for his people, as he saw with frightful clarity Israel's astounding guilt. Yet he could not believe that it would be cast aside forever and have no further significance in the scheme of salvation.

Paul had aroused himself to this outburst of passionate feeling. He needed a rest pause, as did also Silas, who now probably changed places with Timothy. This pause in dictation is indicated, apparently, by the new address, "Brethren." Paul now poured forth all his human sentiment to the Thessalonians, but all this human feeling was imbedded in his relationship with God. He knows how they are all bound together, not only in faith or worship, but in love, as a holy brotherhood, held together by Christ's love.

Often he wished to visit them, but, as he says, "Satan has hindered us" (2:18). Today we would say that circumstances or political conditions hindered us. But for Paul there were no untoward circumstances, whether of political, climatic, or personal nature. For Paul there was nothing impersonal or neutral. He viewed everything that happened in the world as the result of some personal activity that worked either for or against God.

It was either God or Satan. Paul knew no other alternative. It was a philosophy of the simplest sort. Such was Ignatius Loyola's utterly simple view of the two banners: here Jerusalem, there, Babylon. In Paul's mind it was not the influence of the stars, of nerve conditions, of heredity, or any other earthly force that determined the fate of mankind. He concluded these thoughts with a solemn prayer leading up to the thought that Christ will come again. This passage concludes with "Amen," an indication that another pause occurred in the dictation.

In the second part of the letter he treats of his chief theme, the second coming of Christ, to which he referred at the end of each previous section. Two great thoughts alternately try to dominate the ancient Christian Church. The expectation of the final establishment of the kingdom of God, and the accomplishment of the work of salvation in the present through the graces given through the Holy Spirit. The first idea is of the Old Testament; the second is specifically Christian.

But both ideas receive their force from Jesus, who was conscious of this twofold role. To establish the kingdom of God in the present, and to complete the kingdom by his second coming when he would sit, as Messianic king, in judgment over the world. This passing world would be absorbed into the glory of the world to come. The faithful in Thessalonica looked too much to the future, to the imminent dawning of the Last Day. They saw the red colouring in the evening sky announcing the

Day of Judgment. Such excessive preoccupation with the future endangered the present and made this life seem empty and worthless.

We shall be able to understand the eschatological passages in the two letters to the Thessalonians if we keep in mind that Paul, too, had in mind Christ's prophecies about his second coming. Further, we must begin with the supposition that all great prophecies, especially those dealing with the last things, had a twofold sense and permitted a twofold fulfilment. One proximate and one remote, one tentative and the other definitive, one temporal and the other eternal. Paul had nothing definite in his mind about the proximate fulfilment of his words. Nor, for that matter, did he have any idea of how close or how distant the last things might be. One thing he knew: that, according to Christ's will, the apostles and the faithful alike were ignorant of whether the end would come tomorrow morning or a thousand years hence. At times it appears that he thought the proximate fulfilment would occur in the near future, and indeed all the apostolic writings seem to infer the same thing. Whether the final catastrophe would follow close on the first, or whether an interval of thousands of years would intervene, was a mystery about which people could have only surmises, hopes, and fears.

At this time both the writings of the Jews and the works of Josephus Flavius indicate a universal belief in the proximity of the end of the world. In the Jewish mind, every generation seemed to consider itself the last. Human as they were, the apostles were unable to escape this widespread feeling, although our Lord's words about the uncertainty of the Last Judgment kept them from saying anything authoritative or definite about his second coming. On the other hand they could admit the possibility of Christ's early return. Paul, like many of the faithful, seemed to be under the impression that he would still be alive when the Parousia occurred. Only later he began to count on a longer period and the possibility of his own

martyrdom. Often he thought that the world had every
indication of hastening to its ruin. But he realized the danger of
such a one-sided view of life, and insisted on a realistic,
wholesome view of the present.

This present life has its own value, because it is a life in
Christ, already permeated and filled with heavenly forces. Jesus
had said: "Walk while you have the light" (John 12:35); and
Paul, perhaps better than any other, was able to develop the
hidden meaning of these words. By living this life "in Christ,"
the Christian already possesses the joys of salvation. Thus Paul
directed the view of the faithful to the present. He made
Christianity a thing close to everyday life, and close to reality.

Undoubtedly the expectation of the second coming of
Christ gave his preaching a certain impetus. Sometimes Paul
seems to have thought that he would be able to spread the
gospel all over the world during his lifetime. He wished to have
the harvest under cover before the "great day" came. He even
wished to hasten the harvest remembering perhaps an obscure
saying of the Lord, "the kingdom of heaven suffers violence
and the violent bear it away" (Matt. 11:12). But it cannot be
said that the eschatological idea is the decisive thing in his
preaching. Christianity lost little of its appeal when the great
suspense was over and Christ's second coming was more and
more delayed. The expectation for the Parousia remained;
every generation of Christians has prayed, "thence he shall
come to judge the living and the dead."

Paul, therefore, tried to set up a moral ideal of life before
he explained Christ's coming. The sanctification of the inner
man by life "in Christ," particularly in its two main departments:
man's sexual life and his business life. The new Pauline ethics
may be expressed in the words, "Become what you are." The
Christian is to become that which he already is through the
possession of the Holy Spirit, and he should express the holiness
of his state by holy living. The Apostle's words in 1 Thess. 4:4
may refer to the affairs of business as well as to the sexual life,

since the Greek word for "vessel" may mean either wife or one's own body.

It was still necessary after all this to say something about the fate of those who die before the Parousia. Instead of the second coming of Christ, the early Christians more often spoke of the advent of Christ or Parousia. During the imperial era, *parousia* meant the state visit of the emperor to some city. Heralds announced his coming, festivities were planned, games were arranged, and sacrifices made to the gods. Statues were erected, coins were minted, and a new period of time was reckoned to commemorate the event and fix it in the mind of the people. The expression *parousia*, therefore, was an excellent one for the triumphal return of Christ.

Some of the Thessalonians also may have thought the condition after death was an extinction of consciousness. A kind of sleep of the soul from which there was to be no awakening. The dead, then, would have been robbed of this great fulfilment. They would be deprived of seeing Christ triumphant. Hopelessness and uncertainty about the fate of the dead were the outstanding marks of paganism, and both Jews and pagans spoke of death as a sleep. For Paul death was a sleep only externally. As God saw it, it was a life more real than this earthly life, it was life "in Christ," as expressed in the catacomb inscription: *Vivas in Deo, in pace, in aeternum.*

For Paul, the state of man after death is not merely the reflected brilliance of this life, an afterglow, but a state dynamic through the glory of Christ. The state of soul of those who die before the Parousia, is an anticipation of what we hope for in the Parousia. Then souls are "present with the Lord" (2 Cor. 5:8). Death has no power over the risen Christ or over those who are his. What Christ purchased on the Cross, he will never again surrender. The line of death does not run between this earthly life and the state afterward. Only he is dead who is outside the community of Christ.

And the Thessalonians forgot one other thing: all those

who died in possession of Christ and the Spirit will participate
in the Parousia in the general resurrection when their bodies are
clothed with immortality. "Wherefore," he says, "comfort one
another with these words" (1 Thess. 4:17). These words seem
to be an exact opposite of those found in a model letter of
condolence of the Egyptian Irene: "Against something like this
we can do nothing. So comfort yourselves mutually."

The colours and scenes with which Paul describes the
Parousia are partly those we read in the Gospels. Partly taken
from the prophets and partly from contemporaneous Jewish
apocalyptical writings; namely, "the trumpet" that will announce
God's coming, "the clouds," as the triumphal vehicle, "the
commandment and the voice of the archangel. The words "we
who are alive" include Paul himself, the Thessalonians, and all
future generations yet unborn, whether he himself shall see the
Parousia or, as he seems to fear in the second letter to the
Corinthians, if he dies before it happens.

In conclusion he speaks of the uncertainty of human
existence, the inevitability of the fate determined by God, and
the attitude of the faithful and of unbelievers. The latter are
children of the night who delude themselves by talking about
"peace and security," and are intoxicated by the drugs of the
age, their culture, until one day God destroys the spider web of
their security. The *pax Romana,* that Roman order forced upon
all the world, seemed to be taken as a guarantee for the security
of human existence.

But "the children of the light" are sober and watchful,
like the soldier on patrol, with breastplate and helmet. Today
man again no longer counts on God's interference in human
life. Modern man in spite of his great technique feels keenly the
uncertainty of human existence. We do not feel safe in God's
hand any more. We want hundred-percent coverage of a
technical, mechanical, and organizational kind. We want silos
and barns for the future like the rich farmer in the Gospel.

He concludes the letter by striking the chords of joy,

prayer, and thanksgiving. He begins that hymn of Christian joyousness that he will sing until his Roman imprisonment. Early Christianity was a ceaseless joyous giving of thanks.

"Hold fast that which is good." The business men of Thessalonica understood that advice in a day when every coin had to be examined closely. The kiss and the embrace were the usual forms of greeting, which were introduced by Paul into the Christian service.

Silas read the letter for Paul. The sheets of paper were pasted together to form a roll, and Silas was already rolling up the document when Paul asked to make an addition: "I charge you by the Lord, that this epistle be read to all the holy brethren." Some of the brethren might be absent when the letter was first read. The letter was to be read several times, therefore, and then sent to the neighbouring Churches. This was the first letter that Paul wrote to a congregation, and such direction was probably necessary.

Finally, Paul took the quill from the writer's hand and, with energetic strokes and large letters, he wrote, "The grace of our Lord Jesus Christ be with you. Amen."

The roll was placed in a cover, the address was written, the roll tied with cord and sealed. Who was to deliver the letter? The state postal service carried no private mail. The writer had to attend to the letter's delivery. Rich people had slaves or freedmen for this purpose. Soon the Christian congregations, like the Sanhedrin in Jerusalem, established their own courier service. Otherwise it would be hard to explain how Paul was so accurately informed about the important happenings in distant Churches. But when Paul wrote his first letter, the service had not yet been established. At the first sailing, Silas and Timothy went to Thessalonica, or perhaps some merchants who happened to be in Corinth took the letter back with them.

The First Epistle to the Thessalonians ushers a new literary form into the Sacred Scriptures: the letter form, the most intimate and direct form of writing. Perhaps it is significant that it was Paul who introduced the letter form into the Scriptures. His was a nature that had no leisure for literary composition, but the letter, with its unadorned expression, was the form most suitable for his impulsive nature, his quick change of mood, his feverish haste, and the thoughts that tumbled so stormily from his mind. He had a high regard for the art of composition. According to the rabbis, the writer's quill was one of the things that God had created in the dusk of the last day of the creation.

Tertullian says that Thessalonica was one of the cities in which Paul's letter was still read from the original, and the brethren thought then that they could still hear his voice and see the expression on his face.[24] But Providence did not wish that even one fragment of Paul's original should come down to us, although hundreds of less interesting papyri have been preserved. In this instance, too, it is true that the "written code kills, but the spirit gives life." (2 Cor. 3:6).

---

[24] Cf. *Praescr.*, 36

CHAPTER THIRTY-FIVE

ANTI-CHRIST

The Second Epistle to the Thessalonians

Only three months had passed since Paul's first letter to the Thessalonians, when new misunderstandings and disturbances arose. Idlers and gossip mongers, whose pious prattle seemed to them more important than making a living, went about with long faces telling about the signs they had seen and announcing solemnly that the "day of the Lord was at hand." In short, they acted like people whose days were numbered. They referred to some obscure prophecy given by one of the brethren, or to something that Paul had said, or to some apocryphal letter. A second letter had become necessary.

To understand Paul as an apocalyptic writer, we must have an adequate idea of his religious-historical viewpoint. Every age has its peculiar concept of the universe, its own philosophy. That philosophical view represents the temporal-spatial framework in which we live our spiritual and sensible lives. And that world concept or view can easily be changed without disturbing the substance of our faith. After all, these notions are only the garment clothing an idea, as the six-day period in which God created the world clothes the concept of creation. A radical change in the world view will, however, often entail grave disturbances in men's minds. Such was the case when the Copernican system was announced in Galileo's time, and when great advances were made in the natural sciences in the nineteenth century. In the eschatology of the early Church, we must distinguish two things: the belief in the future coming of Christ and the completion of God's kingdom, and the traditional apocalyptic framework in which these hopes and beliefs were suspended.

We know how much early Christianity had its eye turned to the future from the fact that the New Testament really begins with St. Paul's apocalypse and closes with the great Apocalypse of St. John, and between these two lie the lesser apocalypses of the Gospels (Matt., chap. 24; Mark, chap. 13; Luke, chap. 21). Catechetical instructions always included a section about the last things. It is so difficult to understand Paul's curt references to some of these things because he was presupposing the instructions he had given orally. He refers to his talks to them by saying, "You know, brethren," "You are witnesses," and "Remember you not that, when I was yet with you, I told you these things?" (2 Thess. 2:5.)

These expectations of the future were begun by old prophecies and were concerned about two events: the coming of the kingdom of God, and the two separate aeons or eras, namely, the present and the future, between which the Saviour would appear. Only Judaism had cherished the idea that two great eras would occur in succession and that the day separating them from each other would be the most important day in the history of the world – the "day of the Lord." Beginning with Isaias and Daniel, this idea about the two aeons goes through all the Jewish apocalyptical writings, of which the Fourth Book of Esdras was the most famous.

Paul, too, had accepted this dualism about the present evil world, whose ruler was Satan with his angels, and the coming glorious world. But he believed that the era had already begun and that the faithful possessed it through the Spirit. According to Paul, then, the two eras overlapped, and the period of over-lapping was a transition period of indefinite length. The chief mission of the apostles was to penetrate this world with a renewal of the spirit, which was nothing else than the battle between light and darkness. Thus we are in an interregnum which is marked by a greater or less amount of Christianization and which will be concluded by the final catastrophe at the time of Christ's second coming.

In this letter Paul purposed to lay the spirit of the rumour that the end of all things was already here. That could not be, since three preliminary events had not yet occurred: the great apostasy of the faithful, the appearance of the "man of sin," and his profanation of the Temple in Jerusalem. Paul certainly ex-pected these three events, and he knew who it was that retarded the appearance of the "son of perdition." He knew, too, that the mystery of iniquity was already at work.

Two great "mysteries," therefore, are already actively in conflict against each other: the mystery of Christ, of which Paul would speak later (Eph. 3:4), and the mystery of "that wicked one," the Antichrist. These two mysteries are developing side by side, with this difference: that Christ revealed himself at the beginning of his mystery, whereas Antichrist will reveal himself only at the end of his mystery. Now the work of Christ is being spread over the whole world, all peoples hear him, but the opposition of Antichrist has also begun.

Paul does not use the name Antichrist. It appears first in the Epistles of St. John (1 John 2:18, 22; 4.:3; 2 John 7). The idea of Antichrist reaches far back into antiquity, coming from an old Jewish tradition into Christian thought. In Isaias 11:4 the son of David kills the "wicked" one. Some of the features of Antichrist are taken from the description of Antiochus Epiphanes in the Book of Daniel (11:36). Others recall such figures as Balaam, Nabuchodonosor, Gog and Magog. Jesus did not expressly mention Antichrist, but his reference to the

appearance of false Christs, the Satanic opponents of the
Messias, gave new impetus to the old tradition.

Paul speaks of a secret tradition, mysterium (2 Thess. 2:7),
and he is the living testimony of that conviction in the primitive
Church. He speaks of the matter as of something that needs no
further explanation. When he says that the "mystery of iniquity
already works," he probably means some progressive moral
disintegration that is breaking down all peoples and classes;
some destruction of all the bonds of order. From this moral
chaos will arise the son of perdition, the enemy of Christ, the
son of chaos, as the representative of all that is diabolical, in
whom all that is against God will be united. He will perform
deeds that border on the miraculous, and he will demand divine
honours for himself.

Then the final battle will begin. The world will have
reached its last period. The fall of Antichrist will be the signal
for the coming of Christ. But before all this, the great revolt
must take place. The nations of the world will more and more
depart from Christian principles, and then only will Antichrist,
who until this time has had many forerunners, appear and
reveal himself in his true nature. This wicked and godless man
is different from Satan, whose instrument and tool he is. In an
obscure passage, Paul speaks of a factor that prevents the
appearance of Antichrist. This force, whatever it is, is already
active and became known since Paul's departure from Thessalonica.

The Apostle was extremely cautious in what he said about
Antichrist. He was careful to veil his meaning. The Thessalonians, of course, knew what he meant, but we are forced to
rely on mere conjecture. Some have supposed that Paul was
speaking about some secret with a historical background that
could not be mentioned in a letter without considerable risk. If
the letter were intercepted, horrible persecutions might ensue.
The same caution was observed in the Apocalypse, and this
secret matter might have been the beginning of a secret

discipline. In the whole Bible, there is perhaps no passage about which all commentators, beginning with the Fathers, are so much at variance.

Three possible explanations are suggested: one historical, another prophetic, and the third a combination of these two. The Apostle's words have the character of prophecies only when they refer to the distant future. When they refer to some proximate event they are not prophetic but an interpretation of the conditions of the time in the light of Christ's prophecies.

In the course of centuries liberal use of this epistle has been made to interpret the times. Every age claimed the right to interpret the signs of its own time in the light of Paul's eschatology by referring his words sometimes to some historical personage or again to some intellectual movement. This kind of interpretation reached the heights of absurdity when the Waldensians and Reformers of the sixteenth century declared that the pope was Antichrist, that the restraining power was the Holy Roman Empire, and that the Jesuit Order was the mystery of iniquity.[25] We must not forget that Paul is speaking of a proximate event. He wished to interpret, for his Thessalonians, the disturbing signs of the time and to remind them that great tribulations awaited them in connection with the fulfilment of Christ's prophecy, and that the ultimate end of all things was wrapped in deep obscurity.

When he speaks of "the man of sin, the son of perdition" (2:3), he is apparently speaking of something which he himself experienced fourteen years previously: Caligula's decree that a colossal statue of himself be erected in the Temple at Jerusalem and that the Temple be called the Temple of Caius, the new Jupiter. Caligula resorted to these measures in revenge for the fact that the Jews were the only ones who did not recognize him as god. Paul knew that the worship of the emperor was increasing progressively throughout the world. Whole communities in Greek and Asiatic cities felt it a high honour to be called

---

[25] Cf. Prat, S.J., *La theologie de Saint Paul*, Paris, 1929

neocores, temple guards of the emperor-god. "Kill me, or I shall kill you," Caligula is reported to have said to Zeus. This was anarchy in the highest sense, and Paul apparently had some pagan monarch like Caligula in mind. Like Caligula this ruler will have the reins of all power in his hands and will force everything else into subjection. "Remember you not," Paul stops to say, "that when I was still with you, I told you these things? And now you know what withholdeth, that he may be revealed in his time" (2:5).

When Paul wrote these words, Caligula sat on the imperial throne. His stepson, Nero, had already been acclaimed his successor. Seneca had just returned from his exile in Corsica and was appointed by Agrippina as Nero's tutor. Seneca was to teach the prince oratory ostensibly, but we know that such tutors in the highest family had a primary duty of caring for the moral education of their pupils. In this way Seneca became a counsellor to the Emperor.

People knew these things in Corinth and in Thessalonica. The "withholding" power (literally, the ruling power) could be nothing else but that legal order of the Roman state which was incorporated in Claudius. In the first five years of Nero's reign, Seneca acted as the "withholding" force by his prudent advice and by his successful efforts in keeping down the imperial volcanic temper. But after Seneca and his friend Burrus had been overtaken by a tragic fate, the fury of Nero, now under the domination of Tigellinus, knew no bounds. To Vespasian, Nero committed the conduct of the war and thus opened the way to the profanation of the Temple. The appearance of the pagan cohorts on sacred Temple soil, the erection of the image of the Roman eagle and the statues of the emperors, and the establishment of emperor worship on the site of the ancient Temple was, according to our Lord and St. Paul, the fulfilment of the prophecy of Daniel (Matt. 24:15).

The impression of Nero's tyranny was so overwhelming on men's minds that, even after his death, many men were afraid that Nero would reappear and come up from the nether regions. An English scholar[26] remarks that "if Paul had lived long enough to read the Apocalypse of St. John, it would have broken his heart." But that remark betrays a misunderstanding of Paul's prophetic character. Basically Paul and John were in agreement. They differed in their viewpoint: Paul wrote before the great turning point, John wrote after it, since under Domitian the dice had fallen definitely against Christianity. Paul immediately understood that the enthronement of the emperor as god was the apotheosis of a lie. He knew also that the Roman concept of the state with its totalitarian claims would be the archenemy of the primitive Church. But Roman justice was still the "withholding" force, and besides, the Church still lived under the shadow of the synagogue and was still regarded by the Roman authorities as a Jewish sect. The Christian organization had not yet become so articulate as to appear as an autonomous organization. It was in the beginning of its development, although it was hastening rapidly to that point where conflict with the Roman state was unavoidable.

Back in Philippi and in Thessalonica Paul had perceived indications that the Jews would not rest until they had opened the eyes of the Romans to the fact that the Christians were not identical with themselves. And that it was the Christians who, by their rejection of the state religion, were undermining the Roman government. In A. D. 64., the Jews were finally successful in drawing the attention of the Roman authorities to the Christians.

In later times some students understood by the "withholding" power the Roman order itself inasmuch as it opposed anarchy and suppressed the power of evil. For that reason, as Tertullian tells us,[27] the Christians prayed for the security of the Empire. When the Nordic races came pouring out of the north, the Roman Empire collapsed. At that juncture of history, St.

---

[26] W. M. Ramsay, *Cities of St. Paul*, London, 1922
[27] Tertullian, *Apol.*, 39.

Augustine transmuted Paul's concept of the mystical body into the idea of the city of God: two loves have built each a different city, the love of God went so far as to forget itself, human love went so far as to despise God. The Church, as the heir of antiquity, assimilating the social and legal talents of Rome and the philosophy of Greece, took the concept of the city of God with its social order, and transmitted it to the new nations and thus took a hand in their education. The old *pax Romana* was changed over into the *"pax Christi in regno Christi."*

Today we have some idea of what happens when the religious foundation of the state and the educative force of religion are removed in a nation. If ever the forces of Bolshevism are let loose on the world, no power on earth will be able to hold off the cataclysm. Christianity is the source of order, peace, and harmony, and its chief task is the safeguarding of the eternal salvation of its members. But it is also the principal foundation for all social order and stability. If the Church's authority is undermined, no one will be able to hold the power of evil in check. Then we shall see a barbarism of unchained godlessness equipped with every instrument of science and technique. The irony of it all will be that man, who would not believe the truth of God, will believe lying and will consent to iniquity (cf. 2 Thess. 2:11). That will be the hour when Antichrist will appear; but his reign will be short, for the Lord "with the breath of his lips he shall slay the wicked" (Is. 11:4).

We must not forget that each of these historical explanations is replete with difficulties. We can say with St. Augustine: "I must confess that I do not know what Paul meant."[28] We must remember that Paul was speaking as a prophet and, like St. John, he had in mind the whole development and the ultimate fulfilment at the end of time. To obviate all difficulties, some modern students have adopted the interpretation that refers to the end of time, and thus the events are lifted to a higher supra-

---

[28] *De civ. Dei*, 20, 19.

historical plane. Paul, it is true, moved in the atmosphere of the Old Testament and Christian eschatology and, like Daniel and St. John, he was also thinking of that mysterious, eternal, supercosmic battle between good and evil, which appears under various forms at different historical epochs, and is often echoed in the conflict between faith and infidelity.

Satan is the force of evil in this battle, using now this man, and then another. But the "withholding" power must belong to the same plane. According to Daniel and St. John it is the Archangel Michael who will support the Church in the day of her greatest tribulation. According to this explanation, the "withholding" power is some spiritual, supramundane power: perhaps the Archangel Michael, who will give the signal for the resurrection and for the last judgment, and who conducts the war against Satan through all times.

We can see, therefore, that in spite of the fact that the framework of this prophecy is Jewish, the spirit of it is not Jewish. We do not find the idea of Jewish world power, mentioned in the apocryphal psalms, in the Ascension of Moses, and in the Fourth Book of Esdras. The Messias is not pictured as a statesman and general as in Jewish eschatology. For Paul, as for Jesus, only spiritual gifts are considered, and these are partially already in the possession of the faithful.

Thus Paul, in this epistle, is waging a war against the devaluation of this earthly life proposed by the meddlers of Thessalonica. A Christian's earthly existence, according to Paul is a twofold thing: the secular activity in common with other citizens, and the more real, hidden, mystic life in Christ which draws strength and vitality from the spiritual forces of the coming aeon. A man's civil life is not reduced to a mere shadow. The Christian must participate in all civic affairs, and he must do his part to transform the world in Christ. When Paul said, "our conversation is in heaven," he did not intend that the Christian should relinquish the conduct of civic affairs to the pagan. At that time Paul did not even consider that aspect. The question of the Christian concept of the state or the question of an active participation in politics had not yet come into the focus of the early Church.

The problem of the Christian statesman and of Christian political science arose only after Constantine. Paul's whole philosophy, his whole evaluation of the world, was religious. The world, and all that is in it, belong to God. A Christian has this duty: to give to God what is God's, to seek the kingdom of God, and to do his duty with regard to the state. But the world has by an accident become the playground of the devils. And so in the world the Christian is thrown between the old aeon with its apotheosis of the Roman state, and the new aeon of the kingdom of God.

Christ redeemed only individual men. He did not redeem the race or the state as such, and therefore social forms and the whole social order must be permeated with the Christian ideal through man's efforts. At one time the whole human sphere seemed to be about to realize in itself the Christianization of all political forms, and religion and politics were about to become a united entity. But since that brilliant attempt, the ideal of a theocratic government lives only in Dante's poetic vision.

CHAPTER THIRTY-SIX

PAUL AND GALLIO

"But when Gallio was proconsul of Achaia, the Jews with one accord rose up against Paul and brought him to the judgment seat" (Acts 18:12).

The break with the synagogue attracted attention. At that time there was a strong wave of anti-Semitism in Corinth, and thus the break would favour the Christians. The increase of membership drawn from the pagans became greater day by day. Even some additions were made from the synagogue. After a short time, Crispus, the president of the synagogue, presented himself for baptism. Paul speaks of a certain Caius, who was his host during his second stay in Corinth (Rom. 16:23). For these two converts, Crispus and Caius, Paul made an exception from his usual practice of not himself administering baptism (1 Cor. 1:14-16). And on another day, an important city official, Erastus, the city treasurer, came to be baptized (Rom. 16:23).

The Church at Corinth contained a mixed population. From the First Epistle to the Corinthians, we can distinguish three social planes: the better class made up of landowners and government officials, whose houses were large enough to receive the congregation and who were wealthy enough to entertain the congregation at the common love banquet. To this

class belonged those mentioned above, and later a certain Sosthenes, and Zenas, a Jewish lawyer (Titus 3:13). The widow
Chloe, with her servants, might also be mentioned in this group.

The middle class, which was principally Latin, included
Tertius, who later served as Paul's secretary and to whom Paul
dictated the Epistle to the Romans, and Quartus. But the largest
number of the converts belonged to the lowest classes, poor
freedmen, labourers, and slaves. Corinth had many slaves, even
if the number given by Atheois, 460,000, is excessive. "For see
your vocation," wrote Paul, "brethren, that there are not many
wise according to the flesh, not many mighty, not many noble
... And the base things of the world and the things that are
contemptible, has God chosen: and things that are not, that he
might bring to nothing the things that are" (1 Cor. 1:26, 28).

Never before had Paul come into contact with the lowest
and most abandoned classes of society as here at Corinth. Sometime later when the Corinthians seemed to have become
somewhat arrogant, he reminded them from what classes most
of them had come, and the picture he drew was in no way
flattering: "Nor the effeminate nor liars with mankind nor
thieves nor covetous nor drunkards nor railers nor extortioners,
shall possess the kingdom of God. And such some of you
were" (1 Cor. 6:10). Paul's proud and self-justifying spirit must
have had to do violence to itself to deal with this rabble. Some
men have accused him of having gathered the dregs of every
race and the rabble of the Mediterranean countries about
himself. But, if the world ever needed a Saviour, he was needed
by sinners more than by the just. And if Christianity was able
to save this scum of the Mediterranean, no one would be able
to resist the power of the gospel. Was it not a masterpiece of
the Apostle's genius that he was able to bridge over so many
social, racial, and moral antagonisms, and that he was able to
consolidate freemen and slaves into one community, and make
Greek and Jew and Roman and Asiatic into one Church? It was
not smooth work. Paul had many difficult moments, but he

taught his followers to consider disagreements a sin, such as "putting them to shame that have not" (1 Cor. 11:22). That was when Paul was present. But later, alas, when he was gone, things were different.

Gradually the Corinthians began to understand not only that they made up a single congregation, but that they were part of a world-embracing federation of Christian Churches. Twice they had seen delegates from Thessalonica come to Corinth to see Paul. The consultations with these Macedonians took place in the presence of a large group of the local brethren. At such times, it was not lost on the Corinthians that their Apostle was a famous personality. In his hands he seemed to hold the reigns of power; on him rested the responsibility for the other Churches. They were amazed to see how inseparably his life was bound up with the life of the whole Church, how all the cares and concerns of the Church everywhere seemed to flow together in his heart. St. John Chrysostom had a beautiful expression for it: *Cor Pauli, Cor mundi.* The great concept of the unity of the Church was beginning to appear. Anything that affected one Church, affected the others. And as the Corinthians were beginning to understand these things they were also learning another important truth: that, while they were unmolested in Corinth, indeed well received, the reports from Thessalonica showed that adherence to Jesus implied a conflict with the embittered opposition of the Jews, and sometimes with the heavy arm of governmental authority. They were soon to have experience with these matters.

Paul's successes were not unnoticed by the fathers of Israel. Paul had a feeling that the clouds were gathering over him. He wrote at that time to the Thessalonians: "For the rest, brethren, pray for us, that the word of God may speed on and may be glorified, as it did among you; and that we may be delivered from importunate and evil men" (2 Thess. 3:1). Sometimes he felt that his soul was paralyzed within him when he saw out of what poor human material he must build the Church, and how so often converts fell back into their old pagan vices. Then, too, his soul was weighed down by the care for the other Churches, and often he was at the point of leaving Corinth.

Such thoughts pursued him even in sleep. One night, after he had wrestled in prayer, the Lord appeared to him in a vision and comforted him: "Do not fear, but speak. And hold not your peace, because I am with you and no man shall set upon you, to hurt you. For I have much people in this city" (Acts 18:9). After that vision he was encouraged to stay at this difficult post, for "if God be for us, who is against us?" (Rom. 8:31)

In the spring of A. D. 52 the governorship of Achaia became vacant. It was Rome's policy to fill places such as this with prudent and conciliatory officials, just as, for instance, English attempts to send diplomatic persons to India. The Roman Senate in 52 was extremely fortunate in being able to appoint as proconsul of Achaia one of the most lovable and cultured men of the time, Marcus Aenneus Novatus, who took the name Junius Gallio after his foster-father. His name and his office are clearly established by a letter of the Emperor Claudius, written sometime between April and August of 52 to the city of Delphi. The letter was preserved as an inscription on a stone discovered in Delphi and is one of the most important documents for the history of the New Testament.

Claudius calls him, "My friend, Gallio, the governor of Achaia." If, according to this inscription, Gallio was proconsul in the year 52-53, then Paul's stay of a year and a half in Corinth must be placed from the spring of 51 to the autumn of 52. Gallio's appointment was enthusiastically received throughout Greece. He came from a family long renowned for culture and breeding, he was the favourite brother of Seneca the philosopher, the tutor of the imperial prince Nero, and the uncle of Lucan, the famous Latin author. He possessed a great mind and a noble personality, and his contemporaries picture him as one of the most fascinating personalities of antiquity. Seneca along with the whole literary world was loud in praise of

Gallio. Statius called him "my sweet Gallio." He was regarded as the most excellent example of manhood produced by the Stoa. He was the undisputed ideal Roman gentleman. Seneca's devotion to his brother went so far as to prompt him to say: "No mortal can be more gracious to his friend than Gallio is to every man. My brother Gallio cannot be loved enough."

The Jews at Corinth learned of the amiable disposition of the new proconsul, and immediately they made plans to exploit his goodness for their own purposes, but they did not know that Gallio's family had long had a dislike for Jews. They were too blind to understand that their fanaticism would have little effect on a man of Gallio's character.

One day they sent a paid mob to attack Paul in his work-shop and drag him to the agora before the tribunal of the governor. The accusation that they were shouting was, "This man persuades men to worship God contrary to the law." But they had miscalculated. Paul's poise and dignity impressed the great Roman. Gallio immediately saw through the shabby trickery of the Jews and, before Paul could speak, he rejected the charge against the prisoner. "If it were some matter of injustice," said Gallio, "or an heinous deed, O Jews, I should with reason bear with you. But if they be questions of words and names, and of your law, look you to it: I will not be judge of such things."

Paul was eager to speak to the governor, and he looked intently up to this magnificent man, whom Jesus himself would have loved as he had loved the rich young man. It was an opportunity of grace that lightly touched the soul of the Stoic, but Gallio, the proud Roman, scarcely noticed the poor Jew. Smiling coldly, he gestured imperiously to the accusers to leave the Stoa, and directed the lictors to clear the hall. The scene ended in a bit of comedy. Sosthenes, the new president of the synagogue, was wrapping his long cloak about himself as he hurried down the steps; but he stumbled in his unaccustomed drapery while the Greeks had a little horseplay by flogging him

out of the building. This is one of the few humorous scenes that
Luke, in his fine Grecian sense of humour, wove into his story.

But Sosthenes' little chastisement turned out for his own
good. Somehow it caused him to reflect about the whole affair,
and finally became the starting point for his conversion. Grace
can even make use of such trifles.

The platform was cleared of Jews. For a moment, Paul
and Gallio, the proud Roman and the little Jew, stood face to
face. Did the soul of the Stoic this time feel the light rustling of
grace? It was Gallio's second opportunity, and his last, to hear
about Jesus. It is a saddening thought that this magnificent Stoic
thus missed the one opportunity of his salvation; and indeed the
course of his life was marked with tragedy. Like Seneca, his
brother, he died the death of a Stoic. At Nero's command he
died by his own land. That was the ultimate wisdom in the
teaching of the Stoics when pain became unbearable. Seneca
expressed the idea in a famous letter thus: "The eternal law has
arranged nothing better than this, that it has provided but one
entrance into life, but many exits. If I should be forced to await
a dreadful disease or a horrible man, I am still free to escape it
all. Here is one point in life about which we cannot complain.
No man need be unhappy except through his own fault. Live if
you are content; if you are dissatisfied, you are free to return
whence you came."[29]

The Church at Corinth was enjoying a period of calm. In
contrast to his treatment by the officials in other places, Paul
was well treated by the Roman authorities here. This experience
increased his liking for the Roman state, and it also enhanced
the Church's position among the pagans. Paul's activities were
being extended ever farther. He did not forget the countryside
out beyond Corinth, where he founded many Churches. Besides
Timothy and Silas, he had now a large number of assistants,
whom he was able to send out in all directions into the large
territory of the peninsula: to Sikyon, Argos, perhaps even to

---

[29] Ep, 70, *ad Lucilium*.

Olympia and Sparta. We know the name of only one of these Churches: Cenchrae, where the faithful deaconess, Phoebe, laboured like an angel of charity among the seamen on shore. But Corinth with its vast population, its five market places, five baths, two basilicas, numerous theatres and amphitheatres, one of which seated 22,000, Corinth with its two harbours was the appropriate field of labour for the adventurous spirit of St. Paul. Nor was he lacking in the manifestation of his charismatic gifts, especially in a city possessing a famous shrine of Asclepius where many sick people cultivated the temple sleep and sought health. The museum in Corinth still possesses some of the votive gifts donated by those who were cured.

But far removed from the spirit of the Apostle were those Christians of the fourth century, when it was no longer dangerous to be a Christian, who wreaked their unenlightened zeal on the pagan Soter and won a cheap victory over paganism by destroying the pagan temple.

CHAPTER THIRTY-SEVEN

TO EPHESUS

"And he came to Ephesus, and left them there" (Acts 18:19).

Paul had stayed in no city as long as in Corinth. He had been there for eighteen months prior to the hearing before Gallio, and he stayed on for some weeks after that. It was a brave thought to make the grace of Christ leap forth in the forsaken population of Corinth. On the other hand, a population such as he found in Corinth was not without certain dangers for a new congregation if the founder did not remain to see it grow strong. Sometimes we think that Paul should have remained longer with his Churches, but he looked on himself as the great sower who sows the seed but leaves the harvest to someone else.

When the Church at Corinth was able to stand on its own feet, Paul no longer felt any attraction to remain in depopulated Greece, which had no cities of importance beside Athens and Corinth. A strange restlessness urged him to visit his old fields of labour and to seek out new ones. Twice before, the "Spirit of God" had turned him away from Ephesus when he planned to go there. Would the "Spirit" turn him away for the third time? He was deeply grateful for his deliverance from the threats of his enemies and for the noble tolerance of the Proconsul Gallio.

For that reason he made a vow (whether it was the so-called vow of the Nazarenes, is doubtful) to go to the Temple in Jerusalem. This vow reveals how much Paul was still bound to the old religious customs of his ancestors. His unexpressed destination, however, was his adopted home of Antioch in Syria. From there he wished to start out on a new missionary enterprise.

Paul found it hard to say farewell in Corinth. Aquila and Priscilla decided to accompany him as far as Ephesus and arrange for lodgings for him there when he should return. Their business seems not to have prospered in Corinth. At least while Paul lived with them; they seem to have been quite poor, and they hoped to fare better in Ephesus. Silas and Timothy also went with the Apostle. Anyone who has ever made this voyage through the Aegean Sea in spring or autumn will never forget the enchanting scenes among the Cyclades and the Dodecanese Islands that swarm so closely about the sacred island of Delos, the legendary birthplace of Apollo. The passage took about ten days, since the ancients never sailed at night. One beautiful day in late summer, Paul saw the mountains of Ionia, especially high Tmolus, rising in the blue distance behind the island of Samos.

Ionia! The name still resounds with ancient legend and story. We hear the harp of Homer, Sappho's lyre, and the melodies of Anacreon in the sound of the word. Here in Ionia ancient Hellas looked across the sea and beheld its image just as it did in Sicily and lower Italy to the west. This was the home of the Ionian column and Ionian architecture. In the streets of Ephesus, Homer, the blind minstrel, used to sing. Here Heraclitus meditated on the origin of all being. Here for the first time the word "logos" was uttered. Here Pythagoras founded his school of ascetic thought; here Herodotus laid the foundations for the science of history. It was here that Thales of Miletus declared that water was the ultimate basis of all things. Here in Ephesus were the origins of pre-Socratic thought; here the chaotic dreams of the Orphics and their weird cosmogonies were overcome by Greek thought.

Paul did not despise reason, the Greek *nous*. Though no enemy of the intellect, he opposed a degenerate toying with intellectual acrobatics. But Paul brought something much more valuable than all these fabulous gifts of Ionia. He brought the sacred *pneuma,* the spirit that does not come from man, but comes upon him and overpowers him.

In the harbour of Panormus, which was the lagoon-like mouth of the Kaystros river, our travellers left the ship and took a small boat through the mile-long canal to the inner harbour. They landed directly in front of the most imposing buildings in Ephesus. Like Palermo, Ephesus was a *Conca d'oro,* a large shell with mountains rising up behind it: the steep Coressus to the south, the Pion mountains to the east, and the Gallesion to the north. As in Antioch, the villas of the rich dotted these mountains, and on the ridge of the mountains the ancient city walls of Lysimachos encircled the city.

Ephesus had a prosperous Jewish colony with its own government and entire freedom of religion. All the monies contributed by the Jews of Asia for the support of the Temple in Jerusalem were handled through the Jewish bank in Ephesus. In 61 B.C. Cicero had appeared here in Ephesus in a famous lawsuit as the defence attorney for Flaccus, the governor of the province of Asia who was accused of preventing the export of the aurum *Judaicum,* the Jewish Temple funds. Our travellers probably had no difficulty in finding lodgings with some of their wealthier countrymen. Until this time, the Jews in Ephesus had had only a scant acquaintance with Christianity, and they were eager to hear more from Paul. Since his ship was sailing on to Syria the following week, Paul was able to spend only one Sabbath in Ephesus. But his Messianic sermon was well received, and the people made him promise to return.

His reception in Jerusalem, however, was somewhat disillusioning and certainly not cordial. Luke does not even mention the name of the Holy City, but remarks laconically that Paul "went up and saluted the Church." The condition of the mother Church was not encouraging. More and more it wrapped itself in its own cocoon. It is sad to recall that in its own Palestinian homeland the religion of Jesus seemed unable to strike root: "Something in this religion was more akin to the free spirit of Greece ... To what hard tests this religion was put in its earliest years! 'Go forth out of your country, and from your kindred, and out of your father's house, and come into the land which I shall show you.' Islam originated in Arabia, and it remained ever an Arabian religion. But the Christian religion, almost as soon as it came into being, was driven out by the people to which it should have belonged."[30]

We are approaching the climax of Paul's life, that time when the opposition became furious against him, when the great catastrophe occurred. Everything great in the Church was born out of great sorrow and pain. So, too, the complete liberation of the Church from its Jewish habiliments was a painful thing. The extreme Jewish party was never able to forget that day in Antioch and was not able to forgive Paul. Since that day its movement gained momentum and had become a powerful propaganda in the Church. The enemy now started a systematic campaign of erecting a counter mission again Paul, trying to set up an opposition Church in each of Paul's missions. Only when the Apostle was dead and Jerusalem was destroyed were these opponents silenced.

But how cordial was his reception in Antioch! Paul was their Apostle, he was their beloved leader and hero. He had formed them and made them the capital of the universal Church. Here in Antioch, Paul probably met Peter, John, Mark, and perhaps also Barnabas. Here according to an ancient tradition was a *cathedra Petri*. It was autumn; winter was fast approaching, and the expression, "after he had spent some time there," seems to indicate that he spent the winter there.

Paul liked to begin his journeys in the spring. So the next

---

[30] Cf. Ad. von Harnack, *Die Mission and Ausbreitung des Christentums*, Leipzig, 1924

spring he bade farewell to his friends, never to see them again. He strode out bravely into the greatest and most fruitful period of his life which would end with a martyr's death in Rome. It seems that another young friend joined him here, Titus (2 Cor. 8:23). But strangely, he is not mentioned in the Acts of the Apostles although from this time on he plays a prominent role in the Apostle's life. Silas no longer appears in Paul's company. Paul had probably relinquished him to Peter, whose confidential secretary he now became.

Before he sailed, Paul seems to have received word about the plan of his enemies to erect a counter mission in Asia Minor. That may have been the reason why he did not immediately go to Ephesus, but, in spite of all difficulties, crossed over the Taurus mountains through the Cilician Pass and hurried into Galatia to meet the attacks of his enemies and confirm his Churches "in order." Since Luke has nowhere told us of a series of North Galatian Churches, we must understand the South Galatian Churches of Derbe, Lystra, Iconium, Antioch, and their affiliates. This second diagonal trip across Asia Minor was not, therefore, for the purpose of making new foundations, but to strengthen the Churches already founded and also to arrive at the Ionian coast. It is unthinkable that Paul would not have hastened to these Churches when they were in danger, particularly if we remember that he had so much affection for the people of southern Galatia.

He cannot have arrived at Derbe before the middle of June in the year 53. Here he was joined by a new disciple, Gaius of Derbe. As long as Paul was in Galatia, his opponents were silent, lying in readiness to do their destructive work when he was gone. While Paul was present, all opposition disappeared; even those who were weakening acted loyally (Gal. 4:18). Sometimes he feared that the Galatians might be offended by his straightforward speech and not understand how much love and affection he had in his heart. During this journey he was also busily engaged in taking up the collection for the brethren in

Jerusalem (1 Cor. 16:1). Here again, we cannot suppose that Paul would be taking up this collection in the rather unknown North Galatia Churches (Ancyra, Pessinus?) and not in the well-known Churches of southern Galatia. It seems probable that both Paul and Luke used the term Galatia to mean the Roman province of Galatia, which included southern Galatia.

With necessary rest periods on this inspection tour, Paul may have continued his journey by way of Apamea, over the plateau of Phrygia and through the Meander valley sometime in the next spring. After a march of 330 miles he arrived at Ephesus in April of 54. The whole journey from Tarsus to Ephesus was a matter of 720 miles.

Those who argue that Paul went to northern Galatia, must conclude that he ignored the danger in which the southern Churches were and that he went by forced marches by way of Cybistra (Eregli) or Tyana, Caesarea, Ancyra, Pessinus, and Dorylaeum, across so-called "scorched Phrygia," covered with lava flows, to the Persian highway and so to Ephesus. Connections between Eregli and Ancyra were exceptionally poor; they still are. At any rate, it would have been a breakneck journey through mountain passes, canyons, swamps, salt steppes. It was the way St. John Chrysostom, one of Paul's fervent admirers, went into exile 350 years later, and during his first winter in Cucusus in Lesser Armenia, he wrote, "I am really coming back from the gates of hell."

The trip into northern Galatia would have added about 375 miles, and the entire journey from Tarsus to Ephesus would have totalled 1,060 miles. A journey of about 70 days, since the ancients reckoned 15 miles a day for the ordinary foot-traveller, and 20 miles a day for the imperial courier. Why undergo such hazards, especially since nothing came of it? We need not exaggerate the Apostle's journeyings into the incredible. They are amazing enough in reality. If we add up the mileage of St. Paul's three journeys in Asia Minor, we arrive at the following figures: the first journey, from Adalia to Derbe and

the return, 625 miles; the second journey, from Tarsus to Troas
(without the side trip to Ancyra), 875 miles; the third journey,
from Tarsus to Ephesus, 710 miles. If we add to this a large
number of journeys from towns into the neighbouring country,
the differences in altitude, and the increased mileage of
meandering roads over our modern calculations, we arrive at
some idea of the almost superhuman physical achievement of
Paul's missionary journeys.

In Ephesus, Paul was in the heart of the province of Asia.
That city was the metropolis of Asia Minor, the envy of all her
neighbours. The Ephesus that Paul entered now had been
rebuilt by that humane general and successor of Alexander,
Lysimachus, and now it breathed the spirit of late Greek inter-
nationalism. When St. John, in his Apocalypse, was describing
the enormous wealth and luxury of the Roman Empire, he
undoubtedly had in mind the vast storehouses and the world
commerce of Ephesus, so that we could rightly say that
Ephesus was indeed the Babylon of the Apocalypse. Not the
city of Rome, but the goddess Roma who ruled over Ephesus.
The Apostle's words could apply only to a port: "For in one
hour all this wealth has been laid waste. And every shipmaster
and all that sail into the lake and mariners, as many as work in
the sea, stood afar off, and cried, seeing the place of her
burning, saying: What city is like to this great city? And they
cast dust upon their heads and cried, weeping and mourning,
saying: Alas! alas! that great city, wherein all were made rich,
that had ships at sea, by reason of her prices. For in one hour
she is made desolate" (Rev. 18:17 ff.).

But there was another Ephesus. With Jerusalem and Athens
it was one of the three great holy cities of antiquity. Because of
its Artemisium, the sanctuary of Diana, Ephesus was the central
point for all Asiatic magic. It was the paradise of the pleasures,
vices, and mysteries of the Orient. The statues of gods and
goddesses that Paul saw in Ephesus awakened in him the same
feelings as he experienced in Athens. When he passed through

the Magnesian Gate, he soon stood before that gigantic terrace upon which was built the shrine of Diana, one of the seven wonders of the world. But the Artemis of Ephesus was not the divine huntress and virgin of the Greeks. She was a degenerate form of the Phoenician Astarte. The blackened idol carved from vinewood, like the black stone of Kaaba at Mecca, was believed to have fallen from heaven. She looked like a prehistoric nature goddess, as some incarnation of the procreative urge, with her countless breasts, her massive thighs covered with magic sayings, crowned with the mural crown, and her muscular arms resting on a crude cudgel.

Her temple was also a large banking institution, because of the blind trust people had in her. Behind her image and under her protection the entire treasury of the province of Asia had been deposited. Here, as in the Temple in Jerusalem, all the savings and endowments of the priests were placed for safe-keeping. The temple itself, which had burned during the night when Alexander the Great was born, had been rebuilt, and was approximately the size of the present St. Peter's in Rome. The roof was supported by 127 Ionian columns which rested on artistically sculptured marble forms. One of these pillars is still preserved in the British Museum. The great sanctuary was adorned with masterpieces from the hands of Phidias, Polycletus, Scopas, and Praxiteles. Lysippus had made the great statue of Alexander, and such artists as Parrhasius, Zeuxis, and Apelles created the murals.

The old part of the city was completely in the hands of the priesthood. An army of priestesses, who originally had been a troop of Amazons appointed to defend the image of the goddess, and an equal number of priests, most of whom were eunuchs, were governed by the chief priest or Megabyzos. Besides these a great number of temple guards, musicians, singers, staff carriers, magicians, and fakirs were employed. The temple also had the right of asylum for criminals, and thus attracted a number of doubtful characters who were fugitives from justice.

No one, of course, had any inkling that this unassuming Jew who today entered Ephesus was about to tumble Diana from her throne after a tenure of more than a thousand years. That he was about to announce the coming of a new day whose light would disperse all this mummery and the priestcraft and trickery of these eunuchs.

Yet all this pagan magnificence disappeared so quickly and so completely that the English archaeologists had to use steam pumps to lift a few fragments of the temple from below the underground water-level. An ancient epigram told how the Temple of Diana of Ephesus was one of the great wonders of the world. Hundreds of years later a medieval scholar declared that now it had become the most deserted and miserable of places by the grace of Christ and the teaching of John the theologian.

But the good man forgot that the destruction of paganism was owing primarily to the man who today was entering the city with his friends, armed with an unconquerable faith in the might of the eternal Son of God.

St Paul's Third Missionary Journey

CHAPTER THIRTY-EIGHT

APOLLO

"Now a certain Jew, named Apollo, born at Alexandria, an eloquent man, came to Ephesus, one mighty in the Scriptures" (Acts 18:24).

The worship of Artemis was not the only thing that gave Ephesus its religious atmosphere. Besides the cult of the goddess, the worship of the emperor flourished here more than in most cities. This part of Asia has been called the birthplace of despotism, that most unworthy of all religions. A few decades ago German scholars discovered and published a remarkable inscription, taken from a decree of the federation of Greek cities of Asia Minor issued during the reign of Augustus. In 9 B.C., the provincial congress of Asia Minor, sitting in the metropolis of Ephesus, used language, about the birth of the Emperor, that will remind every Christian of our celebration of the birth of Christ. By this decree the beginning of the year was changed to September 23, the birthday of the Emperor, and the way this was done indicates that this day was to inaugurate a new era in the world. The main content of the decree according to Harnack is as follows:

"This day has given the world an entirely new appearance. The world would have gone down to destruction if a new hope had not arisen for all men in him who is born on this day. He judges rightly who understands that this day is the beginning of a new life and new powers for himself and all men. Now the time has passed when a man regretted having been born. No other day confers so much happiness as this day gives to each individual and also to the whole community, and it is impossible to give adequate thanks for all the benefits that accrue to us today. Providence, ruling over everything in life, has endowed this man with such gifts for the salvation of mankind that he must be received by us and coming generations as the saviour of the world. He will put an end to all feuds and restore all things wonderfully. In his coming all the hopes of the fathers are fulfilled. Not only has he surpassed all previous benefactors of mankind, but none greater than he will ever come."

We must keep in mind this twofold background of the cult of Artemis and of the emperor if we would rightly evaluate Paul's courageous undertaking in Ephesus. He needed irrepressible courage, a victorious faith in the power of Christ in order to venture into this stronghold of Asiatic black magic. All he could offer in place of the adoration of the overwhelming majesty of the Roman total state was the poor little tale about the crucified carpenter's Son of Nazareth. All he could offer in place of the intoxicating sensual rites of Artemis and the seductive charm of its literature and eroticism, was the chaste mystery of a small piece of bread over which he said a few mysterious words. Paul must certainly have felt that Christ was an invincible force, a power really present beside him, as he entered on this adventure. What was the secret of his courage? From this very Ephesus he wrote to the Corinthians, "I believed, for which cause I have spoken" (2 Cor. 4:13).

That was it: his faith. He saw not only the shameful and repulsive things of the worship of Diana. He saw not only the folly of superstition; he saw more. He saw a people that did not tire of making sacrifices for its gods, a people that longed for any sign of union with the unseen powers of the universe. His sensitive ear caught the cry of humanity's soul for God, even though they sought him in strange places. Paul had faith in humanity because he had faith in Christ, who had considered this race of sufficient value to give his life for it.

So Paul and his companions walked through the streets of Ephesus one day in April of A.D. 54, passed the great gymnasium of the city, the colonnaded agora with its shops and markets. At last he was glad to accept the hospitality of the quarters prepared for him in Aquila's house.

The Christians of Ephesus were a peculiar group with an odd, half-finished, half-Christian, unapostolic, and unecclesiastical religion. It was not really Christianity at all, but a kind of lay movement begun by the preaching of John the Baptist which later developed an antagonism for Christ. These Christians of Ephesus were Christians more by desire than by faith and knowledge.

Here at Ephesus, Paul learned about a highly interesting liberal representative of Johannine pre-Christianity, who had been preaching in Ephesus before Paul's arrival and who had gone to Corinth. He was a Jew of Alexandria, well versed in the Scriptures, a fiery orator with an unusually attractive personality, called Apollonios, or Apollo. He, too, had joined the Baptist's movement, which had come as far as Alexandria. Now he himself had become the forerunner for the full gospel. From now on Apollo appears frequently within the orbit of Paul's activity, and gradually he begins to assume a more important role in Paul's missionary campaigns.

Apollo brought a new cultural element into the primitive Church: the culture of the School of Alexandria, whose philosophical flights and brilliant excursions into the field of exegesis constituted an important contribution for the defence of Christian truth. At that time the city of Alexandria was the centre of a liberal Jewish theological movement which sought to assimilate the wisdom of all nations, the Greeks' teaching of the logos, their theory of germinal ideas, the ethics of the Stoa, and an enlightened form of Mosaic teaching. The recognized head of this movement was the famous Philo, who sought to reconcile the sacrosanct Plato with the Scriptural wisdom of the Old Testament, so that it was said that "either Philo is platonizing, or Plato is being philonized." One of the principal aims of the Judaeo-Alexandrian school of theology was to adapt Greek philosophy and the Greek language as a suitable vehicle for Jewish ideas. Thus the school of Alexandria furthered the plans of Providence by making Greek the classic form of expression for Christian dogma.

By trying to make the Mosaic teaching acceptable to the pagan world, to the consternation of their brethren in Jerusalem the Alexandrians became more liberal in thought. They had even built their own temple in Leontopolis near Alexandria, a Hellenic counterpart to the Temple in Jerusalem. Apollo may well have been a disciple of the great Philo, and in that case his position as a Christian is easily determined. His religion, then, was indeed Christianity with a Platonic tendency, but without any mystical depth. He was an enthusiastic adherent of Jesus' moral teachings, of his new concept of religion as the adoration of God in "spirit and truth," but he had no appreciation for the heart of Christianity, for the mystical concept of the atoning death of Christ, the Resurrection and the mission of the Holy Spirit. Luke says of him that he was "fervent in spirit," and when he says that "Apollo was instructed in the way of the Lord," and that he "taught diligently the things that are of Jesus, knowing only the baptism of John," he meant that Apollo had been instructed in some of the essential points of Christianity, probably about our Lord's life, his Messianic character, and his divine nature.

Thus Apollo became the leader of a group of Alexandrian Christians who read the Bible assiduously, but had not yet found the Church. They still formed one organization with the synagogue. In Ephesus, Apollo became a sensation, and one day Aquila and Priscilla went to the synagogue to hear him. Apollo preached a forceful Messianic sermon, but it lacked the familiar, heart-touching tone of Paul's preaching. Apollo talked about the *logos*, but he said nothing about the sacred *pneuma*. After the service Aquila and Priscilla invited him to their house and told him of the life of the spirit in the Church as they had learned it from Paul. Apollo, the learned teacher, became their friend and catechism pupil. They told him of the Corinthian Church that Paul had established and of its rich charismatic life. Immediately Apollo determined to go to Corinth to see the fullness of the Church's life, and Aquila gave him letters of introduction to the leaders of the Church. It seems that it was only in Corinth that Apollo was received into the Church by baptism and confirmation conferred by one of Paul's disciples. In a short time Apollo became the subject of much attention. He rose to be one of the leading personalities in the congregation. His appearance was something that pleased the sensation-loving Greeks. His refined Attic accent, his flawless Greek, his flair for Platonic phrases, his emphasis on knowledge (*gnosis*) rather than faith (*pistis*) flattered the pride and self-importance of the Corinthians. Without desiring it or being able to prevent it, an Apollo group, formed in the congregation at Corinth, laid great stress on Apollo's superiority over Paul as a speaker. When his followers became loud and indiscreet, Apollo left Corinth and returned to Ephesus, so that he would not jeopardize the unity of the Church.

Besides this, Ephesus had a group of followers of John the Baptist. Paul considered it his first obligation to lead these half-Christians and odd saints to the full knowledge of Christian faith and life. In this connection he had an interesting experience. He met a group of about twelve men, whose strict and retiring life attracted his attention. But he noticed that something was lacking in their Christianity. That the joy and gladness of other Christians seemed never to light their sombre ascetic faces. Paul asked them, "Have you received the Holy Spirit since you believed?" They looked puzzled. They did not understand what he meant. They had never heard of the coming of the Holy

Spirit on Pentecost. Then Paul asked: "In what then were you baptized?" And gradually he learned that they were a little group of people who prayed and fasted in the spirit of St. John the Baptist. Paul explained to them that the baptism of John as an expression of faith in the coming Redeemer had been replaced. These men then asked for further instruction and admission into the Church through baptism and the laying on of hands. It seemed to them now that they had come from some dark underground chamber into the brilliant light of the Church. The Spirit filled their hearts and souls, their minds had a new light, and they felt a new confidence in religion which they soon expressed in tongues and prophecies.

That question of Paul's: "Have you received the Holy Spirit?" was the deciding question in early Christianity. It was not baptism that was the seal and identification of the Christian, but the possession of the Spirit. The transformation into a Christian was merely begun in baptism. It was completed by the transmission of the Spirit in confirmation. For this reason confirmation was the culmination and complement of baptism. In a sense it was the fullness of baptism, just as Pentecost was the completion of Easter. Together these two sacraments make up the dedicatory rite of the Christian, and can be received but once. But once the rite is conferred, the Christian must go on to Christian life. He must be mystically drawn into the communion of Christ's death and Resurrection, and he must continually renew himself in the mystic communion of life and sacrifice in the Eucharist. These three sacraments complete the mystic circle of the redemption. They are called the sacraments of the redemption and even today, in our catechisms, they are still enumerated in that order.

Ephesus was not the only Jewish community in the Diaspora with a group of Johannine disciples. John himself had brought one group to Jesus. But even in the beginning a certain estrangement arose between the disciples of Jesus and those of John (John 3:26). After John's death his disciples formed themselves even more compactly about his idealized personality into independent groups. And the waves of the Johannine movement reached beyond the Jordan out into Asia and Egypt. John the Evangelist refers to this Baptist movement in the prologue to his Gospel: "He was not the light, but was to give testimony of the light" (John 1:8). That sentence would have had no meaning if there had not been some of John's disciples who believed that he was the light. During the second century these Johannine disciples disappeared.

St. Paul's experience with these twelve disciples in Ephesus shows how essential for true Christianity is the organizational connection with the apostolic Church, and how a personal, unecclesiastical, biblical Christianity soon degenerates into sterile sectarianism marked by a joyless asceticism and a distorted idea of Christ. The Christianity that Paul found in Ephesus was only the anteroom. And Paul is rightfully considered the founder of the Church in Ephesus, and here too he was not building on anyone else's foundation.

CHAPTER THIRTY-NINE

SOLICITUDE FOR ALL THE CHURCHES

"And entering into the synagogue, he spoke boldly for the space of three months, disputing and exhorting concerning the kingdom of God" (Acts 19:8).

Paul followed his old method in Ephesus. From the first day he lived from the labour of his hands, spending the time from early morning till noon at the workbench and loom. In Ephesus he thought it particularly important to show that Christianity and an understanding of economics were not mutually exclusive. That the religion of Jesus was not the religion of pale, emaciated dreamers.

A word of appreciation was certainly due his hosts. After Paul moved in, Aquila and Priscilla had no more privacy or quiet. All day long, until into the night, people came and went. Some came to ask a question, some had difficulties of conscience, some came to register for baptismal instructions, messengers came bringing reports and greetings from the different Churches of Phrygia, Galatia, Macedonia, and Greece, and they often waited to take back with them directions from the Apostle. Anyone who was ever caught in Paul's orbit would be caught up into a whirlpool of energetic living.

No one was ever idle around Paul. In the evening he had catechumens' instructions for beginners and for those who were advanced. Then he preached a sermon and whenever possible, at least on Sundays, he celebrated the Eucharist. He was always starting new classes for converts in private homes under the direction of his helpers. He himself gradually could do no more than supervise the whole organization and confer the sacraments of the laying on of hands, confirmation and holy orders. The Jews believed that the first fruits were always to be dedicated to God. In that spirit Paul greeted the first-born of his Ephesian neophytes in the letter to the Romans: "Salute Epenetus, my beloved: who is the first-fruits of Asia in Christ" (Rom. 16:5).

In Ephesus, too, the synagogue, unknowingly and unwillingly, had become the anteroom of the gospel. But it was only after Paul arrived that the Christians became conscious of their essentially different character. While he was preaching in the synagogue, Paul came into contact with different parts of the population, especially that better class of proselytes who made up the nucleus of the Church in Ephesus. During the first three months Paul made great progress. But it was not long until the Jews began to realize that the full, catholic Christianity meant the end of their nationally circumscribed religion. Paul did not avoid any religious discussions when they were sincere, but the discussions in the synagogue almost always ended in ugly scenes and bitter words. The break had come with the synagogue, and from this time on Paul did not again enter the synagogue. In the meantime the interest in the new religion had grown so great that Paul was able to try a new missionary method. The private homes of his friends were too small for meetings, and so Paul now began to give public lectures.

As the winter came on, Paul realized that he could not continue lecturing in the open. He searched for a fitting hall. A certain grammarian, Tyrannus, probably a convert, was prepared to rent a spacious auditorium. This hall may have been in one of the five great gymnasia which were used for athletics and baths, and for the lectures of professors, rhetoricians, and poets. From the Beza text we know the hours of Paul's lectures, although we do not know the title of his lecture series. Tyrannus finished his lectures at eleven in the morning, and after a half-hour pause, Paul had the use of the auditorium, that is from 11:30 until 4:30. That period was free time in the gymnasium, but Paul knew no free time during the day. The whole morning he had been sitting at the loom to earn his bed and board, and then he hurried to the auditorium where his audience awaited him. It was truly a mixed audience: students, storekeepers, merchants, clerks, labourers, officials, philosophers, men and women of the better classes, slaves, and freemen.

For two years Paul maintained this strenuous regime. The great festivals of Artemis, especially in May, brought visitors from all parts of the world to Ephesus. Many of them naturally came into the auditorium to hear Paul: Phrygians from the valleys of the Meander and the Lycos, Lydians, men from Miletus, Smyrna, Priene, Halicarnassus, from legendary Pergamon, from Troas, and from all the islands of the Aegean. While he is talking, someone asks a question or makes an objection, or requests a fuller explanation. Ephesus, it must be remembered, was the cradle of Grecian philosophy, and these people were natural philosophers. And Paul was not afraid to attack the worship of Artemis occasionally, as is evident from the speech of Demetrius, the silversmith, and from the letter to the Ephesians: "This then I say and testify in the Lord: That henceforward you walk not as also the Gentiles walk in the vanity of their mind: having their understanding darkened: being alienated from the life of God through the ignorance that is in them, because of the blindness of their hearts. Who despairing have given themselves up to lasciviousness, to the working of all uncleanness, to covetousness" (Eph. 4:17 ff.).

Besides this public work of giving lectures, Paul was always engaged in many details, in visiting the homes of his converts, and receiving visitors. These were not pietistic social visits. They were a ceaseless wrestling with souls, with the weak, the hesitant, the doubting, the despairing. Many times

Paul went down to the sailors' quarter, to the agora, the military barracks, to the business section, and up to the residences and villas on Pion and Coressus. Many times visitors sat at table with him while his table talk was a form of instruction, leading them to a more intimate knowledge of Christ, telling them of his missionary experiences and the progress of the faith in other lands.

By this time the Church at Ephesus had grown so large that Paul had to think about a definite system of organization and government. He established the presbyters as the basic organization and called them *episkopoi,* a term used for the ordinary communal officer and functionary of the time, and meaning a supervisor (Acts 20:28). After his departure these officials were to become the responsible pastors of the local Churches, while he reserved to himself the supreme direction of all the Churches.

Never before had Paul found a field of labour so adequate to his great expansive powers, or one so docile. Ephesus was the capital of the most populous province of the Empire with about five hundred cities and towns. Here in Asia Minor "a wide door for effective work has been opened to me" (1 Cor. 16:9) into the pagan world. Paul, however, remained in Ephesus, holding the reins of this many-branched territory in his hand and receiving delegations from almost all the Churches. Thus he received the two Macedonians, Gaius and Aristarchus, Secundus from Thessalonica, and Sopater from Beroea. From Phrygia, Pisidia, Antioch, and Iconium swift messengers came on horseback or in wagons drawn by asses and reported to him how things went with his children.

From Philippi, Luke sent his little papyrus sheets on which, with the exactness characteristic of a physician, he had written down the growth and progress of the Church. Merchants and sailors came from Corinth, and personages like Apollo, Erastus, the city treasurer, and Sosthenes, the erstwhile president of the synagogue. If to these we add his older friends, we see that Paul had a distinguished group of co-workers with whom he could discuss the state of the Church and whom he could send out to found new Churches in the outlying cities. Messengers and delegates were continually coming and going to and from the missionary territory in the coastal region to the north and south of Ephesus and the hinterland to the east, the region of the seven Churches of the Apocalypse. Ephesus was the key point for the valleys of four rivers, the Kaystros, Meander, Hermus, and Kaikos, and for the cities along their courses and at their mouths.

The Acts of the Apostles fails to tell the whole story of this vast missionary activity of Paul and his disciples. We can fill in some of the gaps from what we read in the epistles of the apostles and in the Apocalypse. Unfortunately, Luke wrote this part of the Acts without having been present in Paul's circle.

Thus some of Paul's helpers went out to Miletus, the Venice of antiquity, which was still conscious of its intellectual era under Thales, Anaximander, and Anaximenes, and which was now famous because of its oracle of Didyma and its flourishing wool industry. Some went to Smyrna, the queen of the sea, at the foot of Mount Sipylos, the legendary Tantalis. They went to industrial Magnesia whose smithies could be heard from afar. To Tralles and its dealers in raisins and growers of figs, where Philip the deacon is also supposed to have preached.

Others went up the Kaystros to Philadelphia, or farther over the pass of Mount Tmolus to Sardis, to Thyatira, the home of Lydia, the seller of purple, and still farther to Pergamon, where, according to the Apocalypse, the throne of Satan was, that immense altar and temple to Zeus. Whether they went to Troas and Assus, or whether Luke preached there, we do not know, but at any rate Paul soon founded the Church in Troas on his journey to Corinth. Thus the seven Churches of the Apocalypse were founded.

All these cities had flourishing communities of Jews, strong guilds of craftsmen like those of the Middle Ages. Like a crown of seven stars the Churches surrounded Ephesus. Writing to them, Paul was happy to be able to say: "For once you were darkness, but now you are light in the Lord" (Eph. 5:8). It is surprising that in such a short time the gospel was spread over the whole province, but the Acts leaves no room for doubt when it says: "All who dwelt in Asia heard the word of the Lord, both Jews and Gentiles" (19:10). And Demetrius was able to arouse the populace by pointing out that "this Paul by persuasion has drawn away a great multitude, not only of Ephesus, but almost of all Asia" (Acts 19:26).

The faith flourished most abundantly in a region of southwestern Phrygia. In the valley of the Lykos, with its three busy cities, Colossae, Laodicea, and Hierapolis. Colossae (Chonas) was a small provincial town at the foot of Mount Cadmus, whose many mountain lakes fed the Lykos and the Meander. The apostle of this territory was Epaphras, a prominent Greek of Colossae, who had been won over to the faith by Paul himself and who was especially dear to Paul. Writing to the Colossians, Paul said: "As you learned of Epaphras, our most beloved fellow servant, who is for you a faithful minister of Christ Jesus" (1:7). Later Epaphras shared Paul's captivity in Rome. It was probably through him that Paul became friendly with Philemon, a wealthy citizen of Colossae, who, with his wife Appia, owed to Paul the greatest happiness of their lives and gratefully put their house at his disposal for divine worship. Philemon's slave, Onesimus, had probably delivered many a letter to Paul. One day Philemon brought his friend or relative, Archippus, to see Paul, and Paul was so pleased with the young man that he later ordained him priest in Colossae and called him "our fellow soldier" (Philem. 2; Col. 4:17).

From Colossae, Epaphras went to the neighbouring town of Laodicea (Eski Hissar), which was famous for its beautiful purple and for its school for oculists. St. John was probably referring to this school when in the Apocalypse he wrote: "Anoint your eyes with eye salve, that you may see" (3:18).

Here Epaphras founded a congregation which met in the house of Nymphas (Nymphodoros) (Col. 4:15). After fifteen years this Church received from St. John the severest reproach of all seven Churches, "I know your works, that you are neither cold nor hot. I would you were cold or hot. But because you are lukewarm and neither cold nor hot, I will begin to vomit you out of my mouth" (Rev. 3:15 f.). The ruins of the city seem to be a dreadful fulfilment of that prophecy.

On the other side of the valley where the Lykos flows into the Meander, the city of Hierapolis, the sacred city of the Phrygians, is built high on a mountain ledge. Hierapolis was famous for its hot springs, which tumble from ledge to ledge in playful cascades and form a bizarre world of stalactites with little grottos and fairy palaces. Here, too, Epaphras had brought the message of the faith: "Epaphras salutes you, who is one of you, a servant of Christ Jesus, who is always solicitous for you in prayers, that you may stand perfect ... For I bear him testimony that he has much labour for you and for them that are at Laodicea and them at Hierapolis" (Col. 4:12). Probably Epaphras exercised something like the office of a bishop over this neighbourhood.

But the fate of these Christian cities and towns of Asia Minor is a solemn warning. Their Christianity was not able to maintain the high state of fervour and devotion of the time of their founders. Soon it succumbed to tepidity and worldliness. The glistening white deposit from the hot springs of Hierapolis lying like a shroud over everything is a symbol of the spiritual death which spread over all Asia Minor, so that it was an easy matter for the Crescent to overrun the land; today scarcely half a dozen Christians live there. The remembrance of their "divine" Paul, as they sometimes called him, gradually receded from their minds. He was soon completely forgotten, and the warning of the seer was fulfilled: "I will move your candlestick out of its place" (Rev. 2:5).

CHAPTER FORTY

A SPECTACLE TO THE WORLD

"And God wrought by the hand of Paul
more than common miracles" (Acts 19:11).

Paul had reached the zenith of his activity. By the lectures he was giving in the auditorium, by his influence throughout the province, and by the utter sincerity of his character, he must have made a deep impression on discerning men in political life. We know that several Asiarchs, members of the provincial congress, and directors of the festive games were friendly with him. This amiable intercourse with leaders in the community and with the intellectual leaders of paganism is instructive. Following the example of our Lord, Christianity never disdained to exercise its influence in the highest ranks of society, as Paul had already shown at Athens. Christianity is certainly not an exclusively peasant religion. It addresses all classes of society. But the faith and devotion of the lower classes will ever be the most reliable foundation for the Church. Too much friendship with the great ones of this world, too much intimacy with the rich, produces an attitude in the Church which alienates the hearts of the poor. The common people are sensitive to the voice of the Good Shepherd, and they also have an ear for certain false undertones.

At that time a great number of Jewish and pagan charlatans travelled about, exploiting the people's readiness to believe in miracles. That strange mixture of enthusiast and charlatan, Apollonius of Tyana, whom we met in Athens, was now in Ephesus. The famous astrologer, Balbillus, who had such a harmful influence on Nero, was a native Ephesian. The miraculous cures of Asclepius, the innumerable magic draughts and charms, the business of interpreting the stars, and the various forms of fortune telling provided a comfortable living for an array of priests and magicians. Theosophy, occultism, and black magic had numerous followers in Ephesus. A particular kind of secret knowledge, the *Ephesia grammata*, was cultivated there, together with all manner of esoteric and magic literature.

In a world like this, where the people were so devoted to magic and to the demoniacal, Paul was obliged to permit his charismatic gifts to come to the front. The situation prevailing in Ephesus called forth Paul's special gifts. His miraculous acts are a proof of his attitude. The masters of the black art were amazed at the psychic powers that emanated from Paul. Whatever he was not able to accomplish by his preaching, he did by the "showing of the Spirit and power" (1 Cor. 2:4), by healing the sick and relieving the possessed.

In pagan antiquity, as even today in pagan missionary lands, the sick were the poorest of the poor. Swarms of the crippled and diseased were perpetually gathered in the shrines of Asclepius, and sometimes it may have happened that certain nervous conditions, spasms, or apparent paralysis disappeared in the excitement of the pagan rites. But it was Christianity that for the first time attacked the evil of bodily ailments at the root, by removing the moral psychic disturbance, by healing the moral disease of the personality and by relaxing the paralysis of the soul through the grace of Christ.

As Paul walked through the streets, he saw the sick and lame lying in the shadow of the houses, he saw the festering stumps of the lepers reached out to him for help. And he made them well by calling on the name of Jesus, without asking anything in return, except that they should call on the name of Jesus. "Freely have you received: freely give" (Matt. 10:8). His reputation as a wonderworker became so great that people came to Priscilla for articles of his clothing, his work aprons and handkerchiefs, to cure the sick.

Paul's influence became so powerful that some men were able to conjure the devils by calling on Paul's name. Exorcism was practised by the Jews since the beginning. Jewish conjurers went up and down the country everywhere. Jesus had referred to them (Matt. 12:27; Luke 11:19), and the Evangelists speak of those who worked miracles in the name of Jesus (Mark 9:38; Luke 9:49). The Ephesians' peculiar liking for horrifying experiences led to an embarrassing incident that Luke records with some touch of humour. Seven sons of a Jewish priest, called Sceva, made up a travelling group of conjurers, and on one occasion undertook a public exorcism. The possessed person ridiculed all their efforts to dislodge the evil spirit, and when the crowd saw that the conjurers were bungling the affair, they began baiting them. Now the reputation of Sceva's sons was at stake, and in their anxiety they resorted to the charm that Paul used so successfully: they called on the name of Jesus whom Paul preaches. But the name of Jesus is not to be used as a magic charm, and they received the mocking answer from the possessed, "Jesus I know, and Paul I know: but who are you?" (Acts 19:15) Immediately the possessed person began to attack the would-be conjurers, striking down two of them and tearing the clothing from the others, who fled in disgrace. They had been severely punished for their religious insincerity, but for Paul the incident was a triumph. Now the name of Jesus was spoken everywhere, and it was pronounced with awe and reverence. People understood now that Paul was working miracles, not by some charm, but by the power of the heavenly Christ. This was part of a conflict of which Paul wrote: "For our wrestling is not against flesh and blood; but against principalities and powers, against the rulers of the world of this darkness, against the spirits of wickedness in high places" (Eph. 6:12).

The name of Jesus was triumphantly announced in every part of the city. A hundred sermons would not have had the effect of this one incident. Such is the power of reality. Paul noticed how the attendance was increasing at his lectures. As people sat and listened to him, they thought that he was surrounded by some superior power, that he was one of those "divine" men whom the ancients used to speak of. When Paul uttered the name of Jesus, he pronounced it in a manner different from the way those pitiable conjurers said it. When he was carried away with his subject and cried out, "In the name of Jesus every knee should bow, of those that are in heaven, on earth, and under the earth: and that every tongue should confess that the Lord Jesus Christ is in the glory of God the Father" (Phil. 2:10), his audience trembled with awe. Many believed and others shouted: "Paul, call your Jesus down upon me to help me."

He tried to calm the audience and return to the channel of his subject, but they had no more interest in that. They lifted him to their shoulders and carried him out to the agora. From all directions men were bringing their books of magic, their papyrus charms, their dream books, and the *Ephesia grammata*, and threw them on a heap in the street. Soon someone touched a flame to the pile of parchment, papyrus, and strange amulets. One of these papyrus sheets was accidentally preserved with its lettering, a senseless confusion of unintelligible words: "Aski-Kataski-Aiks-Tetraks." These charm tickets seemed to have fallen from the skies, like our modern chain letters, and somehow they were preserved as remedies against all kinds of evil, against rheumatism, gout, witches, and the evil eye. That day others brought out those magic books supposed to have come from Noe and Solomon. It must have been a bonfire of large proportions, since Luke estimated the value of the books burnt that day at 50,000 silver drachmas, about $10,000. As the flames reached up, it became a mighty demonstration that the old power of paganism must now yield to the light of the gospel.

We see here one of the fundamental differences between the revealed religion and a natural religion. A trait of the natural religion that rises out of man's unthinking soul or out of some natural urge, is that it has a disposition to superstition and magic. That disposition seemed to be in the blood of all ancient races, especially in the Semites and Phoenicians. During the period of classical humanism in the eighteenth century, men dreamed up for themselves an ideal picture of the Greek religion. But today we know that beside this radiant element of the Greek's religion there was a dark, irrational, Dionysian element. The Greek religion was a strange union of contrasts. Besides the gods on high, the Greeks worshipped the gods of the infernal regions. Originally, it is true, the religion of Zeus had been monotheistic. But it could not long ward off the infiltration of the Asiatic cult of Astarte. Artemis in Ephesus is a striking proof of how the well-known Greek gods acquired Oriental features.

Paul was too keen a student of the human soul not to know that these exultant moods which he now experienced in Ephesus would not last for long. The cry of "Hosanna" is quickly followed by "Crucify him." For a short time Paul was showered by adulation and flattery, but he was too prudent to stop to enjoy the taste of success and the smell of incense. He knew that the powers of hell were arraying themselves against him. The devil was no mere Dantesque fantasy for Paul, he was a stark reality. The First Epistle to the Corinthians, as well as the second, written about this time in Ephesus, shows us the other side of the picture here in Ephesus. Soon came the time when he was "serving the Lord with all humility and with tears and temptations which befell me by the conspiracies of the Jews" (Acts 20:19). A flood of grief and suffering poured over him so that he was weary of living.

Both the Acts of the Apostles and the Epistle to the Ephesians contain the key for understanding what these sufferings were. Paul knew that, behind the scenes, the forces of evil were massing against him, that different grades of evil spirits were concentrating their attack on him. Such conflicts with the evil one are common experiences in the lives of the saints. Indeed, there is scarcely a saint in whose life the devil did not play some role. And any man who seriously believes in God will have no doubts about the existence of God's great adversary.

When Paul reached the heights of his life with Christ, he was also at the height of his suffering for Christ. It must have been a life of extreme poverty in Ephesus when he wrote: "Even to this hour we both hunger and thirst and are naked and are buffeted and have no fixed abode" (1 Cor. 4:11). Such destitution arose from his magnanimous spirit, which, in contrast to his own people's great thirst for money, left him no time to earn his living because of the pressure of his labours for souls and his heavy correspondence with the distant Churches.

Paul was proud of his poverty, but he was still prouder of being in the service of the crucified Christ. At this time he wrote to the Galatians: "But God forbid that I should glory, save in the cross of our Lord Jesus Christ" (Gal. 6:14). In his letters to the Corinthians, no less than four times he enumerates the list of his sufferings. "For I think that God has set forth us apostles, the last as it were, men appointed to death. We are made a spectacle to the world and to angels and to men ... We both hunger and thirst and are naked and are buffeted and have no fixed abode. And we labour, working with our own hands ... We are made as the refuse of this world, the offscouring of all, even until now" (1 Cor. 4:9-13). Sometimes when he came to talk of Christ's sufferings in one of his lectures he bared his back to show the livid welts of his floggings, and calmly he went on to say: "I bear the marks of the Lord Jesus in my body" (Gal. 6:17).

He refers to his most horrible experience in Ephesus when

he says, "I fought with beasts at Ephesus" (1 Cor. 15:32). Some interpreters take these words figuratively, others literally. At any rate, they remind us of a passage in the letters of Ignatius Martyr, who describes his sufferings as a prisoner on a transport ship: "From Syria to Rome I have been fighting with beasts, I have been chained to ten leopards." Ignatius was speaking figuratively. Yet it was a real experience and so, unless we are willing to call Paul a boaster in this passage, we must conclude that some great catastrophe befell him that almost annihilated him. Every attempt to soften his words recoils against the hard realism of his language: "For I think that God has set forth us apostles, the last, as it were men appointed to death. We are made a spectacle to the world and to angels and to men" (1 Cor. 4:9). And a short time after this he was writing again to the Corinthians: "For we would not have you ignorant, brethren, of our tribulation which came to us in Asia: that we were pressed out of measure above our strength, so that we were weary even of life" (2 Cor. 1:8).

Some modern interpreters conclude, not without reason, that Paul was imprisoned in Ephesus, basing their conclusion on 2 Cor. 6:5 and 11:23. Not long after this time Paul wrote the letter to the Romans, and in it he expresses his deep gratitude to Aquila and Priscilla to whom, he says, he owed his life: "Who have for my life laid down their own necks" (Rom. 16:4). A few lines farther on he speaks of Andronicus and Junias as "my fellow prisoners." These words can hardly be taken figuratively.

What terrible suffering was this that made Paul, so inured to hard labour and suffering, welcome death as a relief in his weariness with life? Four times Paul went to lengths to describe his great sufferings to the selfish and contentious people of Corinth. When he boasts about his sufferings, is there not a touch of Socratic irony in his words?

Add to these external sufferings the anguish that his beloved children of Corinth and Galatia inflicted on him. His soul was pressed down with sorrow when he thought how his

life's work was being destroyed by his Jewish enemies. And
here again his grief was doubled because he was alone and
forsaken. His friends, just at this time, were absent. Timothy,
Erastus, and Titus had gone to Macedonia and Greece. It is not
surprising that he found himself in the deepest depression. We
remember how he felt when he was alone in Corinth. How he
lay awake at night and everything seemed dark and forbidding.
But now, as then, he heard the Lord say to him, "Do not fear ...
For I have much people in this city." He always came back to
his belief in God who could raise even the dead to life. He did
not despair about Ephesus, as he had not despaired about Corinth.
Out of this agony of suffering his soul came forth purified and
strengthened: "I believed, for which cause I have spoken ...
For which cause we faint not; but though our outward man is
corrupted, yet the inward man is renewed day by day" (2 Cor.
4:13, 16).

In Ephesus, too, Paul was supported by the Spirit, who
urged him on to further labours in Macedonia, Achaia, and
Jerusalem, and after that the vision of Rome always recurred:
"Paul purposed in the spirit, when he had passed through
Macedonia and Achaia, to go to Jerusalem, saying: After I have
been there, I must see Rome also" (Acts 19:21). The Spirit
indicated to him that Rome, the capital of the world, was to be
the focus point from which the light of Christ would radiate
forever. That was the vision that spurred him on in these dark
days. Ever closer to Rome!

CHAPTER FORTY-ONE

"YOU HAVE BEEN CALLED TO LIBERTY"

What Paul had been dreading for a long time was now happening. The harmony that existed between himself and his beloved Galatians, the mutual feeling of confidence, had withstood a previous attack by his Jewish enemies. But now reports came in more frequently that the enemy had broken into his favourite Churches north of the Taurus and were succeeding in establishing rival Churches.

Paul often sent out his disciples for extended journeys to study his missions. Perhaps it was Timothy who had brought this disconcerting news. Or some of his Galatian Christians may have come to sit with him at the loom and tell him of the enemy's inroads with the accompaniment of much wild gesturing. At any rate, it was reported to Paul that prominent men had come from Jerusalem, armed with letters from the apostles, and that they were assuming authority in the Churches. They were telling the people that Paul had preached a distorted gospel, that he was not really an apostle at all, and that he had never seen Jesus. They said they had learned about the gospel from the original apostles, who really were the ones to be consulted. Paul, they said, had neglected to tell the most important thing about the gospel, namely, that the converts from paganism were obliged to submit to the law of Moses. Paul did not demand that submission because he wished to revamp the gospel to suit the pagans and thus obtain a large following. Sometimes he followed one rule, sometimes another. In Lystra he had Timothy circumcised to flatter the Jews, but when he was with the pagans he said nothing about circumcision in order to please the pagans. Now they had come from Jerusalem to announce the true gospel in place of this distortion.

Paul was stricken down with grief. The Church he loved so much, his first love, that he had brought forth with so much sorrow, seemed to be lost to him. He longed to go with the Galatian messengers immediately to see his beloved Galatian children, those simple souls with their blue eyes and fickle souls. But the daily press of affairs and his care of all the Churches kept him at Ephesus.

But who were these trouble-makers? Very likely they were emissaries of those lying brethren who had insinuated themselves into the Church at Jerusalem, and were making the last reactionary stand of the Jews. Now they went out to the foundations of the new Church to harness its energy in their drive for their nationalist aims. They tried to tyrannize over the original apostles, and into Paul's peaceful Churches they introduced the contentious argument about the law so that individuals and families, who formerly did the works of the Spirit now devoured and bit one another (Gal. 5:15).

If they had attacked him personally, Paul could have borne it, but it was a heinous thing to rob his children of their greatest possession behind his back. When Paul reviewed what he had done for the Galatians, he saw how his coming had been followed by a long series of charismata and miracle after miracle. His converts prayed, they sang, joyfully they offered their Eucharistic prayers to Christ, they spoke in divers tongues, they healed the sick, and they worked miracles. And now this exultant rhythm of the new life was to be replaced by the sombre and chill observance of the law.

The whole substance of Christianity was at stake. The question was whether Christianity was to be a formalistic, ritualistic religion. A religion of external observances like the old pagan religions, like the religion of later Judaism that had forsaken the spirit of the prophets. Was the Church that had experienced such a promising spring in Galatia to continue like some Ebionite sect worshipping a distorted Christ and disappear after a while? Or was Christ's inheritance to be carried on by the wings of the Spirit and fly forth into the world with its immortal message that God is to be adored in spirit and truth, and that he asks no more from man than his heart and his faith? That was what Paul fought for in Jerusalem and Antioch, and then he went his lonesome way, and since then had made innumerable sacrifices of body and soul.

No man ever fought for freedom as did Paul. Although he had been brought up in the strictest observance of the law, he now placed the Jewish ceremonial law on a plane with the pagans' worship of nature. Here in Phrygia the decisive battle in the war for freedom was to be fought. What happened later in Corinth and in Rome were only minor engagements.

Like a commander who assembles his general staff on the eve of an important battle, Paul called together his co-workers and fellow soldiers for a conference: Timothy and Titus, Tychicus and Trophimus from Ephesus, Gaius and Aristarchus from Macedonia, Sosthenes and Erastus from Corinth, Gaius from Derbe, and Epaphras from Colossae. It was a brilliant gathering of noble warriors, and it manifests Paul as a truly great leader of men who was not too narrow to inform his friends of his impending decisions.

The letter to the Galatians was probably written about the turn of the year, 54-55. We have extrinsic evidence for the date. In the letter Paul chides the Galatians because they had permitted the troublemakers to persuade them to accept the Jewish feast calendar with the Sabbatical year. Now, we know from

Josephus[31] that A.D. 54 was a Sabbatical year. Paul was writing, therefore, about the time of the Sabbatical year which was being observed by the misled Galatians.

A reading of the letter increases our impression of Paul's passionate personality. The letter was written with characters of fire. The basic thoughts, the biblical proofs, and the style of expression make it the model for the later epistle to the Romans. Many expressions can be explained only as coming from his mood of consternation and amazement, such as his twofold imprecation on those who preach another gospel besides his. The letter has two principal themes: the personal theme, defending the genuineness of his own apostolate; the factual theme, of the teaching of the justification by faith.

The first part is a forceful *apologia pro vita sua*, a dynamic defence of his apostolic office. Paul fights with all his powers against being relegated to the second generation of apostles. He resents being called a disciple of the apostles, or an apostle of lesser rank or order. Personal acquaintance with Jesus here on earth is not the important thing. Only one thing is of any importance; the other apostles received their apostolate and the necessary equipment only by revelation and through a commission received from the heavenly Jesus, risen from the dead. For that reason Paul says he did not go to Jerusalem to receive his authority. He wished to avoid even any appearance of doing so.

Paul was conscious of being in every way equal to the original apostles; the Spirit told him so. This attack on his apostolic office forced Paul to descend deep into his consciousness to reveal the theological foundation of his autonomous position and thereby he gave us a profound insight into Christ's mystery. This unshakable certainty about his vocation is something grandiose in Paul's character. Reading the letter we are confronted with mysteries that no psychology seems able to fathom. In giving this paraphrase of the letter we will come upon passages

---

[31] Josephus, *Jewish Antiquities,* XV, i, 2

that rival Mark Antony's speech against Brutus for sheer dramatic force.

Paul, an apostle, not by man's favour, nor by his own will, but solely and alone by the commission of Jesus Christ who has risen from the dead. All the brethren who are with me join in this circular letter to the Galatian Churches. Allow me to come to the point without more ado. I am shocked to hear of your defection from my gospel to another that is directly opposed to mine. Was I not the first and the only one who led you to Christ? And now you have allowed yourselves to be stirred up as if there were some other, better gospel that I had distorted. But there is none. There are people who turn your heads and falsify the gospel. But even if I, Paul, or one of my friends, or even an angel from heaven, should preach another gospel to you, other than I have already preached to you, let him answer before God's judgment. I retract nothing. Indeed, I repeat what I told you when I was last with you: if anyone preaches a gospel that contradicts what I have preached, let that man answer before God's judgment seat. Some men have said that I was a flatterer, a seeker after popularity, a man who looked for the favour of men, and that I did not care about God. That I had yielded to your dislike of circumcision and so omitted something essential. Do you really believe that I cared for the favour of men? If I cared for such things, I would long ago have given up this service of Christ. But that is all untrue; I am the slave of Christ.

My brethren. Let me again explain to you the nature and origin of my gospel. It is not the work of men; I went to no man's school, I am no disciple of the apostles, but I received this gospel by direct revelation. Men reproach me with the way I lived formerly. They are surprised to learn that Christ appeared to me at Damascus and called me to be the Apostle of the Gentiles. They make all kinds of surmises about my changed attitude. But who will correct the decisions that God makes? As I look back on it, I realize that even when I was in my mother's womb God thought me worthy through his eternal grace, not through my willing or non-willing, to reveal his Son through me. Immediately my mind was made up. I took counsel with no man, for when God speaks, flesh and blood have nothing to say. I did not even try to communicate with the famous apostles in Jerusalem.

Then Paul gives a vivid narrative of his experiences: his lonely Arabian sojourn, his appearance in Damascus and Jerusalem, his return to his home in Tarsus, his actions at the Council of Jerusalem on the question of circumcision, the case of Titus, the recognition of his apostolate by the other apostles, and the division of the missionary districts sealed by their handclasp. That should have been proof that his teaching and calling were equal to that of the apostles. As a final argument he tells the story of his encounter with Peter in Antioch. His narrative culminates in this argument: if a man, by following certain religious regulations, such as the ceremonial law, can obtain the right position of grace with respect to God, then Christ's death was superfluous, and God offered his Son to no avail, and thus committed an error.

Coming to the factual part of his letter, Paul discusses the great question of justification by faith. To forestall that historical misunderstanding which caused the Reformation: Paul was not speaking of man's moral actions after justification. He was not discussing man's life in the state of grace. The fact that man does make a contribution and that his moral attitude has a meritorious character follows from Paul's whole ethical system. Nowhere did Paul teach anything like passive quietism. In this polemic encounter with his adversaries, he is concerned with the first justification, with man's rebirth, about the attainment of salvation and the fulfilment of the redemption in the individual soul, with the transition from the state of sin to the state of grace. This is exclusively the work of God by reason of the atoning death of Christ, and in it there is no autonomous human contribution, no independent moral contribution acts as cause or condition of salvation, except the sorrowful, contrite act of faith, which itself is always motivated by the Spirit so that all active motivation comes from God.

With two mighty arguments Paul annihilates the stand of his opponents. One of the arguments was intended for the converts from paganism, the other for the Bible-based Jewish Christians.

He reminded the converts from paganism of their intimate experiences at the time of their conversion. He asks them: "When you began to believe and you received the Holy Spirit, who poured himself out on you so abundantly in palpable ways, in miracles, in prophetic speech, in healing of the sick, in the knowledge of hearts, did you know anything about the law of Moses? Did you attribute your enthusiasm for Christ to your own actions, to some external practices, to some regulations about eating, or was it not all due to your simple acceptance of my preaching? Did I not make the figure of Christ so alive for you, that you almost relived his crucifixion? I wish to ask you one thing: Who has so hypnotized and bewitched you? Shall people say of you that you began your Christian existence in holy enthusiasm and then ended up in Judaism and the observance of a few miserable rules? You have already attended the higher school of the knowledge of God and of Christ, you have known God, and God knew you, and now you would go back to the beginners and recite your ABC's. Those were happy times when you began to love Christ: those happy days when you trusted and loved me. Where are they now? When the first persecutions visited you and you were so proud to have suffered for Christ, who gave you the strength for that? Was that all in vain? Anyone who has had the experiences you have had, should never forget them. No, my beloved Galatians, these things come only through grace and faith, the faith that I enkindled in you.

The second proof was taken from the Bible: it was a typical allegorical interpretation of that great figure of faith of the Old Testament, a figure beloved of the Jews, Abraham. He was the type, the spiritual ancestor of all the faithful. The promises made to him are not conditioned by fleshly descent, inheritance, or blood relationship. The salvation promised to Abraham is not the exclusive privilege of one race, but the common possession of mankind, and it is as universal as the Church itself.

In Abraham the way of salvation was modelled for all times, and that way is faith. Moses with his books of the law came 430 years later. And he had to deal with a people that had been completely confused about God because of their long sojourn among the pagans. That people needed to be educated for hundreds of years under the strict regime of the law. Therefore the law, in God's plan of salvation, had only a transitory, passing character. It was a matter of training people during their spiritual minority. But we have now come to the fullness of time. Mankind has graduated from the elementary school and has entered the higher school of Christ, in which there is no difference between Jew and Gentile, Greek and non-Greek, master and slave, man and woman.

After Paul has cudgelled his opponents down with these sharp arguments, he suddenly becomes tender and soft like a mother and he gives his emotions free rein. Most of all, he said, I should like to be in labour again for you as a mother, and speak to you as a mother to her children. After this affectionate interlude, Paul apparently paused in his dictation, and then returned to the attack.

"Perhaps you think I know nothing of the law of Moses. Listen to this story that I will interpret according to the best rules of Jewish exegesis. You know, Abraham had two sons. Ismael, Agar's son, was the son of the maidservant, therefore the son of sexual pleasure. But Isaac, Sara's son, was the son of the mistress of the house, the fruit of the divine promise. Now, that is a figure of God's two covenants: the old one on Mount Sinai, which produces slave children, and the new one on Mount Sion, which produces children of God. Agar means 'the mountain,' and indicates Mount Sion, the present-day Jerusalem which because of its enslavement of conscience is a slave mother and will have nothing to do with freedom. Sara, the free woman, however, is the model of the new Jerusalem, which is free from all enslavement of conscience; and that is our mother. Your new teachers are sons of Agar, but we are children of liberty. The thing is repeating itself today. Just as then the son of the free woman is persecuted by the son of the slave woman, by the religion of the law.

"Tell that to your seducers. Tell them they are the sons of slavery; that we are free. Christ gave us our freedom. But this freedom does not mean licence, as some of our enemies contend. By Christ's freedom we are freed from the service of the elements, the demons, and the fates, and we have entered the service of Christ, where love rules. And your seducers are the very ones who violate this love. Since they are with you there has been nothing but fighting and bitterness. They have a thousand rules and regulations, but we have one law: Walk in the spirit. Look to Jesus, and then the works of the flesh will not break forth, then the fruits of the spirit will grow on your tree of life. Whoever sows in the flesh will reap corruption. Who sows in the spirit will reap the fruits of the spirit.

"Circumcision or non-circumcision is of no importance. The important thing is a new life in Christ, a new being in Christ. Whoever listens to this message ought to be at peace. And your seducers ought to permit a man who has been stoned for Christ and still bears the marks in his body to live in peace."
In conclusion, Paul intones the canticle of the Cross, "O Saving Cross," a hymn the Church has always been chanting. In the mystery of the Cross was contained everything that stood in opposition to the world.

The wounds he had received at Lystra in Christ's service are the brief and seal of his apostolate. Thus, at the end of this letter, Paul stands before them like an old general of many campaigns. He bares his breast to show the marks of his wounds received in battle. No one need ever be ashamed of such a leader. Indeed, they ought to remember when it was that he had received these marks. According to Herodotus, when a slave fled to the temple of Heracles and provided himself with the sign of the god, he was secure against seizure by anyone. So now Paul, equipped with the marks of Christ, felt himself secure against the attacks of his enemies.

In this great document, Paul once again had been in labour for his beloved Galatians (4:19). We can imagine the touching scenes in the Churches of Galatia when the letter was read, how "his children were moved to tears when they saw at the end of the letter the big letters ("see what a letter I have written to you with my own hand") (6:11). From that time on we hear of no more disturbances or complaints in this section of the Pauline missions. After the letter's arrival, evidently his enemies fled like a swarm of locusts, only to descend on other Churches. Soon we shall see them at work in Corinth.

The Galatian farmers who came to Ephesus took the letter along with them, up the Meander valley to Antioch, the metropolis of Phrygian Galatia. But they had no notion of the importance of the document they carried, for it was a charter of the world's freedom. Here in Phrygia the word of Christian freedom was first uttered. Just at this time in Phrygia a slave woman gave birth to a boy who was named Epictetus. The child was lame from birth, but in his crippled body he bore an irrepressible longing for freedom. Later, as a freedman in Rome, when the philosophers were banished from the capital by the decree of Domitian, this Epictetus gathered about himself the flower of Roman youth at Nicopolis. He instructed them in the way to preserve their human dignity and their inner freedom while they moved among the imperial courtiers and the continual conflicts of Roman officialdom.

It is only when we compare St. Paul's doctrine of freedom with Epictetus' lecture on freedom, that we appreciate the greatness of Paul's teaching. Epictetus' idea of freedom is nothing more than the glorification of self. It recommends the flight of man into an inner subjective realm where he may dispute every barrier, every bond and all the powers of fate. Yet in that inner citadel man remains the prisoner of himself, and the victim of his own pitiable thoughts and desires. Paul's doctrine of freedom, on the other hand, consists in the glorification of God who has given us an objective, everlasting realm of liberty through Christ's grace. Because he is united to Christ, Paul has a share in a higher world, which permits him to admit his external dependence while it assures him of the eventual conquest over all external bonds and ties. The Christian freedom preached by Paul urges man on to activity. Epictetus' liberty resulted in the weary lassitude of a man caught as a prisoner in his own ego.

The greatest difference between Christian and pagan liberty is that in Christianity a man obtains freedom by believing in Christ, who bestows on him the freedom that he already has earned. With Epictetus, liberty was a laborious process of self-liberation by tortuous reasoning and continuous correction of false conclusions, and a fictitious blindness to brutal reality. Christian liberty is freedom from ego and a binding to God. The freedom of the Stoics, and also of modern man, is a slavery by which man is bound to his own miserable, arbitrary fallible ego.

Any other freedom, whether the freedom of the Stoics or the freedom of German idealism as proposed by Kant and Fichte, is ultimately nothing but a flight from reality, a flight into the artificial realm of a make-believe inner world.

CHAPTER FORTY-TWO

THE FOLLY OF THE CROSS

The First Epistle to the Corinthians, chaps. 1-4

At Caesar's command the ancient city of Corinth had been laid in ruins a hundred years earlier. The new city was a Roman colony into which the most diverse elements of the world's population had come. We have already seen that the Christian community had drawn its membership from all classes of a people without any aristocracy or tradition. It was a curious melting pot, full of contradictions and antagonisms. Here you found the Hellenic craze for freedom and the narrowness of the Jewish ghetto, the most sublime spirit of Christianity and petty partisan jealousy, rich charismatic endowments and a furtive search into the dark mysteries of Dionysus. Looking down on this seething mass, is the heroic figure of Paul, thoughtful and apprehensive. Not like the ancient philosopher who looked with contempt on the follies of humanity, but with Christ's sympathy for humanity with all its curious contradictions.

Corinth, unlike the towns of Galatia, had no settled population. It had no honourable class of citizens as did Philippi. Corinth had a perpetually fluctuating mass of people, and over it the cool breezes of Mount Sion did not blow. From the top of Acrocorinth came the sultry atmosphere of Aphrodite. The picture of Corinth that Paul draws in his two epistles to the Corinthians is not encouraging. Some unthinking critics have reproached Christianity because from the beginning its message of peace has been punished by reality as a lie. But all this conflict was external and, for that matter, even in Corinth were many model families: the house of Chloe, of Stephanas, of Gaius, and of others.

As long as Paul was in Corinth he was able to keep the community on its high moral plane and maintain order by the superior force of his spirit. Four years had now passed. The picture of the Church there had changed. Greek frivolity and fickleness and a certain Oriental wantonness had brought about conditions that until now had never been found in the Church.

Every Greek city was riddled with groups and factions. Since the Greeks had lost their political autonomy and could no longer decide anything, they formed factions about all sorts of trivial questions. They argued for this dancer, for this singer, or for this gladiator in the arena. Personal questions were heatedly discussed.

Paul had established the principle of Christian liberty as against the oppression of the Jewish law, and that was no small achievement. Antiquity knew nothing about freedom of con- science, whether it was the Jew or the Gentile. Paul took one of Jesus' thoughts: the truth shall make you free; this he incorpor- ated into the Christian message. He thereby laid the foundation for the spirit of the Christian West and hence may be called the first great educator of Christian Europe.

But it was a gigantic task to secure this idea of freedom against all misunderstandings. Paul had to defend this newly won freedom against two opponents. In Galatia, against the narrow bigotry of the Jews; in Corinth, against the wild apostles of false freedom.

Apollo had just come back from Corinth and reported to

the Apostle about the precarious state of affairs there. Other reports were coming in about the increase of moral scandals among the converts. One day they joined in the Eucharistic meal, and the next day they were seen in Aphrodite's temple or they partook of a meal in the temple of Serapis. Paul had to do something about it. He wrote an earnest appeal to the Corinthians that they should not associate with "fornicators of this world, or with the covetous or the extortioners, or the servers of idols" (1 Cor. 5:10). Our two epistles to the Corinthians are only part of a more voluminous correspondence with Corinth. Unfortunately this first letter was lost, or it was suppressed. In ancient times people had peculiar ideas about literary property. This letter is lost, and shortly before this, one of the Apostle's letters had been forged in Thessalonica. Even the Jews were often guilty of literary forgeries. They put into circulation forgeries of the works of every great classical author – Orpheus, Homer, Heraclitus, Plato, Phocylides – in order to show that these works were really taken from Jewish traditions. No one was secure in the possession of his literary property. It could be forged, it could be completely appropriated, a man could put his name over your work, or put your name over his product. Is it any wonder that even Christians had no conscience in this matter? The apocryphal literature of the time tells a plain story. For the Church it was a laborious task to sift the genuine from the false, and that sifting of the canonical books went on until well into the second century.

Besides his letters, Paul also sent personal messengers. Thus, before he despatched the first letter to the Corinthians, he sent Timothy, as one of the co-founders of the Corinthian Church, to remind the Corinthians of the fundamental teachings of faith and morals and to "put you in mind of my ways" (1 Cor. 4:17). Perhaps Timothy was also sent to take up the collection for Jerusalem on this visit, and for that reason Erastus had been sent to accompany him as a man of finance. Timothy was to go by way of Troas and Macedonia, because some disturbing news may also have come from those districts. When the letter was being written, Timothy was already on his way. But a noble Christian woman of Corinth, Chloe, sent one of her servants to Paul to tell him about the divisions arising in the Church there and about the increase of immorality.

Besides the old, loyal nucleus of the Church in Corinth, three parties had been forming. The first group were setting up Apollo as their leader in opposition to Paul. Both Apollo and Paul were filled with the burning spirit of Christ, but their personalities were different. Apollo's was a speculative character, his discourses were marked with brilliant Platonic reasoning, classical diction, and oratorical elegance. Paul, on the other hand, was a realist, he had come into contact with stark reality, he had been scarred in battle. Apollo's interpretation of the Bible left many things unsaid, it shunned making a decision, it was like a slight movement caressing the surface of the lake. But Paul's speeches were more like storms, as were his letters to the Galatians and Corinthians. They stirred men up from their depths and forced them to make resolves. After a sermon by Apollo, the people looked pleased and when they came out of the meeting they said: "How lovely, how inspiring!" But when Paul preached, people went home silent and serious. Both styles of preaching have their place in the Church. The elegant graces of Bossuet and the thought-laden lines of Bourdaloue, the comforting words of St. Francis de Sales as well as the deathly earnestness of Segneri.

But for the superficial half-Greeks, Paul's methods were too disturbing. The new seekers after wisdom rallied round Apollo and took up the name of their favourite preacher as 'a kind of battle cry, shouting: "I am for Apollo." And thus many people in Corinth began to think that Paul and Apollo were leaders of hostile factions, whereas these two great souls were in the most complete accord.

The Jewish colony in Corinth grew by leaps and bounds because of additions from the east, from Palestine and Jerusalem.

Some seemingly important Jews had landed at Cenchrae, claiming to have letters of introduction from the original apostles in Jerusalem. Some of them said they had been baptized by Peter himself, that they were his intimate friends. They insinuated that Paul was not a genuine apostle, but that his apostolate was second-rate, because he had never lived in the company of Jesus. Paul, they said, was certainly the "least of the apostles," and no one could be sure whether he was an apostle or not. He was certainly much less than Moses, and now he was trying to replace Moses. Had anyone ever seen Paul's countenance shining as Moses' had shone? The fact that Paul did not accept support from the Church, which was evidently the right of an apostle, showed that he was not sure about himself.

An appeal like this is never entirely unsuccessful, and soon a considerable number of Jewish Christians had gathered under Peter's standard, with the cry: "I am for Peter." Paul never doubted for even a moment that Peter was ignorant of this misuse of his name.

Paul always spoke of Peter with reverence. He did not condemn the effort to unite the scattered Churches under Peter's authority, but he fought strenuously when these partisans tried to set up the venerable head of the apostolic college in opposition to his own apostolate.

This nonsense of partisanship in the Church reached a climax when a third group of preachers of freedom called themselves super-apostles and refused to belong to any party headed by a man. They called Christ the head of their party, and their motto was, "I am for Christ." The prime movers of this party were probably some Jewish Christians who believed they were related to Christ in a special way because they had known the Lord in the flesh. In a way, these last were the most dangerous, because they did not admit that Christ spoke through Paul, and that Paul had "the spirit of God" (7:40). This was slightly more than the childish nonsense of the other groups, for whoever plays the Master against his disciple opposes the order of the

Church itself. It was probably these "Christ" groups that followed a higher asceticism by which they considered themselves exempt from all moral restrictions. They shunned marriage, they preached an exaggerated spiritualism which denied the bodily resurrection of the dead. And lastly the Cross, that continued symbol of Christian life, was considered foolishness.

That is how things were in Corinth. Quick action was demanded. Even before Timothy reached Corinth, Paul would have to get word to the Church at Corinth to make things easier for Timothy. As he attacked this unsavoury situation, Paul tried to evaluate it in the light of the whole gospel. He tried to show how miserable were these small men in comparison with the great ideal.

Paul called in Sosthenes, the former president of the synagogue, and Apollo's convert who had come with him to Ephesus. Paul asked Sosthenes to act as liaison officer between himself and the Church at Corinth. He wished Sosthenes to subscribe to the letter with himself, in order to show that Paul and Apollo were in complete harmony. Let the Corinthians know how close he was to these supposed enemies. He was desirous of sending Apollo to Corinth as his ambassador, but Apollo did not feel equal to the task. For one night Paul wept and prayed for his children in Corinth. Was he not their father? "For in Christ Jesus, by the gospel, I have begotten you" (4:15).

Again the little workshop of Aquila became the sacred place where the Spirit of God moved gently over the spirit of the Apostle, as he dictated and Sosthenes wrote.

In the first four chapters he speaks of the discord and dissension in the Corinthian Church and of their causes: too much emphasis on the human and personal element, too little supernatural understanding; too much spiritual pride and a desire for the empty wisdom of the world. He felt it necessary to tell the party of Apollonists some elementary things about baptism because they prated that the baptism conferred by Apollo was more than other baptisms. In the Church there is only one baptism, and that baptism has value only from the death of Christ on the Cross. Now, he was glad that he had not conferred baptism himself as a rule: "I give God thanks, that I baptized none of you but Crispus and Gaius; lest any should say that you were baptized in my name." But wait; the inspiring Spirit warns him, and Paul reflects: "And I baptized also the household of Stephanas; besides, I know not whether I baptized any other" (1:14, 16). Thus, the biblical writers were ever subject to the correction of the Holy Spirit.

"Was Paul then crucified for you? or were you baptized in the name of Paul?" he asks. "Or can Greek philosophy or Greek oratory save your souls? Then the death of Christ would have been needless. Why did not Christ call the philosophers and the great ones first? Look at the membership of your Churches. The majority consists of people from the lower classes, and even many from among the slaves. Is your Greek philosophy anything but sophistry, without any value for practical living? And now you wish to judge the messengers of the gospel by your false standards. 'But the foolish things of the world God has chosen, that he may confound the wise; and the weak things of the world has God chosen, that he may confound the strong' (1:27). Do you not believe that Christianity is the highest wisdom itself? It had no need to borrow wisdom from the Greeks. But before we talk about wisdom, you ought to learn the elements of knowledge, and from your petty quarrelling it is evident that you have not learned even the beginnings of wisdom.

"You have no right to make distinctions of rank among the preachers of the gospel. Such comparisons are wholly useless. All the apostles have the same office, they are in the service of the same Lord, even though each one may have his own peculiar gifts." Clearly Paul pictures the role which the workers for the gospel play in the building up of the doctrinal edifice of Christianity. As a "wise architect" Paul drew the blueprints and laid the foundation, and that foundation was the significance of the act of redemption which he had grasped so fully, that great mystery of the mystical body of Christ. Paul was proud of his discovery of this doctrine which he owed to the revelation received at Damascus, and which it was his life's work to promulgate throughout the world.

All Christian theologians of later years would build on this doctrine, and the superstructure should be harmonious with the foundation. Paul distinguishes between two kinds of builders. The wise builder who erects a solid building on a firm foundation, and the bungler who builds out of clay and straw and wood on the solid rock. When the "day of the Lord" comes, the day when the world will be consumed by fire, the day of the great catastrophe, all this bungling work will be revealed. The structure of the wise architect will stand up, just as the ancient marble temples of Corinth withstood the destruction of Mummius. But the bungler's work will collapse, and the bungler himself will be fortunate if he gets off with only a few burns.

This judging of the value of Paul's work by the Corinthians is foolishness. No human court is competent to judge here. How laughable it is for you to form these groups and parties, how trivial this cult of personalities if you keep in mind the great goal! As Paul was dictating he had before his mind the whole cosmos as a great pyramid at whose point he saw God. "Let no man therefore glory in men. For all things are yours, whether it be Paul or Apollo or Cephas, or the world, or life, or death, or things present, or things to come. For all are yours. And you are Christ's. And Christ is God's" (3:21).

But Paul has a more telling weapon. He now belays the Greeks with their own weapon of Socratic irony of which he was a master, and he shows his Corinthians that even in the Greek sense he was a "wise" man. Socrates' learned ignorance appears now in a Christian dress: "If a man thinks himself wise, let him first become a fool in order to become wise." With exquisite humour he now disposes of certain men not fully converted, who were still walking around attired in the egg shells of their Hellenistic *gnosis*. They looked down on the simple Christians and their simple faith and acted as if they were pretenders to the crown and were to rule beside Christ. Paul speaks to them as a father would speak to a small child who rides his little wooden hobby horse and waves his little wooden sword and thinks he is a king. You have scarcely been baptized, he tells them; "you are now full; you are now become rich; you reign without us; and I would to God you did reign, that we also might reign with you" (4:8). How I wish I might get on the horse with you! If only I, too, might play at being king and "rule with you."

"But we are only apostles, we are like condemned criminals, 'men appointed to death,' while you look down on us from the imperial box in the arena." "We are fools for Christ's sake, but you are wise in Christ; we are weak, but you are strong: you are honourable, but we without honour" (4:10). Then suddenly he goes from this irony to deep earnestness. From out of his soul comes the cry that expresses the sufferings of his life: "Even to this hour we both hunger and thirst and are naked and are buffeted and have no fixed abode ... We are made as the refuse of this world, the off-scouring of all even until now" (4:11, 13).

Then in the goodness of his heart he fears that he may have offended them by this irony: "I write not these things to confound you; but I admonish you as my dearest children." Now he recalls the time when he first came to them and they sat about him, drinking in every word. He says: "For if you have ten thousand instructors in Christ, yet not many fathers. For in Christ Jesus, by the gospel, I have begotten you."

When Paul spoke of the "wisdom of the world" and the "folly of the Cross," he was not expressing the final word of Christianity on its attitude toward science and philosophy. Like the Stoics he was here indulging in paradox. The Greeks understood this. And at that time Paul was not confronted with true Greek philosophy, that genuine inheritance of the great thinkers of Hellas, the *recta ratio*, of which the First Vatican Council and the prince of Scholastics said that it presented the rational bases for the faith, *fundamenta fidei demonstrat.* Paul was dealing with the representatives of a popular philosophy, the same that had ridiculed him on the Areopagus. Here again is a historical circumstance that we must keep in mind lest we conclude that Paul despised the intellect.

Paul did not reject Apollo's style of supporting the truth of the gospel with philosophical reasonings, even though he himself had no great liking for it. He preferred to let God judge the matter. He laid the foundations of the doctrinal structure on Christ alone. This accounted for that conspicuous note of certainty which is never found in philosophical speculations or in the declarations of mystical piety. Paul's certainty arose from the objective data of the fact of the Christian redemption, from the historical fact of the crucifixion, from his own mystical union with Christ and with Christ's crucifixion. As a trained thinker, Paul knew from his inmost experience that the most valuable knowledge lies far beyond all reasoning, that with respect to the realm of the divine as it appeared to us through Christ we must have an entirely different mental attitude and approach from the one we had before. It is the attitude and approach that St. Augustine called essentially Christian.

CHAPTER FORTY-THREE

"DIVERSITIES OF GRACES"

The First Epistle to the Corinthians, continued

Paul had reached this point, when someone knocked heavily on Aquila's door. Three men had come from Corinth: Stephanas, Fortunatus, and Achaicus. They brought a letter from the Church at Corinth. Since these delegates belonged to the oldest part of the Corinthian Church, the letter was probably from the leaders who remained loyal to Paul. Paul felt somewhat relieved. The Church at Corinth was apparently more docile than he thought. "Brother Stephanas," he said, "read the letter from the brethren at Corinth."

But the news was not good. His first letter (the lost epistle), evidently had irritated the Corinthians. The preachers of freedom read into it a meaning that it did not have. They said the letter was impractical. To live in Corinth meant having a mistress. How could people here in Corinth withdraw into some cloudland? Evidently the brethren in Corinth were still inclined to criticize and misunderstand everything he said. In the letter the Corinthians asked the Apostle to decide about some questions on which they were divided.

Those preachers of false liberty (no one seemed to know

from where they came) declared that sexual intercourse was subject to no restrictions, because the new Christian liberty permitted no restraint. Sexual intercourse was said to be an indifferent matter, like the satisfying of other natural desires, such as eating and drinking. One respected member of the Church there was living openly with his stepmother: a union that was forbidden even by the Roman law. But they troubled themselves little about such things as consanguinity, simply because they no longer recognized the bond of marriage. The increase of eroticism among the pagans led quite naturally to less and less respect for the institution of marriage. And as marriage fell in the regard of the people, prostitution increased among the lower classes while the upper classes turned more and more to their courtesans. As early as Pericles' time, cultured courtesans, like Aspasia, had come over from Ionia to Greece and exercised considerable influence on poets, artists, and men of public affairs.

During Paul's time this doctrine of free love took hold in Rome. Even some of the emperors, who were considered more moral than the rest, had courtesans besides their wives. Before his conversion, St. Augustine had lived for years under his mother's roof in such an illicit union. But now in Corinth the destruction of the institution of marriage was proclaimed under the Christian banner. Others went to the other extreme and condemned all sexual intercourse, as something degrading and unclean. These two attitudes arose quite logically from the Hellenistic dualism which regarded body and soul as opposed to each other.

The Corinthians were asking if all sexual intercourse were forbidden. Whether it was better to marry or not, in view of the imminent coming of Christ. What were they to hold with regard to divorce? Could they begin a lawsuit before a pagan court? Could they eat the meat of pagan sacrifices and accept invitations to sacrificial meals? They had many doubts about the conduct of divine services. The women of Corinth wanted equality with the men in church, they wanted to speak in the assembly, and they cast aside their veils. The agapae turned into disgraceful junkets at which the distinction between rich and poor was unpleasantly stressed. Some people were asking which was better: the gift of tongues or prophecy, and one man who had the gift of tongues once cried out, "Cursed be Jesus." Others again had formidable doubts about the resurrection of the dead.

The letter did not make pleasant reading for Paul. But for us the questions are fortunate since they gave Paul an occasion to declare his stand on these questions, thus giving us an insight into the life of the early Church. Thus the First Epistle to the Corinthians is the most interesting and informative of all the Pauline epistles. In declaring his position with respect to these questions, Paul shows the twofold existence of the Christian, who according to Paul lives in two aeons or eras. Paul does not believe that the Christian is actually free from all sin. The Christian is always suspended between the two forms of his existence: as far as his earthly existence is concerned he belongs to a sinful sphere, but supernaturally he belongs to a higher spiritualized sphere. He lives "in Christ" and also in this world. He is a wanderer between two worlds. As a Christian he was buried with Christ in his death, and in Christ's Resurrection the Christian arose also and put on Christ. The Christian now has died to sin, and sin has no claim on him, but, in spite of this mystical supernatural state, Paul does not close his eyes to the fact of hard reality. He is not alarmed that sin still appears in Christians. Nowhere does he say that sin has died. Sin continues and lies in wait for an opportunity to reconquer the territory it has lost.

The leaders of the Corinthian Church had shared in the guilt of the incestuous man by tolerating his presence. On this point Paul's provocation knew no bounds. His invariable practice had been to put all those who gave public scandal under the ban of the Church, and that implied expulsion from the local

Church and the breaking off of all relations with them. Thus he had dealt with the gossipers at Thessalonica, and later he ordered Titus to break off relations with certain stubborn heretics and trouble-makers. The leaders at Corinth had been guilty of supine toleration of evil, and now he sends them an order: "Remove the criminal from your midst." Paul has a still greater punishment than excommunication: the delivery to Satan. The Church is to assemble (he says he will be with them in spirit), and by a solemn curse the sinner is to be exposed, for a determined time, to the revenge of the devil. And Satan will strike him with some disease, as he did Job, or kill him, as he did Ananias and Saphira.

The sinner is to be brought to penance and saved by this action. Once, at least, during his lifetime Paul made use of this terrible power: when he punished the blasphemers Hymeneus and Alexander. His horror for immorality was increased by what he saw of the break-down of morality in the pagan world. But it was founded on the belief that a Christian's body is no longer his own property, it is now a member of Christ's body, and must not be desecrated by a harlot.

Paul also took up the question of private law. He could not approve the settlement of civil suits in a pagan court. For some time the Jews in the Diaspora had had their own courts, and the Roman state tolerated the arrangement. Paul based his prohibition against going into a pagan court, not only on practical reasons, but on the belief that a Christian possessed a higher judicial character than any pagan judge. That judicial power flowed from the mystical union with Christ who shares his judicial office with his members. Soon this principle of the Church's independence from public courts, even in civil cases, was recognized, and it seldom happened that Christians brought suit in the pagan courts. Only after Constantine did this condition change.

Paul solves the marriage difficulties not only from the standpoint of natural ethical principles, but also with regard to the mystical and supernatural viewpoint. He measured and judged all things in their relationship to the mystical body of Christ and to the life of the religious community. For him marriage and virginity were not opposites. His high regard for both states arose from the same principle: the great Christian mystery. Marriage is not below the unmarried state as such. It is only outranked by virginity. But virginity implies an act of sacrifice for the sake of the highest good. It is, in Paul's mind, the heroic act of religious surrender out of the purest motives. The eternal goal of the married state and of virginity are the same; and marriage takes the second place only when it is surpassed by a higher good, such as the undivided surrender to God.

Paul does not say that the unmarried person is higher than the married person. In concrete instances it may easily occur that, by reason of the sacrifices involved and the contribution made to the community, a married person will rank higher than others. From what he has said it follows that the temporary abstinence from marital intercourse in order to serve God better is a good thing. It is remarkable how a man with Paul's mystical views was at the same time a great realist. He never closes his eyes to hard realities, he always calls things by their right names.

A Christian's calling does not change his social standing. Inwardly a Christian is liberated from these external circumstances. Christianity never tried to change a man's social status. It is interested in his attitude, and if the attitude of men is right, the social relationships will right themselves. If you are a slave, do not take your baptism as an occasion to attempt to be free, but rather fulfil your duties more conscientiously. This advice is somewhat surprising in the light of a rabbinical opinion that a Jew acted despicably if he did not try to become free. If you are a Jew, do not try to hide the marks of your circumcision that you may go to the public baths. If you are uncircumcised, do not submit to circumcision. All these external things count for nothing with Christ. The important thing is that you become a new man.

Suppose that you are living in a mixed-religious marriage with a spouse who prefers to remain a pagan. In this case the marriage bond is not to be dissolved, at least not through the action of the Christian party, unless the Christian's faith is in danger. Here Paul does not refer to any teaching of apostolic tradition; he is relying on his own insight into the spirit of Christ. He is not violating Christ's law, because this case was not considered by the gospel. In the future there will be many such cases, and the Church, under the guidance of the Holy Spirit, must be able to solve new cases in the light of the spirit of Christ. We are not concerned here with a sacramental marriage, solidified by the mystery of mystical union with Christ. In an instance of this kind, the Christian ought not to have less liberty than the pagan. By virtue of his own inspiration, the Apostle declared the Christian party to be free. This is the famous "Pauline privilege," which is still important in mission countries.

Another delicate question proposed to Paul was the question about sacrificial meat. This matter concerned the daily life and the social contacts of almost every family. Almost all the meat offered for sale in the shops was sacrificial meat, because the pagans, too, had a ritual for slaughtering. In fact, the whole pagan religion consisted of external observances like this rite. Every occasion in the family was observed with a sacrifice and a sacrificial meal, as also, of course, every public event or celebration. Whatever meat was not used for the sacrifice was used in the home or sold to the markets. Every public function or festivity included a public meal, and since many of the Christians belonged to the poorer classes, it would have caused them hardship to forbid them to attend these meals.

When Cleisthenes' daughter was engaged to be married, he sacrificed a hundred calves. On a certain holiday in Syracuse, 450 calves were slaughtered on the altars. Livy tells of a sacrifice in which 300 steers and 40 goats were killed; and when Caligula ascended the imperial throne in Rome, the universal joy extended the celebration in Rome to three months and during that time 60,000 animals were killed. People with scrupulous consciences were always tormented by this meat question. Should they refuse to eat meat from the markets? Should they refuse invitations to eat in the homes of their friends and relations?

Paul pointed the way out of the difficulty. He recognized the territory of moral indifference. As far as certain things in themselves were concerned, such as eating and drinking, they were indifferent. In these things a Christian is free to do as he wishes. He can eat anything that is offered in the shops, and he can accept an invitation to eat at the table of a pagan friend. The gods to whom these things were offered are not really gods at all, they are only imagined things. But as soon as these things come within the realm of conscience, they take on a moral colour. As soon as I believe in these imagined gods, or as soon as a brother is offended by my eating this meat, I must desist, because I would then be disloyal to my own conscience, and I would not have the proper regard for the conscience of my brethren.

Taking part in the ritualistic sacrificial meal in a pagan temple is quite another thing. That is never a neutral action. It is an expression of communion with demons who, according to Paul, were always close to pagan rites. Whoever sits at their sacrificial meals joins their magic circle, and no Christian may do that because Christ has come to him in his own holy banquet.

In the ninth chapter, Paul breaks off the train of his thought, only to take it up again later. They try to deny that he is an apostle because he was not a disciple of Christ in the very first hours, because he had not seen the Lord; and therefore he hesitated to accept support from his Churches. This was an attack on Paul's sorest wound. Does Damascus mean nothing? Does the fact that he was honourable enough to support himself deprive him of his apostolic rank? On the contrary, ever since Damascus he has been in a unique part of the service, as a special ambassador of Christ. To be an apostle does not mean being served and honoured by the Churches, nor does it mean sitting on the treasures of Christ, keeping them from being discovered, and secretly enjoying your own conversion and redemption. To be an apostle means to speak, and to speak evermore of the kingdom, of the superabundant knowledge of Christ, of how Christ's life streams into all the organs of the mystical body in which all of us are little arteries that live only because they nourish other parts of the body.

He had been made an apostle by no act of his own. In fact, he had been taken against his will when Christ seized him there near Damascus. A hand had been laid on him, and woe to him if like Jonas he had tried to escape. Amos had felt that seizure: "The lion shall roar: Who will not fear? The Lord God has spoken: Who shall not prophesy?" (3:8) Jeremias had felt this intervention. He knew how a man is overwhelmed by God: "You have deceived me, O Lord, and I am deceived: You have been stronger than I, and you have prevailed. I am become a laughing-stock all the day … Then I said: I will not make mention of him nor speak any more in his name: and there came in my heart as a burning fire, shut up in my bones: and I was wearied, not being able to bear it" (Jer. 20:7, 9). Paul, too, felt that weight upon him. "A necessity lies upon me. For woe to me if I preach not the gospel" (1 Cor. 9:16). But it was always an inexpressibly sweet necessity that showered him with a glow of happiness even in his greatest grief. Therefore it was that he felt so sharply wounded when his apostolate was attacked, "for it is good for me to die rather than that any man should make my glory void" (9: 15).

In Paul there was no desire for spiritual domination. He never wished to play "keeper of the great seal," "not because we exercise dominion over your faith: but we are helpers of your joy" (2 Cor. 1:23). The gospel is not a straightjacket; every man is to develop in his own way under the gentle rule of grace. The law of grace is not imposed from without like the Mosaic law, it is not an immanent thing as with the Stoics, or a cold concept of an imperative like that of Kant. It is born in us in our rebirth. It comes not from Sinai, but from Sion and Golgotha. The true Christian needs not to read the law from a book. He carries Christ's law in himself.

Order was not one of the outstanding traits of the Corinthians. That was clear from the descriptions of their tumultuous conduct during divine services. It must have been a sorry spectacle when the women forgot their natural modesty and threw aside their veils and, without regard for decorum in the holy place, insisted on preaching, or when a charismatic shouted, "Cursed be Jesus." A woman who cast aside her veil denied her sex, her social position, and announced her lack of reverence for the holy angels who were appointed by God to watch over the good order of the sexes.

The agape was the finest expression of the early Church's brotherly love, but in Corinth it quickly degenerated into a disgraceful exhibition of the social inequalities of the brethren. That condition led Paul to speak of the heart of Christianity, the sacred Eucharist, which was the source of its social unity and strength, the inexhaustible fountain at which the Church at all times has renewed herself and from which the spirit of the apostolate has flowed out into all the members of the mystical body. The Eucharist was the pledge to the faithful that the Lord of heaven was present with them as their invisible Ruler. It was the fountain of the Church's purity.

A generation later, when the Roman Governor Pliny wished to tell what Christianity was in a few words, he remembered one characteristic: that the Christians ate the "bread of innocence" (*cibus innocuus*). He could not have given a better description of the religion of Jesus. The times when the Eucharistic heart enlivened the Church were days of high religious endeavour, days that lifted up humanity, like those days of the thirteenth century when St. Thomas was composing his glorious hymns to the Eucharist. They were days of faith, science, knowledge. But when the pulse beat of the Eucharist became weaker and weaker in the Church, there came days of spiritual lassitude, of tepidity, of Jansenist coldness, of liberalist aridity of spirit, of the doubting and despair of the Enlightenment. The times when the faithful fearfully looked at the tabernacle from a distance, as the Jews had looked up to the fire-spewing peak of Mount Sinai in the desert, were days of spiritual death, "therefore many among you sleep" (11:30). In the words of Pius XI, the apostolic soul is the Eucharistically pious soul.

We know how Paul prized and encouraged those charismata which set afire the souls that were hardened by paganism and dried up by Judaism. They were a proof of the power and spirit of the new religion and were valuable in the spread of the Church. Paul enumerated twenty-seven charismata in his letters, which he himself possessed in all their fullness. He asks the Corinthians later: "For what is there that you have had less than the other Churches? . . . The signs of my apostleship have been wrought on you, in all patience, in signs and wonders and mighty deeds" (2 Cor. 12: 11).

Many people in Corinth were often intoxicated by their religious ecstasy. They thought they were religious supermen, and they sought perfection in such things as the gift of tongues. Paul, however, made a clear distinction between the genuine gift of tongues, which had been manifested on the first Pentecost and was the expression of the reception of the Holy Spirit as he appeared in the emotional depths of the apostles' souls, and a degenerate form of that gift which rose from the dark regions of man's subconsciousness. Paul condemned these emotional excesses which seemed to be appearing in Corinth. The thing was hard to control, but Paul tried to point out another way of life, higher and better even than faith and hope and knowledge.

His canticle to charity is probably an echo of something that had come forth from his soul during one of the services and it is an excellent model of a prophetic sermon. It represents the highest peak in the New Testament literature and approaches in sublimity to the words of Christ. In Paul's soul a fire was ablaze. A fire that had been enkindled by Christ himself with a spark taken from the flaming sea within the Trinity's life. It was that sublimest passion that filled his whole being, that burning desire to make known to all men the all embracing redemptive love of Christ, to kindle the cold world with Christ's love. Perhaps when Paul was younger he had entertained plans of his own, ambitions, interests, and he had friends, but all those human things had been burnt to ashes in the fire at Damascus. Now every human interest, every human achievement, was nothing compared with this sacrificial love.

If he had the power to speak with the tongues of men and angels and did not have this love, this charity, he would be like those priests of Cybele, striking their hollow drums and cymbals. And if he had enough faith to move mountains, or to pile Pelion on Ossa, and if he gave away all his little possessions: his parchments and his Scriptures which were so dear to him, yes, and if he were made to stand in Nero's circus as a living torch or be burnt on a pyre, all this would be nothing if it were done out of selfish zeal. For him only one thing was worth while in this life: to be consumed in the service of the highest love whose symbol is the Cross and the pierced heart of the Son of God. Such a love does not look out for itself. It is abysmally different from that love which is content with itself. This charity takes on different forms. It is able to absorb, reform, and permeate every personality, yet it does not destroy individuality. Paul was not the kind of disciple that rested on the Lord's breast. His nature was not tender like John's. Paul's love meant service to an idea, service that consumed a man's last drop of blood. But ultimately there was no difference between Paul saying: "I live in the faith of the Son of God, who loved me and delivered himself for me" (Gal. 2:20), and John saying: "Let us therefore love God: because God first has loved us" (1 John 4: 19).

The hardest doctrine for the Greeks was the resurrection of the dead. Paul had learned that in Athens when his mention of this teaching caused the laughter of his audience on the Areopagus. Later, when he stood before the procurator Festus, he would experience the same thing. Therefore he appended here a dissertation on the resurrection.

The message of salvation deals with three events, and the history of the world moves about three points: the death, Resurrection, and second coming of Christ. Paul repeats the proofs he had previously given in his sermons to the Corinthians. Even the original apostles had made the death and Resurrection of Christ the central points in their proclamation of the gospel, and they had also pointed to the connection between the Resurrection of Christ and our resurrection. But Paul had gone deeper into the nature of these facts of our salvation, and dis- covered their significance in the scheme of salvation. "For if the dead rise not again, neither is Christ risen again" (1 Cor. 15:16).

What is the logical connection in this statement? Whenever Christ did anything he acted for our salvation, and the Resurrection is the complement and culmination of his death on the Cross. Without the Resurrection the Cross and the sacrificial death of Christ would have been inefficacious and incomplete. The fact that the Father raised the Son up again was for Paul the irrefutable proof that Jesus is the King of God's kingdom and the founder of the new kingdom, that the power of the new era had begun to be effective. The proof for this conclusion, given later in his letter to the Romans (chaps. 6, 8), is a typical Pauline piece of mystical reasoning.

The life-giving principle is the divine pneuma or spirit. When a Christian possesses this pneuma he participates in Christ's death, in his Resurrection, and also in the future glory of Christ. By his incorporation into Christ's mystical body a Christian is assured of his future resurrection. Christ's Resurrec- tion was the inauguration of the new aeon, and the second coming of Christ will be the completion of that era. Death and resurrection are not only facts of salvation in which we must believe, they are also forces in the scheme of salvation and they reach out into the life of every Christian. Every Christian is drawn into the death and Resurrection of Christ in some supernatural way.

Finally, Paul resorted to a rather drastic argument *ad hominem* to convince these supposedly enlightened and yet superstitious Corinthians. It happened in Corinth that some of the faithful were being baptized for the second time for their relatives who had died in paganism. How can you reconcile the fact that you are trying to baptize for immortality and still deny the resurrection? Anyone who denies the resurrection has no knowledge of the holy pneuma or of the efficacy of baptism. He falsifies the Christian hope and makes false witnesses out of God's apostles. If your faith is nothing more than the monstrous product of a diseased mind, then all self-conquest, every noble flight of the soul, the life of the apostles which is a daily dying, would be nonsense, and the proverb would be correct: "Let us eat and drink, for tomorrow we shall die" (1 Cor. 15:32).

The Corinthians also had doubts about what the body would be like after the resurrection. Paul replied that the body would go through a profound change, like the seed whose hidden life springs forth only after the shell has been broken and its external cover has been corrupted. The supernatural seed of life, deposited in us in baptism, will develop into various degrees of conformity to the glorified body of Christ, depending on the individual state of each person. Paul lifts the veil from this particular mystery in three of his letters using various arguments, but each time he concludes with the same triumphant certainty (1 Thess.; 1 Cor.; Rom.).

The resurrection seems to take place, therefore, in two different phases: as the resurrection of those who sleep in the Lord, who because they possess the sacred pneuma have the first claim to glory, and the resurrection of the rest of mankind after the destruction of all forces opposed to God and the destruction of the great enemy Death, by Christ the King. Then the new aeon will have been completed, which was begun in Christ's Resurrection.

With a mighty triumphant fanfare Paul concludes his train of thought with the exclamation: "Death is swallowed up in victory. O death, where is your victory? O death, where is your sting?" Since Christ is risen from the dead and the Spirit has been poured out on us, death is like a bee that has lost its sting.

Timothy may have arrived at Corinth in the meantime, and Paul feared that the young man might be exposed to insult on this delicate mission. Paul asks the Corinthians to receive Timothy and to show him all respect. He himself intended to remain in Ephesus until Pentecost and would wait there for Timothy's return. He had plans for Christian propaganda during the great celebration during May in honour of Artemis, "For a great door and evident is opened to me; and many adversaries" (16:9).

The letter is finished. Paul has Sosthenes read it to him. Then he grasps Sosthenes' pen and writes: "The salutation of me, Paul, with my own hand. If any man love not our Lord Jesus Christ, let him be anathema, *Maranatha*" (16:21 f.).

CHAPTER FORTY-FOUR

"GREAT IS DIANA OF THE EPHESIANS"

*"Now some cried one thing, some another. For the assembly was confused:
and the greater part knew not for what cause they were come together"*
(Acts 19:32).

Tragedy is never far from the lives of the saints. We are
not surprised, therefore, to see that Paul's life was full of
tragedy. And the tragedy in the lives of the saints is a fabric
woven by elements that are divine and human, by the interplay
of destiny and personal factors. Many tragic situations and
involvements in Paul's life must be attributed to his character
and temperament. Incessantly that congenital unrest made him
move on. He was never able to remain long in one place. It
seems that some strange desire made him feel that he must go
elsewhere or his life would not be complete. His ambitions
went as far as the known horizons. And sometimes even the
saintliest and the wisest men err in their choice of the instruments and the means they choose, or they do not understand the
true value of what they have in hand, and that error spells
tragedy. Besides this tragedy, ordinary men know the tragedy
of malice and weakness, but certainly it can be said that Paul
knew little of this tragedy of evil and weakness.

May of the year 57 had come. Paul had just returned from

a short visit to Corinth, as many scholars believe, and his return coincided with the great Ephesian May celebration held every fourth year. This famous observance turned the city into a vast fair and bacchanal whose centre was the magnificent temple of Artemis. The month of May was dedicated to Artemis and the whole countryside was covered with blooms from the gardens of the suburbs to the heights of Pion and Coressus. Great throngs came for the celebration from all the coast cities and islands and from the interior of Asia Minor. Lodgings in the inns and private homes were reserved months ahead. When the first day of May came, the days were filled with sacrifices, masked processions, prize fights, contests, and at night people danced and serenaded by the light of the stars.

The affair was directed by a board of ten wealthy citizens who also underwrote the expenses. It is remarkable that ten such millionaires could be found every four years in Ephesus, but the merchants of Ephesus were fabulously rich, and the distinction of being one of the ten Asiarchs, as they were called, was probably reward enough for the great outlay. Ephesus was proud to call itself the "Neocore" or custodian of the cult of Artemis. In the ruins of Ephesus an interesting decree referring to the celebration in honour of Artemis was discovered written on a white marble tablet:

"Whereas temples, groves, statues, and altars are dedicated to Artemis not only in Ephesus but also throughout Greece, and

"Whereas a special month is set aside, to honour Artemis, called Artemision, and

"Whereas it is fitting that this whole month that bears the goddess' name should be observed in her honour,

"The people of Ephesus have decided to regulate the cult of Artemis by this decree. Every day of the month shall be a holiday, and throughout the month festivals, panegyrics, and sacred observances should be arranged. These things will shed a new glory and lustre on our city for all times" (*Core. Inscript. Graec.*, II, 2954).

The games held during Artemision were called *Ephesia,*
Artemisia, and *Oecumenica.*

Paul knew from experience that this great concourse of
people would be an excellent opportunity for the spread of his
ideas, and he was determined to make the most of it for his
Christian propaganda. His viewpoint, however, was too idealistic,
in the sense that he did not realize that the strongest opposition
would come not from the eunuchs and temple prostitutes, the
actors and musicians, and from other hangers-on of the temple,
but from the businessmen and the merchants, from the association of art dealers and the guild of silversmiths, who were
concerned about their profits and for whom Artemis was nothing
more than Hecuba. The storm came from a quarter whence
Paul had not expected it.

The recent bonfire in the market place of Ephesus which
Paul had at least encouraged had not been without effect on the
sale of obscene literature. If we recall that because of Paul's
ceaseless activity in all the surrounding cities and towns of Asia
Minor, and in the neighbouring islands, Christian communities
had been established that no longer attended these celebrations
in Ephesus, it is conceivable that this year the number of
visitors was smaller and the business enterprises connected
with the temple suffered. The silversmiths noticed a decline in
the demand for their products. Formerly the pilgrims who had
come from the neighbouring towns bought a little silver statue
of Artemis or a picture of her shrine to take with them to their
families and friends back home, and in that way the goddess
provided a livelihood for the native artists and shopkeepers.

People soon grasped the connection between the poor
state of their business and Paul's preaching. Demetrius, probably
employing a large number of artists and smiths who manu-
factured little temples and niches and statues out of lead, silver,
and gold, appointed himself spokesman for the aggrieved
businessmen and artisans. He called on the workers to demon-
strate, in much the same way that a modern union leader would

arouse his fellow union members, and Demetrius knew how to direct the anger and resentment of the workers against Paul and the new Churches.

A thousand or more idle workmen and perhaps ten thousand curious onlookers made a favourable audience for Demetrius' inflammatory remarks. Soon the ancient city around the temple with its innumerable booths erected for the fair had become a furious mass of milling humanity. Demetrius climbed on the high platform before the temple. Behind him was the gaudy shrine with the gigantic statue of the goddess, as he shouted to the mob: "Sirs, you know that our gain is by this trade. And you see and hear that this Paul by persuasion has drawn away a great multitude, not only of Ephesus, but almost of all Asia, saying: They are not gods which are made by hands." In his speech, Demetrius cleverly mingled motives of gain and religion, a certain amount of local patriotism and superstition: "So that not only this our craft is in danger of counting for nothing, but also the temple of great Diana shall be reputed for nothing! Yes, and her majesty shall begin to be destroyed, whom all Asia and the world worship" (Acts 19:25).

It has been said that hunger sharpens a man's vision. At least that was true here in Ephesus when the workers, gathered in the first workers' convention recorded in the Bible, saw what the future had in store for them. What Demetrius foretold was still in the future, but it came about as he said. The worries of the silversmiths were not entirely groundless, even though their defence methods were foolish. What did it avail their cause when they began stamping their feet, making a tumult, and shouting for hours, "Great is Diana of the Ephesians"? At last they seemed to know what they wished to do. They began shouting: "To the theatre; bring Paul to the court of the people. Throw Paul to the lions."

As if at a given signal, the mob moved through the Jewish quarter, where Aquila and Priscilla lived, to the temple grounds. The amphitheatre, with its seats rising up against the slope of Mount Pion, was able to accommodate 25,000 persons. Pilgrims walking on the streets, the personnel of stores and shops along the way, were carried along by the mob, serious-looking men came out of the Celsus Library, young folk came from the stadium, the gymnasium, and the baths. From the platform, the white statues of the gods and goddesses, heroes and emperors, looked down on the frantic mob. There on the platform stood the accused, pale and trembling and bleeding: Gaius and Aristarchus, Paul's Macedonian friends and co-workers, whom the mob had snatched up as it swept through the city. It may even have been that these two disciples willingly offered themselves to the fury of the mob, as did Aquila and Priscilla to whom Paul later expressed his gratitude for having exposed themselves to death for his sake: "Salute Prisca and Aquila, my helpers in Christ Jesus, who have for my life laid down their own necks" (Rom. 16:3).

Paul escaped death because he was not at home. Probably he was giving his lectures in Tyrannus' auditorium, unaware of what was happening. When the mob reached the temple grounds, the sound of their fury droned into the hall. Perhaps he paused for a moment in his discourse, and then went on. Soon some of his disciples came with the news: that the mob wanted a public trial and that he, together with Gaius and Aristarchus, had reason to fear for their lives. As a Roman citizen, Paul wished to go immediately to the theatre to present himself and free his friends. At the same time he must have known that his citizenship would not protect him against the raving mob. But he was not consulting his head at the moment. He was listening to his heart, and his heart was filled with the desire for martyrdom.

His friends held him back; they stood in the doorway. More messengers arrived from some of the Asiarchs who had become Paul's friends to say that he should not come (19:31), because that would only complicate matters. These Asiarchs, who made up a board of governors for the festive games and contests in the province, also had possession of the keys for the cages of the wild animals, and the mob was determined to end this affair with a bloody spectacle in the arena.

Things were all confusion and turmoil in the theatre. Demetrius had lost control of the situation. Some of the mob went back to the Jewish quarter and dragged some Jews up to the platform, and now some of the prominent Jews came on the scene because they feared they would become involved in this uprising against the Christians. They pushed forward a certain Alexander, one of Paul's bitterest enemies, to address the crowd and tell them that Paul did not belong to the Jews, that they had long ago cast him out as a heretic and traitor.

Alexander stood forth to talk and held up his arm for silence. Someone started the cry, "A Jew, a Jew," and soon the mob took up the shout, sending mighty waves of sound up against the marble proscenium like the breakers of the sea. And then, as if it were their battle cry, they broke forth into the wild acclamation, "Great is Diana of the Ephesians." With his fine sense for the ironical, Luke points out a characteristic of the mob: "And the greater part [of the mob] knew not for what cause they were come together." The people of Ephesus had succumbed to mass suggestion, as have the people of many communities since then. Paul had had experience with mobs before, and when he came to Jerusalem he would meet another mob. The chancellor of the city, whose official title is recorded on many inscriptions and coins, was a practical psychologist. Fortunately he was not a demagogue, but a responsible official. Evidently he had learned from the treatment of wild animals that, after they had exhausted themselves in their rage, they could be easily tamed, and so he allowed the mob to shout for two hours. When finally the volume of sound rising up to the proscenium began to decrease, he came out calm and serene on the platform and gazed out on the ebbing fury of the mob. His poise and quiet dignity impressed the mob. Slowly the consciousness of their own human dignity returned. Then for some long moments came silence, a pause in which reason came back to her throne.

The last passionate outbursts recoiled from the cold reasoning of the chancellor: "The issue has nothing to do with religion. No one has attacked the honour of Artemis. No one has robbed the temple or blasphemed the goddess. It is only a question of economics. This is really a civil case in which a suit might be brought for damages. Ephesus has been and is still today the great custodian of Artemis. If Demetrius and his fellow craftsmen can establish their charges, they ought to apply to the court. If you have any other accusation to make, you know the court is ready to hear you; but, when you conduct yourselves as you did today, you prejudice the honour and the respect and the privileges of this city." It was prudently spoken. The people roused themselves from their mob intoxication and felt ashamed of themselves. With one gesture, the chancellor dismissed the crowd. The uprising had exhausted itself, but above the clouds of dust the two slogans remained: "Great is Diana," and "Great is Jesus Christ."

What a firebrand and revolutionary Paul had become! He began by attacking the law of Moses and men's allegiance to the Temple in Jerusalem. Now he was beginning to tear down the sanctuary of Artemis, and with it the whole structure of paganism would come tumbling down. The silversmith was right in his fears for Diana, for where is Diana today? Where is her temple? Her majesty is gone and with it the social order and the culture of paganism. Jesus conquered and triumphed over Diana and the cult of the emperors. Ephesus exchanged the glory of Diana for a higher distinction: the fame of a great Christian community founded by Christ's greatest disciple and the honour of possessing the tomb of an equally famous apostle. Here in Ephesus, in a little side street, St. John would write his Gospel and his letters: "And this is the victory which over-comes the world: our faith" (1 John 5:4).

While we recall the memory of Paul and John, another of

Christ's truly apostolic disciples comes to mind: Ignatius of Antioch, who while resting on that last fateful journey to Rome received a delegation from Ephesus in Smyrna. In that group were Onesimus, the bishop of Ephesus, the deacon Burrus, and Crocus, Euplus, and Frontonus. In his letter to the Ephesians, Ignatius warmly praises their Church. As the capital, Ephesus was the metropolitan see of all Asia Minor. All the other sees were suffragan to the metropolitan of Ephesus who was consecrated in the presence of all his suffragans.

Within its walls, Ephesus witnessed no less than nine councils of the Church. In 431, Ephesus reached a high point in its religious history in that great council which signals the victory of the devotion to Mary as the Mother of God, and laid the basis for the dogma that the two natures in Christ are united in one person. But only eighteen years later, in 449, that tragic fate caused by human malice made itself felt in Ephesus. The city gained the sorry fame of being the place where that infamous "Robber Synod," as Leo the Great called it, was held, during which religious differences between certain fanatical monks and heretical bishops were settled by fisticuffs. In the seventh century a new force, the power of Islam, appeared on the scene to fulfil the dire predictions of the Apostle on the seven Churches of Asia Minor. The ancient episcopal sees were humbled and brought low. In 1403 the famous city of Ephesus was overrun by the Mongol hordes of Tamerlane, and today, as a consequence of the Turks' unexampled campaign of suppression, only a handful of Christians can be found in Asia Minor. Fearful tragedy lies in those three rallying cries that succeeded each other: "Great is Diana!" "Great is Jesus Christ!" "Great is Allah and his prophet!"

In a human way, we may ask, "Why were all those conquests of Paul and John lost to Christ in the end?" The answer is one of the most astounding lessons of history. Humanly speaking, it has been Christianity's greatest tragedy that its bitterest enemies have come from its own ranks. Paul was hunted down like an animal by his Jewish-Christian confreres. His ardent admirer, John Chrysostom, was dragged through the salt steppes of Asia Minor by jealous bishops and monks. The faith was no longer a thing close to a man's heart as it had been with Paul. Political theologians and theological emperors made it a pawn in imperial politics. Thus Christianity in the East lost the admirable vigour of its early years. Now that the spirit was gone, what use were all the dead parchments, the bones of many martyrs, the beautiful legends, the miraculous dust from John's tomb in Ephesus, and all the garments woven by the Empress Helena? All these outward things, all the regulations and customs and observances, are as effective as the shouting of the crowd of Demetrius, "Great is Diana."

CHAPTER FORTY-FIVE

FLIGHT FROM EPHESUS

The Second Epistle to the Corinthians

"And after the tumult was ceased, Paul calling to him the disciples and exhorting them, took his leave and set forward to go into Macedonia" (Acts 20:1).

The occurrences between the first and the second letter to the Corinthians are not easily understood, but indications in the second letter lead us to the following surmises. Between Easter and Pentecost of A.D. 57 Timothy had returned from Corinth, but the news he brought was not encouraging. Although Paul's letter had made a forcible impression on the trouble-makers, it had not been able to silence them. Paul was now thinking of sending Titus with full powers to Corinth. A member of the Church at Corinth, or perhaps one of the newly arrived trouble-makers, had committed a crime which, if left unpunished, would have challenged the authority of the Apostle and made it impossible for him to return to Corinth again (2 Cor. 7:12). Paul does not give any details about the crime. He merely indicates that someone suffered an injustice. Was Timothy perhaps subjected to some gross insult in the presence of the assembly? The expression "You suffer ... if a man be lifted up, if a man strike you on the face" (11:12), seems to indicate that some violence was committed.

Paul's faithful friends in Corinth sent him an urgent appeal to come quickly. But he could not make up his mind to go. Once before he had gone to them in time of trouble and had reminded the leaders of the Church of their duty. He could not go for the second time. In his anxiety he turned to Titus, asking him to go to Achaia in his place. Paul had to call attention to all of the Corinthians' good qualities to persuade Titus to go (7:13), but it was Titus' love for Paul which eventually overcame his hesitation. Titus set out for Corinth, armed with the necessary documents and credentials and with a special letter to the congregation, in which Paul earnestly begged them to return from their evil ways. It is this letter which is often referred to as the Epistle of Tears ("I wrote to you with many tears") (2:4), which was lost, probably because it discussed some personal matters that were embarrassing for the people of Corinth. The evildoer was to be punished after a judicial trial, and from that trial it would be clear to what extent the leaders of the Church had been at fault.

As Titus left for Corinth, it was agreed that he should return by way of Macedonia and Troas, and that Paul would meet him in Troas. In the meantime, however, the catastrophe had occurred in Ephesus which made it expedient for Paul to leave Ephesus immediately. Early one morning in May of the year 57 Paul left Ephesus accompanied by Timothy, Gaius, Aristarchus, Secundus, Tychicus, and Trophimus. In Troas a certain Carpus was his host and the leader of the congregation (2 Tim. 4:13). Seven years earlier when Paul had been here in Troas the Spirit had forbidden him to preach; this time "a door was opened to me in the Lord" (2 Cor. 2:12). But his heart was weighted down with many worries; he was troubled and dejected. His voice had lost its ring, and his words fell heavily like stones. All the saints seem to have experienced such periods of aridity. We need only read the writings of the mystics, as, for instance, St. Bernard whose spirit seems to have been an inexhaustible fountain of fire and enthusiasm.

In such times of nervous exhaustion and mental dejection Paul was further afflicted with that migraine that he called the "thorn in his flesh." He was not a man given to long waiting. At the first opportunity he took ship for Macedonia to meet Titus on the way. His first stop was in Philippi, where, after a separation of many years, he found his friend Luke. Luke observed the nervous tension and the inner depression of his friend with the keen eye of the physician as well as with the solicitous eye of a friend. But the warm reception accorded Paul by the Philippians soon cheered him up.

One day he heard a knock on the door of his room. One of Lydia's servants entered to say that Titus had come. And when Paul saw Titus again, his worries slipped from his shoulders. When his friends were away, he knew that they were always in danger, and it was therefore no ordinary event when one of his messengers returned. Titus brought good news. Equipped with the full powers of the Apostle with which Paul had armed him, Titus had been received by Corinth with fear and trembling. The letter he carried had brought the congregation to tears. The incestuous man had been expelled by a majority vote of the members, and now he was made to feel the displeasure of the Church. He had eliminated all cause of scandal and had asked pardon of the congregation, which the Church at Corinth was disposed to grant. But it suspended its decision to await Paul's approval.

The evildoer, who had committed "the wrong" (2 Cor. 7:12), had also been severely punished, and from the investigation it had become clear that the leaders of the Church were not at fault. The divisions in the Church had been removed, although the rebels who had recently come to Corinth still remained. Now they were saying that Paul was fickle and unreliable because he was perpetually changing his plans and seemed to travel only when he was in the mood. Others said that he feared to come to Corinth and that he was forceful only in his letters and that he was courageous only when he was at a safe distance. But the great majority were loyal to Paul and ardently desired him to come to Corinth, to have his consolation and his forgiveness (2 Cor. 7:7-12). Such was Titus' report.

Paul was consoled. He arose, extended his arms, and offered his thanks to God. He wrote: "God, who comforts the humble, comforted us by the coming of Titus" (7:6). Paul had not been in such good spirits for a long time. The old fire was in his eyes, his voice had the old familiar ring. "Now you see, brother Titus, it has all come about as I said. My Corinthians have not disappointed me and 'our boasting ... is found a truth' (2 Cor. 7:14). I will not go to Corinth until these clouds have blown away so that I will not 'make them sorrowful' again. First I wish to write to the Corinthians again, and I wish you, brother Timothy, to subscribe with me to this letter so that the Corinthians will know that we are in agreement, that as founders of their Church we hold equal places, that any insult offered to you affects me too, and that when I forgive them you also concur."

A man always writes and speaks with greater facility and spirit when he is impelled by some strong emotion, and especially when his soul is expanded by feelings of joy and love. Because of its wealth of thought, the first letter to the Corinthians may be said to be the most interesting of Paul's epistles, but the second letter is undoubtedly the most touching. Some critics think that the second letter is composed of several different letters, as if the "letter of reconciliation" (chaps. 1-7), the "collection letter" (chaps. 8, 9), and the so-called "four-chapter letter" (chaps. 10-13), were separate letters. Unquestionably the letter consists of distinct parts and, although they may not have been composed at one sitting, these parts were written so closely upon one another and in the same mood that they actually represent one harmonious literary document.

The difference in the tone of the letter in these three parts is accounted for by the fact that these parts were addressed to different groups. In the first part, Paul speaks to his loyal followers in Corinth in a conciliatory tone. But besides these loyal disciples, many Judaizers still remained, and they were still continuing their attacks on him and his apostolate. Those two things, his person and his apostolate, were identical in Paul's mind, and he was resolved to put an end to these attacks and definitely silence his opponents. The principal purpose of his letter, therefore, is the defence of his apostolate. The chief weapon employed by his enemies was the argument that his sufferings, persecutions, and even his scars deprived him of any apostolic dignity. Paul snatched that weapon from their hands and used his sufferings as the great proof and glorification of his apostolic work. That is why he has so much to say about his sufferings and tribulations, the theme that runs through the whole letter and makes it the "Epistle of Paul's Passion."

After a prayer of thanksgiving, Paul reminds his readers of the terrible experiences he had in Ephesus. For the first time, he has come to think that the measure of his suffering is full, that he can bear no more, that his death is near. He asks them to offer public prayers of thanksgiving for his deliverance from death (1:11). He is indignant at that specious reasoning of some of the members in Corinth, who attributed his change of plans in coming to them to fickleness and instability of character and who said that he hovered between yes and no. "Did I use lightness? Or the things that I purpose, do I purpose ... that there should be with me, *It is* and *It is not?*" (1:17.) If Paul had postponed his visit, it was "to spare them."

"Some of you say that I have a craving for power, that I desire to exercise dominion over your faith, and tyrannize over your consciences. But you misunderstand me. My apostolic office is to be a helper of your joy" (cf. 1:23). Here again Paul is expressing the sentiments of his divine Master: "The Son of man also is not come to be ministered to, but to minister" (Mark 10:45). The purpose of ecclesiastical punishment is not to inflict sorrow, but to effect a salutary contrition which in turn will be for life and not for death. That is the Christian view of penalties, and Paul applies it beautifully in the case of the incestuous man. To abuse the Church's power, to be over severe in punishment, would be a greater evil, the evil of being "over-reached by Satan" (2:11). In all his letters Paul speaks of God's willingness to forgive. He presumes it in every case, as here also when he himself assures the culprit of his forgiveness and asks the congregation to do likewise. All through the ages this thought, the forgiveness of sins, has accompanied the Church.

His old confidence in ultimate success returns to him, especially when he looks back on his apostolic labours. "Now thanks be to God, who always makes us to triumph in Christ Jesus and manifests the aroma of his knowledge by us in every place" (2:14). The Greek expression translated here "to triumph in Christ," seems to have the meaning of "made use of me in his triumphal march through the world, as one of the trophies of his victory." At least the word is used in that sense by Plutarch[32] in a scene describing Cleopatra's visit to the grave of Mark Antony where she swears that she prefers death to being taken captive. "No," Cleopatra declares, "I will never allow myself to be dragged in the triumphal procession of your victor." Conquered kings and distinguished prisoners of war were paraded after the triumphal chariot of victorious generals. Incense pots were swung around the victor so that he seemed to be enveloped in clouds like a god. But, lest the incense turn his head, a slave stood at his side to remind him of his mortal nature: "Remember, Caesar, that you are human."

Paul was grateful for the modest role he was allowed to play in Christ's triumphal march. He was glad to serve as one of Christ's trophies or to swing the censer so that he "could manifest the aroma of his knowledge ... in every place." In his glorification of the apostolic office he was led to other considerations. He tells the Corinthians that he has no need of "epistles of commendation" like his antagonists: "You are our epistle, written in our hearts, which is read and known by all men. Being manifested, that you are the epistle of Christ,

---

[32] Plutarch, *Anton.*, 84.

ministered by us, and written: not with ink but with the Spirit of the living God. Not in tables of stone but in the fleshly tables of the heart," not with an iron stylus but with fire, "for the letter kills, but the spirit quickens" (3:2-6). If Paul had written only these words, he would have earned immortality.

His opponents compare Paul to Moses. Had anyone ever seen Paul's countenance with the glory of Moses? "Very well, your leaders appeal to Moses. It is true that Moses veiled his face when he spoke to the people, and even today when they read the law in the synagogue they wrap it in an embroidered cover. That is a symbol of the hull that envelops their hearts, and therefore they are not aware that the Old Testament has been replaced by Christ. The Christian message needs no such covering; we have nothing to hide. We do not adulterate the word of God as some tavern keeper may water down his wine (4:2); 'we preach not ourselves, but Jesus Christ our Lord; and ourselves your servants through Jesus'" (4:5). This last passage expresses the fundamental reason of his apostolic calling: "For God ... has shined in our hearts, to give the light of the knowledge of the glory of God, in the face of Christ Jesus" (4:6), that face that he beheld at Damascus.

"Some of you say that I do not look like an apostle." That reproach gave Paul an opportunity to speak of the contrast between his unprepossessing exterior, marked with suffering and disease, and his inner being all aflame with the Spirit. In mighty antitheses he proceeds to an evaluation of his life. As the life of Jesus was a continual sacrifice, a life of obedience to the death on the Cross, so Paul will manifest his resemblance to his Master by describing the miseries, the dangers, and the sufferings of his apostolic service. Readiness to serve, complete self-humiliation, these were his daily martyrdom. It is a moving catalogue of his sufferings in the letters to the Corinthians (1 Cor. 4:9-13; 2 Cor. 1:8-11; 4:7-12; 6:4-10); but the most impressive of all is in 2 Cor. 11:21-33.

For Paul suffering was a kind of sacrament by which he

was united mystically to Christ. It effected a kind of symbiosis between Christ and himself. He draws all his strength from Christ. The more he suffers, the greater his strength and dignity. The more he feels of Christ's Passion, the closer he is to Christ. He knows he has more to suffer than all the others and he knows too that he has a special function in the Church. Added to all these persecutions is his chronic illness. In Gethsemane Christ prayed three times to be delivered from his sufferings. Corresponding to this triple appeal is Paul's triple prayer to be freed from the "sting of my flesh" and the buffetings of the angel of Satan (2 Cor. 12:7). He presented, himself thus, in the midst of all these sufferings, to his Corinthians, and by this appearance he gained a distinct advantage. Even now we gradually see, as we read, the stature of another Christ, and so he was able to drive off these enemies among his flock by transforming this outward appearance of being defeated into the victory of Christ.

And while he suffers with Christ, he is also suffering for the Church. In the first chapter he refers to this vicarious quality of his suffering: "Now whether we be in tribulation, it is for your exhortation and salvation." If he perseveres, the faith is mightily strengthened. "For you know the grace of our Lord Jesus Christ, that being rich he became poor for your sakes; that through his poverty you might be rich" (8:9). This antithesis runs through Paul's apostolic career. We are the dying, you the living; we are poor to enrich you; we are the scapegoats of the world, the offscouring of all things. Every year of his life he becomes more conscious of this vicarious character of his suffering, concluding this enumeration of his suffering in the twelfth chapter with the declaration, "But I most gladly will spend and be spent myself for your souls: although loving you more, I be loved less" (15).

Inserted between the two principal parts of the letter is a section devoted to the collection for the Church in Jerusalem. This work of charity was close to Paul's heart because he did not wish the thread with the rather difficult mother Church to be broken, a break that would divide the Church into two parts. He wanted the collection to be a solemn testimonial to the mother Church offered by the daughter Churches, and he desired the offering of each Church to be brought to Jerusalem by chosen representatives of each congregation. The way Paul conducted the collection is an illustration of his fine sense of propriety. He was not a collector of money by natural bent. Financial matters were distasteful to him. But he realized how closely he was being watched by his enemies. Therefore he ordered that each Church should seal its gift and deliver it by a delegate chosen from among the members. To avoid any taint of commercialism, Paul speaks of the collection only in religious terms, as a "grace," "a blessing," "supply the wants of the saints." These words about the collection are an excellent model for a sermon on charity. What delicate restraint he displays! He will not appear too obtrusive or insistent: "I speak not as commanding" (8:8). He knew well the straitened circumstances of the lower classes.

If only this same consideration for the condition of those who must wrest a living by labour from the earth had been displayed in the Church in succeeding ages. If there had been more understanding of the poorest of the poor, of the condition of those who dwell in the slums of large cities, instead of this cold concern with profane, worldly business tactics, the relationship of trusting confidence between clergy and people would not have been broken so often. Whenever the time comes that the priest no longer feels with the poor and needy, when he rises above the average in the elegance of his manner of living, whenever he plays fast and loose with the capital of the people's confidence, which is the Church's securest endowment, whenever that time comes, then the Lord will come to clean the threshing floor with his winnowing shovel. In urging their charity, Paul speaks of supernatural motives. The most beautiful fruit of giving, according to him, is that by giving we grow in mildness and mercy and we draw down upon ourselves the blessing of the Lord.

Between chapters nine and ten a period of time seems to

have elapsed during which an event of some importance occurred. Otherwise we cannot explain the transition from the conciliatory tone of chapter eight to the sharp, upbraiding tone of chapter nine. Probably more news was coming in from Corinth. Perhaps the trouble-makers had received reinforcements from Jerusalem, without, of course, being authorized by Peter and James. Evidently they were now accusing Paul of being bold and presumptuous, of being a seeker after his own glory. Some were saying that the collection was only a clever manoeuver to gain an advantage.

Paul now puts on the mask of Greek irony and plays the role of the seeker after fame and glory that they assigned to him. And while playing the role he strikes one telling blow after another on his opponents. They say that he is self-seeking, that he wants power and fame; but they themselves are always boasting about their friendship with the great ones in Jerusalem, they represent themselves as being wise, and if anyone contradicts them they strike him in the face (11:20). With great restraint Paul foregoes mentioning the names of these emissaries from the East, and he makes no reference to those who supposedly had sent them. He maintains a reverent silence even though there was a great ado about the shadow of "some great name."

Titus and two of the brethren, probably Luke and Aristarchus, took the letter to Corinth. The letter seems to have finally settled all the troubles there. It was Paul's bequest to that Church of Corinth, for which he was willing to give everything. But, as early as the second century, the Church at Corinth seems to have forgotten the services of the great Apostle. One aspect of his heroic service, however, will never be forgotten in the Church: whenever men will be tempted to adapt the Church to the world, whenever secularism and conformity to the world appear in the Church, whenever the Church begins to be absorbed in externals, the figure of Paul appears to recall men to true spirituality: "Let not yourselves be overreached by Satan. Remember that you are children of the Spirit."

CHAPTER FORTY-SIX

WINTER IN CORINTH

The Epistle to the Romans

"He came into Greece; where, when he had spent three months,
the Jews laid wait for him, as he was about to sail into Syria.
So he took a resolution to return through Macedonia" (Acts 20:2).

The warmth with which his loyal Macedonians had
received him restored his powers and infused into him a new
desire to live, so much so that he began to plan new enterprises.
From a remark in the letter to the Romans, it seems that he made
some trips into Illyricum, to Dyrrachium, the modern Durazzo
(Rom. 11:19). Illyricum, as then used, was a term applied to the
entire coast from Dalmatia to Epirus. Evidently Paul also
established a Church in Nicopolis where, ten years later, he
spent his last winter. At the beginning of the winter of 57, Paul
was again in the archipelago where several of the delegates
awaited him to accompany him to Jerusalem by way of Corinth.
Among these were Sopater from Beroea, Aristarchus and
Secundus from Thessalonica, Tychicus and Trophimus from
Ephesus, Gaius from Derbe, Timothy, Lucius, and Jason.
Another group awaited him in Corinth. Paul was surrounded by
as brilliant a staff of co-workers as any apostle had ever

assembled about himself. When the faithful in Corinth met 'this retinue they would begin to have some idea of the worldwide importance of their Apostle. In Corinth, Paul stayed in the spacious residence of his good friend Gaius, who indeed had also opened his house to the whole congregation. Winter had set in. Long journeys were out of the question. Paul had ample time to organize the government of the Corinthian Church and secure it against any future disturbances. In describing these days, Luke displays the gentle hand of the physician again in not wishing to open old wounds. He avoids dwelling on the ultimate and conclusive defeat of the Judaizing party.

While Paul was kept here in Corinth by the weather, he was able to look back on the twenty years of his missionary activity and meditate on God's wonderful ways. Now, perhaps for the first time, he could reflect on those most intimate experiences of his own soul and on the strange fate of his own people. And as he sat thinking here, where East and West met, his eye turned often toward that city of Rome, which for years had been beckoning to him on his mental horizon. The secular glamour of the city that fascinated the provincial of the time was not what attracted Paul, but a kind of premonition that Providence had selected that city of Rome, as the centre of the Church. Here in the Orient, he felt that his work was done. Christianity was now established at all the crossroads of the East. It could now spread out into all the adjacent territory, and that was only a matter of time. "From Jerusalem round about as far as Illyricum, I have replenished the gospel of Christ ... Now having no more place in these countries" (Rom. 15:19, 23).

To understand that remark we must recall how sparsely the vast extent of the Roman Empire was populated. Although it was ten times as large as modern France, it had scarcely as great a population. Paul was now making plans to transfer the centre of his activity farther west. World-dominating Rome suggested to his mind that great idea of a catholic Church. One factor, however, caused him to hesitate. He was unwilling to

violate an old principle: never to build on another man's foundation. He had learned that an apostolic beginning had been
made in Rome, and that could have been the work of no one
but Peter.

Emperor Claudius, who had expelled the Jews from Rome,
died in 54. It may have been about the middle fifties, therefore,
when Peter, accompanied by his wife (called "sister" in the language of the time; cf. 1 Cor. 9:5) and Mark his interpreter, came
to Rome. But the division of the various missionary territories
was not considered to be exclusive. That would have been in
contradiction to the universal character of the apostolic mission.

Besides this, Paul needed Rome as a base for his future
activities in Italy and Spain: "When I shall begin to take my
journey into Spain, I hope that, as I pass, I shall see you and be
brought on my way there by you" (Rom. 15:24). Truly, it was a
Herculean undertaking for an aging man to take the whole
Christian world on his shoulders. He was now waiting only for
the time when shipping would open up again. Then he planned
to send a letter to Rome that would establish a bond of friendship and spiritual union between himself and this the central
Church of the West. The good deaconess Phoebe planned to go
to Rome in the spring. He would send his letter with her.

But during these days Paul often found himself looking at
this matter from another angle. Because of his successes and
his great labours, he was unquestionably the greatest man in the
Christian world and he quite naturally felt a deep responsibility
for the cause of Christian unity. Back on the eastern horizon lay
the suspicious congregation of Jerusalem, grouped round the
Temple. On the western horizon was the Roman Church with
its large percentage of Jewish Christians and a certain number
of extremists, such as the Essenes, abstainers, and vegetarians.
Paul called these latter the "weak," in contrast to the normal,
healthy Christians.

Paul was determined now to attempt to make peace with
the community at Jerusalem by a visit to them, and also to offer

the olive branch of peace to the Jewish group in Rome in a letter. In this letter he would attempt to show that he was not a renegade of the Jewish race, that he had no intention to invalidate the promises made to the Jews, that the dissolution of the law was not an act of disloyalty, and finally that day and night he was grieving over the sad fate of his brethren. Sometimes he felt that the gift he was about to carry to Jerusalem would not be received by the saints there as he hoped. He felt that he was venturing into the jaws of the lion (Rom. 15:31).

Paul felt the years heavy on him. It seemed to be urgent that he write down clearly the spiritual testament that he desired to leave the Christian world, that rich harvest of knowledge which he had been garnering during these stormy years, his gospel about the ways of salvation. He had made a beginning in his letter to the Galatians, but that had been merely an expression of a passionate moment. Now he wished to consider these thoughts quietly and calmly and present them in a system well thought out. Thus the Epistle to the Romans came to be a theological treatise on the fundamental question of Christianity: man's new status with regard to God, the status as created by Christ.

Around him were gathered these loyal friends. They were to be witnesses of the writing of this great letter; they were to see how it poured forth from his mind. The Christian slave Tertius was given the high honour of being Paul's amanuensis. He proudly records this honour at the end of the letter.

After a solemn introduction, Paul announces the theme of the letter: "For I am not ashamed of the gospel. For it is the power of God salvation to every one that believes" (1:16). As he looked back on his own life, he saw it divided into two parts: the period without Christ, and the period in Christ. In the same way the history of mankind has two periods, and each period contains a symbolic figure. The first period is under the leadership of Adam, and it is the period of unredeemed mankind. The second period is under Christ, by whom mankind was redeemed and restored. That is the simple framework within which Paul saw the history of the world and the story of salvation.

1. What was man's status in that period without Christ? Is man's ideal relationship to God, the state of justice, realized in it? According to Paul, before Christ mankind, both Jew and Gentile, was under the anger of God.

He explains that by the religious and historical development of the pagan world. The high state of its political, artistic, philosophical, and moral culture was not able to halt its moral degeneration. His indictment is marked by a vehemence and fire that would have been worthy of Tacitus. The pagans had been in possession of the knowledge of God and of the moral law, but they constrained that knowledge, they held it captive by their sterile speculations, they clipped the wings of the proud eagle of their intellects so that he had to crawl ignominiously on the ground. Man, in his intellect and conscience, had been given the instruments to know God. From the mirror of the created world he could know the power of God; from the law within himself he could come to know the Lawgiver above him; from the moral ideal which is somehow born in him he could have known the holiness of God. From the Book of Wisdom (13:5), Paul had learned of the philosophers' efforts to discover God's existence, His attributes of omnipotence, eternity, and omniscience, but this theoretical knowledge brings with it an obligation.

God wishes not only to be known, but also to be acknowledged, not only studied but believed, honoured, adored, and loved. The culpable ignorance and confusion of the pagan world consisted in the fact that it deified and adored creatures that should have served as the stepping stones to God, the forces of nature, the stars, animals, the works of art and the achievements of the intellect, the state, and the emperor. Therefore God withdrew from the pagans the support of his grace.

But, when man is left to his own resources, he is unable

even to preserve his own human dignity. When man deifies humanity, he not only loses the divine but also destroys the human. The gross figures that followed each other on the imperial throne illustrate that truth with dreadful clarity. Paul's indictment becomes especially telling when we look at the sad state of things at the time. Recall the Eleusinian mysteries with their deplorable sexual rites; look at the Egyptian temples and their monstrous idols with dog's heads, the hundred-breasted goddesses of Asia Minor, the Syrian Baal columns with their symbols of the sexual act, the quarrel about precedence between Ibis and the sacred cat and the crocodile, or the arguments between the worshippers of the dog and of the fish. Paul saw these things daily. He had not retired to live in an ivory tower.

The worship of idols, conceived in sin, continually produced more sin, and moved progressively to a further darkening of the mind and a dulling of the moral sense. This manifested itself in the perversions of sexual life, the lesbian sensuality, in the so-called Corinthian immorality, all of which brought on their own punishment of devastating venereal diseases. Paul distinguishes three things on the face of paganism which clearly mark it for death: its inner untruthfulness, its moral corruption, and its lack of love and mercy. Paul sums up the essence of paganism in two phrases: "Without affection, without mercy" (Rom. 1:31). The old pagan world went down because it had no love, because it was an Asiatic despotism in which a small minority ruled over a mass of slaves. Against that background "the goodness and kindness of God our Saviour appeared" as an unexampled novelty (Titus 3:4).

In Athens, Paul had withstood the academic arrogance of the Greek philosophers. In the Epistle to the Romans he summons both Jews and Gentiles to God's judgment seat. Up to this point his Jewish readers were able to applaud what he said. Now Paul turns his indictments against the Jews. Besides reason and conscience, the Jews possessed another guide to God: revelation, the law, the prophets, the sacred books, the

Messianic promises. But now Paul must point out to them, with great sorrow, that precisely those things that should have led them to salvation brought them to their ruin because they arrogated these things to themselves as the exclusive privilege of their race. In spite of their Messianic promises, Paul will grant the Jews no privileged status. The law was not a means to salvation, it was only an educational means, which announced its own invalidation. But the tragedy of Judaism was that the Jews misunderstood the meaning of the law. They thought it effected salvation by itself. Paul made no distinction between the moral law and the ceremonial law; both made up one law, and this law has been replaced and invalidated. The moral part, the Decalogue, now that Christ has come, must be accepted in a new sense. It must be motivated and infused with the force of a new principle of life. The Jew also must seek salvation from Christ, not from Moses. Whoever does not submit to Christ is in sin, no matter how great his moral efforts, in spite of all his sacrifices and ascetic living.

2. Man's new status created by Christ. Christ's atoning sacrifice made it clear how futile were human attempts at self-redemption. In the natural order, anything great or beautiful must be achieved through man's individual efforts, and once achieved it must be earned again and again. The glory of war and the works of peace, science, art, technical progress, social improvements, power and dominion. Man may boast about all these achievements, but in the supernatural sphere he is unable to attain the highest good by his own efforts. That sublime state of being a child of God can be had only as a gratuitous gift. The really different thing about Christianity is that it is absolutely unmerited and undeserved. Christ did not die because of a combination of political and psychological factors that conspired against him. He died for love of us. By this unexampled act of love, God entered into the history of the race to lift men up to holiness. Love is a gift; otherwise it would not be love (5:1-11). But whenever God acts, his action is a creative act that reforms,

renews, and re-creates the believing soul so that it becomes a "new creature."

In view of this grant of salvation there can be no hesitation, no narrow consideration of race or descent, no contractual giving and taking. Only one response can be made: a completely unreserved faith, an unqualified assent to Christ and his salvation, a complete surrender of the whole personality to the divine will and a readiness to accept this life in Christ. In the presence of Jesus all human pride must melt away. Yet this justifying faith, out of which the new life grows as from its roots, is not a blind act, something unworthy of a human being, it is not a sacrifice of the intellect, but it is rather a reasonable service offered by a thinking and willing man, supported by reasonable motives. However, no man can boast about this faith, because essentially it is not a human act, it is not the result of reasonable conclusions, but is something produced by God, a gracious gift of the Holy Spirit. In its innermost nature this faith is a great mystery buried deep in the eternal selection and predestination of God.

For the Jews, Paul substantiated this doctrine about justification in their history and by reference to Abraham. He made use of terms taken from rabbinical theology which they could understand. For the Gentile Christians he referred to the powerful language of the Cross and the testimony of the individual soul and of the Holy Spirit. Whenever God speaks, he acts. All his acts are worthy of his divine nature. All his words are acts, and all his acts are words, as St. Augustine says *Verba Dei facta sunt*. How the total guilt of mankind was gathered in the head of the race, Adam, is a mystery, but it could be atoned for only by a historical act of a second Adam.

Justification, however, is only the beginning. No one gives life to himself. Every man receives it as a gift. Once it has been given it must be developed in harmony with the powers of nature granted along with it. The same thing is true in the supernatural life. No one can earn it, produce it, conquer it, or overtake it in a race. Once the "new creature" exists, it must live in the Christian community, it can no longer be moved by the urgings of the flesh, it must now follow the impulses of the Spirit of God. Each day it must support this new life, reconquer it, expand it, deepen it, and make it more secure. Thus the transfiguration process of the new-born creature ascends step by step until it culminates in the fullness of God's eternal life, out of whose hidden depths this new life draws its strength.

God would have made a headless torso if his work in us had been left incomplete, if after such mighty things as Christ's death and Resurrection, and the sending of the Holy Spirit, death would be permitted to destroy God's work in us. By the seal of the Spirit in us through baptism and confirmation, God gave us his Spirit as the pledge that the last word in human history is not death, but glory. That shows how serious God was in his love for us, for God would not pledge and promise these things if after death the human soul would be resolved into a little cloud of vapour and be wafted off into space (8:11).

As there is no place for human boasting or glorying in the plan of salvation, so there is no failure so long as man does not forsake the order of grace by his free will and place himself again under the rule of death and Satan. Beginning with man's selection, predestination, and calling in the eternal thoughts of God before all time until he is incorporated into the mystical body of Christ and reaches the fulfilment of his nature in the beatific vision of God, everything proceeds organically, according to a definite plan. The story of man's salvation, with his joys and sorrows, his battles, defeats, and victories, is only a short episode in the great drama of eternity. All the tragedy of human existence is only a short cry for glorification, a cry that joins the eternal harmony which all creation is singing to God. Thus the golden cycle is closed, the cycle that has its beginning and end in the depths of the life of Trinity.

Paul's teaching about predestination is not that fearful

doctrine of Calvin. Rather it is consoling and inspiring. It concludes on the chord of Christian hope (8:31-39), holding up a new light for a world that thought itself doomed to destruction. And that Christian hope went down into the catacombs and it transformed that necropolis, that sombre land of shadows, into a place of refreshment and of peace.

Paul expanded his philosophical meditation into the cosmic realm. He views the cosmic effects of the fall of man as a rent in the fabric of the universe. The fall of the angels is somehow connected with man's fall. In the letter to the Colossians (1:20) Paul obscurely implies that Christ completed the work of the redemption for all of creation, including the spirit world. It is a picture of inexpressible poignancy that Paul paints when he describes the whole creation suffering the pains of travail and crying for redemption.

But the whole history of the human race is a mystery. It cannot be explained in itself. It has no immanent meaning, as the pantheists thought. In itself, it is a horrible monster, a sphinx, about which men have always been guessing. Even the redemption and divine revelation did not lift the veil from the world's destiny. Indeed, revelation actually opened our eyes to the realization that our lives reach down into unfathomable depths. Revelation assured us, however, that all this shrill dissonance in creation awaits the moment of liberation. Virgil thought he heard the weeping of lifeless beings. Paul thought he saw how creatures lifted their hands in prayer to the Creator that he might free them from the service of evil, from the servitude of corruption.

In the midst of this profound dissertation on the law and grace, Paul inserted in the seventh chapter his famous personal confession. Certain imaginative students, think that this passage refers to some dark experience in Paul's youth, to some past sin: Certainly it is no book knowledge, but a matter of intimate experience, what Paul tells us about the two men in himself, about the twofold law in his bosom, about that division and schism in every unredeemed son of Adam.

Paul is making use of an ancient figure of speech when he speaks of himself as the type and representative of his own people under the law.

There may have been a moral or religious crisis in his stormy life. It would not be surprising in a man as highly gifted and emotional and excitable as Paul, living in a large city where the contrast between the atmosphere of his parental home and the brilliant Hellenic culture surrounding it was so great. Severe depressions may have moved over his soul. But to talk about some hidden crime sounds too much like sensationalism and seems to be an attempt to project Luther's soul into the young Paul.

Paul's purpose in writing the Epistle to the Romans was to bring about a merger between the Jewish and the Gentile sections of the Church, and he defends himself against the accusation that he was willing to deprive his own people of the blessings of the promise in favour of the Gentiles. At the mere mention of the word "renegade," something seems to do violence to his being, his whole national feeling is in revolt, his love for his people breaks forth with elemental force. He seems to regret his earlier blunt remarks about the law. His soul is saddened by the tragic destiny of his people which for thousands of years was the depositary of the promises and now had lost the Messias. It is a touching spectacle to see how he tries to solve the mystery of his race in the light of predestination.

God will not allow himself to be called to an accounting by his creatures. He will not be used to further narrow nationalist aims. The free-flowing stream of God's grace cannot be forced into some national channel. The promises were not made to the Israel of the flesh, but the Israel of God. The Jews' failure was, in a sense, a happy fault, *felix culpa,* inasmuch as the entrance of the Gentiles into God's kingdom should make the Jews doubly zealous. God makes use of the infidelity of some to save others, and then He also saves those who for a moment were untrue to their calling. Thus Paul seeks to dry his people's tears. His mind was calm, but his heart still suffers. Whose heart would not bleed at this mystery? "He has mercy on whom he will. And whom he will, he hardens" (9:18).

Paul looks down into the dizzy abyss of eternal pre-destination and, overcome by the yawning depth, he cries out, "O the depth of the riches of the wisdom and of the knowledge of God!" (11: 33.) In his long life he had not overcome his amazement, a sign of his ever youthful spirit.

As an accomplished author who has an ear for the cad-ences of thought and word, Paul closes this dogmatic part of his letter with a liturgical formula: "For of him, and by him, and in him, are all things" (11:36).

In the moral exhortations of the letter Paul shows how a man's moral attitudes are derived from the spirit of his faith. When Paul speaks of man's service of God, he is interpreting his Master's words about adoring God in spirit and truth. The ordinary translation, "reasonable service," is not quite correct. Morality does not depend on things, it is a matter of conscience. Everything depends on the disposition of the soul and on the quality of love. Thus Christian morality becomes a simple affair. Christian ethics also determines the Christian's attitude toward the state. Jewish apocalyptic writings regarded the state as the kingdom of Satan, and held themselves aloof from the world of politics. With all his high spirituality, Paul was the first one to adopt a just attitude toward the things of this world and the Roman state.

In the second letter to the Thessalonians he spoke of the state as the restraining power that held Antichrist at bay, but in the letter to the Romans he goes still farther. The authority of the state is, in his view, one of God's deacons, a representative of God, instituted for the suppression of evil. When Paul was writing these sentiments of friendliness to state authority, the Empire was in the fourth year of Nero's reign. The imperial auth-ority was still in high repute. It was the famous quinquennium, the first five-year period of the young Emperor whose diseased mentality had not yet revealed itself since he was still under the influence of his tutors, the genial Seneca and the noble Burrus. But Paul saw the face of the future.

His admonitions were intended first of all for the Jewish Christians whose compatriots in Jerusalem were heating their national passions to the boiling point and would soon find themselves in bloody revolt. Paul's teaching was not opportunism. He maintained his stand of fidelity to the state even after the animal in Nero had been unleashed and the Roman state had changed its attitude toward the Church (1 Tim. 2:1; Titus 3:1).

A glance at the last two chapters of the letter gives rise to several surmises. These chapters contain four conclusions to the epistle (15:33; 16:20, 24, 27). The solemn finale (16:25 ff.) is found at the end of chapter fourteen in two of the best manuscripts. Some scholars think that the long list of names in chapter sixteen is really a part of another letter, now lost, that Paul wrote to the Ephesians. How would Paul have known all the people he greets here? These people, it is thought, actually lived in Ephesus, as for instance, Epenetus, the first fruit of Asia. Later Paul wrote to Ephesus from Rome. Were Aquila and Priscilla still in Ephesus or had they returned there? (2 Tim. 4: 19.) No satisfactory explanation has yet been found for the greeting to this long list of persons.

In retrospect we may say that the Epistle to the Romans contains the whole of the Pauline theology. No other letter of Paul's played such a tragic and fateful role in the history of the West. Because of a monstrous misunderstanding, one part of the letter – Paul's words about justifying faith – was violently torn from the living context and represented as the heart of Paul's theology, as the most decisive tenet in the Christian teaching. But for Paul those words were only an episode of one of his polemic periods. He meant them to be understood in the context of his controversy with Judaism. In his later letters he never again refers to the thought. This will explain many of St.

Augustine's harsh conclusions and certain other exaggerated statements in the course of the history of the treatise on grace.

The young Luther was too much absorbed in the state of his own soul to understand the real nature of the question. Objective truth does not exist for the passionate man. In Luther's sense of the term, faith was nothing more than a sickly self-suggestion that God was a forgiving Father. But Paul saw all these things objectively. For him faith was the humble submission of oneself to the order of salvation. Luther took a transition point and made it the central point of Christianity, and thus he moved the whole perspective. Luther's was an egocentric distortion that took mere man with his contingent ego and made him the central point of religion. That was the great discovery of the Reformation, arising from the moral dislocations of the time and the monstrous suggestive powers of one poor mind. This subjective staring, this sickly fixation of the spiritual vision on the soul's poverty, this preoccupation with the untamed movements of man's unregenerate heart, has finally brought mankind to the relativity of moral standards and the ultimate irrationalism of our own day.

It would have been a great sorrow for Paul if he had seen how his words would be used to inflict such grievous wounds on the body of Christ 1,500 years later. In his mind justification was a transition, a stage in the spiritual process. Beyond justification he saw a sunny land where men lived "in Christ," a land watered by the stream of God's grace, and fructified by the creative powers of the risen Christ and the Holy Spirit.

CHAPTER FORTY-SEVEN

LAST JOURNEY TO JERUSALEM

"But now I shall go to Jerusalem, to minister to the saints" (Rom. 15:25).

The winter was past. On 5 March, Rome had solemnly opened the sailing season with religious ceremonies and the launching of the *navigium Isidis,* the Egyptian guardian of the sea. Paul made ready to leave for Jerusalem and from there he planned to sail for Rome. He was to reach that destination eventually, but in a way that he did not dream of now. He realized fully how great a venture it was for him personally to deliver this collection which he had so laboriously gathered. But the great cause of Christian unity seemed to demand it. Christian unity was for him a pledge of the truth of his cause. So the way to Rome must be through Jerusalem, if he wished to stand beside Peter in Rome.

If until now Paul's wanderings were a reflection of the journeys of Jesus, from now on Paul's life bears an even greater resemblance to the life of Jesus. In so many respects this last journey to Jerusalem, in its premonitions of death, in the heroic spirit with which he turned his face to Jerusalem, that murderess of prophets, in the warnings of his friends, resembled the last journey of Jesus as he resolutely, in obedience to his Father's will, went up to his death in Jerusalem (Mark 10: 32). It is remarkable how this city again and again drew the Apostle within its walls. But the Master and his great Apostle were united most of all in the poignant tragedy of their hearts: to be condemned as enemies of their people because of a higher loyalty to that race.

To evaluate the Apostle's courage, we ought to have an idea of the savage tactics of the zealots in Jerusalem. In their fanaticism they were waiting for the great day of revenge, the day when the Messias would come to slay the Gentiles, and for that day they had organized their robber bands. They burned any village that opposed their will. They appeared at every feast in Jerusalem, mingling in the crowds, their daggers hidden in the folds of their garments. Suddenly they struck out at their victims and silently they moved out of the crowd of devout worshippers.[33] The high priests had allowed the religious and political leadership to slip from their own hands. Josephus, who was serving as one of the Temple priests at this time, describes these days under the Governor Felix as the most dismal in the history of the Holy City. He relates how a certain demagogue incited large numbers to rise against the city. How some years later another mountebank from Egypt tried to storm Mount Olivet, to show that at his word the walls of the city would collapse. Felix met the rebels with an armed force. Hundreds were killed, two hundred escaped, but the Egyptian was never captured.[34]

In the port of Cenchrae, Paul had a foretaste of what awaited him in Jerusalem. At paschal time, all the sea and land routes were filled with pilgrims going to Jerusalem. As he came down to the port to take ship, Paul noticed the hateful looks and heard the murmured curses intended for the great "renegade." Many of the ships' owners were dependent on Jewish money, and it was an easy thing to buy off a captain and

---

[33] Josephus, *Antiquities*, XX, viii, 10
[34] *Ibid.,* 6.

his crew. Once on the high sea, a ship crowded with passengers offers an ideal opportunity to plunge a dagger in an enemy's back and silently slip the body overboard.

But the brethren had an excellent information service. Someone overheard the plot against Paul, and his plans were quickly changed. According to several manuscripts, Paul and Luke went immediately by land to Macedonia while the rest of the party, to throw the conspirators off the trail, went by way of Ephesus to Troas, where they were to meet Paul again. The original plan of celebrating Easter in Jerusalem was discarded. But Paul planned to celebrate it with his good friends in Philippi. From this point we find Luke in Paul's company again. Because of Luke's medical knowledge and his maritime experience, Paul realized how valuable and desirable a companion he would be for the missions in the west. As we return again to the "we" section of the Acts of the Apostles (20:6), the itinerary is more accurately kept, facts are recorded with classical exactness in the journal, and the whole narrative manifests unusual powers of observation and a rare charm.

In the year 58, Easter fell on Tuesday, 28 March.[35] On the following Tuesday, 4 April, Paul bade farewell to his friends in Philippi. In the harbour of Neapolis they found a little freighter going to Troas. "But we sailed" (Acts 20:6). That word "we" is filled with a world of emotion and affection. Although Paul's life was filled with suffering, we must not think of it as an unhappy life. He was a master of the art of making friends, and friendships were a need in his apostolic labours. At all times we find great friendships in the Church. The brighter aspects of the lives of the saints are really hymns in praise of friendship. The most amiable of all the saints, St. Francis of Assisi, and the most cosmopolitan of the saints, St. Francis de Sales, are classical examples of great friends. Paul had neither wife nor child. He had no family ties. But God gave

---

[35] Cf. F. K. Ginzel, *Handbuch der mathematischen and technischen Chronologie*, Leipzig, 1914.

him good friends. And what friends they were! Few men had
more bitter enemies, but few men had more devoted friends
than Paul. And that meant unspeakable good fortune in the
midst of great suffering.

Because of an unfavourable wind, they did not reach
Troas until Sunday, 9 April. They stayed seven days in Troas,
and the end of their visit was marked by a dramatic occurrence.
In spite of the contrary opinion of many scholars, we believe
that Luke is describing a Sunday Eucharistic service in the
upper room at Troas. The Sabbath was over. The sun had gone
down in flames into the sea behind the island of Tenedos. Men
and women were hurrying up the outside stairs of a large
residence to the upper room. The windows were open to the
warm air of the spring evening, and from the sea cool breezes
came into the room. Luke is a keen observer. We see the
attentive audience, the many small oil lamps hanging from the
ceiling, the curtains swaying in the breeze. The agape is over.
Paul is preaching about the Saviour who conquered death; his
text: "I am the resurrection and the life."

Young Eutychus was sitting on the window sill, fighting
sleep. Suddenly a shriek rent the air. Eutychus had fallen three
stories to the courtyard below. Paul went down and, like Elias
and Eliseus (3 Kings 17:17 ff.; 4 Kings 4:18 ff.), threw himself
upon the lifeless body and called the youth back to life. How
vivid those words of the sermon's text seemed now to the
assembly: "I am the resurrection and the life." Paul made no
reference to the miracle. He went on calmly with his sermon,
and then he broke for them the bread of life.

No one had any thought of sleep that night. The ship that
was to take Paul's friends to Assos lifted anchor at dawn. (The
Beza text remarks that Eutychus was present as they sailed,
safe and sound.) Paul made the journey of about fifteen miles
on foot, perhaps because he wished to visit some Christians on
the way. Besides, he needed some time to think, and some
time, too, for intercourse with God. He felt how forebodings

had increased, how frequent now were prophetic warnings. Would he have to forego the journey to Spain? When he was alone he felt the weight of his declining years. There before him in the midday sun, lay Assos. "Go to Assos," said the ancient poet, "if you have thoughts of suicide." Paul climbed down the steep rocks, and in the city below he met his companions. There is reason to believe that his party had hired a small coastal vessel in order to lose no time in loading and unloading. It was the first Christian pilgrim ship to go to Jerusalem. At night they drew the little ship up on shore and slept either on board or in tents.

The next day they came to Mytilene on Lesbos, the island of Sappho. The following day they reached Chios fragrant with flowers. The third day they raised the temple of Artemis in Ephesus. After a landing on Samos they reached Miletus, 20 April. Paul sent messengers, probably Tychicus and Trophimus, to Ephesus to invite the elders of the congregation to a last meeting with their Apostle.

The farewell scene at Miletus is one of the most touching passages in Luke's journal. Paul, in his farewell speech, gives expression to his apostolic solicitude. How great a sense of responsibility, how much fidelity to duty are implied in each word! He could have lightened his burden if he would have passed over the difference between Judaism and Christianity in Antioch, in Corinth, and in Ephesus, if he had kept silence because of human respect or timidity. But what would have happened to the Church? The Church needs not only prudent and circumspect leaders. It needs also martyrs of conviction.

Knowing that unpleasant things awaited him in Jerusalem, Paul continued on his way "bound in spirit," his goal ever before him, and that goal was Jerusalem and Rome. "Neither do I count my life more precious than myself;" in his ministry his life was of small value. Paul had a supernatural scale of values: the blood of Christ, then the Church, the human soul, his own calling, and lastly his own life. Paul did not know that the way he was travelling would take him to prisons and chains, to blows and insults, to shipwreck and mortal dangers, and finally to execution. He was content to know that his Master knew where he was going. "It is a more blessed thing to give, rather than to receive," he told them. But those words are true only in the realm of love.

Paul stretched out his hands in farewell. How much blessing came from those hands of Paul! They were always open to give, never to receive. We can see them, stiff and trembling, grasping the quill to write an affectionate greeting at the end of a letter. Those calluses and scars are his stigmata. We can understand that his brethren could not tear themselves from him, "being grieved most of all for the word which he said, that they should see his face no more." (Acts 20:38).

On 25 April, a favourable wind carried them to Rhodes, that charming island of roses about which the ancients boasted that here the sun shone every day of the year. In Patara they had the good fortune to find a ship bound for Phoenicia. The crossing lasted five days. They passed the west coast of Cyprus on their left, Cyprus the home of Paul's old friend Barnabas. "Ah, Barnabas, I wish I had been more patient with you that day in Antioch." Paul had shed tears over so many men (2 Cor. 2:4; Acts 20:31), and now when he looked over to Cyprus, perhaps his eyes were moist again. They stayed seven days in Tyre. The Church here owed its origin to that Christian persecution which Paul himself had occasioned twenty years before.

Now that they had set foot on the soil of Palestine, Paul's mood became ever heavier, the prophetic warnings were more frequent, and he seemed to feel on his face the hot breath of Jerusalem's hatred. From Ptolemais (Acre) the caravan set forth on foot. Fourteen days before Pentecost they reached Caesarea and now they were only three days' journey from Jerusalem, 63 miles. In Caesarea, Paul planned to spend several days in quiet recollection in the home of his friend Philip, a man after his own heart. Philip referred to himself as an evangelist, as an apostle of lower rank, but he was nevertheless "one of the seven," to whom the spirit of Stephen had been given in large measure. Twenty years previously he had been obliged to flee from the persecution that Paul had provoked in Jerusalem. He had gone into Samaria and along the coast near Joppe to preach the gospel, settling finally in Caesarea.

In later years Philip adopted Paul's more liberal ideas. These two apostles spent precious hours together in Philip's upper room, looking out to the sea. What memories came back to them! How the good God had disposed all things for the best! Paul was deeply impressed by the Christian atmosphere of Philip's household. Philip's charisma, the gift of exhortation and consolation, had been given also to his four daughters. These four virgins, the forerunners of so many consecrated virgins in the Church, sat at the feet of the famous Apostle. Not long after this they would be privileged to offer their womanly ministrations to Paul in his imprisonment.

The shadow of sorrow moved like a cloud over these happy days in Caesarea. The prophet Agabus, whom Paul had known in Antioch, came one day to Caesarea. Taking Paul's cincture, he bound his own hands and feet, and said: "Thus says the Holy Spirit: The man whose girdle this is, the Jews shall bind in this manner in Jerusalem and shall deliver him into the hands of the Gentiles" (Acts 20:31). His friends could no longer contain their anxiety for him. They begged him not to go on. But Paul was resolute: "What do you mean, weeping and afflicting my heart? For I am ready not only to be bound, but to die also in Jerusalem, for the name of the Lord Jesus" (21:13). Paul's readiness to suffer was not something fanatical. He knew clearly that, like his Master, his career would find fulfilment in Jerusalem.

On the Wednesday before Pentecost, Paul's caravan covered the last lap of the journey. Some of the brethren from Caesarea had come with them to Antipatris, through the fertile plain of Saxon where the farmers were cutting the first sheaves. Then they went up to the stony plateau of Judea and on to

Jerusalem. On the eve of the great Sabbath they approached the
Holy City. Along every road groups of pilgrims in bright
coloured garments and head-dresses, farmers driving sheep and
young steers, moved on to the capital. Thus some forty years
earlier Paul, as the merchant's son from Tarsus, had come with
his father on his first visit to Jerusalem, perhaps at the time
when the divine youth from Nazareth in his humble garment
walked the stony road to the city. The city was filled to overflowing with strangers. Most of them slept in tents. Paul found
lodging in the house of one of the Lord's disciples, one
Mnason. The official Church of Jerusalem had no place for its
greatest Apostle.

CHAPTER FORTY-EIGHT

An Ominous Counsel

"Do therefore this that we say to you" (Acts 21:23).

Paul was back again in Jerusalem, for the fifth and last time since his conversion. The Jewish terrorists were in command of the city streets, and Paul, who thwarted their plans for national glory, was their bitterly hated enemy. Some of the Jewish Christians shared this hatred for Paul. James was now a very old man and he had no longer any energy to hold in check those violent spirits in the Church that had come over from the Pharisees. St. Clement of Rome, in his letter to the Corinthians, says that Paul's unjust treatment was on account of envy. No doubt can exist in anyone's mind that Paul was the victim of a conspiracy between the "unbelieving" and "false" brethren.

From the roof porch of his host's house Paul looked down into the street and saw the Pentecostal crowd: "Parthians and Medes and Elamites and inhabitants of Mesopotamia, Judea and Cappadocia, Pontus and Asia" (Acts 2:9). Yes, they had come again from Asia Minor, and Paul was not pleased to see them here, these fanatical groups of Asia Minor, Jews from Ephesus, easily recognized by their colourful garb. The hired murderers from Corinth were here too, waiting for him. The news of the arrival of the "renegade" went swiftly through the city, down every alley, into every bazaar, to every caravansary. It seemed hardly possible to escape death at the hands of these zealots.

Paul was careful not to venture out alone. His friends in Jerusalem were pitifully few. That group, of whom Luke says, "the brethren received us gladly," was probably a small number of Hellenists. They came to his lodgings to greet him, but the great council felt no need to welcome him. Paul's appearance the next day before the great council was like a trial by fire. The Church in Jerusalem had grown large. The elders spoke of thousands of members.

Luke draws an impressive picture of this remarkable assembly before which Paul was to appear. In the chair of the presiding officer sat the white-clothed figure of James, surrounded by the presbyters. What were the thoughts of Paul's eight companions, mostly converts from paganism, when they saw for the first time this great Apostle who was a blood relative of the Lord, who as a child had played with him on the hillsides of Galilee?

Each of the delegates from the Gentile Churches now came forward and presented his gift. They observed their leader with amazement. Was this the same Paul who now stood so humbly and quietly in the presence of the emaciated form of James? Solemnly Paul and James gave each other the kiss of peace. Then the presbyters gave Paul the kiss of peace. Paul's companions stood near him expectantly. Their faces fell, the sign of brotherhood was not given to them. The gifts they brought were taken from them silently, as if the offering were a matter of course, something that was owed. Luke is silent about the matter, but his silence indicates the disillusionment of the delegates. The fears that Paul had expressed in his letter to the Romans had not been entirely groundless.

Everything was formal and stiff. The atmosphere changed somewhat when Paul gave a comprehensive report about all the great and wonderful things which the Lord had done for the pagans through him. Paul went on, not mentioning names, but unable to hide his pain and sorrow, to tell about what he and his converts had had to suffer from the false brethren, how they had abused him because of his appearance, how they had undermined his authority, preached a perverted gospel, exploited the Churches, and blasphemed the grace of God. But God had turned all things to good. In spite of all this the glory of Christ had been even brighter. Now like a string of pearls there were Churches from Syria, to Greece, all about the Aegean Sea.

As Paul spoke, hearts became warm for his cause, indifference grew into interest, the interest grew into amazement and enthusiasm. When he finished, James nodded to him and smiled and from his aged lips came the cry: "Praised be God, the God of Abraham, Isaac, and Jacob, who has done such things for his beloved Son" (cf. Acts 21:20). They all took up the cry.What else could they do? The success had been too great that they should not give thanks to God. But for Paul and his co-workers no word of commendation was uttered.

Luke leaves little doubt about his disappointment at what happened now. In his journal he wrote: "But they said to him." "But": it was like a stream of cold water on their warm enthusiasm. "But you see, brother, there are thousands of Jews here. You must consider them, you must be cautious. Our people here are much disturbed by your teaching. They see how you lift the barrier between Jew and Gentile. Yes, and you have even gone farther: you have deposed Moses and invalidated the law." It was the prodigal son's elder brother talking. He could not be glad when his brother came back home, he could not join in his good father's joy, and he would not sit down with his brother even after his father had begged him to come in.

We can easily understand the Apostle's disappointment when, after his glowing report, the first question implied a serious accusation. It was as if some famous missionary had won half of Africa for Christ, and after years of unspeakable labour and hardship had come home to a Church council to give a report of his activities and then heard words like these from the synodal officer: "May God be praised! But, beloved brother, it has come to our ears that in teaching plain chant to the Negroes you did not make use of the Vatican Edition." Unfortunately things like this have happened in the history of the Church only too frequently. When the two famous Apostles of the Slavs, Sts. Cyril and Methodius, came to Rome to make a report to the Pope, they were greeted by an arrogant and antagonistic attitude of the papal court because they had made some concessions in favour of the Slavic tongue at the expense of the Latin rite. But luckily a prudent, far-seeing Pope stood at the Church's helm at that time.

And now they proceeded to give Paul that strange counsel. "Do you know what you ought to do?" they asked. "Take our advice. Purge yourself of this suspicion. Do not discredit the religion. Show publicly that you are a good Jew after all. Here is our plan. We happen to have here four men who have made the Nazarite vow and are not able to pay the expenses involved. Join them in their vow which is nearly complete. Pay their expenses and take them to the Temple for the next seven days. Then everybody will see that there is nothing to these accusations and that you walk in the observance of the law." Then they took their little prick of revenge. They reminded Paul of the four statutes of the Council of the Apostles. Eight years ago they had yielded to Paul. Now it was Paul's turn to make a small concession. It was all well planned. The advice may have been considered prudent at another time when everybody was not agitated to fever pitch. And the reasoning behind the advice was most humiliating: he should rehabilitate himself by making what amounted to an open profession of Judaism.

It was an extraordinary demand they made on Paul. Even the physical performance was no small matter: to spend seven days in the courts of the Temple with men who were total strangers, and then pay for the expenses, which were also heavy. The Temple offering for five Nazarites was fifteen sheep, fifteen baskets of bread, cake, oil cakes, and the same number of jugs of wine. Besides this, Paul would have had to pay the living expenses of the four men for seven days. During his last visit to Jerusalem, Paul had fulfilled such a vow for himself. But that had been of his own volition, now it was to be an external observance against which his whole being rebelled. He was being asked to do a sort of public penance.

And if it actually pacified the Jews, how would it be interpreted by the Gentile Christians? Might it not be interpreted as a tacit retraction of all that he said with so much emphasis? Would not his lifework suffer by carrying out this plan? His conscience may have reproached him: "Paul, what are you about to do? For years you fought for freedom from the law and you called those Jewish ceremonies 'weak and miserable elements.' Now you are walking on the edge of the sword. In itself, it is true, the matter is indifferent, but will it not appear as a subterfuge?"

How easily a man can be placed in an embarrassing position, and sometimes even by his friends? Paul was undoubtedly fighting a bitter spiritual battle, but Luke makes no reference to it. It was Luke's business to write down the events of the day, not to reveal the secrets of his hero. But knowing Paul as we do, how sensitive he was about truthfulness and honesty, and knowing also Luke's delicacy at times like this, we feel sure that something occurred between verses 25 and 26. Paul must have made some reply, and some discussion must have followed. But about all this Luke says nothing. He goes factually on with his report: "Then Paul took the men ..." Between those two verses occurred a spiritual tragedy. Paul made his decision for reasons that remain hidden to us. Was it perhaps because of that noble desire to become all things to all men and to reconcile the mother Church with the Gentile missions? "For whereas I was free as to all, I made myself the servant of all, that I might gain the more" (1 Cor. 9:19). Even Renan was forced to admit that in Paul's entire apostolic career he had made no greater sacrifice than this. Here at Jerusalem he manifested greater magnanimity than in his labours at Corinth or Thessalonica where he had been able to unfold all the force of his genius in complete freedom.

CHAPTER FORTY-NINE

"I AM A ROMAN CITIZEN"

"And the tribune coming, said to him: Tell me, are you a Roman?
But he said: Yes. And the tribune answered: I obtained the being free of
this city with a great sum. And Paul said: But I was born so" (Acts 22:2).

Easter and Pentecost were trying days for the Roman garrison in Jerusalem. It is said that one year, during Nero's reign, 2,600,000 persons came to Jerusalem to eat the paschal lamb: The number is, of course, a gross exaggeration. But even if we divide it by ten, it is still considerable. At such times the garrison at Jerusalem was reinforced by cohorts drawn from Caesarea. While Cumanus was governor, 20,000 persons are said to have lost their lives during the Easter celebration in Jerusalem.[36] Most of these agitators for liberation of the Jews were Galilean hotheads. With innocent looks on their faces, carrying daggers in the folds of their cloaks, they stood around the altar of sacrifice; but on one occasion, at least, the governor had been informed of the plot and had ordered them massacred on the spot (Luke 13:1). Because the radical national party for liberation was growing year by year, these conditions on the festival days in the capital grew worse. These agitators were

---

[36] Josephus, *Antiquities*, XX, v, 3.

the forerunners of the final Jewish revolution against the power of Rome. All during these years a threatening cloud was hanging over the Holy City and the Temple.

On Pentecost, accompanied by his faithful Trophimus, Paul went with the four Nazarites to the Temple mount and entered the famous Court of the Gentiles, which occupied all the present Haramesh Sherif in which has been erected the Mosque of Omar. From the northwest corner of the court, Herod's fortress looked down defiantly. In honour of the Roman general, Herod had called the fortress Antonia. It was a vast stronghold with battlements and towers, parade grounds, courts, barracks, and in the interior was a superb residence rivalling the splendour of a palace. By the might of this fortress Rome was able to keep its iron grip on the throat of a rebellious people. From the fortress Antonia a walk led out to the roof of the gallery that surrounded the Temple court, and a grand staircase led down into the Court of the Gentiles.

Three large terraces had been built on Mount Moria, the Temple hill. The lowest of these terraces was the Court of the Gentiles, where Jesus twice dispersed the buyers and sellers. From this court a wide staircase of fourteen marble steps led up into an inner court, the Court of Israel, through the "Beautiful Gate," where Peter healed the lame man. This Court of Israel had a division called the Court of the Women. The Court of Israel was a large rectangular place surrounded by a colonnade and contained the chest for the offerings with its thirteen trumpet-like openings near which our Lord had been sitting one day when he saw the widow offer her "two brass mites."

Immediately in front of the Temple buildings stood the altar of holocausts on an elevated platform surrounded by troughs through which the blood of the animals was led off. Around the Court of Israel were the quarters of the priests. Into this inner Court of the Priests the ordinary people were admitted only in the morning and evening at the time of sacrifice (Luke 1:10). Above the steps leading from the outer to the

inner court were two beautiful doors made of bronze that could
be moved only with the help of twenty men. A short distance in
front of these massive doors a barrier had been erected with a
tablet bearing a notice in Greek and Latin as a warning to the
Gentiles: "No stranger is permitted to cross this barrier into the
holy place. Whoever does so must take upon himself the consequences of his act: the penalty of death." Out of deference to
the feelings of the Jews, the Romans had ratified this warning.
And even today, the present owners of the Temple place, the
Mohammedans, enforce the same rule. Woe to that Christian
who should dare to set foot in the Temple place on Friday. The
fanatical crowd would tear him to shreds.

When Paul and his companions entered the outer court,
he found it filled with a confused din and a mass of people:
money-changers, butchers, and pilgrims from all over the
world. In the background was the sound of the bleating and
bellowing of the animals destined for sacrifice. Here and there
in the crowd could be detected the slinking figures of the
Galilean conspirators. When Paul went into the inner court, he
was careful not to take Trophimus along. In the inner court it
was almost silent compared to the confusion of the outer court.
Only the throat rattle of the sacrificial animals could be heard.
Priests in white robes moved about swiftly with their long
butchering knives, flinging the leg pieces of the slaughtered
heifers with uncanny accuracy up on the high altar. Levites
stood at the gates, serving as porters. The court was filled with
an unpleasant odour. From this altar of holocausts the smoke
and vapour from the warm blood of the animals had been rising
almost incessantly for centuries to heaven.

Paul gave notice to the priests about the final day of their
vow, before which their sacrifices had to be offered. Every day
he had to be present for these sacrifices, being permitted to
return home only in the evening. During this week when he was
engaged here at the Temple, the Jews from Asia Minor were
able to perfect their plot. They appointed some fellow

conspirators to station themselves in the inner court on the seventh day, and at a given signal they were to create a disturbance and under cover of the ensuing confusion make their attack on Paul.

Luke's accurate reporting of the incident leads us to believe that he and others of Paul's friends had come to the inner court on the last day of the vow, because they feared for Paul's safety. The morning sacrifice was being offered. Suddenly, at some signal, the Jews from Asia Minor began a fearful outcry: "Men of Israel, help! This is the man that teaches all men everywhere against the people, and the law and this place. Moreover he has brought Gentiles into the temple and has violated this holy place" (Acts 21:28). Words cannot describe the demoniacal fury of an Oriental mob once it has been aroused to the pitch of fanaticism. Terror is portrayed on every face because of the violation of the holy place; the priests stop in their functions, and a screaming, pushing, gesticulating mass of people moves toward Paul and swallows him up, as sinewy arms reach out to him, tearing his clothes and raining blows down on him. The Levites sound their trumpets, fearing a desecration of the Temple. The Temple guards arrive and push the angry, screaming mass through the gates down the marble steps. The great bronze gates close with a loud clang, and above all the other noise Paul may have heard it as symbolic of his ejection from his people.

Paul lay on the floor of the court. This was precisely the place where twenty years ago they had dragged young Stephen, and for a moment Paul felt in his being some ecstatic joy: soon he would be with Stephen and with his Master. But his hour had not yet come. The mob, even in its orgy of hate, hesitated to kill its victim within the outer court. They began to drag him to the gate, but that hesitation of his murderers was Paul's safety. The Roman sentinels on guard on the enclosing gallery had seen the whole affray and had informed the corporal of the guard. Immediately the cohorts in the barracks were called into action, the alarm was sounded in the fortress Antonia, and soon the sharp bark of Roman commands could be heard. Colonel Lysias was already hurrying down the stairs with a detachment of soldiers. He had been hoping for a long time to arrest the Egyptian agitator who had escaped some years before and he now thought he had the culprit in his hands.

He strode into the mob, had Paul arrested and bound with chains, and ordered him removed to the fortress. But the howling mob followed him, shouting: "Away with him, to the death." When the soldiers reached the steps with their prisoner, they were forced to lift him to their shoulders because of the pressure of the crowd. During all this time Paul had remained aware of all that happened. His garments had been torn to tatters, he had lost his cloak, blood was streaming into his eyes, but he was still master of the situation. Calmly he caught the tribune's attention and asked him in Greek: "May I speak something to you?" Lysias was surprised that it was not the Egyptian but an educated Greek who was his prisoner. "Can you speak Greek? Are not you that Egyptian who before these days did raise a tumult?" he asked.

Paul identified himself: "I am a Jew of Tarsus in Cilicia, a citizen of no mean city. I beg you, let me speak to the people." It was an unusual request coming from a man who had just been trodden under foot by the mob and had hardly come off with his life. In spite of the unprepossessing appearance of the prisoner, Lysias felt the influence of a strong personality. A brave man recognizes bravery. Perhaps the man has something to say that will throw light on the disturbance, and so, Lysias orders: "Speak." Paul looked out serenely on the mob that surged back and forth like a stormy sea.

Directly below him he now saw some members of the Sanhedrin. Some of them may have been old school companions of his. Now they were dignified rabbis with broad hems and heavy tassels on their robes. At a gesture from Paul, strangely enough the mob became subdued. When Paul began to speak in

Aramaic, they listened with rapt attention. It was an odd pulpit for the preaching of the gospel, the preacher was strangely garbed, shreds of cloth to cover him, chains dangling from his wrists, and he faced an unusual congregation.

Whenever Paul was able to address a crowd of people, he felt sure of himself. He now tried to show the angry men before him that it was not hatred for his people or for the law or for the Temple, but the will of God that had made him an apostle of Christ and the missioner to the Gentiles. Every one of the Jews knew that Jahve was a God who interfered in history, every day in the psalms the Jew read about the wonderful, the great, and terrible things that God had done. Would anyone withstand the will of Jahve? His reference to the law-abiding Ananias, as well as to the stoning of Stephen, would serve to mollify his hearers, but when he mentioned the word "Gentiles," "Go, for to the Gentiles afar off, will I send you," blind passion furiously unseated whatever reason had tried to assert itself in the mob's mind. Fanatics and Pharisees tore their clothing throwing the pieces about them, the frenzied rage of the mob knew no bounds. And even the Romans felt somewhat uneasy. Lysias understood nothing of what Paul had said, but he knew now that it was a fight about some Jewish religious question.

To satisfy the passions of the people, Lysias resorted to the same measure as that used by Pilate. He ordered the captain to scourge and torture the prisoner "to know for what cause they did so cry out against him." Paul was taken through the inner courtyard where once the Roman soldiery had placed the purple cloak about the Master's shoulders, slipped the crude scepter between his bound hands, and pressed the crown of thorns on his head. Whether Paul was to be scourged in the torture chamber where the pillar for the scourging and the rack were, is not clear from the account. The instrument for the scourging was a whip having metal points and lead balls, the *flagellum,* not the rod or *virga.* Paul was stripped, made to lie face down on the rack, and bound with thongs at wrists and ankles. The torturers understood no Greek. When the captain came to see that everything was in order, Paul asked him, calmly and not without some suggestion of humour: "Is it lawful for you to scourge a man that is a Roman, and uncondemned?"

According to the Roman law, one of the most important things to be remembered by those who exercised police authority was to have special regard for any man who was able to say: "I am a Roman citizen." The words always worked like magic. The centurion ran to the tribune, whose respect for the prisoner now grew still more. He came immediately to the place of torture and asked Paul: "Tell me, are you a Roman?" And Paul replied: "Yes."

Any false claim to this proud and noble title was punishable by death, and thus the claim was seldom made fraudulently. Lysias eyed the prisoner dubiously, remarking: "I bought this citizenship for a large sum." To which Paul replied with a smile: "But I was born a citizen." Lysias was more than embarrassed, he felt uncomfortable. The Roman criminal law forbade an official to begin a hearing with torture. Paul was immediately unbound, and lightly fettered to the wrist of a soldier.

What a night it must have been for Paul, he who had so often and so vividly talked to his converts about the sufferings of Christ! Here was the actual place where Christ had suffered the scourging, and as he reflected on these things, his own expression, "to be crucified with Christ," assumed a new and deeper meaning.

CHAPTER FIFTY

BEFORE THE GREAT COUNCIL

"But on the next day, meaning to know more diligently for what cause he was accused by the Jews, he loosed him and commanded the priests to come together and all the council: and, bringing forth Paul, he set him before them" (Acts 22:30).

In analyzing the psychology of danger it is interesting to observe how different temperaments react to it. For some so-called romantic and adventurous spirits, danger has a certain attraction, it offers fascination. Such persons go jubilantly into danger. Others tremble at the thought of danger, their knees turn to water. Still others are too phlegmatic to fear danger. They lack imagination to picture the peril or its consequences. Your true hero, however, sees the danger as it is. He does not rush headlong into it. But when he realizes that the danger is midway in his path, that it is inescapable, he goes bravely forward, dropping his visor, that is, he does not permit his imagination to exaggerate the danger. Like the knight in Albert Duerer's woodcut, he rides straight on between death and the devil. When Paul realized that this danger was unavoidable, he faced it bravely. He did not lose his self-possession for even a moment. When he lay on the pavement of the court with the trampling feet storming over him, when he was stretched upon the rack, he coolly considered what was the best course to follow.

The next day Paul showed the same presence of mind when the commandant of the fortress brought his prisoner before the Sanhedrin, consisting of the high priest and seventy-one councillors, in order to have some light thrown on this trouble. Claudius Lysias accompanied Paul, under military escort, to the same tribunal that had once condemned Jesus. This time, however, it did not meet in the council chamber, Gazith, in the Court of the Priests, but in some hall in the outer court where Stephen had been tried. Among the members of the council were several familiar faces. Among them, too, was the former high priest Caiphas. The heavy weight of crimes on his conscience seems only to have hardened the old scoundrel, although deep lines furrowed his face.

Evidently the high priest Ananias (47-59), whom Herod had himself placed in office, was not presiding at today's trial. At no time in its history had the office of high priest of the Jews fallen to such a low state as now. Ananias was a member of the family of Annas which, even in Jewish writings, was often referred to as a "breed of vipers," and Ananias himself is described by his contemporaries as a greedy, gluttonous man about town, known for his unbridled sensuality, who shunned no means to satisfy his lusts. Paul had been out of touch with Jerusalem for many years now, and therefore did not know the high priest personally. Today he was also making his first acquaintance with that aristocratic section of the priesthood called the Sadducees, that party of refined gentlemen, shrewd ecclesiastical politicians, and enlightened spirits.

The Sadducees were principally concerned about keeping down any national or religious movement among the Jews so that their own position would not be jeopardized. Luke, who was not present at this meeting of the council, is silent about the details. It seems, however, that Lysias requested the president to define the accusation they were making against Paul. Because of the frivolous view which the Sadducees took with regard to religious teachings, they immediately declared that it was ridiculous to characterize Paul's teaching about the Resurrection of Christ and his vision at Damascus as politically dangerous. Whenever such words as resurrection, angel, or spirit were mentioned, they indulged in derisive laughter at the expense of the Pharisees, who held dearly to these beliefs. In a flash, Paul saw the point where his enemies were divided, and he felt that the battle was half won.

At the very beginning of the speech he was making in his defence, a painful incident occurred. As Paul referred to the privilege of his good conscience, Ananias, bereft of all sense of human decency, ordered one of the Temple servants to go to Paul and strike him on the mouth. A blow on the mouth, particularly in an open assembly, was one of the worst insults that could be inflicted on a son of Israel. It meant that this man ceases now to belong to the people of Israel. We can easily understand how Paul, in whose veins flowed the blood of noble Jewish ancestors, almost lost control of himself at this indignity. Excitedly he cried out to Ananias: "God shall strike you, you whited wall. For you sit to judge me according to the law, and contrary to the law command me to be struck?" Here again we see the inconsistency of the Pharisee's moral judgment. Paul was immediately reproved for "reviling the high priest of God," but the high priest's unjust action is passed over. In excuse Paul replied, "I knew not, brethren, that he is the high priest." This excuse is variously interpreted, but very likely Paul implied with considerable irony: "It never entered my mind that this could be the high priest, or that a high priest could so far forget his dignity."

A comparison of Paul's action here with that of Jesus in a similar case shows that the disciple cannot approach the moral perfection of his divine Master. Of course, Paul was under no obligation to painfully copy what Jesus did. That is not what is meant by the imitation of Christ. Paul's figure of the "whitened wall" may have recalled to some of the Pharisees sitting here a

similar remark by Jesus when He called them "whitened sepul-
chres." It was a telling blow, for the word aptly characterized
the high priest as a decadent phenomenon giving the outward
appearance of virtue, righteousness, and power, while beneath
it all was rottenness. Paul's dire prophecy found fulfilment. A
few years later when Ananias was hiding from the Sicarian
conspirators, he was murdered.

Paul realizes that from a council made up as was this one,
he could expect no fairness or justice and therefore he made
use of the opportunity of setting the members of the council
against one another by throwing the moot question of
resurrection among them as the apple of discord.
Fundamentally, Judaism's opposition to Christianity was
rooted in Christ's Resurrection, which had invalidated the
Jewish religion and its political power, and the whole position
of the priests. Grasping the situation immediately, Paul called
out to the assembly: "Men, brethren, I am a Pharisee, the son of
Pharisees: concerning the hope and resurrection of the dead I
am called in question." The Sadducees then broke out in
resounding laughter, deriding the Pharisees, who still believed
in such things. In the end it seemed that Paul was no longer the
accused, but the Pharisees who turned the hearing into a
disgraceful theological squabble with the Sadducees.

Things went so far that some of the rabbis were defending Paul and saying that it was entirely possible that an angel or
some spirit had appeared to him at Damascus. Claudius Lysias,
in the meantime, had understood nothing of all this argument,
and when the discussion grew heated he began to fear for the
safety of his prisoner. He called the guard and ordered them to
take Paul to a safe place. According to the Beza text, in his
letter to Felix, Lysias wrote: "I was hardly able to tear him
(Paul) by force from their hands."

Some critics are inclined to say that in this incident
before the tribunal Paul did not conduct himself with his usual
dignity. They refer to his strategy, and they point out the contrast

between Paul and Jesus' silent dignity before the council. But they overlook the essential difference between the Passion of our Lord and the sufferings of an ordinary person. Jesus' Passion had a unique purpose, entirely different from that of any other human suffering. Jesus was effecting the salvation of the human race by a voluntary submission to suffering and death. For that reason he refrained from making a defence for himself, he asked no intervention from either human or divine agencies. He was certainly able to make use of the same strategies as his disciples. But while he suffered he saw before him the great mass of unredeemed humanity, he saw you and me, and he willed to be the silent Lamb of God mentioned by the prophets.

But Paul was suffering and fighting for himself alone. He was ready to die, but the time and place were circumstances to be determined by God. He was obliged to make use of all permissible mean to continue his service of the gospel. Besides, these critics expect too much from mere man. Even in those sublime heights to which the Spirit raises a man like Paul, man must still remember that he is human like the rest of us, that there are human limits, and that only One was able to surpass the limits of human nature.

Let us pay a visit to our hero as he sits in his prison cell in the fortress of Antonia. The events of the day have taken their toll of his strength. He realizes that he might have drunk deeper of the cup of suffering. He might have taken a larger share of his Master's suffering. The word he used with his Galatians and in his writing to the Romans (6:6), "crucified with Christ," echoed again and again in his mind. This was his second night in this cell. Here he sat alone and forsaken, the cell was unlighted, round about him everywhere he felt the hatred of people, and soon he found himself a victim of one of those attacks of sadness and dejection from which the greatest saints were not spared. Once when Peter was in similar circumstances, the Church of Jerusalem had prayed and watched for him (Acts 12:5). It is a saddening thought that this time Luke was not able to record such a loving act of sympathy on the part of the congregation at Jerusalem. The faithful of the Holy City thought they had gone far enough if they tolerated Paul without breaking with him. In one house in Jerusalem that night a light burned till dawn, a light enkindled by love for Paul. It was the house where his friends had come together to pray: Luke, Timothy, Titus, Trophimus, his sister and her family.

Paul's position was serious. Only the strong hand of Rome could save him now. He had come to the point where his attitude to his own people had to be reviewed, and during this night he reached a decision. Until now he had always felt himself safe within the juridical body of his people, he had always submitted to Jewish law and justice, but now he would cast off finally all political and juridical connections with the Jewish people and place himself within the Roman law and Roman justice, of which he had written so loyally in the Epistle to the Romans.

But the Romans had to act cautiously when dealing with a jealous and contentious people like the Jews. A long period of imprisonment awaited Paul. His ambition to carry the glory of Christ to Rome and to the ends of the earth seemed more and more like a vain dream. But dejected and disappointed as he was in the dark cell, he still was able to lay all things before his divine Master. He considered all these things with Christ, *in Christo*, and soon weariness closed his eyes in sleep. But as he slept his thoughts lived on. He continued somehow to talk to Christ. Someone said that when the waves are foaming and frothing on the surface of the sea, the depths below remain quiet and calm. So it was with Paul. Although his external life was stormy like the wild ocean, his inner life remained calm and unperturbed "in Christ."

Who will explain how the human soul, released from the burdens and bands of the day's work by sleep, is able to have intercourse with the demons of the deep or with the luminous spirits from on high according to its disposition? Who can tell how it comes that an angel of light will clothe himself with the gossamer stuff out of which our thoughts and our subconscious minds are made and bend lovingly in consolation over our tired spirits?

Suddenly, during the night, the Lord appeared to Paul in a vision as he had appeared to him twenty years before. "Lord, is it you?" Paul asked, because he knew that the prince of evil can put on the appearance of an angel of light to deceive men. Then he saw the marks of the wounds, as then at Damascus. "Lord," he said, "let your servant speak with you. Did I speak well of you before the fathers of Israel? Speak, Lord, for your servant hears." "Be constant, Paul," he heard in reply, "for as you have testified of me in Jerusalem, so must you bear witness also at Rome." The vision was gone. Paul awoke. All sadness was gone from his soul, he felt new power. If the Lord was with him, it would make no difference that men might condemn him.

CHAPTER FIFTY-ONE

PAUL AND FELIX

"And when day was come, some of the Jews gathered together and bound themselves under a curse, saying that they would neither eat nor drink till they killed Paul" (Acts 23:12).

In the meantime the conspirators had completed their plot, and made it known to the Sanhedrin, demanding its co-operation and support. To such depths had the great council of Israel fallen. This time, however, the information service of the brethren was functioning. Paul felt the proximity of loving, solicitous brethren. Paul's nephew had been able to overhear an important piece of news. Perhaps Paul's brother-in-law, because of his high office and many connections in the city, had learned of the plot and told Paul's sister, who sent her son to the fortress. While Paul was still meditating on what had occurred during the night, his cell door was suddenly opened. His nephew stood before him. "What news," he asked, "do you bring, my son?"

"Important news, Uncle Paul," the lad answered. "Delegates from the Sanhedrin are going to ask the commandant to bring you before the council again for another hearing. But that is only a pretext. As soon as you leave the fortress, you will be a dead man. Forty men have bound themselves by a terrible oath not to eat or drink until they have killed you. They will be lying in wait at every corner and in every nook."

Paul asked the captain of the guard to take the youth to Lysias at once, and thus the commandant received the news about the conspiracy just as he was preparing to receive the emissaries of the Sanhedrin. He felt that the responsibility for this case was getting too heavy for him, and that he now had reason to submit the affair to the Governor.

At nine o'clock that night two captains held themselves in readiness in the barracks of the fortress with two hundred foot soldiers, Syrian and Arabian archers, two hundred spearmen, and seventy horsemen, to take Paul under cover of the night to Caesarea. It was a memorable ride through the night with the stars above and the moon lighting up the reddish rocky landscape of Judea. In the morning they came down from the rocky plateau to the fertile plain of Saron where the reapers were going out to the day's work and farmers were threshing their grain. The ancient Roman road, a masterpiece of engineering, can still be seen near Caesarea, the road on which Paul travelled twelve hours that night. Now in the flat country, they had no fears of an ambush, and the four hundred foot soldiers turned back to the fortress Antonia. Toward evening the little company rode through the flowering gardens of the villas of Caesarea.

The harbour city of Caesarea, built by Herod the Great and named by him for the emperor, was a provisioning centre and a key city for the military government of Palestine. A garrison of five cohorts and a cavalry detachment were stationed here. The Jews were forced to pay by heavy taxes for the support of this army of occupation. Their bitter resentment against this burden was expressed in the question they addressed to our Lord: "Is it lawful to pay tribute to Caesar?" Caesarea was a beautiful city, the residence of the governor. Its architecture by its flamboyance revealed the decadent period of a healthier style of building. As in Jerusalem, the royal palace, called the Herodion, was the residence of the governor. Luke called it the praetorium of Herod. Important prisoners were lodged in the praetorium of the camp, or more precisely in the guardhouse. The cavalry captain commanding the horsemen from Jerusalem delivered Lysias', police report and handed over his prisoner to Antonius Felix the governor. For the first time these two men, representing two different worlds, stood face to face. Felix glanced casually and haughtily at the miserable figure of the prisoner.

He took the letter from the officer and read it aloud in Paul's presence. The letter was quite favourable to Paul. It told merely that the affair concerned some quarrel about the Jewish religion. Lysias was indeed a good example of the prudent, cautious Roman official. Felix asked the prisoner about his native province, and since Cilicia was an imperial, and not a senatorial, province, the court of the imperial governor would have competence in this case. Somewhat condescendingly, Felix said to Paul: "I will hear you when your accusers come." But even this meeting with the power of Rome bore some promise of success.

This was the beginning of Paul's imprisonment in Caesarea, which lasted for two monotonous years. They were difficult years for a man of such great activity, because the life of a prisoner has little variation. Therefore, too, Luke describes the few dramatic incidents of this period with broad strokes of the pen in four scenes. He wished to put the prejudices of Jewish Christians against Paul in their true light by showing how favourable were the judgments of those outside the fold, of the impartial Romans. The principal Roman actors in this tragedy are placed in a singularly favourable light. Luke was not interested in depicting the morals of a decadent period, as were, for instance, Tacitus, Suetonius, and Flavius Josephus, who wrote about the same personalities and not always without some bitterness and acrimony. Luke, influenced by his high sense of Christian morals, graciously covered over the weaknesses and the private lives of these personalities with the mantle of Christian charity. To understand how much restraint Luke was exercising, we must look at the historical background as it is described in contemporary sources.

Felix, from 52 to 60 procurator of Judea, and his more important brother Pallas, were freedmen of Antonia, the mother of Emperor Claudius. Pallas was the powerful favourite and first minister under Claudius and for some years under Nero, and through his influence Felix was able to follow a brilliant career. But his slave soul broke forth again and again. Tacitus says of him: "Sensual and cruel, he exercised royal authority in a slave-like manner. Now he suppressed the robber bands of the Sicarians. Then he made use of them for purposes of private revenge."[37] Thus it was that the high priest was murdered by the Sicarians because he dared to reprove Pallas for his extortions.[38] Pallas' powerful position at court assured Felix complete impunity for his crimes. Suetonius called him the "man of three queens."[39] He first married a niece of Antony and Cleopatra. At present he was married to Drusilla, the seventeen-year-old daughter of Herod Agrippa I. With the help of the Jewish magician Simon of Cyprus, he had won Drusilla away from her husband, King Aziz of Emesa. This, therefore, was that exemplary couple before whom Paul had to appear and with whom he had such awkward relations.

Drusilla's brother, Herod Agrippa II, whom we shall meet later when he visits Felix with his sister Berenice, had been educated at the imperial court after his father's horrible death. Since Herod was a minor, Claudius did not give him his father's kingdom of Judea, but later when his uncle died the Emperor gave him his uncle's little kingdom of Chalcis near Lebanon. When Nero was emperor, Herod increased his possessions by annexing principalities in northern Palestine and in the country east of the Jordan.

After several marital adventures, Berenice lived with her

---

[37] Tacitus, *Hist.*, V, g.

[38] Josephus, *Antiquities*, XX, viii, 5.

[39] Suetonius, *Claud.*, i8.

brother Agrippa. She was a famous courtesan, a lover of splendour. After the destruction of Jerusalem she entered into questionable relations with Titus. But when Titus became emperor, his scandalous connection with the Jewess was too much even for Rome, and he cast her aside. She disappeared finally in the darkness of oblivion, while her sister Drusilla lost her life in the eruption of Vesuvius.[40]

So Paul was now lodged in the palace of Herod. What stories this building could tell! Down its corridors at night could be heard the sobbing of the beautiful Miriam whom Herod had murdered. Here the sons of the old tyrant had met their fate. Unable to sleep at night, the ghastly tyrant roamed about the halls and rooms of the palace calling out the name of his beloved Miriam even after he had murdered her in a jealous rage. Outside this palace the Jews had once encamped and sent their petitions to the King when Caligula was about to desecrate the Temple with his statue.

In this building now the first scene described by Luke, the judicial hearing, took place. After a few days Ananias the high priest arrived with some of the elders from Jerusalem and a Roman lawyer, whose surname Tertullus betrayed the fact that he had formerly been a slave. He was a beginner, one of those who went out to the provinces and undertook the defence of natives in order to gain experience. The introduction of his speech reveals his ineptitude, for his awkward and obvious attempts at flattery were evidently copied after some model in his textbooks. The high priest probably had to suppress his laughter at the palpable lies the young lawyer now began to utter. Felix had granted peace to the whole land. It was Felix' foresight that had established good order everywhere. For these reasons the Jews felt exceedingly grateful to Felix. The Jews gave practical proof of that gratitude exactly two years later when they accused Felix of misadministration and caused Nero

---

[40] Josephus, *Antiquities*, XX, vii, 2; *Jewish Wars*, II, 13; Suetonins, *Titus*, 7; Tacitus, *Hist.*, II, 2

to remove him.

The tricky assumption that the case in question was a political matter reveals the clever machinations of the Sadducees. They argued as follows: that Paul was a dangerous political agitator and guilty of the crime of sedition. He was the leader of a religious sect which had no legal standing, and therefore he was guilty of the crime of *religio illicita*. That he had been guilty of desecrating the Temple. Each of these crimes was punishable by death, according to the Roman law.[41]

Felix was experienced enough to see through the schemes of these bloody dilettantes. He knew a great deal about the malice of these gentlemen and this venerable high priest. He now wanted to know what Paul had to say. Paul arose, the chains hanging from his wrists, and immediately he commanded the attention of everyone in the courtroom. In his treatment of men, in his choice of time and place, Paul showed he was the master of them all. His speech was prudent. It put the matter in its proper light by showing that the case was primarily concerned with a religious question: Paul said that he began his defence with confidence because the Governor had for many years been a judge over these people. Paul insinuated that Felix knew these people only too well. Point by point Paul went over the accusation, but he placed strong emphasis on the point that he had not been unfaithful to the religion of his ancestors. On the contrary, his religious stand, differing as it did from that of the Sadducees, his Christian worship of God, was really based on the law and the prophets, that is, on the dogmatic contents of the Old Testament. According to Paul, the Old and New Testament formed one dogmatic unity.

As the Roman law viewed the matter, the teaching of Paul about the Resurrection (and the Resurrection contained the whole doctrine of Christianity) was a matter entirely within the confines of the state-protected religion of Judaism, and could not be treated as an illegal religion. The Roman government was

---

[41] Josephus, *Jewish Wars*, VI, ii, 4

not concerned about differences of opinion within the Jewish religion. Twenty years earlier the proconsul Gallio had taken that stand. Paul's speech in his own defence was the first official apologetic document of Christianity before the Roman state. It outlined the stand which the early Christians took later and which the Roman authorities at first accepted. The Romans took no official cognizance of the essential difference between Judaism and Christianity in the beginning. Only later, about the middle sixties, did the Romans learn through the Jews that the Founder of Christianity had been crucified because he had "contradicted" Caesar, and then Roman jurisprudence recognized the essential difference between the two religions. When Domitian ascended the imperial throne, the attitude of Rome had already changed radically, leading to the first Christian persecutions. Hence St. John in his Gospel (19:7-16), written after the outbreak of the persecutions, no longer felt obliged to pass over the fact that apparently Jesus had been put to death as an enemy of Caesar. That knowledge was then a great comfort for the early Christians.

Because of the many years as an administrator in Judea and because of his marriage to a Jewess, Felix understood the religious quarrels of the Jews better than the average Roman official. After hearing Paul's defence, he had to admit that Paul was right. He could have handed down his sentence immediately. Indeed he should have done so. But he did not, partly because of his fear of Jewish revenge, partly because of his greed, for he hoped to extort the payment of money. According to Roman provincial law it was for him to decide whether any further custody of the prisoner was required. Felix decided that custody was still necessary under the pretext that he still needed further information from Lysias, and he closed the session of the court with the expression, "*Amplius*"; which meant as much as: the case is remanded for further testimony. Naturally Lysias never came again, and the Jews thought it wise to do no more about the case. Felix ordered that Paul's imprisonment should be made as light as possible, and from then on Paul was permitted the freedom of the barracks without fetters, and he was allowed to receive visitors whenever he wished. But the injustice of this imprisonment without a judicial sentence irked Paul.

Luke describes a second scene in this period at Caesarea. Evidently in the beginning when Christianity was still a novelty it had become the subject of polite discussion and conversation among the upper classes. Because of ennui or a longing for the sensational, the upper classes interested themselves in any new theory or religious movement. In the provinces, the governors were generally surrounded by groups of literary and artistic dilettantes, magicians, occultists, philosophers, and actors, according to the mental bent of the governor himself. Syrian manuscripts indicate that the governor often entered into discussion with Paul at his wife's instigation. As a Jewess she naturally wished to know more concerning this compatriot of hers about whom the whole eastern world was talking. She was a daughter of Herod Agrippa who had tried to thwart the new religion in James and Peter. She was a niece of Herod Antipas who had beheaded John the Baptist. Was she completely happy in her brilliant position as the governor's wife? Did not her soul long for something loftier than the embraces of a noble rake? Was she perhaps reaching out for that mysterious something that filled this poor prisoner with happiness? Desiring to come by this great secret of Paul's, she liked to hear him talk about "faith in Jesus." Returning from an official tour of the country, Felix arranged a social evening in the festive hall of the castle, at which Paul was to speak about Christianity. They had all heard about his spiritual powers, and what had happened at the court of Sergius over in Cyprus. It might turn out to be a jolly evening, something like that day when Jesus stood before Herod.

It was not easy for Paul to appear before this decadent assembly as the object of their curiosity. Still he longed for their souls. He felt that he was Christ's ambassador who must still exhort men to be "reconciled to God" (2 Cor. 5:20). He knew this kind of Jewish-pagan society, he had known them in Greece, in Ephesus, and back in Tarsus. He knew what ailed these people. After talking about the historical proofs of the faith, about the wonderful life of Christ, about the appearances of the risen Saviour, and about his own experiences, he suddenly gave his talk an unexpected turn by directing the attention of his hearers to the practical consequences of Christianity in the moral sphere: to a man's inner rectitude, his control of his sexual life, and a man's responsibility to the coming judgment of God.

He probably explained the sexual aberrations of the pagans as consequences of their religious confusion. He went on to paint a picture of the coming of the judge with apocalyptic colours. Felix was restless in his chair, he was pale and flushed by turns, he exchanged sly glances with his concubine while she opened her big eyes like an inquisitive child and watched the sacred fire that seemed to spray sparks from Paul's eyes. We do not know what was happening in the soul of the young woman. Ordinarily Paul refrained from saying anything harsh to a woman. Whenever he makes an accusation, he generally blames the man. But we know what happened to Felix. He was trembling now with fear, he was "terrified." He had reason to tremble, for his conscience rose up within him to accuse him. Before his eyes arose the bloody crimes of his past, the innocent victims of his violence, of his sensuality, of his rapacity, he saw the figure of the high priest whom he had murdered, the women whom he had seduced.

But Paul did not call down on Felix the punishment of the Furies, those avenging goddesses of the pagans who tortured an evildoer and drove him to madness. Paul referred to the friendly voice of God, who spoke to man of penance. For a moment it seemed that the grace of God had touched Felix. But it was not to be so. Penance and contrition are not thrilling experiences, they are not dramatic, they are hard reality, and Felix had no time for harsh realism. Under the pretence of feeling ill, Felix suddenly adjourned the meeting and said to Paul: "For this time, go your way: but when I have a convenient time, I will send for you." But that convenient time never came. Whenever we come into contact with Christ and the higher world and then postpone the matter for a more convenient time, almost always that time never comes, and each rejection of grace hardens the heart still more.

As Felix walked from the hall with his young wife on his arm, the demons of sensuality and rapacity were already waiting for him. In flattering tones they urged him never again to expose himself to such embarrassment, and Felix never again allowed himself to hear more in public. But he gave himself the pleasure of talking with his interesting prisoner in private meetings. He was impressed by Paul's extensive knowledge of Greek culture, of the cities of the world where he had travelled, of the experiences he had had in his many journeys: But he wished to go no deeper. He was too superficial, too much lacking in even ordinary idealism.

Hard times were coming for this poor man. In a few months he was deposed, and he disappeared in disgrace and oblivion. And his beautiful young wife with their child, the little Agrippa, perished in the searing lava of Mount Vesuvius. But that other man, Paul's friend who often sat with him in a corner of the courtyard with his notebook on his knee, would write the story of poor Felix, and as long as the world lasted people would read that sad story. Occasionally Felix made veiled suggestions to Paul about ransom for his release, and perhaps behind all the apparent religious interest on the part of Felix there was nothing more than ordinary pagan avarice.

Paul did not spend these years in Caesarea in complete inactivity. On the contrary, they were extraordinarily fruitful years for the Church. A man with Paul's appreciation of the value of time (Eph. 5:16) would find a way to use the time. His friends had come from Jerusalem and they were continually with him. Because of this enforced rest, Paul's health also improved. Indeed his life was more secure now than it had been for many years. Because of his long imprisonment, the hearts of some of the Jewish Christians were softened, and in his later letters we see few evidences of the old bitterness. Due to Caesarea's favourable location, Paul was able to keep up his contacts with all the Churches in the harbour cities of the Mediterranean. His correspondence during this period was unfortunately not preserved. But these days may have provided the time for the preparation and composition of one of the most beautiful books in the world: the Gospel according to St. Luke.

Paul had begun to realize that his oral proclamation of the gospel, now discontinued for so long a time, ought to be replaced by a written account. In his sermons he had always referred to the great events in Christ's life, but his spiritual disposition always led him to dig deeper into those divine thoughts that Christ had made known to him. Paul's was a mystical and prophetical nature, whereas Luke had rather an inclination for historical writing. Thus these two men comple- mented each other to the great advantage of Christianity. Matthew had already written his Gospel in Aramaic for the Jewish Christians. Mark was about to complete his narrative of Christ's life as he heard it from Peter's mouth. Luke was there- fore in the fortunate position of being able to weave these two accounts and others also into his Gospel. Besides this he was able to investigate other documents and sayings and to question many "eyewitnesses and ministers of the word" (Luke 1:1-4). He was able to extend his researches into the very beginnings, back to the childhood of our Lord, and to set down the earliest records in his book.

Here, in Caesarea, Luke may have met that newly con- verted Roman officer, called Theophilus, to whom Luke dedicated both of his books and who probably provided the means for the many journeys Luke made to reach every possible source of information. Luke may have gone many times from Caesarea into the Holy Land: to Jerusalem to interview James, to Nazareth to see the relatives and contemporaries of Jesus, and especially to see the Mother of Jesus, if she was still alive.

Mary would now have been an aged woman of eighty years. But from whom else would Luke have been able to obtain the wonderful story of Christmas, if not from the loving memory of Christ's Mother? When Luke wrote, "But Mary kept all these words, pondering them in her heart" (Luke 2:19), he designated Mary as the depositary of the most ancient tradition and the source of the Gospel of the divine childhood. In 2:35 ("And your own soul a sword shall pierce"), Luke painted the picture of the Sorrowful Mother, and when he records the *Magnificat* (1:46) and the humble praise of the woman (11:27), he lays the foundation for the veneration of Mary.

A troublesome question arises here: Why is it that we find nowhere in Paul's writings a cordial word about Mary, the Mother of the Lord? That short dogmatic reference in the letter to the Galatians (4:4), "God sent his Son, made of a woman," does not satisfy us. Where is the connection between Mary and Paul? We find it here in Caesarea. St. Luke is the bridge uniting Mary and Paul. Luke, the Pauline Evangelist and the historian of Christ's childhood. The master and the pupil complement each other: Luke the historian and Paul the theologian. More than the influence of the brethren of Judea, we see Paul's influence in Luke's Gospel: the same viewpoints, the same expressions, especially in the narrative of the Last Supper, so that the earliest writers of the Church referred to the Third Gospel as the Gospel of St. Paul.

A second work seems to owe its existence to these days of the captivity at Caesarea: the Acts of the Apostles. The "evangelist" Philip and the Christians of Caesarea and Joppe provided rich material for the early history of the Church. The actual composition of the Acts, however, took a number of years, and as the years went by Luke realized that many things which once seemed important should be omitted because of the changes time had brought. At this time another historian was living in Caesarea: Flavius Josephus. He was visiting some priests who were imprisoned there at the time. To him we are indebted for the most detailed descriptions of that period.

The imprisonment in Caesarea was now far into the second year, and apparently no change in the Apostle's position would have taken place if events had not been set in motion by a bloody occurrence. Caesarea was a city where Jews and Gentiles had equal rights, and because of this equality violent conflicts often took place in the city.

Such a fight took place now, and this time the Greeks were defeated. Felix arrived on the scene and ordered the Jews to be cleared from the streets. When the Jews refused to obey, the Roman cohorts went into action, massacred a large number of Jews, and burned many Jewish homes to the ground. The howling protests finally reached Rome, where the Jews had great influence.

Felix' patrons in Rome had died, his brother Pallas was in disgrace. Felix was recalled. One of his last official acts was to put Paul in irons again and leave him under arrest for his successor. The year when Felix left office, A.D. 60, is one of the most reliable dates in the life of the Apostle.

CHAPTER FIFTY-TWO

"I APPEAL TO CAESAR"

*"Then Festus, having conferred with the council, answered:
Have you appealed to Caesar? To Caesar shall you go"* (Acts 25:12).

The new governor, Portius Festus, who arrived in Caesarea at the beginning of autumn A.D. 60, was a descendant of an old senatorial family from Tusculum near Rome. He was a member of the old Roman nobility, an official of the old school. He was known to be a firm, just, and loyal administrator.[42]

After a three-day rest Festus went up to Jerusalem to meet the Jewish authorities and to hold court and dispose of any trials on the docket. Immediately the leaders of the priests, especially the new high priest, Ismael ben Phabi, began swarming round him. That highest religious office in the country was now obtainable for the payment of money. An old Talmudic tradition said: "Woe is me because of the house of Ismael ben Phabi! They are the high priests, their sons are the treasurers of the Temple, the sons-in-law are the rulers of the Temple, and their servants beat the people with rods."

The interval of two years had not quieted their hatred for Paul. Now indeed they had fresh hopes for his conviction by

---

[42] Josephus, *Antiquities*, XX, viii, g.

the new governor, who knew nothing about Jewish affairs.
Festus was like a new English official who goes out to India and
must decide between two quarrelling Hindu sects. The Jewish
priests asked Festus for a favour at the beginning of his term, a
gift: to hand over to them the prisoner Paul, so that they could
try him in their court in Jerusalem. They had already planned
how they would murder him on the way to Jerusalem. But
Festus was not nearly as inexperienced as they thought. He had
read the proceedings of Paul's case. "No," he told the priests,
"Paul will remain where he is. Roman justice does not permit
anyone to make a gift of the life of a prisoner. If you have a
case, bring it to my court in Caesarea." Thus Paul was obliged
to submit once more to the procedure of a futile court trial.

This new trial, which took place after ten days, is the
third scene that Luke describes in his journal. For Festus it was
a new and unaccustomed experience, his first contact with
fanatical Judaism, with that howling, gesticulating, threatening
mob that milled round the prisoner, insulting him and calling
for his blood. Two things were at once clear to Festus. He
perceived that the case concerned the Jewish religion, its law,
or its Temple, all of which were unintelligible to a Roman.
Festus felt that the case belonged to some religious tribunal, but
without Paul's consent he could not take him from an imperial
court to be tried by a Jewish tribunal. Everywhere and at all
times a Roman citizen had the right to be tried only by an
imperial court.

Festus therefore suggested to Paul that he ask for a change
of venue. This unexpected suggestion confronted Paul with a
difficult problem. Festus was right. The issue was essentially
religious. But it had a political aspect because of the Roman
law's cognizance of religion. It was therefore a mixed case.
Paul had always taken the stand that religious problems should
be solved by religious means. If he refused to go to Jerusalem
for trial, would he not be violating his own principles? Or should
he also countenance a mixture of religion and politics? It was

not an easy matter to decide.

But Paul had long ago rejected the competence of the Jewish courts in religious matters. He no longer acknowledged the competence of the Sanhedrin in this issue of his conscience. As far as the religious aspect of his case went, Paul felt that it could be adjudicated only by a higher authority, before God's tribunal, and in that court, he knew, the sentence had already been handed down.

Only one issue remained in Paul's mind: whether he had violated the law of the Roman state. If the imperial court decided that he was guilty, he would not refuse to die, for then he would be dying for his faith and not as the victim of a miscarriage of Jewish justice. Since, however, the governor refused to admit that the religious issue was solved, and he himself felt incompetent to give a decision, Paul was obliged to eliminate the governor's jurisdiction with his famous declaration, "I appeal to Caesar."

Magical words. They represented that most precious privilege of a Roman citizen of being tried by the imperial court in Rome, no matter where he was. That supreme court in Rome enjoyed the confidence of all men. As soon as a Roman citizen pronounced these magical words, all other courts in the world became incompetent. Since the time of Augustus, the Roman law permitted such an appeal even during the trial of a lower court, and not only after such court had given sentence. The appeal set aside not only a conviction but also an acquittal. By this appeal, Paul had outmanoeuvred his opponents. Festus breathed a sigh of relief. After a short conference with his legal advisers, the governor announced the appeal in the customary legal form: "Have you appealed to Caesar? To Caesar you shall go."

All Festus had to do now was to send Paul under military guard to Rome, with an accompanying letter describing the issue. But Festus was in doubt how to sum up the case. Just at this time, fortunately, King Herod Agrippa II of northern Palestine arrived for a state visit, with his sister Berenice, to

congratulate the new governor. Agrippa was an influential
personage in Rome. In fact, he had been instrumental in having
Festus appointed to his present position. Like no other, Agrippa
was qualified to advise Festus in this complicated case: by birth
a Jew, but a Roman of the Romans by training and education.
On his coins he called himself, "Philocaesar–Philoromaios"
"Caesar's friend–Friend of the Romans." For political reasons
he had studied the Jewish religion and was considered an
expert in that field, but personally he belonged to the elegant,
cultured group of liberal Jews. He had the right to appoint the
high priest and was himself the supervisor of the Temple
treasury, an office which turned out to be lucrative.

He always travelled with his famous sister, the beautiful
Berenice, who had deserted her husband, the Cilician magnate
Polemon. Since then Agrippa and Berenice lived together as
king and queen. Now they had arrived in Caesarea, where only
a few months ago their sister Drusilla had been mistress of the
palace, and where sixteen years before their father had suffered
a horrible death as a judgment of God. This dynasty was the
only one in the world's history to have had close contact with
Jesus: their great-grandfather was the murderer of the Innocents
in Bethlehem. Their great-uncle was the murderer of John the
Baptist and the derider of the Saviour. Their father was the
murderer of James and the persecutor of Peter. Since the day
that the founder of the dynasty had persecuted the Child of
Bethlehem, the whole family had become inextricably involved
in tragic guilt. Of this family the words of Jesus were true:
"Whosoever shall fall upon that stone shall be bruised; and
upon whomsoever it shall fall, it will grind him to powder"
(Luke 20:18).

Agrippa had ample reasons for making a study of religion.
Festus told his royal guests about his famous prisoner, and as
soon as Agrippa heard the names of Jesus and Paul he was
consumed with interest. "I should like to hear the man myself,"
he said, just as Herod Antipas once had wished to see Jesus.

Festus was glad to be able to please his guest, as then Pilate had been glad to please Antipas. "Tomorrow," said Festus, "you shall hear him" (25:22). Thus one of the most interesting scenes in the history of religion was arranged. It is the fourth scene in Luke's journal.

Paul was notified that on the next day he would be brought before this gathering. He knew Agrippa, he knew his entire history, and he immediately resolved to make use of this occasion for the spread of the gospel. Paul's address on this occasion is his finest apologetic sermon. It was not a juridical trial, but a social event in honour of the King. It was held in the great marble hall, the *basilike,* of the palace. The principal military and civil dignitaries were present, as well as the governor's official council.

Festus appeared in his white toga. The young King wore the purple mantle into which gold and silver threads were woven. Berenice was at his side, radiant in all her beauty. With becoming courtesy, the Governor yielded the place of honour to the King, while the distinguished company ranged themselves along the walls of the hall.

In his threadbare cloak, fettered to a soldier, Paul was led into this brilliant assembly. Pale, poorly clad, the Apostle stood before them in their shimmering satin gowns and sparkling jewels. Two antipodal worlds stood face to face in that room. The gospel stood in the prisoner's box. Paul knew it, he knew that it would always be thus until the heavenly *Kyrios* would come to annihilate the princes of this world.

Festus began the session with an introductory speech about the purpose of the meeting: he desired to obtain information for the opinion he had to write on Paul's case for Rome. He referred to the "lord," "*Kyrios,*" in Rome. Augustus and Tiberius had declined that title of divinity, but it was in constant use since Caligula and Nero had come to the throne. Condescendingly Agrippa then turned to Paul and said: "You have permission to speak for yourself" (26:1).

The prisoner stood up. All eyes were fixed on him. A feeling was abroad in the noble edifice that they were about to experience an important event. The experienced orator in antiquity always began an address with certain well-known gestures: he swung his toga about him, he raised his right arm and extended three fingers of his right hand. When Paul raised his right arm, the raw rattling of his chains was heard against the soft tinkle of the golden bracelets of the ladies of the court. This man who had talked on the Areopagus, in whom the divine *pneuma* dwelt, felt no embarrassment before this audience. The Beza text says: "He began with good courage as one who had been strengthened by the Holy Spirit." With the noble bearing of a free man, he turned to the King as to an equal. He knew the sad history of that King's family. He knew the family's tragic relationships with his Master. But now he was not influenced by these memories. Now he remained strictly factual.

Before Agrippa's mind he unfolded what the prophets had written about the spiritual heritage of the twelve tribes of Israel, he spoke of the contents of the thousand-year-old hopes of Israel that had at last been fulfilled in Christ. And then, when he mentioned the fateful word "resurrection," the King sceptically shook his head, for he belonged to the liberal wing of the Sadducees. Then Paul cried out: "Why should it be thought a thing incredible, that God should raise the dead?" For the true Israelite, the Resurrection of Christ is no obstacle. It is a proof of his religion and a beautiful triumph.

"I am no gullible visionary," said Paul. "Once I hated Christ, for a long time I did many things contrary to the name of Jesus of Nazareth." And then Paul was forced to talk of that most embarrassing period in his life. He tried to show that his conversion to Christianity was not a defection from the true spirit of the law and the prophets, it was a fulfilment of the Old Testament. In the presence of a man like Agrippa who knew the history of Judaism, Paul was able to reach back to all the scriptural proofs.

Festus sat through all this as if he were petrified. It was a completely alien world for him. It seemed sometimes as if he had come into a madhouse. Paul, however, was being carried away by enthusiasm when he cried out, "It is my mission to witness to both small and great and to the whole world that they may believe in the risen Lord." Such words had never before been heard. In ancient times nobody cared whether or not a religion was true – men often belonged to several religions as today in the Far East, in India, China, and Japan. The important thing to seek in a religion was not truth, but an advantage for the individual such as some mystical ecstasy, some consolation, or preferment in the government.

Christianity was the only religion that proposed the question of truth. That was why Pilate asked in amazement: "What is truth?" And here in Caesarea, Festus thought that Paul was a fanatical seeker for truth, and he interrupted him: "Paul, you are beside yourself: much learning does make you mad." Paul, not offended by the remark, with perfect courtesy replied: "I am not mad, most excellent Festus, but I speak words of truth and soberness. For the King knows of these things, to whom also I speak with confidence. For I am persuaded that none of these things are hidden from him. For neither was any of these things done in a corner" (Acts 26:25).

Then Paul ventured to address the King directly. "Do you believe the prophets, O King Agrippa?" No Jew was permitted to speak against the prophets. Agrippa was struggling for an answer, but Paul answered immediately for him, "I know that you believe." Now if a man believed the prophets, he also had to believe in Christ. But how hard it is for a man to draw the practical consequences from his intellectual convictions when it entails a sacrifice? What a far way it is from the head to the heart? Agrippa, embarrassed, had an uneasy feeling within himself. It seemed that somebody had struck a chord somewhere in his soul that had never been touched before. But he was an accomplished man of the world and he knew how to get out of uncomfortable situations. All you needed to do was remember some catchy phrase, a little joke, some *bon mot*, with a little admixture of irony, a little humour, and a little compliment for the speaker, and you threw dust in his eyes. The disposition to irony was in Herod's blood, it was a family trait. "Paul, you think you could make a Christian out of me in a moment?" The current translation, "In a little you persuade me to become a Christian," does not reproduce the original meaning. It was not the outcry of a soul nearly convinced of the truth. It was merely a pleasantry uttered by a proud and arrogant spirit trying to escape the painful consequences of Paul's reasoning.

Perhaps the assembly laughed politely at the King's clever sally, but Paul had no ear for witticisms. The hall was silent as Paul took up the King's remark and deftly gave it a serious turn. "I would to God," he said, "that both in a little and in much, not only you, but also all that hear me, this day, should become such as I also am, except" – and Paul raised his fettered arm – "except these bands." It was a dramatic moment. It seemed as if an angel of God hovered in the room. The Romans smiled at Paul's wish, but they had no idea of the happiness in Paul's soul. Some of the ladies giggled behind their kerchiefs. With a forced smile the King passed over the incident. Suddenly he arose, Berenice stood at his side, he bowed to the assembly as a sign that the meeting was over.

For Paul the speech was a success. It decided his future. After the meeting, Agrippa volunteered his opinion to Festus: "This man might have been set at liberty if he had not appealed to Caesar." Accordingly Festus wrote his opinion to Rome, and what he wrote contributed a great deal toward Paul's acquittal by Nero in Rome.

CHAPTER FIFTY-THREE

SHIPWRECKED

*"Going on hoard a ship of Adrumetum, we launched,
meaning to sail by the coasts of Asia, Aristarchus,
the Macedonian of Thessalonica, continuing with us"* (Acts 27:2).

The twenty-seventh chapter of the Acts of the Apostles contains the famous passage that has been called "the sailor's chapter." A German scientist of the Bremen School for Nautical Science, after extensive study of the chapter, called it "the most valuable nautical document that has come down to us from ancient times, and a literary document that could have been written only by an eyewitness." On the morning of the Battle of Trafalgar, Nelson had it read to him on his flagship. The son of an English clergyman, Nelson was well acquainted with the Scriptures since his boyhood and like many other brave spirits, such as Stanley, he always found encouragement and comfort in the Scriptures especially in difficult times.

The great hero of Trafalgar did not live to see the sun go down that day. That night he lay dead in the cabin of the Victory, but only after he had secured Britain's dominion of the seas for all time by the annihilation of the united French and Spanish fleets.

Sacred Scripture is a remarkably practical book for all

walks of life. It is a heroic book, a book about heroes for
heroes, a book for the training of heroes.

The autumn of the year 60 had come. The equinox had
passed. The transport of prisoners to Rome could not be delayed
any longer if the ship was not to lay up for the winter on the
way. The Roman captain, Julius, of the Augustan Cohort, the
Prima Augusta Italica, was entrusted with the safe delivery of
the prisoners in Rome. The Imperial Police Commissariat, of
which Julius was a member, was a masterpiece of Roman
organization. Its most important task was the protection of the
imperial family. But it had other duties: it was also the Empire's
secret police, the imperial courier service, and the imperial troop
for the safe conduct of prisoners everywhere in the Empire. The
privates of this organization were called *frumentarii,* and sometimes also *Peregrini,* because so many were aliens. Julius
selected a merchant ship bound for Adramyttium in Mysia in
Asia Minor. There he hoped to find a ship bound for Italy.

On a morning in September, a detail of Roman soldiers,
their helmets and spear tips flashing back the first rays of the
rising sun, took a group of prisoners down to the ship. They
were partly political prisoners and partly criminals and brigands
destined for the wild animal performances in the Circus
Maximus. It was evident that the latter belonged to a different
class from that prisoner who walked alone, only lightly
manacled to one of the soldiers, a Roman citizen obviously by
his proud and free bearing. But he, too, was a gladiator,
fighting for "the prize of the supernal vocation of God in Christ
Jesus" (Phil. 3:14). Toward Paul, Julius was friendly, almost
respectful, from the outset. Julius was one of the noble Roman
officers of the cast of the captain of Capharnaum and of
Cornelius in Caesarea. He had come to know Paul during the
latter's imprisonment, probably he had commanded the guard
on that occasion when Paul made his remarkable address in the
marble hall of the governor's palace.

All Paul's disciples and friends came down to bid him

farewell, and three were permitted to accompany him to Rome – Timothy, Luke, and Aristarchus – who are probably included in the "we" of the account. It was a great concession that they owed the captain. Only prominent prisoners with considerable influence were permitted to take slaves with them. A Roman citizen, however, always had two slaves to serve him.

As the ship pushed off from the Asiatic mainland, Paul stood on the deck, watching the land of his fathers receding in the distance. Perhaps in this moment of recollection, the years of his apostolic labours passed in review before his mind, the years since he had begun this Odyssey with his friend Barnabas. Even without him, of course, Christianity would have made its march out into the Mediterranean area, for God does not need any particular man for his plans. But when he makes use of a man, this man is permitted to imprint on the work the mark of his own personality. Today it is almost impossible for us to have an adequate idea of how much courage, daring, and tenacity was required, when all others began to waver and yield to the established and vested powers of the past. But this persevering energy had been crowned with complete success, because the man who is adamant in will power, who will make no compromise with the foe, is in league with the future. Now that Paul was leaving the eastern world, he looked back on his struggles with a holy joy in his heart. All around the Mediterranean, every country was now dotted with enthusiastic, zealous Christian Churches that were united with one another in a lasting bond of charity. Only Jerusalem stubbornly adhered to the past, but it had shut itself up in its own shell and become, sterile with respect to any influence on the world. How insignificant the opposition of a few Jews in Jerusalem seemed now!

Paul knew what to expect of this voyage. From experience he knew how exhausting such a voyage would be. Moreover, now he was a prisoner, although his treatment was milder than that of the convicts. To see how these poor creatures were treated by the soldiery, how poor was their fare and lodging,

while he was given special consideration, caused Paul much
suffering. When he was able to lighten their lot, physically and
spiritually, he was happy to do so. Did some of these poorest of
the poor learn from Paul the way to Christ? Nothing, of course,
is said about this in the Acts of the Apostles, but those who
know the heart of the great Apostle as he reveals it in his epistles
can read between the lines. It is a charming picture: Paul, the
ship's chaplain, and Luke the ship's physician.

To understand what followed we ought to know something about the seamanship of the ancients and their attitude
toward the sea. Nautical knowledge was, of course, exceedingly
primitive. Hardly any instruments had yet been invented. The
ancients did not have the compass, and were obliged to rely on
their observation of the sun's position and that of the stars. It
would be quite unfair to call the ancient ship captains "summer
captains". It would be underestimating their courage. In the
winter, it is true, all trans-Mediterranean sailing was discontinued, because it was almost impossible to see the stars on account
of the clouded skies. Already in the autumn, the eastern Mediterranean is swept by severe storms, and a sailing westward on
the bulky, broad-backed freighters of the day was not to be
thought of.

In ancient times man hated and feared the sea. For him it
was the essence of chaos out of which the beautiful and ordered
land had emerged. Neptune, the god of the sea, was full of
trickery and revenge, his unpredictable moods had to be pacified
by sacrifices. Besides this, the ancients were plagued by a
thought from religion: that the dead have no rest except in a
grave in the solid earth. No people associated the sea with chaos
more closely than the Jews because of the narrative of the
creation. In the psalms, in the Book of Job, and in the Prophets,
the waves of the sea are a figure of disorder and confusion, and
the ideal picture of the future as described in the Apocalypse
eliminates the sea, "and the sea is now no more" (21:1).

For a long time Paul looked back at the mountains of

Judea on the horizon. Behind them lay Jerusalem with its many sacred and painful memories. He saw Herod's marble palace in Caesarea where he had recently spent so many happy hours in pious conversation with his friends. In a few years, Caesarea would replace Jerusalem as the metropolis of the Palestinian Church. It would later become the seat of a famous school of theology where a great admirer of the Apostle, Origen, and Luke's first successor in the long and brilliant line of Church historians, Eusebius, would labour. Thus Paul's spirit, and Luke's too, would hover long over this city. Today nothing remains of the marble palace and the crusaders' castle except the cliff on which they were built.

Steadily battling against strong west winds, the ship was not able to hold its course, but with the help of occasional coast winds and currents it was able to sail around Cyprus to Myra on the southwest tip of Asia Minor. They had been at sea now fifteen days. Myra was a large and important port in the Egyptian grain trade. Some of the ships on this line reached two thousand tons or more. In Myra, Julius made a contract with a ship's owner to take over the transport of his prisoners. And as an imperial captain of police, Julius became the commanding officer on board. The ship carried 276 persons. Heavily laden it laboured to the northwest, and after three weeks out of Caesarea it had reached only the heights of Gnidus. The most difficult part of the voyage still lay ahead. They wished to round Cape Matapan, the southernmost tip of the Peloponnesus, in order to enter the Ionian Sea. But they were driven off, and they were glad if they could skirt around Crete and come under a favourable wind south of the island. Crete has the shape of an outstretched finger, measuring in length about 160 miles, and by its position it would ward off the blustering storms coming down from the archipelago. Thus they came to the harbour of Kaloi Limenes near Lasaea, a wide bay guarded by two islands across its entrance, on one of which a small chapel built in St. Paul's memory still stands. Here they decided to await better weather.

That year the Day of Atonement, *Kippur*, fell on the twenty-eighth of October, a few days before they landed on Crete. Julius called a conference between himself, the ship's owner, the captain, and the pilot. He also invited Paul. Paul proposed that they winter here on the island, but the ship's owner opposed the plan because he feared the loss of the cargo since no barns were available on the island. The alternate plan was to try to reach Phoenix, a winter port some distance to the west, and winter there. According to a modern seaman, this latter proposal was really a stab in the dark and would have been foolhardy. Paul was overruled, but they never reached Phoenix, the modern Port Lutro. A treacherous south wind lured the ship out of the bay, but they had scarcely rounded Cape Matal to the north when they were terror-stricken at the sight of Mount Ida with its ominous cap of white clouds. Suddenly a terrible tornado struck, a typhoon-like northeaster pounced upon the ship. "The Euroclydon, the Euroclydon," was the terrifying cry from everyone on shipboard.

The sails were lowered, the helm was drawn up. A few miles from shore they sighted the little island of Cauda (Gavdos), where they hoped to draw their little lifeboat up on shore. For a moment the ship was held high on the crest of a wave, the next moment it was dropped sickeningly into an abysmal valley between towering mountains of water. When it was high on the crest, only the middle part of the ship was supported while bow and stern were suspended in mid-air, and they thought the ship would be broken in two. A heavy cable was lashed around the gunwale of the ship to keep it from falling apart. The device was called "girdling the ship." It was a night of terrors.

A new danger arose. Since they had lost directions they feared that at any moment they would be thrown on the high sandbanks of the North African coast. The four heavy driving anchors were let down to slow the ship's progress. The ship's owner jettisoned part of the cargo, and all dispensable rigging, poles, masts, tackle, and things like the hand millstones. But the worst was still ahead: days of black despair when even the most experienced sailors gave up hope. Darkness is man's worst enemy. For days they saw neither sun nor stars. They had no idea where they were. Luke wrote in his book: "All hope of our being saved was taken away." Any hour the ship might be dashed against some reef or thrown upon some sandbank.

The whole crew lay beneath deck, pale as death. Because of the high seas awash over the deck, the hatches were battened down, and so the air below could hardly be breathed. No one had eaten anything for days, and Luke, the ship's physician, was a busy man. Paul prayed often for the lives of these 276 persons. Exhausted, he slept for a few minutes only to rouse himself again to prayer. How great is the power of one just man with God, a man like Paul or like the Curé of Ars! When despair threatened to engulf him, an angel of God stood at his side: "Fear not, Paul, you must be brought before Caesar. And behold God has given you all those that sail with you." In a dream Paul saw an island emerging from the sea, an island he had never seen before, on the rocks of the island a stranded ship. "On this island," a voice told him, "you must be wrecked." The vision was gone, Paul awoke, and the storm went on unabated.

Another man would have ascribed the vision to his feverish condition, but Paul felt sure of himself. He felt new strength coursing through his body. In the grey fog of all this misery, Paul went among his fellow voyagers, encouraging them and telling them of his vision. "Wherefore," he said, "sirs, be of good cheer: for I believe God that it shall so be, as it has been told me" (Acts 27:25).

On the fourteenth night, they were in the part of the sea between Greece and Sicily, which the ancients called Adria. Suddenly at midnight someone cried, "Land." Through the howling of the storm, the trained ear of one of the sailors was able to distinguish the thunder of some mighty breakers. They dropped the lead and found twenty fathoms, and shortly after fifteen fathoms. To slow the ship so it would not be beached on a reef, they dropped the four anchors off the stern. Luke never forgot the strain of that night. Strong men in the crew gave way and became panic-stricken. We must not imagine that ancient crew to have been anything like a modern ship's crew. They were mostly hired for the voyage, men picked up on the shores and wharves, often escaped slaves, who had no interest in the ship, or its cargo, or in the lives of the passengers.

In the dark of the night, Paul heard stealthy steps and whispering. A group of sailors were busy near the lifeboat, evidently planning to take off with the boat and leave the passengers to their fate. The same danger turns some men into cowards and some into heroes. Paul hurried to the captain and informed him of what he had seen, "Except these stay in the ship, you cannot be saved." Julius commanded the soldiers to cut the ship's cable, thus securing at least that much unity among those working for safety on board ship. Paul was always a man who believed in the community. He hated selfishness. This was the first time a ship was saved by Christian solidarity, such as it was, but it was the symbol and figure of another ship. The Church is also a ship on which a community sails, and he who deserts the ship is a traitor.

Because of these long days of fasting and the long night vigils, the crew was reaching a state of exhaustion. The next day would require steady nerves and physical endurance. Again Paul was the saviour of the ship, the only one to remain cool in the face of a new trial. He went about talking to the crew, the officers and the bedraggled passengers, trying to encourage them. In times such as these, position or rank is of little avail. What counts in time of peril is real manhood, and Paul was indeed the greatest man on board. He promised them that every man would be saved if every man did his duty, and for the work that lay ahead, every man should now take some food. Knowing the force of example, he proceeded to order food brought. Bread it was, and solemnly before all of them he said a prayer of thanksgiving over the bread, he broke the loaf and began to eat. And now they all followed his example.

For the first time a hopeful look could be seen on their faces. Then, when dawn came, through the grey curtain of rain they saw a bay enclosed by steep stone walls, and a sandy shore near the mouth of the bay, the modern Bay of St. Paul. Here they decided to let the ship run into the bay. But they did not know that, because of the action of the spring tide the mouth of the bay had been blocked, and sandbanks had been thrown up. To lighten the ship for the run into the bay, the remainder of the grain cargo was thrown overboard, the anchors were lifted, the mainsail was hoisted, and the course of the ship held into the bay. Suddenly the whole ship was violently shaken as if some giant hand had laid hold of it. Men were thrown against each other, timbers and masts were wrenched apart. The ship bored its bow deep into the sand of what was a bank over which the flood tide of the bay was flowing. The sudden impact together with the force of the waves shattered the stern, and water poured in. The ship was a loss. The passengers rushed to the bow of the ship, but no other way was left to save their lives than to swim to shore. And then, when safety seemed so near, the greatest peril came for Paul and the other prisoners.

It speaks for the excellent discipline of the imperial troop that even in the midst of this disaster one of the officers guarding the prisoners, realizing his horrible duty, presented himself before the commandant and asked whether he should put the prisoners to death. The law provided that in instances of this kind the prisoners should be put to death rather than permit their escape. Among the prisoners were murderers and bandits, violent men, and the centurion would have sacrificed their lives without further thought. Here again, we see the cold harshness of the Roman law of which Paul had said that it was "without love." But the influence of Christianity had begun to be felt.

The soldiers stood ready with drawn swords, the captain looked at Paul, and within a conflict was fought between two duties. Human sympathy won over soldierly duty. A ray of Christianity had reached into Julius' soul. He ordered the fetters struck from the prisoners, and called out: "Every man save himself."

That scene of 276 men, exhausted by long fasting, cold, and strain, many of them in full armour, plunging into the stormy sea near the furious breakers, clinging to "boards, and some on those things that belonged to the ship," defies the powers of the imagination. Some were finally carried to shore on the backs of soldiers, some came with shattered legs and arms, some fell like dead on the wet sand after an hour's struggle with the elements. Our sympathy goes out to that man and his companions, who had been cast out by his own people, and had taken upon himself all this labour and suffering, in order to remain true to his Master. Now Paul was even poorer than he had ever been. He had lost his few possessions. Above all, he had lost what he prized most dearly, his Bible.

Fortunately the inhabitants of the island were friendly. They came running from all sides to help. They brought bread, fruits, and hot drinks. But the members of the crew were not able to understand a word they said. Paul and one or two of the Phoenician sailors thought they could distinguish some familiar sounds of their Punic tongue. They learned after a while that they were on the island of Malta. The modern Bay of St. Paul on Malta is precisely at a place such as is described in the account of the Acts: "a place where two seas meet" (27:41). Now that they were on land they discovered that narrow channel between the island of Malta and a smaller island which gave the appearance of leading into another large body of water. When Luke speaks of "barbarians," he speaks as a Greek author, meaning that these people spoke neither Greek nor Latin.

A fire was built. The whole ship's company, including Paul, gathered twigs for the fire. Warmed by the fire, a poisonous viper leaped out from the twigs and fastened on Paul's hand, coiling itself around his arm. The superstitious islanders immediately concluded that Paul was a murderer pursued by Nemesis, and that the vengeful goddess had now attacked him on land after his rescue from the sea. Calmly Paul flung the snake into the fire. They now stood waiting for his arm to swell up, and they supposed that "he would suddenly fall down and die." But when nothing happened to him, the antagonism of these naive people was changed into superstitious worship. Now they thought Paul was a god.

Perhaps Paul made use of this occasion of their superstitious adoration to preach a sermon about how a Christian would be able "to take up serpents" and would not be harmed (Mark 16:18). The pious Maltese still believe that it was through Paul's prayers that their island was rid of poisonous snakes, just as the Irish ascribe the same benefit to St. Patrick.

Malta was a part of the province of Sicily. The chief Roman official on the island, Publius, offered his assistance to the shipwrecked company, and gave them shelter for three days on his estate until they could find suitable winter quarters. Apparently Paul soon drew the attention of Publius to himself, for it seems that soon after the landing Publius took Paul to the bedside of his sick father. In such a congenial and sympathetic atmosphere Paul was able to manifest his charismatic gifts to the full. It is hardly probable that he neglected to found a Christian community here on Malta. The silence of the Acts speaks neither for nor against such a founding. The wonderment of these simple people at Paul's powers was certainly the beginning of that wisdom and knowledge which prepares the way for Christ. The people of Malta still celebrate, on 10 February, with great enthusiasm the feast of St. Paul's Shipwreck.

CHAPTER FIFTY-FOUR

"SO WE WENT TO ROME"

"And when we were come to Rome, Paul was suffered to dwell by himself, with a soldier that kept him" (Acts 28: 16).

The second part of the Acts of the Apostles might be called a Christian Odyssey, with Paul as the Christian Ulysses. For more than ten years Rome had been his goal, for all that time he had been striving to reach Rome, but unfavourable events had always brought his plans to nought. Now, when he believed he was almost within sight of the city, the powers of Neptune tossed him high on a rocky cliff. Hostile "principalities and powers, ... the rulers of the world of this darkness" (Eph. 6:12), stood in the way, but a mighty hand conquered all these forces and led him to his goal. The day when Paul set foot in Rome was an important day in the history of the human race. From that day the Church of Rome became the common foundation of the Princes of the Apostles, Peter and Paul.

The mild winter of Malta was over. At the end of February, A.D. 61, Julius was down in the harbour of Valetta ready to embark on an Alexandrian grain ship which had also been forced to winter in Malta. The images of the Dioscuri, Castor and Pollux, the protecting deities of ancient seamen, whose constellation guided the pilots at night, were the ornaments on the ship's stern. The first port was Syracuse. The people of Syracuse still revere the memory of Paul's three-day stay and of his sermon in their city. Stern and majestic, the snow-covered peak of Mount Aetna looked down on the ship. Passing the rocks of Cyclops, they entered the Straits of Messina. Paul was thoughtful as this magnificent panorama of natural wonders passed before him, but he was no poet of nature. Behind all these phenomena he saw causes and reasons and symbols. He saw how the universe had been marked for destruction.

Two days later they passed the beautiful marble palace that Tiberius had built for himself on Capri. Then into the Gulf of Puteoli, north of Naples where the shores were dotted with the villas and summer residences of the great ones of Rome. He saw Pompeii and Herculaneum with the great estates of the rich merchants of the Empire. There was Baiae where Pliny the Elder, the uncle of the famous writer, lost his life as captain of the fleet in the eruption of Mount Vesuvius. There was the famous imperial villa where the Empress mother Agrippina had plotted her crimes and where she had been strangled in bed at Nero's command. Now they passed the charming islands of Procida, Ischia, and Nisida, and came abreast of Misenum where Tiberius, too, had been strangled. In the background, Vesuvius was asleep. Then he did not yet wear his plume of smoke. The slopes of the mountain were covered with gardens and country houses that would have only twenty more years until destruction poured down on them. Here in the Gulf of Puteoli grain ships from Egypt unloaded their cargoes. Seneca relates how the population of Puteoli came down to the wharves when an Egyptian grain ship was sighted in the Gulf.[43] Only these ships were allowed to sail into port with their flags flying from the masthead. They were jubilantly hailed by the populace because they brought bread for Italy. And this ship brought bread, too, bread of a higher kind, "the bread of life," for it carried to Italy's shores Paul, who was Christ's greatest disciple.

---

[43] Seneca, *Letters to Lucilius*, 77, 1.

Fifty years earlier the imperial barge had been poled slowly up these shores bearing the dying Emperor Augustus. The people came to meet the barge with flowers and incense and honoured him as a god; but the dying Imperator, who wisely exercised his office of first citizen of Rome, merely smiled at all this homage as though he were weary of it all. Ancient Rome went down to its grave when Augustus died. Today the herald of the greatest of all kings was landing on Italy's shore. He wore chains and no one knew of his coming. A departing civilization, a world that is going down to its ruin, makes much noise, it collapses with a mighty crash. Few people are sensitive enough to detect the coming of a new world, and so no one noticed the energetic little Tarsian who had already penned the great Epistle to the Romans.

The traveller knew he was approaching the great city. She showed herself to be the "beast" of the Apocalypse in more ways than one. Here on the wharf you heard the shouting of stevedores, corn measurers, slave dealers, the hammering of workers in the dry docks and shipyards, and above it all the roaring of lions, panthers, and tigers coming in on African freighters. They were destined for the animal games in the arena in Rome and Puteoli. Paul saw the look of despair on the faces of his fellow prisoners when they heard the sounds from the animal cages. For them it was a vivid reminder of the dreadful fate that awaited them in the arena.

Other ships were docking, loaded with marble blocks, obelisks, monolithic columns, porphyry from Egypt, *giallo antico* from Numidia, and statues from Delphi for the gigantic structure that Nero was building and called his Golden House. Amid all this confusion and noise, Paul may have been conscious of the significance of the moment, and yet he felt mystery in the atmosphere, that mysterious aura of the conqueror of the world.

Puteoli was full of Jews and Orientals. Syrians had brought along their idols, especially their Syrian goddess Atargatis, to whom Nero was now devoted. "Here on the way to Rome's

Tiber, the Syrian Orontes had thrown up on its coasts the flotsam of humanity."44 But the mustard seed of the Gospel had also taken root. In Pompeii at that time Christians had been the subject of the town gossip. That Christianity had come early to these shores is evident from an inscription on a wall in Pompeii, since then, of course, obliterated. But three independent witnesses testify that the word "HRISTIAN" had been written on the wall, sometime before the destruction of Pompeii (August 24, A.D. 79).

Julius was glad to allow Paul to accept an invitation from the Christians and to stay a week with them. In the meantime the Christians were able to send messengers to the brethren in Rome and announce the arrival of the Apostle, and so the last part of Paul's journey was something like a triumphal progress.

From Puteoli to Rome was a six- or seven-days' journey, about 130 miles. The first day they seemed to be travelling through a fertile oasis, overflowing with wine and oil. At Capua they turned into the road that came from Brundisium, the famous Via Appia, the queen of all roads. Along this road Paul saw signs of the sad social conditions of the Empire. On both sides were the extensive estates of the great Roman landowners which were cultivated by large armies of slaves. Each farm employed a thousand or more slaves. Agricultural slaves were always closely watched during the day, and at night they were put in chains because they were the most dangerous and most likely to attempt escape. The farmers of Italy had helped to conquer the world, but others were now reaping their harvest. The farmers had disappeared, driven out by the great capitalists.

Paul saw how the vintagers were beginning to prune the vines. The hillsides were still wooded. Long ago the fig tree had immigrated from the East, and the olive tree was the Greek's gift to Italy. In Formia they stopped. Here was the cenotaph and the country house of Cicero, the *Formianum,* where the famous statesman had been murdered. As they came

---

44 Cf. Juvenal.

to one of the high spots on the road, they had an enchanting view of the Gulf of Gaeta. At Terracina Paul heard again the familiar melody of the waves of the sea. Soon afterward they found themselves in the Pontine Marshes. Here Augustus had dug a straight canal alongside the road as far as Forum Appii. The canal barges were drawn by donkeys. Horace described with excellent humour an amusing trip he had on this canal.[45] Julius had probably decided to make the trip by water because it was faster. In Forum Appii they stopped for the night at the inn. The country was infested with mosquitoes and there was danger of malaria. For that reason a shrine had been built here in honour of Aesculapius.

Ancient authors have little to say in commendation of the inns of antiquity. Few arrangements were made for the comfort of the traveller. The inns offered shelter and an unfurnished bed, no more, and travellers were expected to bring their own cooking utensils and bed clothing. The clan of innkeepers had an unsavoury reputation. They were known principally as furtherers of games of dice and ready thievery. Horace said the innkeepers of Forum Appii were scoundrels. Once in the inn, a guest found it almost impossible to sleep because of vermin and the croaking of the frogs in the marshes. The servant maids had the reputation of witches. They engaged shamelessly in the trade of prostitution, they kept slave girls to pander to the guests, they adulterated the wine, and cheated the guests at every turn. It was in a wine tavern that Nero met his first wife. Most inns were filled with stable boys and donkey drivers. From the kitchen smoke pervaded the whole building, irritating the eyes, and if you wished to fall off to sleep a rowdy crowd of travellers started their loud singing of indecent songs, and the mattress stuffed with reeds became alive with vermin. Paul's stay in the inn, therefore, was certainly not a delightful experience.

Along the road Paul had his first pleasant surprise: the Roman community sent its greetings to him. The grateful

---

[45] *Satires*, I, 5

readers of his Epistle to the Romans sent two delegations out to greet him. He met the first group at the forty-third milestone. How good it was to have this gracious attention! Tears came to the eyes of the greying Apostle when the Christians from Rome came forward to embrace him and give him the kiss of peace. He had already seen some of them. Others were known to him by hearsay. If we wish to know their names, we need only refer to the list of names at the close of the Epistle to the Romans. Perhaps Aquila and Priscilla were there, too. Mark speaks of Alexander and Rufinus, the sons of Simon of Cyrene, as though they were well-known personalities in Rome. Paul greets them and their mother in the letter to the Romans. It may be, therefore, that they also were among the delegates who met Paul. And in these difficult days in Rome, when age weighed heavily on his shoulders, it was a comfort for Paul to have the tender ministrations of the mother of Alexander and Rufinus.

We can easily understand Luke's remark, "whom when Paul saw, he gave thanks to God, and took courage" (Acts 28:15). He must have been suffering hours of severe depression again. At the next posting station, *Tres Tabernae* (Three Taverns), another somewhat more official delegation awaited him, consisting of the elders of the Roman Church. Julius and the rest of the company must have been more and more surprised as they witnessed these solemn welcoming scenes. Their regard for their famous prisoner grew steadily.

On the heights of Velitrae (Velletri) they entered the classical territory of the Albanian mountains. In Aricia (according to the pseudo-Acts of the Apostles) the last stop was made, and then Paul set foot on the sacred ground of Latium. Out of this sterile soil came the Latin genius of Rome which, in alliance with the Attic genius of Greece and the genius of Christianity, created the culture and civilization of the West. And the man who brought the precious seed of Christianity to this place and had prepared the way for the union of these three disparate forces was standing now on the border of Latium.

Below them lay Alba Longa, the legendary mother of Rome. On the heights of the Alban hills they saw the temple of Jupiter Latialis to which the victorious generals of the Empire went in triumph. In Aricia was the temple of Diana, whose chief idol was said to have been brought here from Tauris. Here again the goddess Diana stood along Paul's path as then in Ephesus. The next morning the travellers set out on the last lap of the long journey. Soon they looked on the Roman Campagna in its stern and sombre melancholy, the arena and graveyard of the ambitions of so many nations. But what was it that their eyes began to discern in the northern distance? Jubilantly the Roman Christians pointed to the great sprawling city: "*Ecce Roma..*" "See, there is Rome."

How different was the Rome of the first Caesars as compared with the modern Rome! Where now the tourist sees the cupola of St. Peter's, was the oval of Nero's Circus with its Egyptian obelisks. Apart from the splendour of the Forum and the Palatine, Rome was then an ugly, dirty, evil-smelling city filled with many-storied houses. But seen from a distance, it gave an impression somewhat majestic and artistic, when the yellow and brown tones of the city were framed by the fine lines of the Alban and Sabine hills. From the dull background, the Capitoline temple and Nero's palace stood out white and shimmering, just as the snowy whiteness of the National Monument on the Piazza Venezia does today. The famous aqueducts, the proud boast of the city, the Aqua Appia, Claudia, and Marcia, crept like centipedes across the countryside, drawing ever closer together as they approached the city.

As they neared the city, the Via Appia became more and more a triumphal avenue, announcing the greatness of Rome. At the same time, it was the greatest burial road in the world. Among the ancients, reverence for the dead was the sustaining idea of all religion. It also gave an opportunity for the expression of the vanity and pride of the noble families, such as the Scipios, the Metellii, the Valerii, as, for instance, in the monument of Caecilia Metella. Cemeteries were never quiet or secluded places. The dead were supposed to want the company of the living. The ancients knew nothing of the idea of rest in God, or of a communion of saints. As he walked on, Paul may have read the epitaph; "Here by the road lies T. Lollius Masculus so that passers-by may say, 'Greetings to you, Lollius.'"

Where now the basilica of St. Sebastian stands, the Via Appia went through a valley to the catacombs of Callistus and the Jewish catacombs. Perhaps as Paul was led through this Jewish quarter, his fellow Jews looked with disdain on the chained prisoner. Once the Romans had cried in terror, *Hannibal ante portas* ("Hannibal stands at the gates"). On this day they might have shouted, *Paulus ante Portas* ("Paul is at the city gate"), when Paul entered through the Porta Capena. But they were not aware of the danger of his coming until later, when they beheaded him beyond the city walls so that at least after death he would remain outside the city.

"And when we were come to Rome, the captain turned his prisoners over to the stratpedarch, the prison-camp command-ant," is Luke's entry in his journal. Whether Julius delivered his prisoners to the Pretorian camp on Mons Caelius, the so-called *Castra Peregrinorum,* or to the headquarters of the Pretorian Guard on the Via Nomentana, is uncertain. The head of the imperial police for the last ten years had been the noble Burrus, a capable general, a wise statesman, beloved by the people, and the most powerful man, next to the Emperor. These two noble Stoics, Burrus and Seneca, had been Nero's tutors, and until now they had been able to hold his worst ambitions in check.

Burrus also held the office of examining judge in all criminal cases that came before the imperial tribunal. Paul was probably arraigned before this man. The e*logium*, or commit-ment papers, written by Festus and the report of Julius about the conduct of the prisoner were so favourable that Burrus ordered Paul to be treated as a prominent imperial prisoner and that he be allowed every privilege. For the first ten days Paul had to stay in the police headquarters for the preliminary hearings during which the appeal to Caesar was certified. He was permitted the mildest kind of custody, the *custodia libera*. He was allowed to rent an apartment for himself, somewhere near the police offices, but remained always subject to police surveillance. Undoubtedly the Roman congregation considered it an honour to pay for Paul's lodging and support.

CHAPTER FIFTY-FIVE

THE CRADLE OF THE ROMAN CHURCH

"Be it known therefore to you that this salvation of God
is sent to the Gentiles: and they will hear it" (Acts 28: 28).

The world monarchy of Rome will always appear as one of the greatest phenomena in the story of the human race alongside the origin and spread of Christianity. And this religion, with its roots in the narrowness and exclusiveness of Jerusalem, but in principle completely cosmopolitan, entered into the world capital of Rome as into a seat prepared for it by history. From the ruins of the political monarchy it developed the gigantic structure of the Church, the moral monarchy.[46] The depository of that world-embracing concept, Peter, had only recently come to live in the suburb of Trastevere, and now one of the most dynamic instruments in the world-wide diffusion of that concept lived in rented quarters under the surveillance of one of the Pretorian Guards.

In accord with his custom of long standing now, Paul first made contact with his Jewish compatriots. He had no wish to appear as a renegade of his people, nor did he wish others to say that he had cheated his own people of their Messianic

---

[46] Cf. Gregorovius.

promises. Since the second century before Christ a large colony of Jews had settled in Rome. After Claudius' death they had returned and soon they numbered about twenty-five thousand. Because of their religious and national peculiarities, they settled near the edges of the great city, but they maintained the liveliest intercourse in business matters with every part of the city, and soon they also exchanged their mother tongue for Greek. They lived in little groups on the periphery of the city, near the ends of the consular streets, and in those outlying districts they also had their catacombs and cemeteries (about six).

In their religious organization they followed strictly the model of the Sanhedrin in Jerusalem. Under the central authority they possessed at that time about thirteen synagogues. The synagogues adopted the names of their noble patrons: Augustenses, Agrippenses, Herodienses, or sometimes they took the name of the section of the city where they were located: Suburenses, Campenses, and still others took names from the old country: Palaestinenses, Vernaculi of Tripolis, of Lebanon, etc. The presiding officer of the council of the synagogue (*Gerusia*) was the Gerusiarch, the most important personage next to the "Father of the Synagogue." Besides these two officers the synagogue had a "Mother of the Synagogue," a correspondent (*grammaticus*), a treasurer, priests, servants, and executive officers. From the latest researches among the inscriptions of this period in Rome, it appears that the old scientific view that the first Christian congregation in Rome modelled itself after the synagogue is now untenable. On the contrary, the model adopted for the organization of the Roman Church was the Roman religious organization called "*collegia.*"

Paul probably realized early enough that the Jewish colony in Rome possessed much influence, and that this influence even reached into the imperial palace. The greatest dramatist of the time, who was one of Nero's favourites and instructed him in the art of acting, was a Jew, one Alityrus. Through Alityrus' good offices, Flavius Josephus was presented to Poppaea Sabina, the most powerful favourite at court, of whom it was said that she was a Jewish proselyte.[47] If the Jews wished to destroy Paul, all they needed to do was invoke this woman's hatred against him. For these reasons, too, Paul thought it expedient to conciliate the leaders of Jewry in Rome. Otherwise it would be somewhat difficult to explain the haste with which Paul invited the leaders of the Jews on his third day in Rome.

When they came to see him, he could effectively point to his chains and say that it was for the defence of the most precious heritage of his people, "for the hope of Israel, I am bound with this chain" (Acts 28:20). The venerable fathers acted as though they knew nothing about the case. If that were true, then the decree of excommunication of the Sanhedrin had not yet reached the outlying synagogues. Quite innocently the reverend fathers asked Paul what his attitude was concerning the recent controversy about Christ, "But we desire to hear from you what you think; for as concerning this sect, we know that it is everywhere contradicted" (28:22). It was the finished language of the diplomat. How could they claim to know nothing about Christianity when only recently Christian propaganda under Claudius had provoked serious disturbances in the ghetto? At any rate, a date was set for a religious discussion in Paul's quarters.

Since Paul was talking to men who knew the Scriptures, he was able to display his own extensive knowledge of the sacred writings and his consummate ability in scriptural exegesis. The discussion lasted "from-morning until evening". It seemed that now Paul wished to give expression to all that he had been meditating about, all that he had learned about Christ, during these years of his imprisonment. But it was to no avail. Were they to believe that the glorious history of their people was to culminate in the incident of the Crucifixion on the tree of shame? These gnarled old rabbis could not step over this stumbling block of the Crucifixion, and it was to be the last

---

[47] Josephus, *Antiquities*, XX, viii, 11

time that Paul offered the salvation of Christ to the synagogue. It was the last hour of grace, when the Jews would have to decide whether they would continue as the chosen people or as the people of the great rejection.

Luke knew beforehand that the hour of the ultimate rejection of the Jews was not far off. He describes how they went down the steps of Paul's lodgings, arguing with one another, bargaining with God, distrusting one another. And as they went out of that house they began that wandering of the eternal Jew, marked with the stigma of the divine rejection, which became a widespread proof of Christ's coming. As they left him, Paul called down upon them the anathema of the prophet Isaias, those words penumbrated with the mystery of divine predestination: "Hear, and understand not: and see the vision, and know it not" (Is. 6:9).

That controversy about Jesus soon broke out again. Some of the Jews finally turned about and became Christians, but the opposition of others changed into implacable hostility which threatened the Roman congregation with utter destruction. The antagonism of the Jews seems even to have tainted the loyalty of those Jews who had become Christians. These Christian Jews, it is true, were not the violent free thinkers of Corinth, but they were deeply attached to their old ideas, Essenism and Pharisaism, which eventually led them to inaugurate an opposition party against Paul. Paul had these men in mind when he wrote: "Some indeed, even out of envy and contention. But some also for good will preach Christ" (Phil. 1:15).

The principal danger from Judaism had been squashed by the Apostle's great encyclical letters. These engagements with the enemy were mere rear-guard actions. "But what then? So that by all means, whether by occasion or by truth, Christ be preached: in this also I rejoice, Yes, and will rejoice" (Phil. 1:18). Such, too, had been the magnanimous and generous attitude of Jesus when John came to him indignantly to say that some men who were not from their ranks were daring to cast out evil spirits in his name: "Forbid him not; for he that is not against you, is for you" (Luke 5:50). The two sections of the Roman congregation, however, were held together chiefly by the friendship of the two Princes of the Apostles, but it was only after these had shed their blood in common martyrdom that the last differences between the two factions were extinguished.

Luke was evidently unwilling to close his book on a discordant note. He preferred to end it with a comforting look into the future of the Christian Church. Luke indicated briefly that Paul's poor lodgings in Rome were becoming the focal point in a Christian movement. Until this time the gospel had been handicapped by the weight of Judaism, and it was being announced timidly and with hesitation, but now, fanned by the impulse that Paul gave it, it burst forth into a roaring flame. Already A.D. in 64, according to Tacitus, the Christian community had become a vast multitude (*multitudo ingens*). If the Jewish population in Rome at that time numbered about 30,000, at least half were Christians, and the number was increasing daily. Paul himself attributed the growth of the Church to his imprisonment: "And many of the brethren in the Lord, growing confident by my bands, are much more bold to speak the word of God without fear" (Phil. 1:14). In the letter to the Romans he enumerated the various domestic communities in Rome where services were being held. The members of one such group comprised "Asyncritus, Phlegon, Hermas, Patrobas, Hermes, and the brethren that are with him," another group gathered around Philologus, and Julia, Nereus, and his sister, Olympus, "and all the saints that are with them."

Paul's Roman friends also paved the way for him to meet members of the Roman aristocracy. The acumen of Christian archaeologists, with the help of their spades, has disclosed several secrets which contemporary writers were eager to conceal. De Rossi and Marucchi seem to have made certain that the residence of Aquila and Priscilla stood on the Aventine where the ancient basilica of St. Prisca still stands. An inscription unearthed there, bearing the name of Pudens Cornelianus, indicates that the ground on which the house stood belonged to the Cornelian family. Further, in the catacombs of Priscilla were found the tombs of Pudentiana and Praxedis, the daughters of Senator Pudens, and also the tombs of Aquila and Priscilla. This fact indicates that the catacombs were a common burial place for the families of Cornelius and Acilius. Since they were so close in death, it may have been that some members of the *Gens Cornelia* had joined the Church even before Paul came to Rome. Two of the oldest churches in Rome on the Esquiline bear the names of these two daughters of that Roman Senator. It was believed that Peter held services in the house of Senator Pudens. During his second imprisonment in Rome, Paul received a visit from a certain Pudens (2 Tim. 4:21). This Pudens was apparently not an obscure person in the city.

Undoubtedly Christianity found converts among the higher classes of society who had lost respect for the pagan gods because of the derision of poets and philosophers. Many superficial and blase natures, however, surfeited with wanton plays and spectacles of the arena, were looking for a change in some metaphysical thrill, and they turned to the conventicles of Oriental religions, or to the synagogues of the Jews, or to the meetings of the Christians. Frequently, however, they were disillusioned by the multiplicity of saviours and gods that were presented.

In the lowest classes of the population Christianity took a firm hold, for these unfortunates saw in Christianity the basis for the re-establishment of their human rights and freedom. Just at that time a sensational thing happened in Rome: the Prefect of Rome, Pedanius Secundus, was murdered by a slave who was jealous about his master's attention to a slave girl. According to the law, all the slaves living in the same house with the murderer at the time of the crime were to be put to death. In this instance over four hundred slaves were affected by that law. The people of the city protested against this injustice, but the Emperor and the Senate decided to permit the law to take its course.[48] It is not surprising that the new gospel attracted the attention of the imperial slaves on the Aventine and that Paul's name was mentioned with reverence. Toward the end of his first imprisonment Paul was writing to the Philippians: "All the saints salute you: especially they that are of Caesar's household" (Phil. 4:22).

Who were these Christians on the Palatine? In the list of greetings at the end of the Epistle to the Romans, we note two groups: the Christian domestics of the house of Narcissus and Aristobulus. These Christians must have belonged to the households of these two aristocratic gentlemen, although they themselves were not Christians. In antiquity the word *familia* embraced everybody in the household, including servants and slaves, and the head of the house was called *paterfamilias*. The average family, such as, for instance, that of the common citizen, possessed fifteen slaves, but rich men like Narcissus and Aristobulus owned hundreds of slaves. Tacitus remarked that the "families" of the rich were a great mixture of all nations. Harnack[49] declares that the two most powerful men in Rome at the time of Emperor Claudius were a certain Narcissus, a freedman and the private secretary of the Emperor, and a certain Aristobulus, a nephew of Herod the Great and a friend of the Emperor. When a man having such close connections with the imperial court died, his entire household, including his many slaves, was added to the imperial household. If these two men mentioned by Harnack are the men that Paul speaks of in the letter to the Romans, it would be another indication of Paul's close connection with the slave sheds on the Palatine.

Sometimes the reproach is uttered against Paul that he had knowingly gathered together the political and intellectual

---

[48] Tacitus, *Annales*, XIV, 42.

[49] *Die Mission and Ausbreitung des Christentums,* 4th ed., Leipzig, 1924

outcasts from every country in the world in order to bring about
an uprising of the lower elements of humanity, that he had
surrounded himself with the "intellectual offal of the Hellenistic world and with the dispossessed of all nations." But, to
realize that any progress humanity was ever to make depended
on the Christian community, all we need do is read the moral
requirements Paul laid down for his converts. "Under the
impact of these sermons that seized upon both body and soul,
sermons about the coming judgment of the race and the power
of the spirit of Christ, the morality of the people rose ever more
to purer and higher states ... The Christians were not to be men
who clung to possessions, they could not be self-seeking, and
yet in other ways they were to be genuine, courageous men ...
Paul and Christianity were not working for the disintegration of
society. On the contrary, they halted the swift progress of
society's ruin."[50]

Sometimes historians speak disparagingly about the moral
morass and the racial chaos of the Mediterranean area where
the Church originated. Then the achievement of the apostles
must be regarded as still greater. It was the Church's task to
sanctify and Christianize the cultures of the various peoples, to
give them a moral ideal, and form them according to that ideal.
And that was what Paul did. He rescued from the chaos whatever could be rescued. The fact that nevertheless the Roman
state went down to ruin was not the fault of the Church. The
blame lies on the Roman state itself because it no longer had a
religion to give it a moral ideal and because it refused to ally
itself with the religion of the future. But even in the Roman
state, the Church saved what it could, and it was no small
achievement to attract to itself men with gifts like St. Augustine.

---

[50] *Ibid.*

CHAPTER FIFTY-SIX

IN PRISON FOR CHRIST

In Rome at that time only three classes of people felt any kind of security or enjoyed any well-being: the rich classes, the so-called "clients" who were fed by their rich patrons, and the dark figures who came from the Orient. If a man had any desire for recollection and quiet, he found Rome a terrible place. At that time there was little of that breath-taking beauty which Rome acquired later and which the poet Fulgentius praised: "How beautiful is the heavenly Jerusalem when Rome here on earth is radiant with so much glory."

In the business sections of the city, living quarters were very uncomfortable and unhealthy because of the narrowness of the streets, the lack of ventilation, the evil smells of garbage which was thrown into the streets. Besides, there was always great danger of fire. Because the Tiber was a sacred thing, a god in fact, it could not be regulated, and its floods caused frequent epidemics. The houses were high and poorly built. Martial tells of a man who had to climb two hundred steps to reach his room. The noise in the streets was almost unbearable. Even the wealthy Seneca in a long letter complained about the street noises. At night, from about seven o'clock in the evening until sunrise, heavy freight vehicles rumbled over the rough streets, and during the day Syrian musicians and begging priests of Isis and Cybele, clanging their raucous brass instruments and castanets, went up and down the streets. Poor renters had to be content with the rooms on the street side, while the wealthier owner occupied the inside rooms around the peristyle. Certainly life in a rented room facing the noisy street through the hot Roman summer was no small hardship for Paul.

On the wall of his chamber hung the chain, the symbol of his imprisonment. He was permitted to go out and to receive visits during the day, but as soon as night came on, the moment he ventured from his room, the chain was placed on his wrist and attached to his guard who walked behind him. It was no trifling thing never to be allowed to be alone, not even for one moment. It is hard to say which is the greater trial: to be always alone or to be never alone. Dostoevski, who during many years of imprisonment in Siberia shared a room with another convict, described it as one of the most maddening trials, that he was never permitted to be alone with himself and his thoughts. Whenever anyone came to talk to Paul, when the delegates came from the various Churches, when his friends came, the guard was always present, and sometimes these *frumentarii* were coarse, uncultured mercenaries who may have vented their ill will on Paul. The royal Prince Herod Agrippa I, who during his youth was a prisoner in Rome, was forced to pay a large sum of money in order to have respectable men as his guards. A bad feature of the imprisonment was that the guard was changed every day. But Paul saw an advantage in this arrangement: it gave him an opportunity to meet more men in the Pretorian Guard. Sometimes Paul probably went with the guard to the barracks to make the change.

And the guards came to know Paul. He was the most re-markable prisoner they had ever met. Some of the guards came to like their prisoner and enjoyed talking with a man who had travelled all over the world. None of these men went away from Paul without feeling that he was a better man, and that his thoughts had been given a better turn. For Paul, like Socrates, was able to tune the mood of others to his own. Back in the barracks, the guards talked about this unusual prisoner and his interesting religion, and perhaps some of them, listening to his impassioned appeals in his room, fell to their knees and cried, "Credo." Paul wrote to the Philippians: "The things which have happened to me have fallen out rather to the furtherance of the gospel: so that my bands are made manifest in Christ, in all the court (Praetorian Guard)" (1:12 f.).

But a man who has sown the seeds of love and kindness, as generously as Paul did, is never alone. His disciples were always with him. He was that kind of man whom the Stoics described as a wise man, "an artist in making friends". Like Socrates he had his friends near him even in prison. Two of his friends were engaged at this time in a work of great significance for the New Testament: Luke and Mark, the former the Evangelist of Paul, the latter Peter's Evangelist. Peter seems not to have been in Rome at this time, and Mark was probably designated to represent him. Relying on the oral preaching of Peter, Mark had already written his Gospel for the Roman Christians. Again and again he had heard from Peter the same narratives of Christ's life and teachings, so that they had taken a definite form in his mind and had been impressed on his memory. Now Luke was able to make use of Mark's material in the composition of the Gospel that he had begun in Caesarea. Often these two men, Luke and Mark, sat together in Paul's cell, conferring about the new Gospel which was to complement the other two.

The fundamental theme of Luke's Gospel, its concept of Jesus' life as the masterpiece of divine love and condescension, is clearly the result of Paul's influence. But Luke's charming individuality is not suppressed. It appears in beautiful harmony with the Pauline imprint, depicting Jesus as the heavenly physician of soul and body. Luke's Gospel was intended as a farewell gift and as a permanent reminder of Paul's spirit for the Pauline Gentile Christian Churches, and it may have been published to the world even before the end of the first Roman imprisonment.

Luke's presentation of Jesus as the divine physician shows the fine touch of the Greek as well as a reproach against the Roman contempt for the medical profession. Since the beginning, physicians had no standing in Rome. They were compared to the mountebanks and jugglers that appeared in the Roman fairs. Cato the Censor was most unfriendly to them because they were Greeks and came from the Orient and were a nomadic class. Cato feared for the corruption of the Latin race. He expressly forbade his son to consult a physician: "The Greeks have ruined everything by their literature as the philosophers have ruined everything by their idle prattle, but the physicians are much worse. Mark, my son, I forbid you to go to a physician." The first physician who came over from Peloponessus was stoned. The antagonism against the physicians disappeared somewhat when a Mauretanian physician, Antonius Musa, saved the life of Augustus. The Emperor Tiberius preferred his old home remedies to the advice of a physician. Pliny, who himself had written some medical works, although he did not practise medicine, said that Rome had not had a physician for, over six hundred years. A Roman who had any regard for tradition would not have anything to do with such a despicable profession, which was generally left to the slaves.

The removal to Rome, therefore, brought no material advantages to Luke, the first Christian physician in Rome. However, remembering what Jesus had done, the Church professed to see something almost sacerdotal in the art of the physician. She had a sacrament of healing and a charisma of healing, which were available without cost, in obedience to the Lord's command: "Freely have you received, freely give" (Matt. 10:8).

If we wish to have a picture of how the day was spent in

a prison like Paul's, we must first have some idea of the daily customs of the Romans. A historian of antiquity declares that the ancients were early risers. Vespasian was said to be busy with his affairs before daybreak.[51] The beginning of the day and of each hour was announced by a slave. When the sun rose another slave opened the doors of the house. Work could be done only during the day because artificial illumination was exceedingly poor. No work was done after the evening meal, except in the case of busy statesmen and scholars who sometimes worked at their tasks during the period of the long nights between the first and second crowing of the cock, between three and four o'clock in the morning. In this respect the Christian Church made a radical change by its night service, its sanctification of the night hours. The early Greek Church observed the so-called *Eucharistia lucernaris*,[52] and the Roman Church found the service so beautiful that it incorporated it into its liturgy once a year, in the Easter vigil.

Trained in the ancient Jewish tradition, Paul was accustomed to divide the day into definite periods of three hours each, separated by prayer. Christianity's new evaluation of time was by no means the least of its influences on the civilization of the race. The pagan looked upon time as a monster that threatened to devour his life. Christianity sanctified the notion of time; it put order into even the workday and its humble duties, and it impressed upon the whole year a new sacred order, "redeeming the time, because the days are evil" (Eph. 5:16). The Christian Middle Ages conformed to that religious order. Thus, for instance, Henry I and Otto the Great divided their day into periods of three hours and after each period they went to their domestic altars for prayer. In that way they submitted their energies to the higher power of God. Very likely Paul's friends came early in the morning to his lodgings for morning devotions.

In Rome the forenoon was devoted to labour, the after-

---

[51] Cf. Theo. Birt, *Zur Kulturgeschichte Roms,* Leipzig, 1911
[52] Ildefonso Cardinal Schuster, *Liber Sacramentorum,* IV

noon was the time of rest and leisure. In the afternoon the horrible noises of the streets were stilled for a time. Quiet and peace descended on the forums and public places. The evening was given over to the family meal. In ancient times the average man lived quite simply: he was often a vegetarian, and his diet consisted principally of cabbage, beans, artichokes, cheese, and a kind of *polenta.* Paul always contributed his grain of salt to season the meal (Col. 4:6). He must have been an unusually amiable and interesting conversationalist and narrator. From his letters we know that he possessed the Greek's gift of harmless irony and good humour, the gift of pleasant and gracious entertainment, what the Greeks called *terpnon.* How interesting it would be to read his table talk!

For the evening meal a few oil lamps of pewter or bronze were placed on the table, but the ancient lamp gave little light and much smoke. Only on Saturday night, when Paul celebrated the sacred mysteries, lights were not spared. We can imagine the mood of reverie evoked on such an evening. The lights and shadows trembled and hovered on the drawn faces of his guests while Paul masterfully drew the portrait of the heavenly Lord or described his mystical body which is "the fullness of him who is filled all in all" (Eph. 1:23).

In general, this period of Paul's first Roman imprisonment was among the most fruitful periods of the Apostle's career. It had all been worth while, for Christianity was now penetrating into the Roman army by means of the Praetorian Guard, who would sometime be sent to all parts of the world, to the Rhine, to Gaul, to Britain, and to Spain. But above all else, it was during this, period that Paul's theology and his mystical vision of the eternal Christ and the Head of the Church was nearing full maturity.

CHAPTER FIFTY-SEVEN

CHRIST'S WORK OF UNIFICATION

The Epistle to the Ephesians

Even in Rome, Paul remained the head of an organization with numerous branches throughout the world. Here we see what a man can do in an unfavourable situation. Now the news went into every Church in the Orient: Paul is in prison in Rome. Everybody prayed for him in their assemblies, they wrote him encouraging letters. They sent delegates to report about their congregations and to stay and share his captivity for a while. Macedonia was represented by Aristarchus, Galatia by Timothy, Ephesus sent Tychicus, Colossae sent Epaphras, its founder, and Philippi sent Epaphroditus. Paul's cell became a shrine to which pilgrims came from all over Christendom.

The letters written in the captivity take up a new trend of thought. With his keen synthesis, St. Thomas Aquinas indicated the difference between the various letters. Paul, in his early letters, treated of the work of Christ's redemption in the individual soul. That series of letters was concluded with the Epistle to the Romans. In the letters written during his captivity, Paul considered redemption as a whole in the social organism of the Church. In the pastoral letters he treated of the

hierarchy of the Church. The Epistle to the Hebrews, even
though it was not written by Paul, expresses Paul's thoughts. It
returns to the central point of the supernatural life, to Jesus
Christ, the high priest.

As a wandering apostle and founder of Churches, Paul
had been busy with men and their problems, but now from this
vantage point in his life he could look back on his work. The
old battle smoke had cleared away. Paul himself had become
an older, calmer, and maturer man. Like the thunder of a
receding storm, small disturbances sometimes broke out (Col.
2:16, 20; Phil. 3:1-6). The world-wide power of Rome now
awakened other thoughts in his mind. He had always been a
man highly conscious of the community, and in Rome he was
accorded a unified view of the whole, he was made to think
often of the social whole, the whole Church, the whole of
humanity, and the cosmos. His view of Christ, too, had become
more mature. In the Epistles to the Thessalonians he pictured
Christ as the Word that judges mankind at the end of time. In
the second group of letters he pictured Christ as the Word
redeeming man and revealing the truth to him. In the last letters
he speaks of Christ as the creative Word before all time.[53]

The traditional address, "To the saints who are at Ephesus,"
was not originally a part of the letter. Many scholars believe, as
did Marcion in the second century, that the letter to the
Ephesians is really the letter to the Laodiceans mentioned in the
Epistle to the Colossians: "And when this epistle has been read
among you, have it read also in the Church of the Laodiceans:
and that you read also the letter from Laodicea" (Col. 4:16).
The name of the Laodiceans was erased from the letter because
of the condemnation expressed in the Apocalypse (3:15) as a
kind of *damnatio memoriae*. The letter, however, has the
character of a circular letter which was intended to be read in
many of the Churches near Ephesus. For that reason no special
greetings are found at the beginning or at the end. The Fathers

---

[53] Cf. Prat, S.J., *La theologie de Saint Paul*, Paris, 1929

of the Church record that in the oldest manuscripts a space was left after the words, "To all the saints," for the name of some particular Church, such as, Ephesus, Laodicea, Hierapolis. Since the Epistle to the Ephesians contains a number of expressions found also in the letter to the Colossians, both letters may have been written about the same time. For what reason, we may ask, did Paul feel justified to address communities like Ephesus and Colossae which he himself had not founded? (Col. 2:1) It was probably because of the responsibility he felt for the unity of the whole Church. God's election had fallen upon him, and that choice, he believed, gave him the right to address any Church.

No letter of Paul's is tuned to such a solemn pitch as this letter to the Ephesians. It seems to have been the echo of some solemn and majestic sermon that Paul delivered in Rome. The blessing at the beginning has the form of a religious hymn. The writer seems to have been overwhelmed by some ecstatic vision.

The triune God has drawn man to himself in a threefold cycle of eternity, by the threefold work of the creation, redemption, and sanctification. Such a thing as an escape of the universe from God's hand into absolute nothingness, or an escape of man from the order of salvation of Christ, is now unthinkable. Three thought series can be distinguished in the Epistle to the Ephesians, which, although not logically distinct, continually flow into one another: 1. the dedication of the created world pre-existing in the eternal thoughts of God. 2. the dedication of created things by the incarnation and the redemption of the Son. 3. the dedication of the community in the Church by the sacred *pneuma*.

Christ did not come into the world like a flaming meteor, nor did he come to establish a new system of knowledge. He was sent by the Father from the depths of the living Trinity into the world according to an eternal plan of salvation to "re-establish all things," to create a new human race in his blood, in which he was to continue, prolong, and complete his own life.

Human thought was always exposed to the danger of either making the world the most important thing or making it nothing, either inflating the world into a deity or allowing it to disintegrate into nothingness. Both extremes, the apotheosis of the world and the flight from the world, were the result of sin. Then the Son came and accomplished the work of unification. He is the "beginning of the creation," he attached the world again to God, he himself is the bond of union between God and the world. According to Paul, the new humanity proceeded from the bosom of the Father (Eph. 1:3-6), from the heart of the Son (1:7-12), and from the Holy Spirit (1:13 ff).

God is not, therefore, the Platonic idea or the Aristotelian *actus purus*, who knows only himself. He is not the Gnostic father who sits high on his throne above the world and the *pleroma*. No. God sends down blessings upon his world, and the world sends up to him its canticle of praise. The fundamental cause of all things is the eternal and uncreated Love. The Son cries, "Father," and he permits us also to say, "Father." At that time the Stoics had awakened a general feeling of human solidarity founded on the concept of Zeus the father of all things. But the doctrine was mere abstract theory which never became flesh and blood in a concrete personality.

But Christ established a supernatural, heavenly order. The eternal cradle of the human race lies in the loving thought of God and in his election of the human race. God blesses us in time because he knew us before all time and predestined us. We were never pure nothing, or some universal Platonic idea. We were always a definite something in God's thoughts, something individual and unique. Every blessing that is poured out upon humanity in time is merely the continuation of the original loving act of election by God.

The original order of creation, however, was violated and destroyed, and now it was to be re-established, restored, and again related to its central point. The spirit world, too, received a new head in Christ's incarnation. With the "redemption through his blood," a new supernatural era was begun, a new world came into being, and the Incarnation was the dedication of that world, while the Crucifixion was the sanctification. The material world, too, needs this re-dedication of its being, but here God found no opposition. Nature is as pliable as clay in the potter's hand. Man is the one great rebel against God.

In the individual soul, the redemption is a difficult work. How great a work is the redemption of peoples with their racial and national prejudices! But the mighty force that manifested itself in the Resurrection of the Son will overcome all secular opposition. In a majestic antithesis, "now-then," without Christ-with Christ, Paul contrasts these two periods in human history. Then humanity split into Jew and Gentile, into Greek and barbarian, tortured by demons, ruled by the spirit of the world as in the case of the Gentiles or by the spirit of proud exclusiveness as were the Jews. Now the new people of God, humanity united in Christ, the new *civitas Dei*, whose keystone is Christ (1:10). The blood of races divides men. Christ's blood unites them: "But now in Christ Jesus, you, who some time were afar off, are made near by the blood of Christ" (2:13). Paul thinks of Christ's work of unification as a cosmic thing, yes, something supercosmic, having an effect even on the angelic powers. Christ snatched the universe from despair. At the beginning of the Christian era, even the Nordic peoples were beginning to doubt their gods, they felt the advent of a *Goetterdaemmerung*. And today, without Christ, how black would be the world's despair!

The dedication of created things is completed by the dedication of the community. God revealed to Paul his secret: how he was to break down human opposition. Christ established an organism of salvation that embraced the whole of humanity, the Church, which was his body as a social and mystical phenomenon. Primarily salvation was not concerned with the individual. It was first for the whole. Paul knew well that Christ had sacrificed himself also for him personally (Gal. 2:20), not as an isolated human being, but rather as a member of humanity incorporated in Christ's mystical body. Just as the original guilt of the individual was only a participation in the common guilt by reason of the individual's blood relationship with the sinning head of the race, so personal salvation can be conceived only as a participation in the common redemption by the mystic relationship with Christ the Head of redeemed humanity.

This thought ushers us into the heart of Paul's theology. This central thought of Pauline theology is so un-Jewish and so new that scholars have vainly sought to derive it from the confluence of two streams of thought: the organism concept of Hellenistic philosophy and the Indian-Iranian theory about a primitive man who had a collective soul which included all individual souls. Just as Christ is the fullness of God so the Church is the fullness of Christ, his timespace integration, "the fullness of him who is filled all in all" (1:23).

This is Paul's canticle to the Church in which all the wonders of the redemption are gathered. What a supernatural optimist Paul must have been! Here in his poor rented lodging, the Church an organization with a few members without influence or power, Paul envisioned a mighty picture of the Church of the future. His optimism was akin to that divine optimism of our Lord: "Fear not, little flock, for it has pleased your heavenly Father to give you a kingdom" (Luke 12:32). Out of Paul's gigantic vision of the unity of the Church came quite logically the idea of a uniform moral way of life. The new, reformed man must have a new style of living. From the inner spiritual being a new Christian morality, a new attitude, would proceed. All of the moral prescriptions in the second part of the letter are based on our real union with Christ and the Church.

Paul's total view of the Church in the idea of the mystical body appears to us today as a beautiful metaphor, or as a purely symbolic expression, but for Paul this mystical unity was as real as the natural unity of the human race. In human beings there is a solidarity of evil and of guilt, as well as a solidarity of the good and of grace. Christian antiquity and the Christian Middle Ages were much more conversant with this idea of unity than we are. The nominalism of the late Middle Ages, which watered down the idea of the universal into a mere figure of speech, and positivism, which said that facts alone were valid, have dissolved the bond of humanity's unity. For Paul the solidifying bond of unity was love. According to him the whole creation of the world and all human history are nothing but a movement of love from the heart of God and back again to God's heart. All the tribulation of human living, all the narrowness of human beings, will yield only to love.

Keeping before his mind this grand total view of the Church, Paul proceeds to solve the chief problem of his age: the problem of marriage and sexual love. Among the Greeks, concubinage and pederasty were accepted as a matter of course. The noblest thinkers and statesmen, such as Socrates, Plato, Aristotle, and Pericles, countenanced pederasty and ascribed to it great educational advantages. Gradually Greek eroticism led to contempt for marriage and to the suppression of the natural rights of women. Marriage, therefore, the creative fountain of humanity, had to be re-established in its relationship to the original divine fountain of life, and so Paul went from his mystical doctrine of the Church to his treatment of the sacrament of marriage. In the words of Genesis (2:24) giving the historical account of the institution of marriage, Paul professed to see a model and prophecy of the future. "In this word of the Scriptures," he said, "is contained a great mystery (sacrament), an allegory which I interpret as referring to Christ and the Church" (3:32).

As all earthly things are mere figures, so the relationship between the sexes, the union of man and wife, is a figure of the mystical marriage between Christ and redeemed humanity. In the Eastern Church the groom receives a crown *(repraesentatio*

Christi), and the bride receives a branch from the tree of life
(repraesentatio Ecclesiae). The relationship between Christ
and the Church cannot be more beautifully expressed than by
the figure of marriage, and marriage could not have been more
ennobled than by this mystical reference to the Incarnation and
the Church's espousals.

Thus by that intimate union of souls in marriage, Christ
wished to give the life of the woman a higher dedication and a
new significance in society. Among the Greeks no one would
have praised a faithful wife, although men often praised their
courtesans. But now among Christians a new feeling was
awakened for the wife. In the catacomb inscriptions we find an
expression of a new concept of the family, we find phrases like,
Dulcissimae uxori. Paul did not desire to "sublimate" sexual
life from below by psychoanalytical methods; he desired to
spiritualize it from above, and he could so elevate marriage only
because of the basic thought in his doctrine of the redemption:
that Christ had assumed to himself all of humanity including its
sexuality. Out of Paul's teaching about Christian marriage came
a new notion of the family, a notion toward which the Stoics
had long been groping.

Paul was proclaiming to the world a noble, sublime idea
of life at the very time when the "beast" of the Apocalypse was
about to be let loose on the world.

In the corner of the cell sat the stolid Pretorian Guard. He
remained silent during the dictation of the letter. But when Paul
saw him, the soldier provided him with a forceful figure of the
battle of the spiritual life. Paul closed the epistle with this
reference to the warfare of the soul.

CHAPTER FIFTY-EIGHT

CHRIST'S WORK OF RECONCILIATION

The Epistle to the Colossians

One day Epaphras, the founder of the Church in Colossae, came to Paul for advice and assistance. The people were zealous for the faith and they were filled with fraternal love, but they were somewhat subtle and hypercritical. They liked to spend much time in unreal dreaming and useless subtleties.

Paul immediately grasped the situation. Phrygia, he knew, was a place where storms were apt to be brewing, and when he had been in Miletus he thought how threatening clouds of heresy might easily arise in Phrygia. The people of Phrygia always looked at the world as a place filled with demons; the skies were full of Thrones, Powers, Dominations, and Principalities (Col. 2:15), and the sublunary space was filled with lesser spirits (Eph. 6:12). The higher spirits they called *pleroma,* the "fullness," and the word came to be a catchword in Colossae. Everybody, workman and slave, was talking about spirits, although most men knew nothing of the whole issue. The lower spirits were called the *kenoma,* "the vacuum." Ionia was the place, after all, where, philosophy originated, and Phrygia had nurtured all sorts of Gnostic speculation, and now they were both in a religious ferment. Even the topography seemed to favour such fantastic and extravagant theorizing. The country was often visited by earthquakes, it was scarred and torn by ugly ravines and canyons and craterlike openings, from which sulphurous vapours sometimes issued. Near Hierapolis, visitors were shown a large crater in the earth, called the *Plutonium,* where evil spirits were supposed to cavort. Thales was born here, and it was his opinion that the world was filled with demons.

From the scant indication of the Apostle, we are now unable to gain an exact idea of the nature of the heresies in question. It seems sufficiently clear that the matter had to do with a warped kind of theosophy derived from Jewish and Hellenistic speculation. The Jews, who had settled in Phrygia in great numbers since the time of Antiochus the Great, were attempting to make their Judaism more palatable by covering it over with philosophy. They claimed to know everything about angels and spirits, who were supposed to have transmitted the Decalogue to Moses on Mount Sinai. They developed an exaggerated and superstitious worship of angels and spirits, and they declared that Christ was also one of the intermediate angels. That was why he had obeyed the law, and therefore the Christians must also obey the law. Until this stage the heresy was comparatively harmless, but it would soon become a poisonous draft, mixed with Jewish, late Platonic, Neo-Pythagorian, Orphic, Persian-Zoroastrian ingredients, and it was to survive for several centuries of Church history, causing great harm to the Church.

This was the first stage in the religious fermentation. In the beginning there were signs of Samaritan influence from the school of Simon Magus, and also signs of the religion of Zoroaster. The idea of an esoteric belief was unusually acceptable to people who were disgusted with earthly things and had a strange thirst for redemption. The issue seems to have turned about these points. What is to be thought of earthly matter? Is it created? Or does it derive from a source opposed to God? What about evil? Does evil arise from matter? In answer the new enlightened spirits said: Earthly matter is too coarse, too far removed from God, and God is too sublime to be concerned with the creation, direction, and rule of the world. Such things would only besmirch God. These activities are therefore to be ascribed to lesser spirits, the so-called *aeons* (Col. 2:8).

If God took care of these things he would be drawn away from his self-contemplation. From God proceed, by emanation, all beings from the greatest to the smallest, including the demiurges and architects of the universe who have made this world through which the evil spirits go storming at all times. The human soul is a spark of light that lost itself in this world of matter, and one of the better aeons, the higher Christ, who united himself with the earthly Jesus by the baptism in the Jordan, decided to save this spark of light. The crucified Jesus is not the redeemer, but the Christ who returned to the *pleroma* before the Crucifixion. Those who had been initiated into this teaching considered themselves enlightened and called themselves Gnostics. They looked down with pity on the simple believers whom they called Pistics. The initiation into this esoteric group took place only after a strict regime of mortification, abstinence from wine, meat, marriage, etc.

Paul would not have been the keen thinker if he had not immediately recognized the danger this doctrine was for the clear concept of faith. Because of his deep insight into the mysteries of Christ, into the inner Trinitarian life, he knew that the act of creation was not unworthy of God, but that together with the act of redemption it flowed from the goodness of God. The primal fountain for these external acts is the eternal generation within the Trinity by which the Spirit of God embraces himself in the knowledge and love that course eternally between the Father, the Son, and the Holy Spirit. And creation is, as it were, an effervescence, the running over of God's love to the outside, and the image of his Son appears in myriads of new forms, from the highest cherubim down to the last weak shadow, to the last island on the periphery of the realm of being that borders on nothingness. This is the ultimate and fundamental why of the creation: the Son is the creative, formal, and final cause of the universe, all things are in him, for him, and by him (1:16).

The earthly sojourn of Jesus is surrounded by such a brilliant light of glory that it can be understood only if we pursue its bright course backward and forward into eternity. The speculation in Colossae tended to eliminate the mediatorship of Christ and threatened to deprive Christ of his central position as high priest of the universe. It sought to make Jesus a creature among creatures. That was the beginning of the Gnostic heresy which aimed at dissolving Christ, as St. John said, and the heresy developed into the greater evils of the heresies of Arius and Nestorius. The whole series of heresies attacked the kingship and primacy of Christ, and with that they attacked the dignity of man which Christ had restored. In forceful sentences Paul proceeded to define the primacy of Christ (1:19). God did not disperse his power among subordinate spirits, but he poured out his "fullness" to dwell in Jesus. The divine essence has not been shattered into a million sparks. The whole furnace of love is concentrated in the Son. We do not obey a subordinate spirit or some vicar. We are immediately subject to the beloved Son of the eternal Father. Those angels that ministered at the giving of the law on Mount Sinai, and any other powers, principalities, or dominations about whom the Jews and Persians are talking have been disarmed and they, too, must obey Christ.

Just as it collapsed when confronted with the problem of creation, so Gnosticism failed in the face of the problem of evil. The evil demons are so numerous in the world, suffering is so universal, that every attempt to solve the problem by natural means leads only to intellectual despair. Any dualistic solution leads inevitably to hopeless pessimism. There is only one solution: the Cross of Christ. Without the Apostle's mystical concept of suffering, this problem of suffering cannot be mastered. He himself has not finished with suffering because his is not personal suffering. He is suffering as a member of the mystical body of Christ and he is filling up the measure of the suffering of Christ (1:24). To every member of the mystical body a share of suffering has been assigned, according to his nearness to the Head of the mystical body, and therefore the greatest suffering has come to the apostles, for they are champions of God (1 Cor. 4:9). And that thought gave Paul much pleasure.

Paul depicts Christ as the creative image of the Father, uniting in himself the fullness of the Godhead, as God of God, Light of Light, and still a man among men, who by his blood closed the gap which sin had made between God and the world. For Paul, the world was not derived from the devil, nor did it belong to the devil. We may not sacrifice the world and give it up to its fate, in spite of its sad history, its misery, and its burden of sin, for the world needs salvation and it is susceptible of salvation. We cannot refrain from all action and activity and leave the world to its own designs.

Thus by his very definite and express dogma about Christ, Paul saved Christianity from sinking into some kind of Oriental quietism, and he made it to be a creative factor in Western culture. Without this teaching of Paul's, the West would have become intellectually a province of Asia. Zarathustra or Mohammed, under Mongol domination, would have decided the fate of Europe. Just at this time the Celts and the Nordic peoples were sickening of their gods, and no salvation therefore was to be expected from the north. Then the angels of the nations appeared before the throne of the Almighty and said: "Have pity on the hope of the human race." And Paul was given full authority and a commission: "The hope of the gospel which you have heard, which is preached in all the creation that is under heaven, whereof I, Paul, am made a minister" (Col. 1:23).

The initiation into the inner religion, into that life which is "hid with Christ in God" (3:3), does not take place, according to Paul, after some hypocritical regime of asceticism. Those who "are translated into the kingdom of the Son of his love" (1:13) should not be hampered by the old elements that belong rather to the childhood stage. God has expunged the Old Law, He took the handwriting of the law as a trophy won on the battlefield and affixed it to the Cross. The Christian conscience is concerned with more sacred things than the Old Law. Instead of thinking about whether the milk jug touched the meat bowl, see to it that men do not come into conflict with one another. Instead of having rules that say: "Don't grasp this! Don't taste this! Don't touch this!" say rather, "Bear with one another, forgive one another" (3:13). Instead of refusing to handle a coin because the emperor's image is on it, divest your old man of his pagan thoughts and desires, and erect the image of your Creator in your hearts.

Paul told them to cherish the unity of Christians more than any differences of station or social position, to value it more than blood relationship. Such was Paul's answer to those who would make Christianity a secret doctrine and a secret cult for the few, and a kind of mass religion for the rest. By these words, Paul preserved the Church from an asceticism that fled from the world. Simeon Stylites, standing for forty years atop the narrow platform of a temple pillar, leaning on his staff, without sleep or nourishment in an ecstatic state while his body gradually withered away – this miracle of asceticism that lifted itself high above everything earthly and human and cared not whether the world went down in ruins, and all the other ascetics of the Eastern Church that flared up like torches to light the decline of the world – these were not Paul's ideal.

Paul thought it important that the religion of Jesus should defend its universal character as the training school for all mankind, and as part of that theory he held open the door of the Church to receive into it the higher knowledge of Christian philosophy and Christian mysticism. As centuries went by, the door would be opened still farther to let in the full stream of reason and research until that great age when faith and reason would join hands in the Summas of St. Thomas Aquinas. Soon after Paul's day, the Alexandrians experienced "the intellectual joy of Christian thought,"[54] to which Paul had opened the door for the first time. In high confidence in the superiority of Christianity over pagan philosophy, these scholars employed the results of Greek thought as an interpreter to make God more intelligible. To what a high state of scientific achievement the Alexandrian School must have attained! For Clement of Alexandria was moved to exclaim: "Since Christ has come, we have no need of pagan schools. Our new Teacher teaches all things. Through Him the whole world has become Athens and Greece."

Paul prepared the way for the reception of St. John's concept of the Logos into the world of Christian thought.

All Paul's friends from the East were standing round the table while the Apostle dictated his letter, as we can imagine from the list of greetings. These rented quarters of the Apostle often became his house chapel in which his friends remembered the absent brethren in prayers, in hymns, and in the breaking of bread (1:3, 9). In the choir of those who sing and pray, we hear the voice of Epaphras, the founder of the Church of Colossae, praying for the souls of his children. Paul was deeply impressed by the zeal of this truly apostolic man (4:12).

Thus we have a picture of how things went with Christ's prisoner in Rome. There was an incessant coming and going, brethren were departing for distant Churches, others were returning, messages were being received, letters were being dispatched. From the street below came the raucous, strident noises of this restless city, but here in the prisoner's room were peace and love. The stolid Praetorian sat in the corner. Perhaps he had some inkling that this man whom he was guarding was not a dangerous agitator and leader of some international conspiracy, but the spiritual head of a world-wide organization that prayed unceasingly for the welfare of the Empire, and in their hands the fate of the Empire would have been much more secure than in the hands of the soldier's imperial master.

---

[54] Cf. Harnack, *Die Mission and Ausbreitung des Christentums,* 4th ed., Leipzig, 1924.

CHAPTER FIFTY-NINE

ONESIMUS THE SLAVE

The Epistle to Philemon

Among these visits that Paul was receiving day in day out, the most interesting and the most touching was the visit by a young escaped slave. It was interesting because it shows how early Christianity handled the social problem, and it was touching because it shows us a new and highly sympathetic side of the Apostle. It reveals Paul's noble humaneness and the way he was able to elevate ordinary things to a supernatural level. The Epistle to Philemon is an immortal memorial to Paul's goodness of heart.

Philemon was a wealthy merchant in Colossae. At some slave market he had bought an unusually alert and intelligent young slave for a considerable sum. He called this nameless orphan Onesimus (profitable). Now, Onesimus had done a stupid thing. He robbed his master and then, afraid of the punishment, he had run off and finally made his way to Rome, the meeting place of all fugitives and the cloaca of all vice. But now that he was in Rome things were different from what he thought they would be. His money was gone, and the Roman police were close on the trail of fugitive slaves. As a fugitive, Onesimus was outside the law, he was even lower now than a slave and, free as he was in Rome, he was exposed to every vice. But the grace of God touched the soul of this poor slave.

Philemon and his wife were converts and intimate friends of the Apostle. They were friends to whose home Paul felt free to invite himself and expect lodging, as he actually did: "But withal prepare me also a lodging" (Philem. 22). Philemon's house was also the place where divine services were being held. Some scholars think that Archippus who led the services was a son of Philemon. It may have happened that Onesimus met Epaphras on the street in Rome. Perhaps, in his desperate situation, he remembered the goodness of Paul to whom he probably had often delivered letters from his master. What better place to take refuge than in the heart of a Christian! But Onesimus found more than he thought: he found the greatest good fortune of his life. So, this escaped slave represents one of the most beautiful triumphs of divine grace, and the letter which was occasioned by his escape and from which we know the story must be looked upon as a monument of grace.

At any rate, one day Onesimus knocked on Paul's door. Paul asked him if he had a letter from his master, Paul's good friend Philemon. Onesimus was shy and embarrassed, but he could not long hide anything from the eyes that looked so kindly and yet so piercingly into his soul. Onesimus told his story of the prodigal. Onesimus' position was extremely serious. When an escaped slave was caught, he was immediately branded on his forehead with an F, meaning *fugitivus*.[55] And as a thief his master could have him flogged to death, or send him to the *pistrinum* to turn millstones for the rest of his life. From the second half of the fourth century we have a metal tablet worn about the neck of a slave who had escaped from one of the sextons of the church of San Clemente in Rome, with this inscription: *"Tene me quia fugi et reboca me Victori Acolito a Dominicu Clementis,"* that is, if this slave should escape again

---

[55] Cicero, *De Off,* II, 7; Martial, VIII, 75, 9; Val. Maximus, VI, 8.

he is to be returned to the church of St. Clement. Onesimus could feel quite certain that he need not fear the worst from his master, but if Philemon advertised his escape and if he were caught by the police, things might go very badly for Onesimus and place Paul in an uncomfortable position.

When Paul told Onesimus that he must go back to Philemon, Onesimus winced at the thought. If only someone would free him. At that time the slaves had set up in the temples collection boxes for their redemption, and these receptacles were under the protection of one of the gods. The slave's master went with him to the temple, and took the redemption price, as it were, from the hand of the god, and thus the slave became a freedman of the god. Paul reflected for a moment.

"Onesimus," he said, "I know someone who will buy your freedom for you. I myself am a poor man, but he is so rich that he could redeem the whole world."

Onesimus looked up anxiously. "Who is that? Who could do that?"

"Have you not heard of Christ, the Redeemer of the world?"

"Oh, yes," Onesimus replied. "Philemon often spoke of him, and since he became a Christian he was much kinder to us slaves. Some of the slaves became Christians like Philemon."

"Now look, Onesimus," said Paul. "I will tell you about him, about our glorious Christ. He is the eternal Son of God, the freest of all free men. But nevertheless he gave up his freedom and his glory and took the form and condition of a slave. He died a slave's death of his own free will in order to free us from a more dreadful slavery."

Paul went on to tell Onesimus how once he had suffered in the slavery of the law, and that now he had found liberty in Christ.

"My dear Onesimus," Paul went on, "we have a good Master. With Christ there is neither slave or free man. In fact, we are all slaves; but look at our slavery. The least of Christ's slaves is freer than the freest man on earth. His burden is sweet and his yoke is light. You need not tell me, Onesimus, about the freedom of men. Once I boasted that I was a free man, and I was really a miserable slave, a slave of the letter, a slave of a vain dream. I thought I was living, and I was dead. But since I died with Christ, since I was crucified to the world, I really know what life is. Once, when everybody thought I was a happy man, I was actually miserably unhappy and I spent the nights in dread and terror. Once I cried out, 'Who shall deliver me from the body of this death?'

"Since that time I was scourged five times for Christ, three times I was flogged, and once I was stoned. I was driven from city to city, I was subjected to every hazard on land and sea, to all kinds of weather, to every kind of hardship, and for the last thirty years I have led a life of toil and sacrifice, but in the midst of all this I lived and was happy. All that I can say again and again is: 'Rejoice in the Lord.' Once I was young, too. Now I am old and grey, but the Lord has renewed my youth like that of the eagle. Onesimus, do not be afraid of the brand on your forehead. Those who are branded on their souls are the ones who ought to fear, those who have 'their consciences seared' (1 Tim. 4:2). Glorious is that freedom 'wherewith Christ has made us free'" (Gal. 4:31).

Onesimus listened to Paul with wrapt attention. No man had ever talked to him like that before. Paul had a warm feeling for the boy. He always had a sympathetic ear for the young, and there was something likeable about this young fugitive despite his mischievousness. Onesimus was aware of the kindly heart beating in the breast of the man who was talking to him. He came back to Paul's room frequently. Soon they were close friends, and one day, when Paul had again poured forth his love for Christ, Onesimus dropped to the floor beside Paul and whispered his "Credo." That was not the first or the last time that a visitor fell to his knees beside Paul. The Praetorian Guard sitting in the corner could tell of many other scenes like this.

The rest of Onesimus' story illustrates a special character-istic of Christianity, its close relationship to ethics. In Christian-ity the sublimest flights of thought are accompanied by the soberest sense of reality. Christianity is sometimes a most un-comfortable religion and sometimes it is quite congenial. With the pagans, religion and morality were separate things. Some of the gods were immoral. Religion and morality existed without relationship to each other and sometimes were even in opposition. A man could be morally depraved and still be a devout client of the gods. Christianity was the first to demand that the fullest harmony exist between the religious and the moral attitude because religion and morality are derived from the same source. Paul's religion was an eminently practical affair. He was not content with only an intellectual attitude.

"Onesimus," Paul said, "you will have to go back to Phile-mon, you will have to confess your wrong and take whatever punishment Philemon inflicts. It will be hard for you to go, I know, and it will be hard for me to see you go. Now we have become good friends and I could use your services, but I may not interfere with the rights of a third man. But I will do one thing for you. I will write a note to Philemon. When you go back with Tychicus you can take it with you to Philemon."

Paul sat down at the table in his cell and dictated the note to Timothy. Of Paul's letters that we possess, this is the only one about a personal matter. It permits us to look deeper into Paul's heart than the other letters, so burdened down with great thoughts. Here is a man who need not hide his private letters from public gaze. Everything that Paul wrote, every note, every notation, bore the imprint of his spirit and came from the depth of his apostolic heart.

Paul omitted every official title in the letter, every reference to his apostolic office, but he did rattle his chains significantly when he wrote, "Paul, a prisoner of Christ Jesus." Philemon had a large house with dozens of slaves, and Paul knew that Philemon would read the letter at the domestic religious services.

Therefore he added the greeting, "and to the Church which is in your house." Paul actually had a claim on Philemon because of his spiritual fatherhood, and he had something practical to ask of Philemon. But he knew that Philemon was a man of fine sensibilities (v. 5), and that no command would be necessary. Therefore Paul makes his request on the basis of the law of love. Anyone having the care of souls will accomplish more by a request than by command.

Paul accumulated his motives with a fine sense for their increasing force. "I, Paul, an old man," he wrote (v. 9). The aged, furrowed face of the Apostle came before Philemon's eyes. How touching is Paul's humility as an old man with respect to this younger man! Here Rembrandt's striking portrait of the aged Paul comes to mind. He was old and grey in Christ's service:

But besides his years, he was "now a prisoner of Jesus Christ" (v. 9). With him all Christianity is in chains. He knows full well that if he asks in that name, and if he asks for his "son," then Philemon will not be annoyed at him, even though he for whom he asks is called Onesimus. Now he has uttered the fateful name. He could say it only after some psychological preparation, because the mere mention of the name Onesimus would arouse in Philemon bitter thoughts on account of the slave's ingratitude for Philemon's goodness to him. Paul could see Philemon wrinkling his brow with displeasure, and immediately he tried to smooth out the furrows with a little humour, a play on words: "who has been heretofore unprofitable to you, but now is profitable both to me and to you." Philemon almost felt Paul's cool hand smoothing his brow.

"Whom I have sent back to you. And do receive him as my own bowels." That is asking for a great deal, but if Paul speaks this way there must be something good in Onesimus. And then Paul goes bravely on to sing the praises of the slave: "Whom I would have retained with me, that in your stead he might have ministered to me in the bands of the gospel, but

without your counsel I would do nothing." Paul acknowledged
the laws of antiquity and Philemon's rights that were based on
that law. He could have kept Onesimus, presuming Philemon's
permission. But that would have been using some force, and
Paul was an outspoken enemy of all force, he was against all
moral duress, especially in material things, so that no shadow
should fall on the gospel.

Then Paul turns quickly to a supernatural consideration:
"For perhaps he therefore departed for a season from you, that
you might receive him again forever: not now as a servant, but
instead of a servant, a most dear brother." It is a fine character-
ization of Christianity as the communion of those who may
have been separated before but who have now found brotherhood in Christ. Onesimus had done wrong, of course; but when
God forgives, man must also forgive and in God's eyes his
wrongdoing had become the occasion for his conversion. Onesimus has caused you some annoyance, but it was worth the
trouble. Philemon, you thought you had suffered a loss, but you
really made a handsome profit. Instead of a slave you now
receive back a brother.

Because of his spiritual fatherhood Paul believes that he
has a common interest with Philemon in his possessions, or, as
he expresses it, he is in partnership with Philemon: "If, therefore,
you count me a partner, receive him as myself. And if he has
wronged you in any thing, or is in your debt, put that to my
account. I Paul have written it with my own hand: I will repay
it: not to say to you, that you owe me your own self also. Yes,
brother. May I enjoy you in the Lord. Refresh my bowels in the
Lord" (17-21).

We may search all the epistolary literature of antiquity
and we will not find a human document that can compare with
this letter. Read Pliny's letter in which he asks his friend
Sabinianus to refrain from torturing an escaped slave. For the
moment, he says, the slave has been sufficiently punished by
the reproaches Pliny has already made to him. If the slave fails

again, then his master may punish him without grace or mercy. Any comparison will be in Paul's favour. How close Stoicism approached Christianity, however, is shown by Pliny's treatment of his own slaves. Pliny's freedman, Zosimus, was suffering from a disease of the lungs, and Pliny sent him to Egypt to recover. Zosimus came back apparently cured, but he again began to cough up blood, and then Pliny tried to find a place for Zosimus to stay on the Riviera. He permitted his slaves to make a last will, a privilege of free men. Cicero, too, was magnanimous to his slaves as appears from the following in a letter to his son Mark (53 B.C.): "When you set Tiros free you afforded me great pleasure because you deemed him worthy of a better fate and looked upon him rather as a friend than as our slave. I thank you and congratulate you."

The letter to Philemon is not only a masterpiece of tact and politeness, it is in a way also the beginning of the Christian declaration of the rights of man. Paul could not contemplate a declaration that slavery should be immediately abolished: the safety of the state, the social conscience, and indeed the welfare of the slaves themselves would have been jeopardized by such an abrupt declaration. At that time the Roman Empire had far more slaves than freemen. The slaves formed a large part of the national wealth. A household with more than a thousand slaves was not rare. Seneca said that the slaves were not dressed differently from free men so that they would not realize their great number. A million busy hands worked in homes, on farms, in factories, tanneries, etc. Slaves were the invaluable servants of Roman culture. Millions of slaves had to plough and cultivate fields, had to plane and saw so that a few thousand could study, paint, and rule. Certainly the tragedies of Sophocles and the Zeus of Phidias were not too dearly paid for by the misery of so many slaves, according to Treitschke. But Paul thought otherwise.

At first, however, he could do little to mitigate the lot of the slaves. As things were then, a proclamation of the emancipation of the slaves would have caused a civil war, and might put the early Church in danger. The experience of centuries, and especially the case of the French Revolution, has taught that a sudden change from servitude to freedom does not bring happiness even to those who are apparently benefited. If today we look on slavery as opposed to our moral sense, we must remember that we are viewing the matter in the light of Christian teaching. Classical antiquity, including Aristotle himself, saw nothing unreasonable in slavery. Actually the condition of the slaves was most wretched. It was a universal principle that no act committed against a slave could be unlawful, although the slave's treatment was generally better than his legal status warranted. On account of their religion, the Jews were the most humane in the treatment of their slaves. The Greeks were generally milder than the Romans. At times it may have happened that some Roman millionaire fed the flesh of his slaves to the fish in his pond, but we must avoid generalizing cases like this.

When philosophy failed, the matter needed to be considered from another angle, from the religious viewpoint. Only the faith in the mystical unity of all redeemed souls in Jesus, a belief in the equality of all men before God, could offer a solution to the problem. First the treatment of slaves had to be more humane, then the slaves had to be regarded as equals, and then slavery could be abolished. Paul wrote the Magna Charta of Christian freedom in the Epistle to the Galatians: "For you are all the children of God, by faith in Christ Jesus. For as many of you as have been baptized in Christ have put on Christ. There is neither Jew nor Greek; there is neither bond nor free; there is neither male nor female. For you are all one in Christ Jesus" (Gal. 3:26).

Even in religion the pagans considered the slaves as being of a lower class. They were allowed only the cult of the agricultural and forest deities, and they were refused participation in the official religion. Paul on the contrary proclaimed full religious equality: "For in one spirit were we all baptized into one body" (1 Cor. 12:13). How could anyone despise a slave after the Holy Spirit had made no distinction in the outpouring of his charismata? In the first letter to the Corinthians Paul took the stand that baptism did not change a man's external condition. In themselves baptism and Christianity do not dissolve the marriage bond or the social order. They change the soul and lift it above these human accidents and social differences. Any other stand would have been dangerous for the Church, because many false conversions would have followed upon a proclamation of universal freedom.

In the letter to Philemon, Paul had an opportunity to put his theory to the test. He was never a man to try general solutions. He would rather treat every case by itself in the light of the general principle. The question in Onesimus' case was this: Could a slave, after he was freed by the blood of Christ, cast off his earthly master? Is the Christian master under any obligation when his slave is converted to Christianity? In answer Paul did not disturb the Roman legal order. He ardently desired the liberation of the slave, but he left that decision where it belonged, in the Christian conscience.

The early Church continued in Paul's high regard for human dignity even though it wore the slave's garments. A slave was admitted to all ecclesiastical offices. It was indeed a novelty that the Roman Church, the most famous of all, was at one time under the leadership of a scion of that illustrious family the *gens Corneliana,* Pope Cornelius, and at another time under the leadership of a freed slave like Pope Callistus.

Whatever still remains in the Christian Church of true freedom is nourished by the spirit of Paul, and is Paul's bequest to the Church. We should forever venerate the man who, at the time when the unspeakable Nero governed the world and when he himself was in chains, was able to speak these words of tenderness toward our humanity: "I Paul, a prisoner of Jesus Christ, I appeal to you for my child, Onesimus, whose father I have become in my imprisonment" (Philem. 10).

CHAPTER SIXTY

THE EPISTLE TO THE PHILIPPIANS

Paul's first conquest on European soil, the Church in Philippi, remained his favourite Church. In this Roman colony there was none of that preoccupation with fantastic speculations that we saw in Galatia. The Philippians had a great deal of practical Christianity. Unexpectedly, one day Epaphroditus, a prominent citizen of Philippi, came to Paul in Rome and presented a generous gift in the name of the Church at Philippi. Paul was highly pleased at this evidence of his children's love and affection for him. He knew, too, who was the moving spirit behind this munificence: that truly apostolic woman, Lydia, whose goodness and solicitude were inexhaustible. She was never content unless she had someone to care for. Some students think that the "sincere companion" (4:3) refers to Lydia, but it may also refer to Luke, who had gone on ahead to Philippi.

"And how were the brethren in Philippi?" Almost all of Epaphroditus' news was good. The congregation was firm and solid in its faith, it was fighting valiantly for the gospel. And it was deeply concerned about Paul. Sometimes, it is true, little jealousies and quarrels broke out between some of the women, like that little difficulty between Evodia and Syntyche. For a time some Jewish Christians had made inroads in the community and disturbed the harmony of the Church, trying to undermine Paul's authority, but they had not succeeded. They had, indeed, been able to put some of the brethren in prison, but that had only served to unite the Church all the more.

Epaphroditus stayed for some time with Paul, sharing his imprisonment. Unselfishly he had given himself entirely to the service of the gospel, and even risked his life for Paul. Because of the poor state of his health, he soon contracted Roman fever. And Paul nursed him back to health. How many nights Paul watched by his bedside and wrestled in prayer with God for his good friend, who "was sick, close to death"! (2:27.) Paul was grateful for his recovery so that he could go back to his good Philippians, but he was still more thankful, "lest I should have sorrow upon sorrow." It may have been near the end of this imprisonment that Paul bade farewell to Epaphroditus and gave him an affectionate letter to the people of Philippi. Mark, Tychicus, and Onesimus had already departed for Asia Minor. Only Timothy was still with Paul. Evidently Paul had been brought back to the Praetorium for the final hearings of his case.

In none of his letters does Paul touch so gently and tenderly on the chords of the human heart as in the Epistle to the Philippians. It has rightly been called the pearl of the Pauline Epistles. In it we find no strict sequences of thought. It is simply the outpouring of his great heart, his heart speaking to the heart of his beloved Philippians. He had but one purpose in writing the letter: he wished Philippi to be his model Church, and from it he wished to banish the least taint of disunion.

The changes of mood in the letter, from joyous confidence to melancholy resignation and premonitions of death, reflect the varied fortunes of his judicial case and indicate interruptions in the writing of the letter. But the dominating emotion is that of spiritual joy. Paul's only desire was Christ's triumph, whether through Paul's living or dying. A long life or imminent death was indifferent to Paul, and in these days of his captivity he rejoiced because that imprisonment did not hinder the spread of the gospel. Some of the Jewish Christians in Rome found malignant pleasure in calling the attention of the Roman public to this prisoner. But that only served to make Christ's name better known. Paul did not surmise, however, that this same publicity would become a serious threat within the next year. The words written in bright golden letters over the *Confessio* at the Apostle's tomb in Rome: *Mihi vivere Christus est et mori lucrum* ("For to me, to live is Christ: and to die is gain"), are the majestic expression of the principal cause for his spiritual rejoicing. He knew no interest of his own, he had no selfish pleasures. All his interests coincided with Christ's interests.

But life had its value for Paul. It was the prerequisite for his apostolic work. Thus Paul was confronted with a difficult choice: two opposite desires besieged his soul, and he could not say which was more desirable, to die for Christ, or to live for Christ. Finally he took the same stand that Ignatius Loyola later adopted: If I had the choice of dying now with the assurance of going immediately into heaven, or a longer life filled with labour and toil for Christ without the certainty of going to heaven, I would choose the latter as the more heroic.

For a moment Paul turned away from his main theme of the complete unity of souls in the Church of Philippi. He told them that their little differences came from their lack of supernatural thinking; they did not take Christianity seriously enough. For Paul the mystery of Christ was not a mere system of thought, the mystical communion of the brethren was not an empty figure of speech, faith was not a way of looking at things, fraternal charity was not something to be practised cautiously. No, said Paul, our union with Christ is the most real of all realities, and if Christ is real for you, then you will avoid any differences among yourselves. The moral attitude of a Christian is not a fancy adjunct to his faith, it grows out of his faith and is integral with it.

And now Paul talks to his Philippians about the central mystery of Christianity. Christ is the uncreated image of the

Father. He has the same essential nature as God. He is equal to God. He has an absolute right to divine honours and glory. The first Adam thought that he could pluck "being-like-God" from the forbidden tree, he intended to steal divine honours. But the second Adam did not consider it robbery to be like to God. That was his rightful possession because of his eternal generation from the Father. Nevertheless Christ freely divested himself of all external glory, and he hid his divine origin under the form of a servant according to his Father's will. If Christ had thought as we do, he would have insisted on his divine rights while he was here on earth. He would have avenged himself on everyone that offended him. He would have had legions of angels to fight for him. He would have rained down fire and brimstone from heaven. And he would have sold his life for the highest price.

But Christ did none of these things. Did he therefore cease to be equal to God? No, his divinity was only veiled under his human appearance. And do you cease to be what you are, if you yield to others? No one can take from you the nobility that is within you. That was "God's first leap," as St. Gregory express-es it, the first leap of the Infinite into human finiteness, the first step in God's self-humiliation. And God went still farther into the depths of self-humiliation. Having taken to himself our human nature, he wished to sacrifice everything that made life agreeable. He became small, poor, obedient, desirous of humili-ation even to a slave's death. He took upon himself everything that was horrible in human life. He allowed the cup of suffering to be filled to the brim and he emptied it to the last dregs.

And we men wish to insist on our rights; we are stubborn, and we will not yield to others. The redemption on the Cross was God's second "leap" into humiliation. And if this view of the divine descent into the human abyss is not enough, then look at the ascent that followed the descent, for the measure of the humiliation is also the measure of his glory. The Father elevated Jesus' human nature to sit equally with him on the throne of

God. He gave him the title of *Kyrios*, Lord, and the greatest of all names, King of kings, Lord of lords, the ruler of three worlds, below the earth, the earth itself, and above the earth.

Some scholars think that the following part of the Epistle to the Philippians is a fragment of another letter to the Philippians, written at another time and afterward attached to the first epistle. These students think that they can discern the exact joining of the two parts between the first and second verses of chapter three. The obvious change in mood can easily be explained by a pause in the writing of the letter, during which some new reports came in.

With sudden indignation, Paul warns the Philippians: "Beware of dogs: beware of evil workers: beware of the concision" (3:2). All that tiresome, empty prattle about Jewish privileges, that silly preoccupation with tassels and fringes, that stupid insistence on family trees and ancestral charts, promises and circumcision, Paul called it all sarcastically "concision." The unloving way the Jews bayed at him in prison like the dogs in the Apocalypse (22:15) and uprooted the vineyard of the Lord like wild boars, was answered with that fierce derision and stinging ridicule of the pagans contained in the expression "*curtis Judaeis*" ("mutilated Jews") and in Paul's "concision."[56] He held up before the Jews his own Hebraic coat of arms and sent it crashing into a thousand pieces at their feet, as one might hurl the heraldic device of the scion of a defunct noble family into an open grave.

Paul was not despising his past or his Jewish extraction, but since his conversion he had found something of such value that it outstripped all other values, and devaluated even what had once been the central thing in his life. That thing of inestimable value was the knowledge of Jesus Christ, "I count all things to be but loss for the excellent knowledge of Jesus Christ, my Lord; for whom I have suffered the loss of all things, and count them but as dung" (3:8). Even after thirty

---

[56] Cf. P. Delatte, O.S.B., *Les Epitres de Saint Paul*, Tours, 1928

years of incessant activity, the aging Apostle was still storming on to the fulfilment of his mission, like a runner in the Olympic races trying for the prize. He was still the ruthless enemy of all mediocrity, still impatient to give all and to make every surrender to his glorious goal.

And as he observed Christians from that exalted viewpoint, he saw the Church divided into two movements or tendencies: he saw that group of Christians who were earthly minded, who had adjusted themselves comfortably to the world, a worldly Christianity that did business with the world with the world's methods and weapons. He saw also that other group that drew its strength from Christ's Cross, those Christians who solved all problems with supernatural means, who did not try to outwit the children of the world with their cunning and shrewdness and did not think they could outmanoeuvre the world with their poor parliamentary devices. To these he said solemnly: "Our state, our politics, 'our conversation is in heaven'" (3:20). The Christians of his time could have no part with the decadent culture of Greece, they could take little part in the public life of the Empire because both were riddled through with tendencies inimical to God. They had to transfer their citizenship into the spiritual order. They were to be members of Christ's body, citizens of a heavenly state.

Paul concludes with an earnest exhortation to joy: "Rejoice in the Lord always; again I say rejoice" (4:4). Just at this time Seneca over in his villa was writing a significant phrase, *Res severa magnum gaudium* ("This question about true happiness is a serious matter"), and almost conversely, it is a great happiness to be engaged in a serious matter. And who is working in a more serious matter than the Christian? Happiness is to be found where faith and God and the eternal and the absolute are taken seriously, and where the little ego is extinguished and absorbed in the happiness of the whole. The degenerate culture of paganism had lost the knowledge of true happiness. Seneca was groping blindly about for the thought.

Paul said, "Rejoice in the Lord"; for him the Lord was the source of all joys; happiness flows from the heart of God.

For, after all, God did not create the universe in an attack of ill will. He created it out of pure joy because of the beauty he beheld in himself. Joy is not, of course, the same as virtue, but it is the atmosphere in which virtue thrives, the light by which it sees. Joy is also one of the strongest motives to invite the faith of those who are without. When others note the joy of a true Christian they will see that here is the source of life; they will say, "The Lord is nigh" (4:5).

Thus Christian joy embraces everything that is good in the world: "For the rest, brethren, whatsoever things are true, whatsoever modest, whatsoever just, whatsoever holy, whatsoever lovely, whatsoever of good fame" (4:8). Christianity, therefore, is in league with everything that is fine and noble and strong. A religion in which these things would have no place would indeed be a sad religion.

We see, too, how nobly Paul acknowledges the generous gift of the Philippians. He is evidently relieved by it. Perhaps the rent of his lodgings had been unpaid for some time. With delicate tact Paul accepted this gift and at the same time he expressed his thanks in such a way as to imply that the donors had also received a benefit: "Not that I seek the gift: but I seek the fruit that may abound to your account. But I have all and abound: I am filled, having received from Epaphroditus the things you sent, an aroma of sweetness, an act acceptable sacrifice, pleasing to God. And may my God supply all your want, according to His riches in glory in Christ Jesus" (4:17).

CHAPTER SIXTY-ONE

NIGHT ON THE WORLD

An ancient hymn for Vespers of Advent begins with the words: *Vergente mundi vespere* ("As night descended on the world"). At the time of Christ one of the great cycles in human history was coming to a close, and, as night descended, Christ came into the world to bring to it the new youthfulness of the children of God.

While Paul was sojourning in Rome the first death lines on the countenance of antiquity became plainly visible. The elder Cato had vainly warned against the emasculating influence of Hellenism. Vainly Augustus had assumed to himself the dignity of *pontifex maximus,* vainly he had tried to renew the culture of Rome, vainly he had tried to stem the storming flood by his marriage laws. Now Roman knighthood began to fail after it saw the high nobility go down. Vainly Maecenas tried to cover up the corruption with his cult of beauty. The sweet poison that Ovid had instilled into the veins of Roman youth was working its way through their beings. Only recently Ovid had published his guide for adulterers, his shameless *Ars amatoria.* Augustus saw the effect of that poison in his daughter Julia. Virgil was lamenting the fact that the old religion of Rome had been driven out by Oriental cults. Virgil bravely described Rome as the Phrygian mother of the gods, crowned with towers, rejoicing because of her divine origin.[57] But soon the Christians would know her as the woman riding on the beast, the mother of whoredom and abomination, drunk with the blood of the saints. The old religion of Jupiter was gone, the Romans took refuge in Babylonian magic and mystical numerology.[58] Instead of religion came the apotheosis of the state, and the government was glorifying itself with monumental piles and dizzy splendour. Rome intoxicated itself with a ceaseless round of festivities and entertainments in the circus. Everything could be bought with money: influence in the government, citizenship, the votes of jurors, a soldier's oath, and a woman's honour. But nations and cultures die slowly, and Rome presented a sturdy framework to the ravages of corruption, and so it collapsed only after several hundred years.

The man who could foresee the Parousia of Christ near at hand in a vision of smoke and flame over Rome and Jerusalem, was now completing his second year in a prison in Rome. We need not be surprised at the law's delay. The case was, after all, about some religious matter of an alien Jew, and the imperial court had little interest in such things. Within the last few months the character of the young Emperor had undergone a fateful change. Nero had shaken off the guidance of his tutors, Seneca and Afranius Burrus, and those wild instincts planted in him by his mother were coming to life. One after the other, those who stood in his way were cast aside: Britannicus, Octavia, and his mother Agrippina. Seneca was told to cover up Nero's matricide with his authority, but the noble Roman withdrew to his country estate, there to await, like his brother, the order to commit suicide. Burrus disappeared in March of A.D. 62. People said he had been poisoned.[59] To eliminate the influence

---

[57] *Aeneid*, VI, 785
[58] Horace, *Odes*, I, 11
[59] Tacitus, *Annal.*, XIV, 51

of the commanding general of the Praetorian Guard, Nero divided the office between two men: Tigellinus, the reputed companion of all his crimes, and Fennius Rufus, a decent but weak character.

Since Tigellinus was deeply involved in all sorts of court intrigues, he had no time for Paul's case, and thus Paul's imprisonment ended in the summer of the year 63 with acquittal. Official Rome acknowledged that Christianity was not a crime against the state. Domitian was the first, years later, to recede from that viewpoint. One morning a centurion came to Paul, took the chain from its place on the wall, and attached it to his belt, with the declaration that the prefect of Rome had dismissed the case. Paul was now free to go wherever he wished. He had barely escaped death. If his case had continued for another year, Tigellinus would certainly not have released him when he was emptying the prisons in order to fill the Circus with martyrs.

It has been asked why Luke did not tell of Paul's acquittal. He certainly was aware of the outcome of the trial; but at the end of Paul's imprisonment Luke was no longer in Rome. He is not mentioned among those sending greetings at the end of the Epistle to the Philippians. The fact that he does not report the death of the Apostle indicates that Paul was released in the interval, and that the Acts of the Apostles was published sometime between the first and second imprisonments. Where did Paul go? The letters of the captivity indicate that he postponed, temporarily at least, his original plan of going to Spain. His eyes were turned again to the east. Timothy had already gone to Philippi, and Paul was to meet him on the way. Now after two years in prison, when at last all restraints were removed from his gathered energies, Paul sensed a second spring in his life, but in reality it was the soft glow of autumn that gives the vine its last drop of sweetness and sparkle.

Since his shipwreck on Crete, that island often returned to his thoughts as a field he had overlooked. In Ephesus he may have heard from some of the brethren concerning the Christians on Crete, about whom no one seemed to care. There was still work to do in the East. With Titus, Paul now set out for that island of the legendary King Minos. As they sailed up to Crete, the island made a more friendly picture than during that storm two years ago. The people of Crete had become soft because of their prosperous trade and the imported luxuries from Egypt and Asia Minor, and at the time of Paul's arrival the Cretans were regarded as the most dissolute people of the world. One of their own seers, Epimenides, had made the Cretans notorious all over the world because of his derisive remark: "The Cretians are always liars, evil beasts, slothful bellies" (Titus 1:12).

But even here the seed of the Gospel had sprouted. Some Cretans who had seen the miracle of Pentecost became the first heralds of the faith to the island (Acts 2:11), but it was a disconnected, confused Christianity, without organization or stability. The Cretans knew little about Jesus, but a great deal regarding the heroes of the Old Testament, about whom the Jewish rabbis had told them all manner of tall tales. Here in Crete, Paul saw a rich field of labour. Titus was to continue in his mission in Crete until Paul would return from his journeys in the far west.

Paul was extremely cautious not to set foot on the soil of Palestine again. The terrible political and religious confusion of the time seemed to be worst in Jerusalem. Josephus reported that at this time "the high priest Ananus called the Sanhedrin to sit in judgment upon a brother of Jesus, the so-called Christ, by name James, and some others, and had them condemned to be stoned to death."60 That happened just as Paul was leaving Rome.

As we observe the course of history, suddenly a mass of fire and smoke obscures the scene while Paul is going from Church to Church in the Orient. In the dim light of the flames, we see dark figures darting here and there. One of those figures

---

60 Josephus, *Antiquities*, XX, ix, 1

is Peter. When the cloud rolls up to the Aventine and the heights of the Janiculum to the huts of the poor Christians, Peter is swallowed up in that fire and blood. Where Paul was at this time, we do not know. On 19 July, A.D. 64, to Nero while he was at his villa in Antium south of Ostia the news was brought that Rome was ablaze. For seven days the conflagration raged, leaving only four of the fourteen sections of the city unscathed. The night the fire started, people remembered seeing Nero's henchmen running from place to place with torches.

The great fire of Rome was the signal for the beginning of a three hundred year probation in which the work of Paul, the "wise architect," and of Peter, and their co-workers, was tested to see whether they had built on the foundation stone of Christ with gold, silver, and precious stones, or with wood, hay, and stubble (cf. 1 Cor. 3:12). Perhaps no single event in history made as great an impression on his contemporaries and succeeding ages as this act of Nero's. Five unimpeachable witnesses from paganism itself record the event: Tacitus *(Annal.,* XV, 44), Suetonius, Hadrian's court historian and a friend of Pliny *(Nero,* 16), the poet Juvenal who belonged to Suetonius' circle of friends *(Sat.,* I, 155), Cassius Dio *(Rom. Hist.,* LXII, 16), and Seneca *(Epist.,* 14).

A terrible surmise, which becomes almost a historical certainty, forces itself upon us. The Jews, who had been driven from Rome because of the controversy about Christ during Claudius' reign, were now wreaking a frightful revenge on the Christians. Nero needed someone on whom to put the blame for the fire. Any disreputable Oriental sect would serve his purpose. The Jews were able to withdraw their own heads from the imperial noose and direct the anti-Semitic feeling of the populace against the Christians. Until this time Christianity had flourished under the protecting roof of the synagogue, but now an enormous price was exacted for that benefit. The full hatred of the Roman people against the Jews was now unloaded on the Christians. Influential persons close to Nero-Tigellinus, Alityrus,

and the Jewish proselyte Poppaea, incited the Emperor against
the followers of Christ, and thus the Church was caught between
the upper and nether millstones of Judaism and anti-Semitism.
The wonder is that the Church was not ground out of existence.

Clement of Rome in his Letter to the Corinthians (I, 6)
seems to hint that the persecutions were the work of the Jews,
when he says: "The persecution was the work of envy." A few
years later, St. John in the Apocalypse called the synagogue of
the Jews, the "synagogue of Satan" (Rev. 2:9; 3:9).

During this orgy of hate, the blessed name of Christ
appears for the first time in pagan literature. Just as Christ died
on the Cross between two criminals as a political offender, so
from now on the Church will be described by the Roman state
as a political criminal, and by Tacitus and other writers as the
paragon of all superstition, abomination, and of everything
hateful to the human race. The fact that the Church withdrew
from public life was proof enough for Tacitus, and soon the
accusation began to do its ugly work. Apion in his book,
Against the Jews, declared that the Jews during their religious
ceremonies ate the flesh of some Greek whom they had first
murdered ritually in a grove. Now the same bloody charge was
transferred to the Christians, and they were accused of a similar
crime during their rite of the Lord's Supper. The pagans shuddered with horror when they heard the words of the Eucharistic
celebration: "Eat you all of this, for this is My body."

Strangely enough in the midst of all his venom, even
Tacitus felt a little movement of pity for the Christians on
various occasions. But that smooth courtier Suetonius, bereft of
all humane feeling, remained unmoved even when he
witnessed those awful scenes from Greek mythology which the
Christian martyrs were forced to enact. He looked on coolly
when a Christian became Hercules in actual flames, or Ixion
torn upon the rack, or Orpheus lacerated by wild bears, or Attis
during his mutilation, or Pasiphae surrendered to the lusts of
some rake wearing the mask of a wild steer (probably Nero

himself). Clement of Rome (I, 6) tells of these horrible sufferings. Seneca, now retired to his country house where he paid for the half-truths he had instilled in Nero's youthful mind, referred to these disgraceful scenes: "Tyranny has at its disposal, steel and fire, chains and wild animals, to set upon the bodies of men. I can recall those prisons, the tortures of the cross, the iron hooks, and that pale driven into a man's midriff and forced out of his mouth. I can still see how limbs were torn from bodies attached to wagons driven in opposite directions, that tunic lined with inflammable stuff, and all the rest of the inventions of diabolical fury" *(Ep.,* 14). These are the words of an eyewitness beholding the heinous crimes of his misguided pupil on the imperial throne. And this cool Stoic who had seen so many gladiators die in the arena, remarked that some of these victims died with a smile on their faces: "In the midst of all these tortures, there was one who did not moan; no, he did not beg for his life; no, I saw more, he smiled as though there was happiness in his heart" *(Ep.,* 78).

Among these unnamed victims of Nero's persecution was probably the greater part of those brethren whom Paul had greeted in the Epistle to the Romans, the men and women who had come to meet him on his arrival at Forum Appii, and those who had preached Christ with no pure motives but only to cause him sorrow in his bands. They also were saved, "yet so as by fire" (1 Cor. 3:15). The common danger and common death had expunged the human element from their hearts. Aquila and Priscilla are the only ones who, to our knowledge, escaped the persecution, for Paul greets them later on when they were in Ephesus (2 Tim. 4:19). This persecution was the first glorious victory of the Roman Church by which it earned for itself the highest place among all the Churches of the world.

Such were the events during the August days of A.D. 64, in the kingdom of the "beast," when the lights of Roman civilization were going out. The end could not be, far off, since "the man of sin" had revealed himself. Whether the persecution abated in 64 or whether Nero issued a general law against the Christians, the *Institutum Neronianum,* is not clear. The worst effect of the persecution, however, was the defamation of the Christian name. Now that the crime of the fire of Rome was attached to their name they were stamped as the acme of criminality and degradation.

The persecution of Nero marks the beginning of a period in which the Roman state and the culture of antiquity engaged in a life-and-death struggle with a spiritual power which must in the end come off victorious. It was Rome's tragic mistake that it did not recognize the power of the future, that power which alone could have kept Rome alive. A world empire, such as Rome, needed some universal spiritual bond like a universal religion to complement it. The old state religion could no longer serve that purpose since it had been completely discredited by the derision and contempt of Rome's philosophers. Christianity was the only religion that could bridge over all national differences and at the same time properly evaluate every national trait, and thus could be the bond that would hold together a falling empire. In its organization the Church fairly paralleled the Roman model. It was formed to fit the Roman state.

But the state alienated those powers and forces which alone could infuse life, and this inner division in the state ultimately led to the fall of the Empire. Even now, leaders and jurists in the Roman government had fearful premonitions that something new was afoot, that the old legalistic views about the totality of the state would not hold, that the old concept of the state was unable to contain the idea of a perfect religious society. The separation between the two perfect societies, religious and political, and the delimitation of their respective spheres would be the principal task of the coming centuries of Western civilization.

CHAPTER SIXTY-TWO

"THE PILLAR AND GROUND OF THE TRUTH"

The First Epistle to Timothy

St. Paul's mission in the Orient was completed. He now took up an old project. His eyes were turned to Spain. We have several indications that he sailed from Ephesus to Spain by way of Marsilia (Marseilles). Since ships generally tied up for some time in the larger ports, Paul very likely set foot on Gallic soil when he visited the Church at Marseilles. If the reading "Gaul" for "Galatia" (2 Tim. 4:10) is correct, it seems that Crescens accompanied him. The oldest witness to the Spanish mission is Clement of Rome, who probably knew Paul in Rome, even though he is not identical with the Clement mentioned in the Epistle to the Philippians. In his letter to the Corinthians, Clement said that Paul had penetrated to the limits of the West. For a Roman that could be nothing but Spain. The famous Muratorian Fragment also leads us to conclude that Luke did not record Peter's martyrdom and Paul's journey to Spain because he was not present at the time. Certain local traditions in Spain point to a visit by the Apostle, as, for instance, in Ecija, Lezuza, and especially in Tortosa where Paul is said to have appointed Rufus as bishop. The results of the Spanish mission, however, are completely shrouded in darkness.

In the spring of 66, Paul is again making a visitation of the Churches of the East. He visited Crete, then he went along the coast of Asia Minor, asking Timothy to wait in Ephesus, and from there he went to Macedonia by way of Troas, where he stayed with Carpus. While in Macedonia he wrote the first letter to Timothy principally because he feared that some unforeseen obstacle would prevent his return to Ephesus.

The style of the three pastoral epistles represents the maturest stage in Paul's writing. The earlier forcefulness arid energy have been tempered down. The old fluency and fullness of expression is gone, as are also those characteristic onrushes of words and phrases which sometimes do violence to the grammatical construction. Paul's vocabulary also shows the influence of the various idioms which he came to know in his travels. The change of secretaries, too, had its effect, since the secretary had a certain liberty in the composition of the letter. The hand of the secretary is clearly seen in Paul's last letter to Timothy when he lay in chains in a Roman prison accused of being a traitor to the state. But Paul's voice and the imprint of his thought are evident. Because of the many opportunities for contemplation while he languished in his first imprisonment Paul became the great theologian and mystic in his epistles, but in the pastoral letters he appears as the practical pastor of souls.

Ephesus had become the centre for a new philosophy of enlightenment. The city was now interested in an unusual hybrid of Babylonian and Persian elements, concocted of star-gazing, Jewish visions, cabalistic doctrines, rabbinical ancestral charts, and sexual stories. The Old Testament genealogies were used as the basis for spinning innumerable old wives' tales. Garrulous old men claimed to know all sorts of stories about every figure in the Old Testament. But belief in the resurrection, as Hymeneus said, was something for the simple-minded faithful. The way to perfection and enlightenment was through abstinence from meat, wine, and marriage. An especially dangerous intriguer was Alexander the coppersmith. Paul excommunicated both Hymeneus and Alexander.

Another group was even more dangerous. Paul said of them: "Their speech spreads like a canker" (2 Tim. 2:17). They were hard to reach with the ammunition of reason because they barricaded themselves in the emotional and imaginative sphere. They thrived especially in pious circles and in the circles of devout women. This new heresy signalled the beginning of that witches' Sabbath of the next few centuries when Gnostic, Manichaean, and Neoplatonic elements were mingled in religion, resulting ultimately in a dualism that professed to see in matter the origin of all evil.

Paul realized the danger of such loose thinking and cloudy beliefs for a simple straightforward expression of the faith. The heresy was hard to fight, it changed continually, and such a slippery form was utterly detestable to Paul. To counteract this enervating heresy, Paul proclaimed the idea of Christian solidarity, and the principal theme of the First Epistle to Timothy is the Christian community in its faith (chap. 1), the Christian community in its worship (chap. 2), and the Christian community in its hierarchy (chap. 3).

The object of the Christian message is not to initiate men into cabalistic visions and into the casuistry of the Jewish law, but the love of a pure and unselfish heart and a simple trusting faith. The law is good inasmuch as it is the honest expression of the divine moral law. But now Mount Sinai is not the norm of the Christian's conduct. He is guided by the gospel of mercy and grace and the Sermon on the Mount, not by the cold imperative of duty. Externally the old law and the law of grace are the same. But even if two men do the same thing, it is still not the same. Once more the vision of his pre-Christian past comes before the Apostle's eye, but now he is milder and more mellow. Now he sees principally God's great act of mercy. He recalls Timothy's ordination and asks him not to disappoint the hopes and prophetic votes that led to his selection.

Without unity in belief there is no unity in prayer and worship. The Church, says Paul, is a world-embracing community of prayer, praising God in the name of all creation. He singles out a special group that needs the prayers of the Church: "for kings and for all that are in high stations." The exhortation to prayer for public authority was especially appropriate at that time. The Jewish element was antagonistic to the *Pax Romana,* that political "new order" which Rome had imposed on the world, and this attitude of the Jews might easily have implicated the Christians as enemies of the state. Revolution was brewing in Palestine. The governor Florus had been forced to surrender the Fortress Antonia, and the priests had refused to offer sacrifices in the name of the Emperor: Jerusalem had become the carrion upon which the Roman eagle under Vespasian's leadership would soon pounce.

The Christian may not make his patriotism depend on the good will of the state or its head. Yet he has a right to defend himself against the accusation of enmity to the state, in Paul's time and in so many instances in days to come. At this time Paul arose to say that the paying of taxes and civil obedience were not enough. We must also pray for the civil authority. And the reason for that statement is that authority has a greater responsibility before God and that it strives to ensure for us "a peaceable life in all piety and chastity." And the Church cannot attain its end, it cannot carry out its worship, except in an orderly peaceful political atmosphere. Both Church and state serve the one God and implement God's will of universal salvation.

Paul envisages a beautiful scene: Throughout the Roman Empire he sees "men . . . lifting up pure hands'. . . and women in decent apparel" in prayer for the welfare of the state. Instead of hacking off these hands, the Roman Empire would have done better to rely on them for support. Paul's picture of these *orantes* was painted on the walls of the catacombs. The lifting up of hands in prayer is the priest's position in the Mass. Thus, too, Christ prayed on the Cross.

From the state and the family, Paul turns to the Church and its social structure. Before this he had described the Church as the mystical community of the elect, Christ's "glorious Church, not having spot or wrinkle" (Eph. 5:27), and as the invisible Church still shrouded in Christ's mystery. Now, speaking as a practical pastor, he calls the Church God's household, a great earthly community, a Church with experience and organization, with authority to teach, a concrete and visible Church which contains some who are unworthy. But all this merges into one vision: The Church is the realization of the mystery of Christ, the continuing revelation of God.

Through the Church, God is always speaking to men. The Church is the unshakeable pillar and ground of truth. Now, the truth will never again be lost as long as the Church exists. But around the base of the pillar it is dark, and that darkness represents the miserable world that runs after the banners of lying and unprincipled propaganda.

Because of his youth and his retiring disposition, Timothy often needed the encouragement of his paternal friend who seemed to have an inexhaustible supply of energy. These two men were very different in their characters; yet Paul drew no one closer to his heart than Timothy, not even Titus. He points out the way to influence other men: by being "an example of the faithful in word, in conversation, in charity, in faith, in chastity" (4:12); by considering position, age, and sex; with regard to women, by observing a supernatural tact. In his charities Paul seems to have had some unpleasant experiences with certain young widows bent on marriage.

Faithful priests deserve Timothy's respect, especially those who teach. With regard to the faithful, Timothy should carefully avoid any appearance of avarice, he should make no financial demands. An occasional glass of wine, and no puritanical asceticism.

CHAPTER SIXTY-THREE

THE CHURCH IN CRETE

The Epistle to Titus

Paul had completed his last visitation in the East. From Crete, where he left Titus, he went to Corinth, where Erastus remained, then to Miletus, where Trophimus became ill, to Ephesus, where he established Timothy as his legate, and finally to Troas and Macedonia. In the autumn of 66 we find Paul on the road to Nicopolis on the Adriatic coast, with a group of friends, probably including Luke. Nicopolis was the most important city and Roman colony in Epirus. It was called "victory city" by Augustus, its founder, in commemoration of the victory he had won over Mark Antony at Actium in 31 B.C.

Herod the Great had embellished the city with many fine public buildings.[61] Here Paul intended to spend the winter, and if possible, visit the Churches of Illyrium, and then, in the spring, to visit the sorely tried Church of Rome. On the way he wrote to Titus, ordering him to come to Nicopolis as soon as a substitute should be sent to replace him. Artemas was probably Titus' successor, since Tychicus was shortly after sent to Ephesus (2 Tim. 4:12).

---

[61] Josephus, *Antiquities,* XVI, v, 3

The solemn address of the letter to Titus is attuned to the seriousness of the occasion. Crete was the most recent of Paul's foundations. It lacked a stable organization, it was without the framework about which an organization could be formed. And without a staunch teaching authority and a definite tradition, a successful war cannot be waged against heresy. The heresies that raised their heads in Crete were the same as those in Ephesus. The heretical movement was led by a number of Jewish half-Christians who were trying to make money out of religion, "teaching things which they ought not, for filthy lucre's sake" (Titus 1:11). Yet we must not say that material things are the seat of evil. Everything that God created is good, and such should man's attitude be. If your inner eye is good, the Master said, then your whole body, and the whole world, will be good. All light, goodness, and beauty come from within.

This doctrine of Christianity has created a new world (1:15). At that time some agitators were urging the freeing of the slaves and were preaching rebellion to authority (3:1). Such men were causing much unrest in families, men who "subvert whole houses" (1:11). The Stoic teaching about the equality of men and the value of the ego was beginning to take hold at that time, even among the slaves. If Christians now began to fan the flame, a social revolution might ensue and also engulf the Church. Paul tried to lift the problem to a higher plane where social differences are immaterial. "The goodness and kindness of God our Saviour appeared" and he opened our eyes to the true dignity of man before God. Once more Paul explained the new ethics of Christianity in antithetical sentences: once–now. A great change has taken place. We can no longer act as if Christ had not come. The new Christian nobility must work from within and leaven the whole mass of society.

The pastoral letters of St. Paul indicate a second stage in the organizational development of the primitive Church. In the first stage everything was under the immediate direction of the apostles, and their charismatic gifts were sufficient for every contingency. In the second stage, the monarchical episcopate has not yet appeared. It is still virtually contained in the apostolic office, just as the whole episcopate was contained in the apostolic office of Peter. As yet there are no resident bishops. Timothy and Titus were apostolic delegates of the Apostle, they acted under his orders, they governed the Churches and appointed priests and deacons by Paul's plenary authority. Under these delegates, a college of presbyters, sometimes called bishops, governed, and from this college later came the monarchical bishops. The essentials of a monarchical episcopate are residence, autonomy, and lifelong tenure of a certain diocese. Paul never granted his Churches any autonomy. His representatives always return to him for instructions, directions, and authority. Paul himself was the supreme shepherd of one immense diocese. Dioceses with definite boundaries did not yet exist. The world was still a great missionary territory. The word "bishop" is older than the office; it was used by Homer[62] and the Greek classical writers in the sense of an officer who supervised the temple property or colonial affairs. The full episcopal office in the monarchical sense appeared some decades later in the letters of St. Ignatius of Antioch.

---

[62] *Illiad*, XXII, 255; *Odyssey*, VIII, 163.

CHAPTER SIXTY-FOUR

LAST WILL AND TESTAMENT

The Second Epistle to Timothy

While Paul was at Nicopolis, his thoughts were repeatedly turning to Rome. During the winter Titus arrived from Crete. He spent the rest of the winter with Paul, and then was sent to Illyrium (2 Tim. 4:10). We do not know where Paul was arrested. Some say it was in Nicopolis, others think it happened in the house of Carpus in Troas, and that Paul had to leave his possessions there. Others think he was taken captive in Ephesus, since he spoke of the disloyalty of the brethren in Asia Minor. Still others surmise that the arrest took place in distant Spain. But it seems more probable, in my opinion, that in the spring of A.D. 67 Paul came to Rome of his own accord and that he had been there some time labouring at the building up of the Church.

This opinion is supported by an ancient Roman tradition which was put into writing as early as the second century in the *Passio Petri et Pauli*, ascribed to Linus. According to this tradition, Paul lived in an inn on the left bank of the Tiber in the eleventh region, *ad Arenulam,* near the island in the Tiber. This tradition also maintains that Paul preached in an empty grain barn near the Porta Ostiensis, and that soldiers were among his hearers. An extremely old chapel built in the Apostle's memory now stands on the site of the inn, *San Paolo alla Regola* (*Regola* is a distortion of *arenula,* which refers to the sand thrown up by the flooding Tiber). This little oratory has served to keep the ancient tradition alive, and recent excavations made near it revealed ruins of some old business establishment. This section of the city was a business district for retailers, ship chandlers, tanners, potters, and truck gardeners. It may have been the place where Paul was one day apprehended by the Roman police as a suspected head of a religious sect.

In the Forum at Rome stood the golden milepost to which all the roads in the vast Empire led, and near it, at the foot of the Capitoline, stood the Mamertine prison. And to this prison, according to an unsubstantiated tradition, Paul was finally brought. This second imprisonment placed Paul in a highly unfavourable position. He now wore chains like a criminal. Classical and Christian antiquity are filled with complaints about the terrible treatment of prisoners and their close quarters, about the frightful conditions in Roman prisons with their lack of light and the unbearable filth. Even the Emperors said that detention in a Roman prison was a fearful ordeal, and it was noted that the mortality rate steadily increased among inmates of the prisons.

Paul, now an old, tired man, lacked everything he needed. He complained about lonesomeness; his Roman friends had difficulty in being admitted to the prison. Eubulus, Pudens, Linus, and Claudia greeted him cautiously. Their caution is explained, according to another ancient tradition, by the fact that they knew where Peter was in hiding and they did not wish to draw attention to themselves. One legend tells that Paul met Peter in prison. But this is probably only the fabrication of some pious soul.

Paul touches on the painful matter of Demas' desertion: "For Demas has left me, loving this world" (4:9). The brethren of Asia Minor also left him in the lurch, none of them came in answer to his appeal, and he mentions Phigellus and Hermogenes by name (1:15) . Only Luke remained with him (4:11) . But one day he had great joy. A citizen from Ephesus, Onesiphorus, who had served him well in Asia Minor, found him after looking through all the lists of prisoners in Rome.

Paul's case was to be adjudicated by the imperial court. Nero was at this time travelling in Greece as a comedy actor, but his place in Rome was taken by the unspeakable Aelius, a second Nero. The first hearing was held in one of the great basilicas facing the Forum. The judge and the officials of the court sat in the apse of the basilica, the prisoners were in the front of the nave with their witnesses and attorneys. Behind them, down the nave, and also in the side aisles and above in the galleries, were the spectators. Among these, ecclesiastical reporters were to be found in later times writing down the proceedings of the hearings of the martyrs.

Paul was most likely accused of complicity in the crime of setting fire to the city of Rome, or of having had guilty knowledge of the plan. His reference to the hearing is a brief dramatic word, and the hearing itself must have been brief because Paul had no legal assistance and no exonerating witnesses. No one would have dared to take up the defence of the Christians at this time: "At my first answer, no man stood with me; but all forsook me" (4:16). But Paul must have made a brilliant defence, as the hearing was adjourned and for this time Paul "was delivered out of the mouth of the lion" (4:17). In the long interval between his first and second hearings, Paul had ample time for prayer and reflection, but his thoughts seem to have been chiefly about two things: one an earthly concern and the other spiritual, the welfare of Timothy and the purity of the Church.

Paul is once more overcome with an ardent longing for Timothy's company. Here in prison he summons his waning energies to write a last letter under these most trying conditions. The letter was an intimate expression of his friendship for Timothy. In it Paul appointed Timothy the executor of his last will. He wishes he could see Timothy once more before he dies, but he fears that it will be too late when Timothy can come. He asks him to bring Mark along, for in his thoughts Mark now represents his friend of long ago, Barnabas.

The aged Apostle must have been always cold in the dark, damp subterranean dungeon. When Jugurtha, the Numidian king, was taken down to the clammy dungeon filled with seep water, he exclaimed: "By Hercules, how cold your bath is!" Paul asked Timothy to bring him the old, threadbare cloak which he had left behind in Troas. In spite of all his trials, his mind was still alert and active. He missed his Scriptures, his precious parchments and notes, and he should like to have put them in order before his death and then put them in Luke's hands. His eyes fixed on his heavenly goal; even here in the Mamertine dungeon, cold and starving, he never lost the strong consciousness of his apostolic mission.

When a man is old his thoughts turn frequently to his early childhood. Recalling his childhood, Paul now breathed a fervent prayer for his forefathers to whom he owed his first knowledge of God (1:3). But as soon as he thinks of his own youth, the youthful figure of Timothy moves into his field of vision. He remembers the bashful boy looking down on him with big wondering eyes as he lay covered with blows on the ground after the stoning at Lystra (3:11). He has fond recollections of Timothy's mother and grandmother. Now in this cold prison he remembers the warm hospitality of their home. Timothy's was a soft, clinging temperament, somewhat inclined to melancholy, and that made him all the more lovable and the object of Paul's fatherly solicitude. The grace of ordination, conferred on him when Paul's gnarled hands rested in bene-diction on Timothy's head, will strengthen whatever is weak by nature, for God has "given us the spirit ... of power" (1:7). Once that "holy calling" (1:9) transformed Paul himself, and now in prison Paul still remembers that soul-shaking event near Damascus.

Immediately Paul winged himself to supernatural heights to view everything in the perspective of faith where the soul is secure against all tribulation. Our eternal happiness is not supported by our weak hands, it is not measured by our poor merits, but it is derived from that eternal act by which God in His love has chosen us. By this act "I am appointed a preacher and an apostle"; and by it you are my disciple. Once the Master pressed His banner into my hands. Now I am old and I cannot hold it aloft for long. You must take the banner now, guard it well, and entrust it only to reliable men. "Labour as a good soldier of Christ Jesus," as a man that is training to fight in the ring, as a farmer who nourishes the soil that nourishes him.

The doctrine that must be set up to oppose the Gnostic heresies is the dogma of the two natures in Christ; His true humanity as a scion of David, and His true divinity by which He rose from the dead. For that doctrine Paul was glad to suffer as "an evildoer," and even die so that he might participate also in Christ's sufferings. But there must be no denial of Christ, no treason, no desertion, for "if we deny Him, He will also deny us" (2:12). The outstanding trait of the Apostle was fidelity. Once more the vision of God's great building, the Church, comes before his mind. Across the facade is written: "The Lord knows who are His" (2:19). The Church is also a great household in which will be found unruly children, "who have erred from the truth" (2:18). A Church that would not be persecuted, a Church that would be a "lover of pleasures," could not be the bride of the Crucified. But the Church has the "Holy Scriptures, which can instruct you to salvation," and that will be comfort enough.

It is autumn of 67, the second hearing has been set. Paul knew that it would end with his entrance into God's heavenly kingdom (4:18). He has abandoned all hope: "For I am even now ready to be sacrificed; and the time of my dissolution is at hand" (4:6). Before the end he writes his epitaph: that figure of the fighter and runner in God's arena. He is thinking of that

time when he was called at Damascus and the burden of the
Apostle of the Gentiles was laid on him. Then he swore his
soldier's oath, and he kept that vow from that day when he
humbly bowed his head beneath Ananias' hand until the day
when he bowed his head beneath the headsman's sword.. "I
have fought a good fight: I have finished my course: I have
kept the faith" (4:7).

"Make haste to come to me quickly" (4:8). Did Timothy
arrive before Paul's execution? If the Epistle to the Hebrews
was issued at Rome, it seems probable that Timothy saw Paul
once more, for in that epistle we read: "Know that our brother
Timothy is set at liberty: with whom (if he come shortly) I will
see you" (13:23). Then in spite of the danger, Timothy came to
Paul and shared his chains. Perhaps there in prison, in the
presence of the other prisoners, they gave each other Holy
Communion.

CHAPTER SIXTY-FIVE

"PRESENT WITH THE LORD"

That Paul was not summarily condemned as an enemy of the public welfare (*hostis publicus*), but as a Roman citizen after a regular trial, is clear from the Letter of Clement of Rome to the Corinthians, written some thirty years later. That passage in Clement's letter reveals an intimate knowledge of the last days of Paul's life and incidentally serves as an excellent summary of that heroic life. Clement says: "Paul also obtained the reward of patient endurance, after being seven times thrown into captivity, compelled to flee, and being stoned. After preaching both in the east and in the west, he gained the illustrious reputation due to his faith, having taught righteousness to the whole world, and come to the extreme limit of the west, and suffered martyrdom under the prefects. Thus was he removed from the world, and went into the holy place, having proved himself a striking example of patience" (chap. 5).

Paul's second hearing ended with the death sentence. In the basilica the best man and the worst of the century stood face to face: righteousness was in chains, crime was on the throne. Paul and death were not strangers to each other. Paul had often met death under many disguises. He had often looked deep into the empty eye-sockets of death, he had looked on the dried skeleton, deep into death's stony heart. He did not fear death; he had learned long ago "to die before his death." Now he meets death for the last time, in a decisive passage of arms.

Paul did not take death lightly. For this great realist, death was the last enemy. Nor did he yield or cringe before death. He had drawn the sting of death when he transferred his life into Christ's. Now, when the last vestiges of earthliness were falling from his soul in this dark prison night, his soul gave back a perfect reflection of his crucified Master. Now he had reached the climax of the sacrificial service of his apostolic life.

One morning the Apostle was led by a troop of lictors through the Porta Trigemina past the pyramid of Cestius. They turned into the Ostian Way; where St. Paul's Church now stands they turned left through a meadow. An old Roman legend says that the blind Petronilla met the Apostle here and offered him her veil so that he might use it as a blindfold. For the last time Paul looks to the right on the Tiber valley. To the left is the Via Appia on which six years before he had come to the city. The marching troop turned off on the Via Laurentiana and after about half an hour they came to the Salvian Marsh *(Aquae Salviae),* at the third milestone, where today the silent Trappists, in their monastery of Tre Fontane, keep watch beneath the tall eucalyptus trees.

Unless there had been ancient tradition to support it, no one would have designated this out-of-the-way place as the site of Paul's execution. Beheading outside the city, however, was a Roman custom.[63] Appropriately the legend goes on to say that Paul lifted his bound hands in his last prayer and that he prayed now in that sacred language in which the risen Lord had called him into his service. Here his head was severed, his tongue forever silenced. That other legend which points out the place where the two Princes of the Apostles met on their way to execution is a symbolic testimony to the fact that the common martyrdom of the apostles closed the breach between Jewish

---

[63] Tacitus, *Hist.,* IV, 11

and Gentile Christians and cemented the indissoluble unity of the Church under Linus.

Christians reverently carried Paul's body to his grave about two miles away on the property of the Roman matron Lucina, where the present basilica of *San Paolo fuori le Mura* stands. The grave was in a pagan neighbourhood. Few Christian graves have been found near Paul's. And that, too, was fitting for the Apostle of the Gentiles. The body remained here in a simple grave *(memoria)* until the persecution of Valerian in the third century. Then attempts were being made to plunder every Christian treasure and to destroy the Christian burial places. But the Roman Christians quickly removed the bodies of the apostles Peter and Paul to the Catacombs of St. Sebastian on the Via Appia. The Church gives thanks each year for the preservation of this great treasure on the feast of Sts. Peter and Paul (June 29).

Pope Sylvester returned the remains of the apostles to the original burial places in the churches built by Constantine. Fifty years later the three Emperors, Valentinian II, Arcadius, and Honorius, replaced the small structure of Constantine with the famous basilica of St. Paul, which was completed in 395. It was the most spacious and daring architectural structure, surpassing every other building of Christendom.

The ancient basilica, dating from the fourth century, was destroyed by fire in 1823, at the time when Pius VII lay dying in the Quirinal. But the tomb of the Apostle and the mosaic of Galla Placida on the triumphal arch were saved from the ravages of the fire. The present church was erected with the offerings of all Christendom, and though it lacks some of the simple grace of the old structure, its majestic dimensions are equally effective. The inscription above the altar of the "confession" expresses the whole message of the Apostle in his own words: "For to me, to live is Christ; and to die is gain" (Phil. 1:21).

CHRONOLOGY OF THE LIFE OF ST. PAUL

The only starting point, supported by documentary evidence, for establishing the dates of the events in Paul's life is a letter written by Emperor Claudius to the city of Delphi. That city inscribed the letter on stone. In it the Emperor mentions his "friend Gallio, the proconsul of Achaia." According to this letter, Gallio must have entered upon his office as proconsul in June, A.D. 51 or 52. I accept the latter date because it provides a better arrangement of the events we know of until the first imprisonment. Since Paul appeared shortly after this date before Gallio's tribunal and remained afterward eighteen months in Corinth, we can now date events before and after this point.

The second date with some bearing on Paul's life is the date when Festus relieved Governor Felix, in the summer of A.D. 69 or 70.

For the date of Paul's conversion, we have two points beyond which we cannot go: the earliest limit is the year of Christ's death, A.D. 30 (or 33), and the latest is A.D. 37. The year 30 is not acceptable because it leaves too little time for the growth and development of the Church before the death of St. Stephen. The later date of 37 leaves little room for the Council of Jerusalem and the fourteen years between Paul's first and second journey to Jerusalem. We must, therefore, arrive at some date between these extremes, somewhere near 33 or 34. With 33 as a starting point, the three years in the Arabian desert and those fourteen years between the visits to Jerusalem can be easily accounted for, and the earlier date of the Council of

Jerusalem in 48 or 49 allows for Paul's early arrival in Corinth.

Since Paul was said to be a young man in 33, at the death of St. Stephen, and also a somewhat prominent personality, he must have been at least thirty years old. That would place his birth between 1 and 5 B.C. This view coincides with Paul's statement thirty years later, when he wrote the letter to Philemon, that he was an old man, i.e., about 60 years old, in 62 A.D.

The following are approximate dates of the events in Paul's life with the contemporary Roman Emperors:

1-5	Paul's birth
30	Christ's death
33/34	Stoning of St. Stephen; Paul's conversion
34-36	Sojourn in Arabia
36/37	First journey to Jerusalem
37-42	Paul in Tarsus
42	Arrival in Antioch
44	Famine in Jerusalem
45-48	First missionary journey
48/49	Council of Jerusalem; the controversy with Peter in Antioch
49/52	Second missionary journey
49/50	Philippi
50/51	Thessalonica and Beroea
51-52	Athens and Corinth; the two epistles to the Thessalonians
53-58	Third missionary journey
54-57	Ephesus
54/55	Epistle to the Galatians
56	First Epistle to the Corinthians
57	Flight from Ephesus; Second Epistle to the Corinthians; journey to Illyrium
57/58	winter in Corinth; Epistle to the Romans
58	Last journey to Jerusalem
59-60	Imprisonment in Caesarea
60/61	Journey to Rome
61-63	First Roman imprisonment; Epistles of the Captivity
63-66	Visitation of the Orient; mission to Crete; journey to Spain
66/67	Return from Spain; winter in Nicopolis; First Epistle to Timothy; Epistle to Titus
67	Second Roman imprisonment; Second Epistle to Timothy; martyrdom